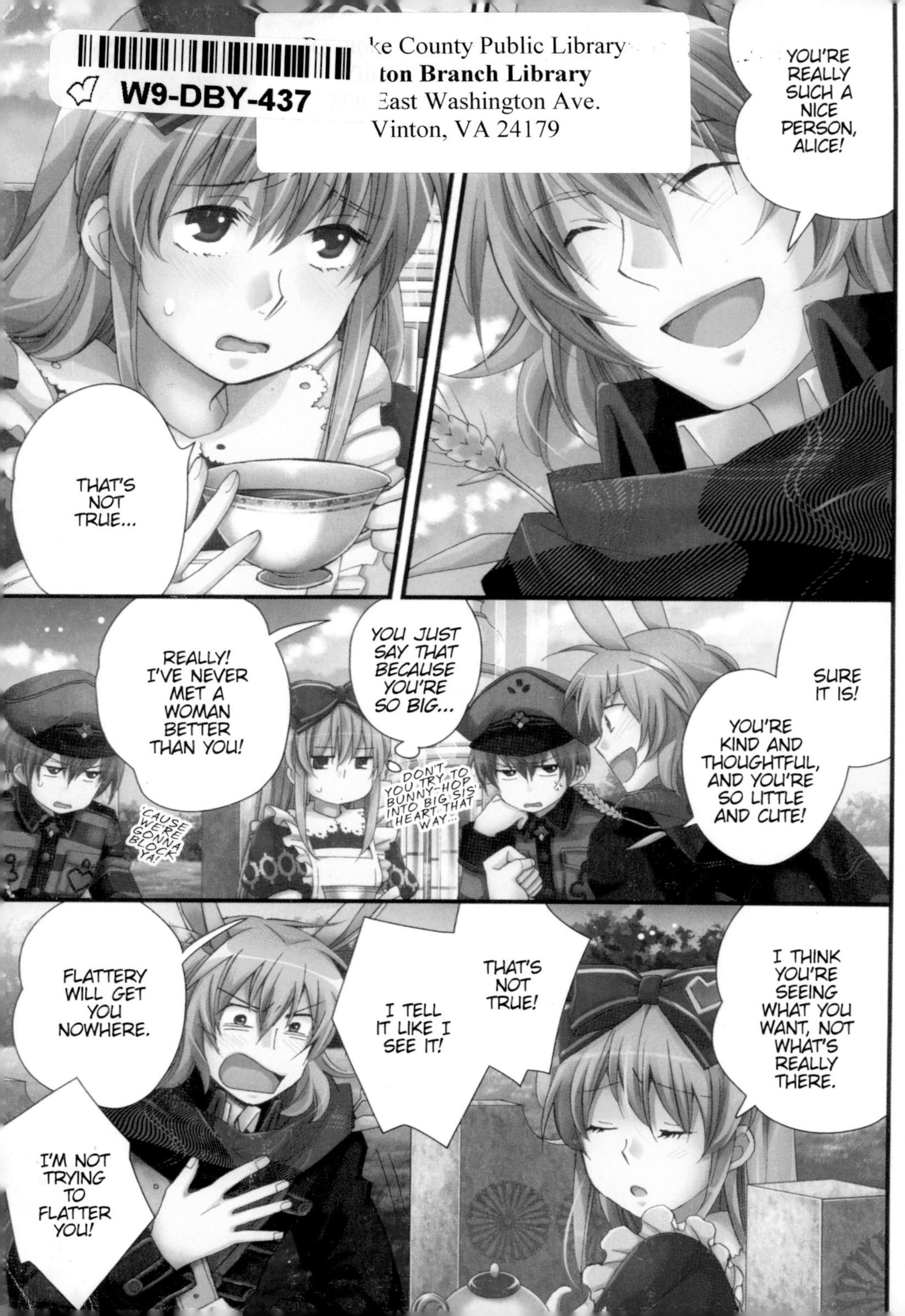
YOU'RE REALLY SUCH A NICE PERSON, ALICE!
THAT'S NOT TRUE...
SURE IT IS!
YOU'RE KIND AND THOUGHTFUL, AND YOU'RE SO LITTLE AND CUTE!
YOU JUST SAY THAT BECAUSE YOU'RE SO BIG...
DON'T YOU TRY TO BUNNY-HOP INTO BIG SIS' HEART THAT WAY...
REALLY! I'VE NEVER MET A WOMAN BETTER THAN YOU!
'CAUSE WE'RE GONNA BLOCK YA!
I THINK YOU'RE SEEING WHAT YOU WANT, NOT WHAT'S REALLY THERE.
THAT'S NOT TRUE!
I TELL IT LIKE I SEE IT!
FLATTERY WILL GET YOU NOWHERE.
I'M NOT TRYING TO FLATTER YOU!

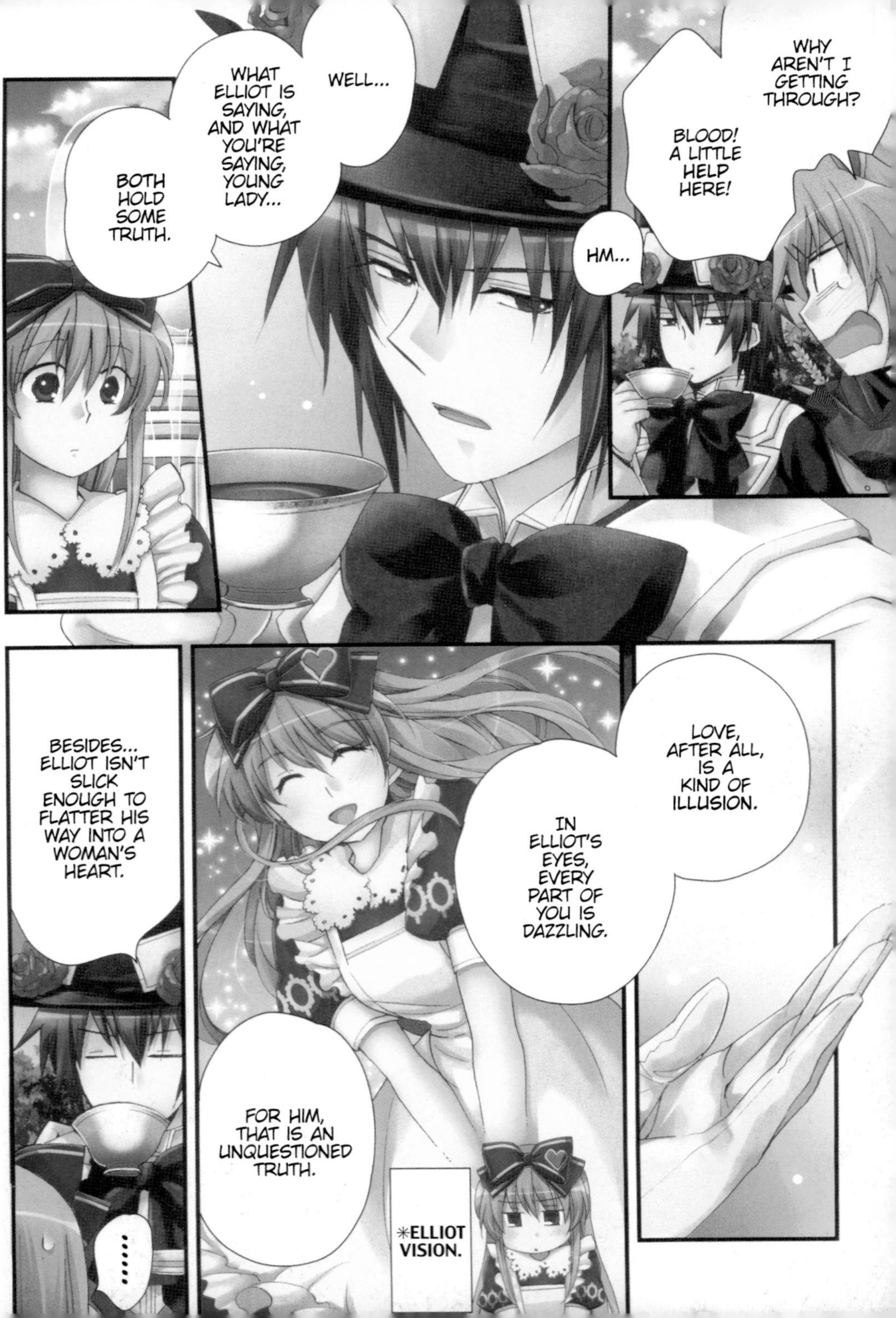
WHY AREN'T I GETTING THROUGH?
BLOOD! A LITTLE HELP HERE!
HM...
WELL...
WHAT ELLIOT IS SAYING, AND WHAT YOU'RE SAYING, YOUNG LADY...
BOTH HOLD SOME TRUTH.
LOVE, AFTER ALL, IS A KIND OF ILLUSION.
IN ELLIOT'S EYES, EVERY PART OF YOU IS DAZZLING.
FOR HIM, THAT IS AN UNQUESTIONED TRUTH.
*ELLIOT VISION.
BESIDES... ELLIOT ISN'T SLICK ENOUGH TO FLATTER HIS WAY INTO A WOMAN'S HEART.
......

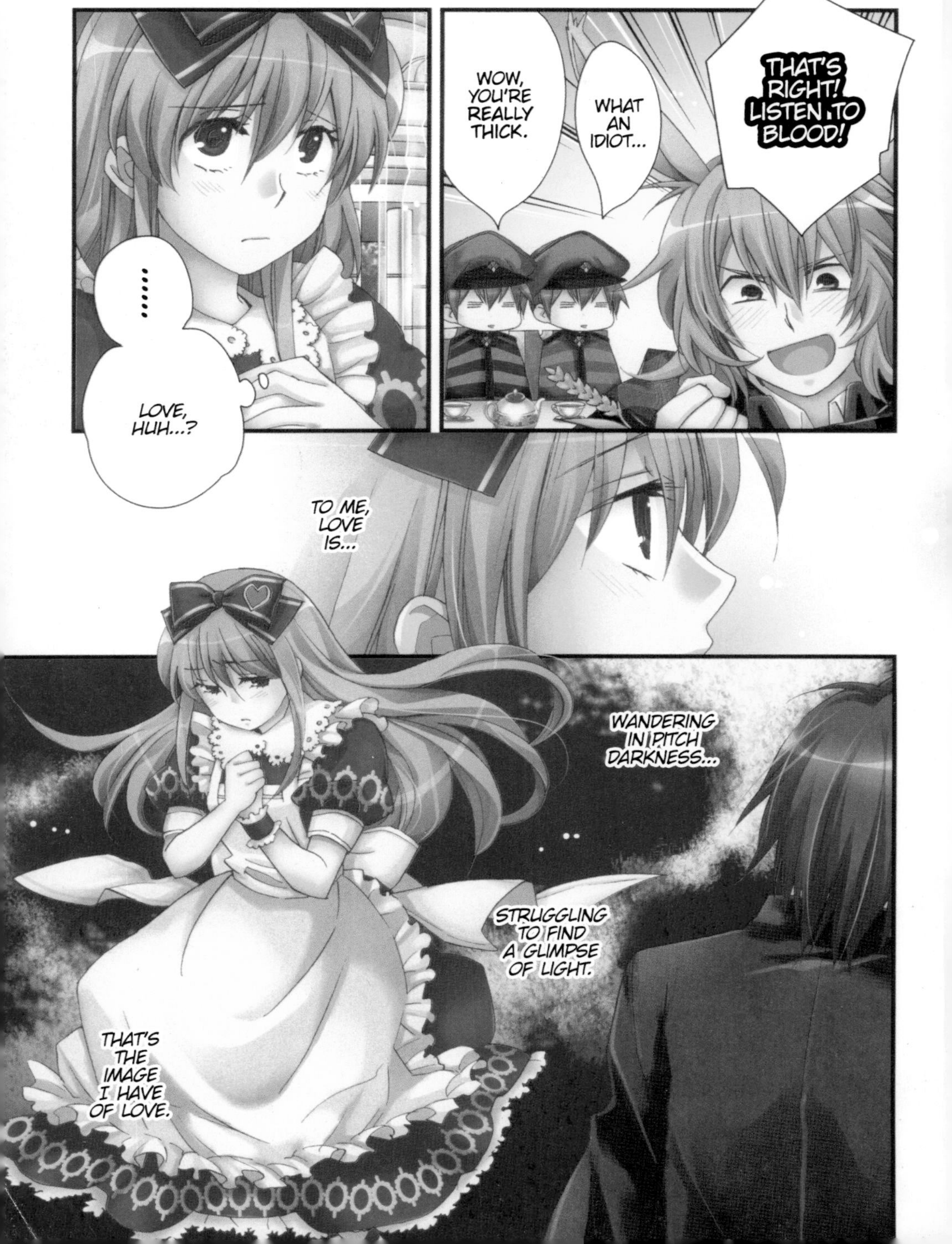
THAT'S RIGHT! LISTEN TO BLOOD!
WHAT AN IDIOT...
WOW, YOU'RE REALLY THICK.
......
LOVE, HUH...?
TO ME, LOVE IS...
WANDERING IN PITCH DARKNESS...
STRUGGLING TO FIND A GLIMPSE OF LIGHT.
THAT'S THE IMAGE I HAVE OF LOVE.

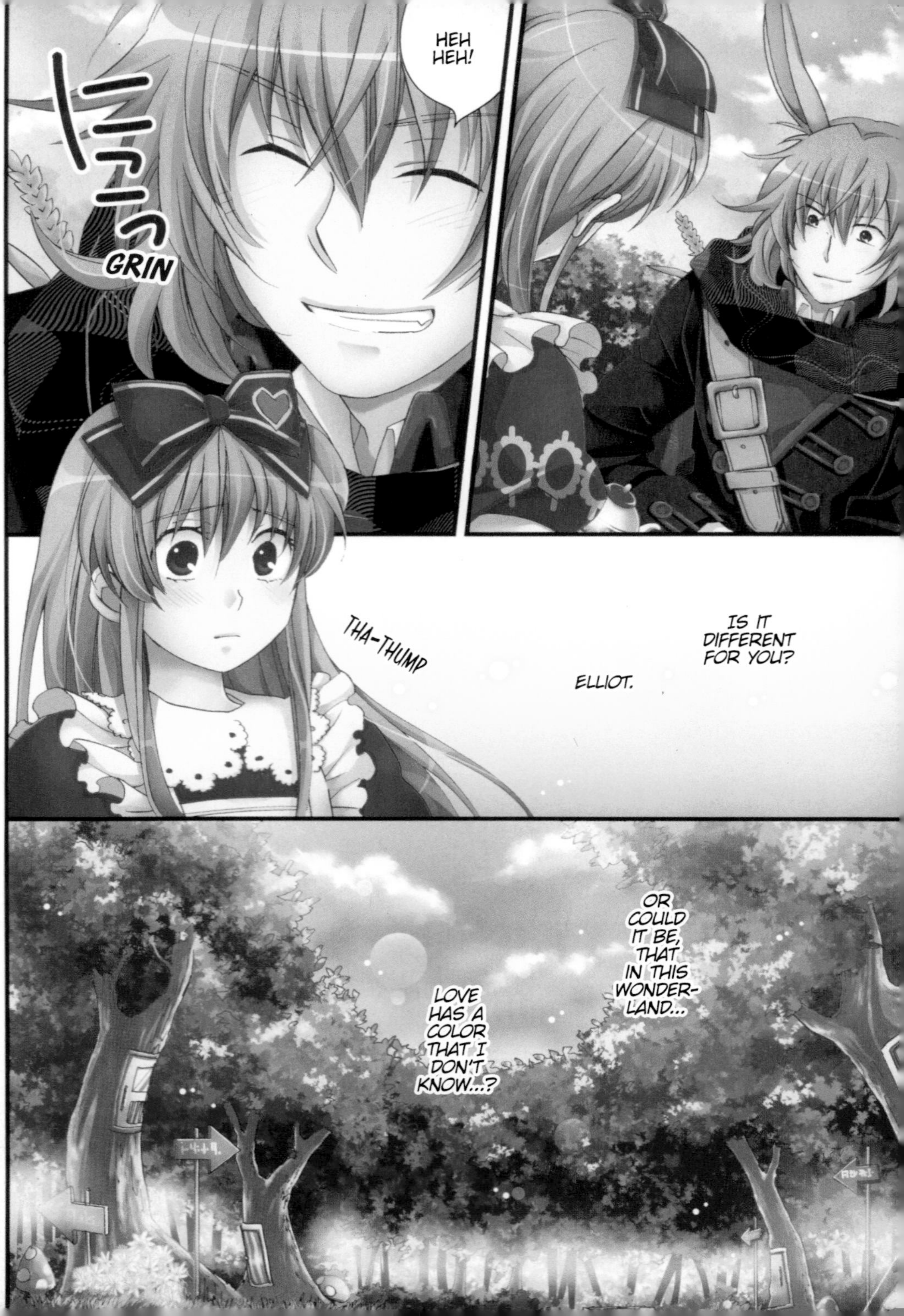
HEH HEH!
GRIN
IS IT DIFFERENT FOR YOU?
ELLIOT.
THA-THUMP
OR COULD IT BE, THAT IN THIS WONDER-LAND...
LOVE HAS A COLOR THAT I DON'T KNOW...?

ALICE IN THE COUNTRY OF CLOVER

~March Hare~

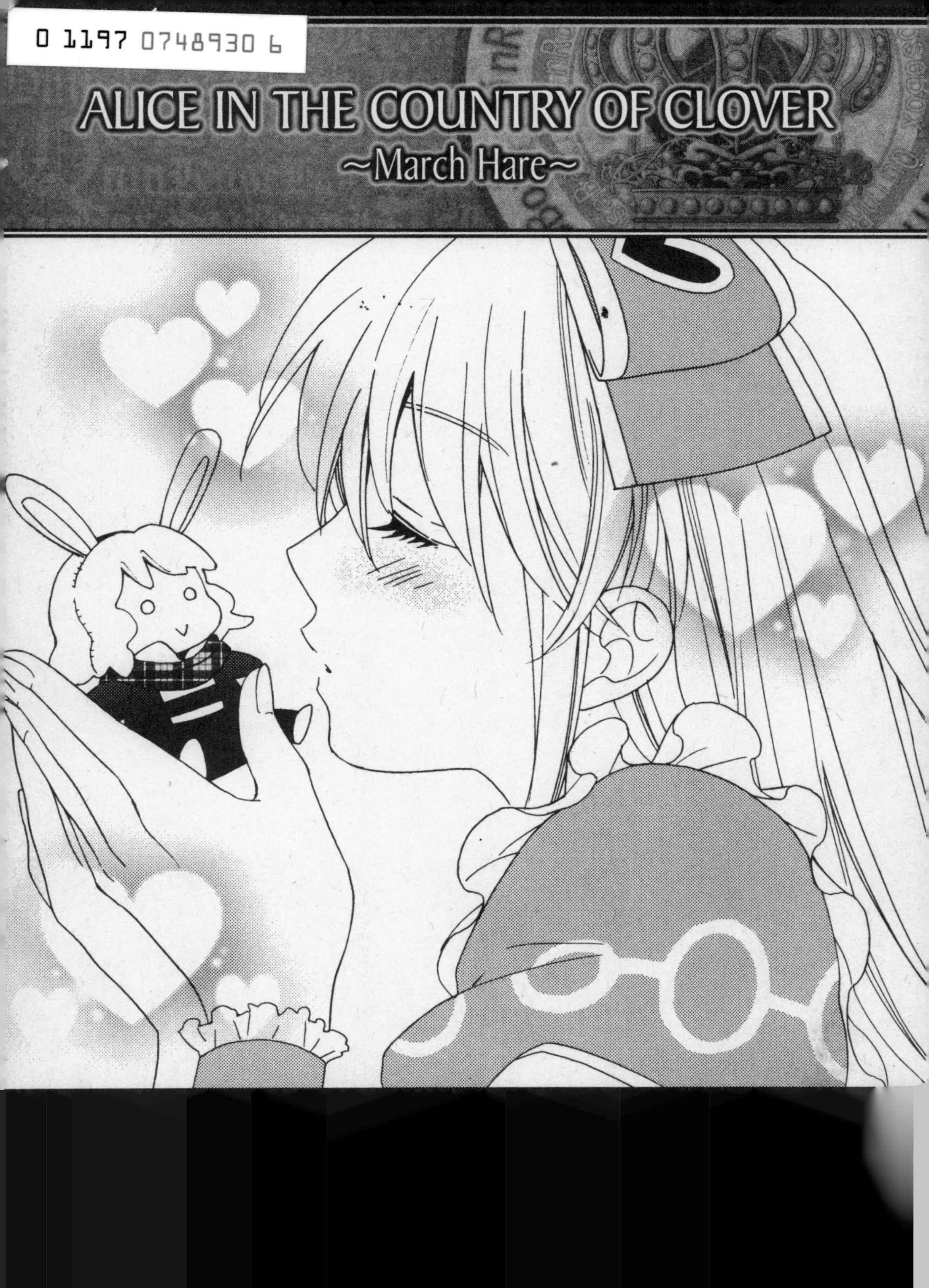

SEVEN SEAS ENTERTAINMENT PRESENTS

Alice IN THE COUNTRY OF Clover
MARCH HARE

art by SOYOGO IWAKI / story by QUINROSE

TRANSLATION
Angela Liu

ADAPTATION
Shanti Whitesides

LETTERING AND LAYOUT
Laura Scoville

LOGO DESIGN
Courtney Williams

COVER DESIGN
Nicky Lim

PROOFREADER
Lianne Sentar

MANAGING EDITOR
Adam Arnold

PUBLISHER
Jason DeAngelis

ISBN: 978-1-626920-52-1

Printed in Canada

First Printing: March 2014

10 9 8 7 6 5 4 3 2 1

FOLLOW US ONLINE: www.gomanga.com

READING DIRECTIONS

This book reads from *right to left*, Japanese style. If this is your first time reading manga, you start reading from the top right panel on each page and take it from there. If you get lost, just follow the numbered diagram here. It may seem backwards at first, but you□ll get the hang of it! Have fun!!

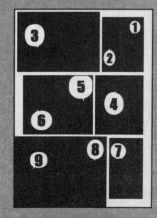

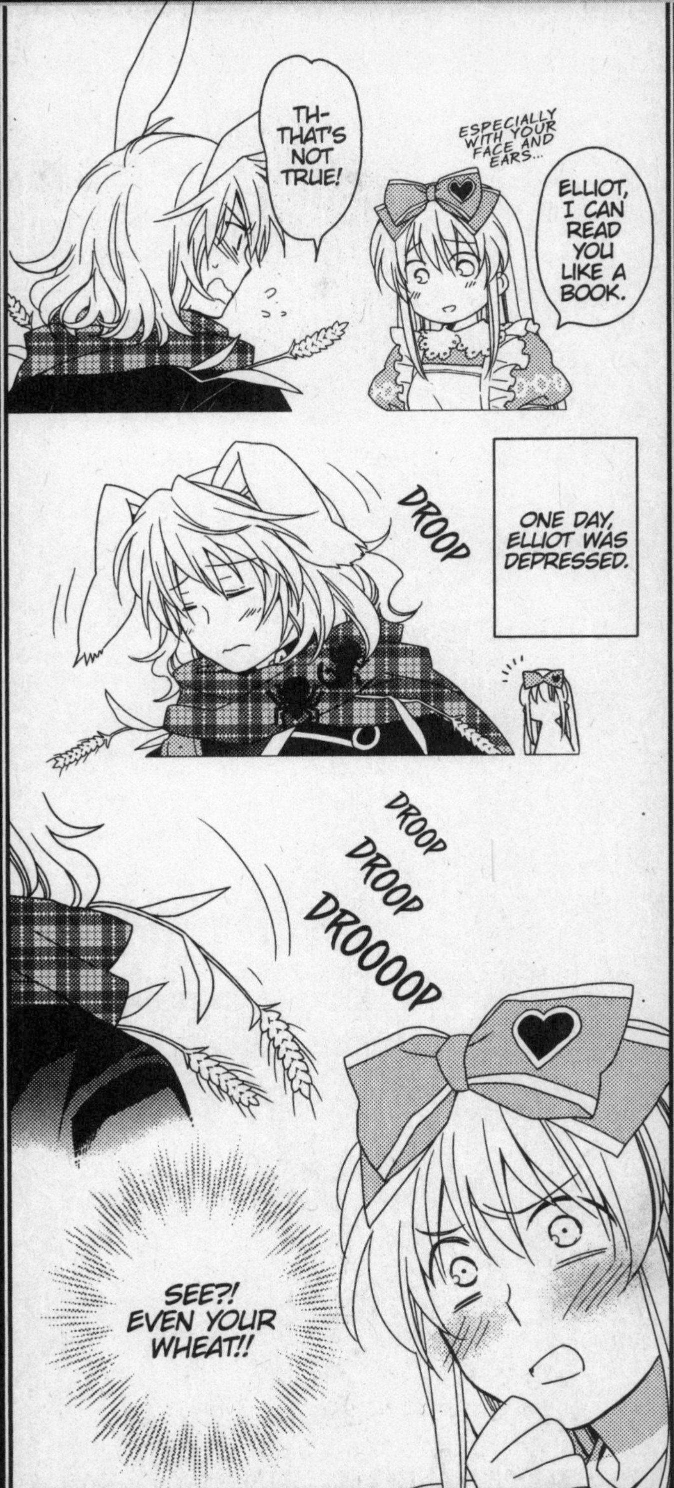
ELLIOT, I CAN READ YOU LIKE A BOOK.
ESPECIALLY WITH YOUR FACE AND EARS...
TH-THAT'S NOT TRUE!
ONE DAY, ELLIOT WAS DEPRESSED.
DROOP
DROOP
DROOP
DROOOOOP
SEE?! EVEN YOUR WHEAT!!

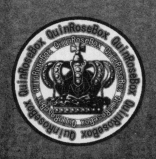

Alice in the Country of Clover
クローバーの国の
アリス
~Wonderful Wonder World~

- STORY -

In *Alice in the Country of Clover*, the game starts with Alice having not fallen in love, but still deciding to stay in Wonderland.

She's acquainted with all the characters from the previous game, *Alice in the Country of Hearts*.

Since love would now start from a place of friendship rather than passion with a new stranger, she can experience a different type of romance from that in the previous game. Her dynamic with the characters is different through this friendship—characters can't always be forceful with her, and in many ways it's more comfortable to grow intimate. The relationships *between* the Ones With Duties have also become more of a factor.

In this game, the story focuses on the mafia. Alice attends the suited meetings (forcefully) and gets involved in various gunfights (forcefully), among other things.

Land fluctuations, sea creatures in the forest, and whispering doors—it's a game more fantastic and more eerie than the first.

Will our everywoman Alice be able to have a romantic relationship in a world devoid of common sense?

Alice in the Country of Clover
Character Information

Elliot March
VA: Tsuguo Mogami

Blood's right-hand man has a criminal past… and a temperamental present. But he's not as bad as he used to be, so that's something. Joining Blood has been good(?) for him.

Blood Dupre
VA: Katsuyuki Konishi

The head of the mafia Hatter Family, Blood is a cunning yet moody puppet-master. Alice now has the pleasure of having him for a landlord.

Alice Liddell
VA: Rie Kugimiya

A normal girl with a bit of a chip on her shoulder. Deciding to stay in the Wonderland she was carried to, she's adapted to her strange new lifestyle.

Vivaldi
VA: Yuuko Kaida

The beautiful Queen of Hearts has an unrivaled temper—which is really saying something in Wonderland. Although a picture-perfect Mad Queen, she cares for Alice as if Alice were her little sister…or a very interesting plaything.

Tweedle Dum
VA: Jun Fukuyama

The second "Bloody Twin" is equally cute and equally scary. In *Clover*, Dum can also turn into an adult.

Tweedle Dee
VA: Jun Fukuyama

One of the "Bloody Twin" gatekeepers of the Hatter territory, Dee can be cute when he's not being terrifying. In *Clover*, he sometimes turns into an adult.

Boris Airay
VA: Noriaki Sugiyama

This riddle-loving cat has a signature smirk—and in *Clover*, a new toy. One of his favorite pastimes is giving the Sleepy Mouse a hard time.

Ace
VA: Daisuke Hirakawa

The unlucky knight of Hearts was a former subordinate of Vivaldi and is perpetually lost. Even though he's depressed to be separated from his friend and boss Julius, he stays positive and tries to overcome it with a smile. He seems like a classic nice guy… or is he?

Peter White
VA: Kouki Miyata

The Prime Minister of Heart Castle—who has rabbit ears growing out of his head—invited (kidnapped) Alice to Wonderland. He loves Alice and hates everything else. His cruel, irrational actions are disturbing, but he acts like a completely different person (rabbit?) when in the throes of his love for Alice.

Gray Ringmarc
VA: Kazuya Nakai

Nightmare's subordinate in *Clover*. He used to have strong social ambition and considered assassinating Nightmare… but since Nightmare was such a useless boss, Gray couldn't help but feel sorry for him and ended up a dedicated assistant. He's a sound thinker with a strong work ethic. He's also highly skilled with his blades, rivaling even Ace.

Nightmare Gottschalk
VA: Tomokazu Sugita

A sickly nightmare who hates the hospital and needles. He has the power to read people's thoughts and enter dreams. Even though he likes to shut himself away in dreams, Gray drags him out to sulk from time to time. He technically holds a high position and has many subordinates, but since he can't even take care of his own health, he leaves most things to Gray.

Pierce Villiers
VA: Souichirou Hoshi

New to *Clover*, Pierce is an insomniac mouse who drinks too much coffee. He loves Nightmare (who can help him sleep) and hates Boris (who terrifies him). He dislikes Blood and Vivaldi for discarding coffee in favor of tea. He likes Elliot and Peter well enough, since rabbits aren't natural predators of mice.

The World of "Alice"

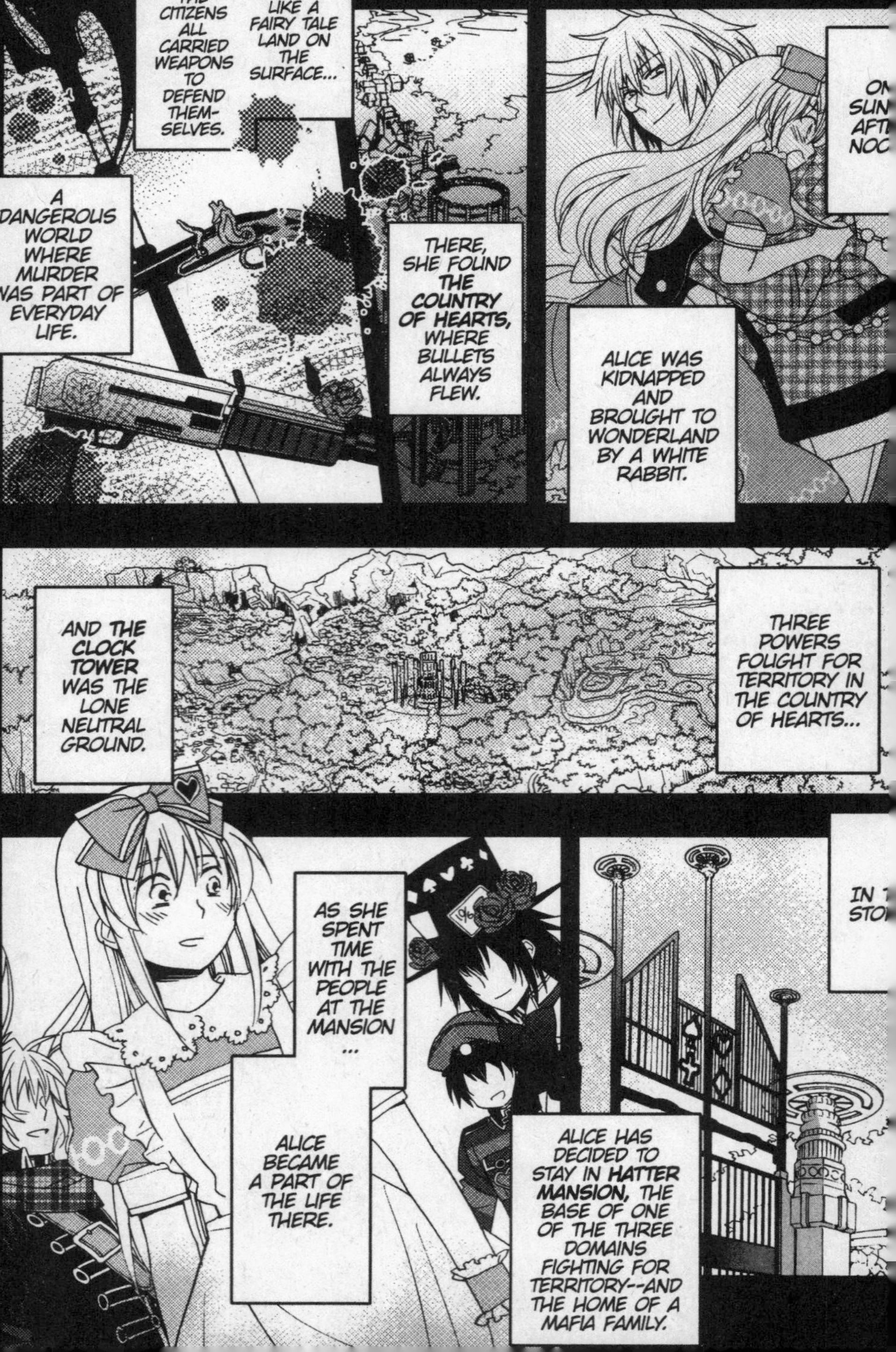
ALICE WAS KIDNAPPED AND BROUGHT TO WONDERLAND BY A WHITE RABBIT.
THERE, SHE FOUND THE COUNTRY OF HEARTS, WHERE BULLETS ALWAYS FLEW.
WHILE IT LOOKED LIKE A FAIRY TALE LAND ON THE SURFACE...
THE CITIZENS ALL CARRIED WEAPONS TO DEFEND THEMSELVES.
A DANGEROUS WORLD WHERE MURDER WAS PART OF EVERYDAY LIFE.
THREE POWERS FOUGHT FOR TERRITORY IN THE COUNTRY OF HEARTS...
AND THE CLOCK TOWER WAS THE LONE NEUTRAL GROUND.
ALICE HAS DECIDED TO STAY IN HATTER MANSION, THE BASE OF ONE OF THE THREE DOMAINS FIGHTING FOR TERRITORY--AND THE HOME OF A MAFIA FAMILY.
AS SHE SPENT TIME WITH THE PEOPLE AT THE MANSION...
ALICE BECAME A PART OF THE LIFE THERE.

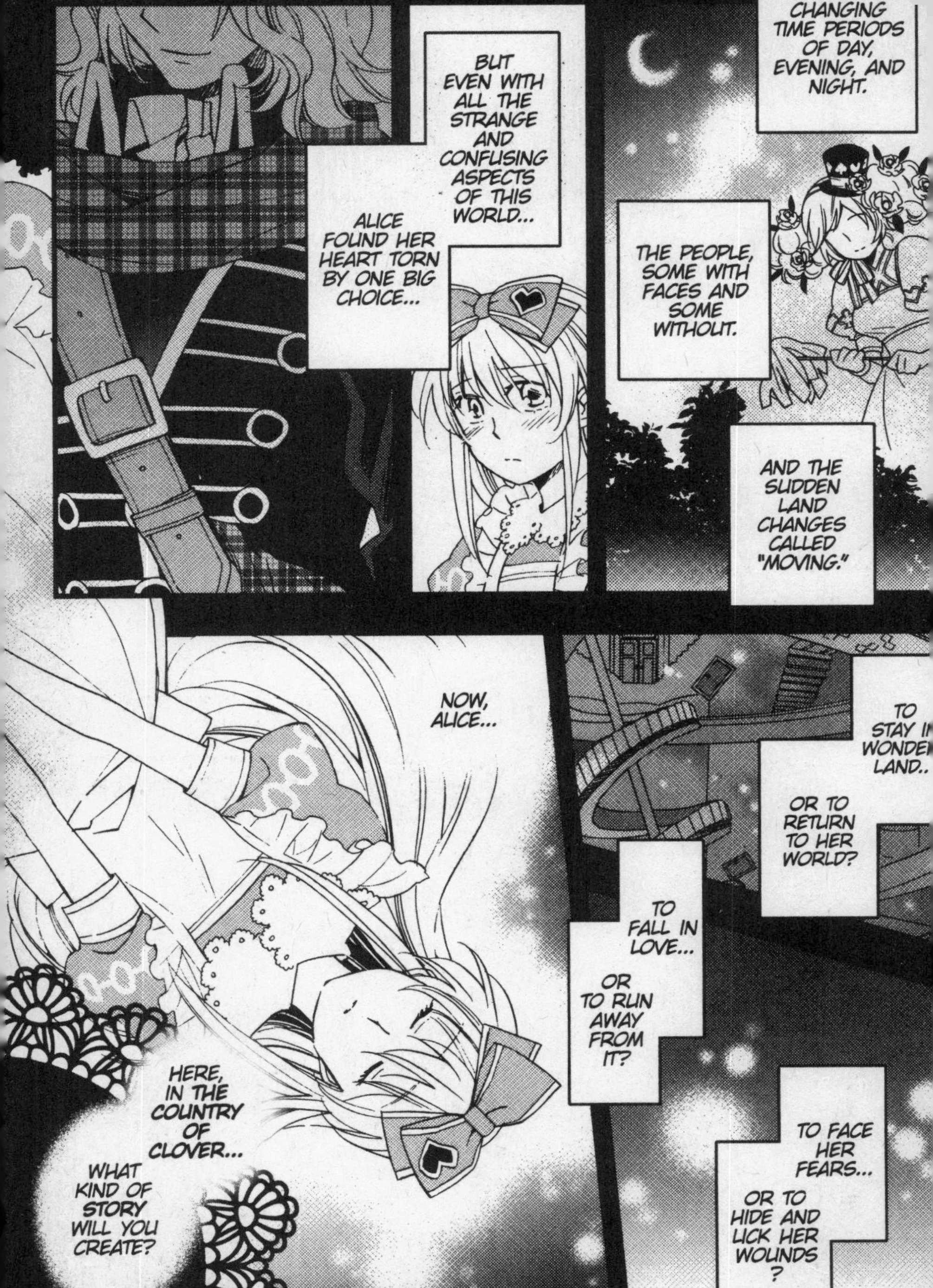
THE RANDOMLY-CHANGING TIME PERIODS OF DAY, EVENING, AND NIGHT.
THE PEOPLE, SOME WITH FACES AND SOME WITHOUT.
AND THE SUDDEN LAND CHANGES CALLED "MOVING."
BUT EVEN WITH ALL THE STRANGE AND CONFUSING ASPECTS OF THIS WORLD...
ALICE FOUND HER HEART TORN BY ONE BIG CHOICE...
TO STAY IN WONDERLAND..
OR TO RETURN TO HER WORLD?
TO FALL IN LOVE...
OR TO RUN AWAY FROM IT?
TO FACE HER FEARS...
OR TO HIDE AND LICK HER WOUNDS?
NOW, ALICE...
HERE, IN THE COUNTRY OF CLOVER...
WHAT KIND OF STORY WILL YOU CREATE?

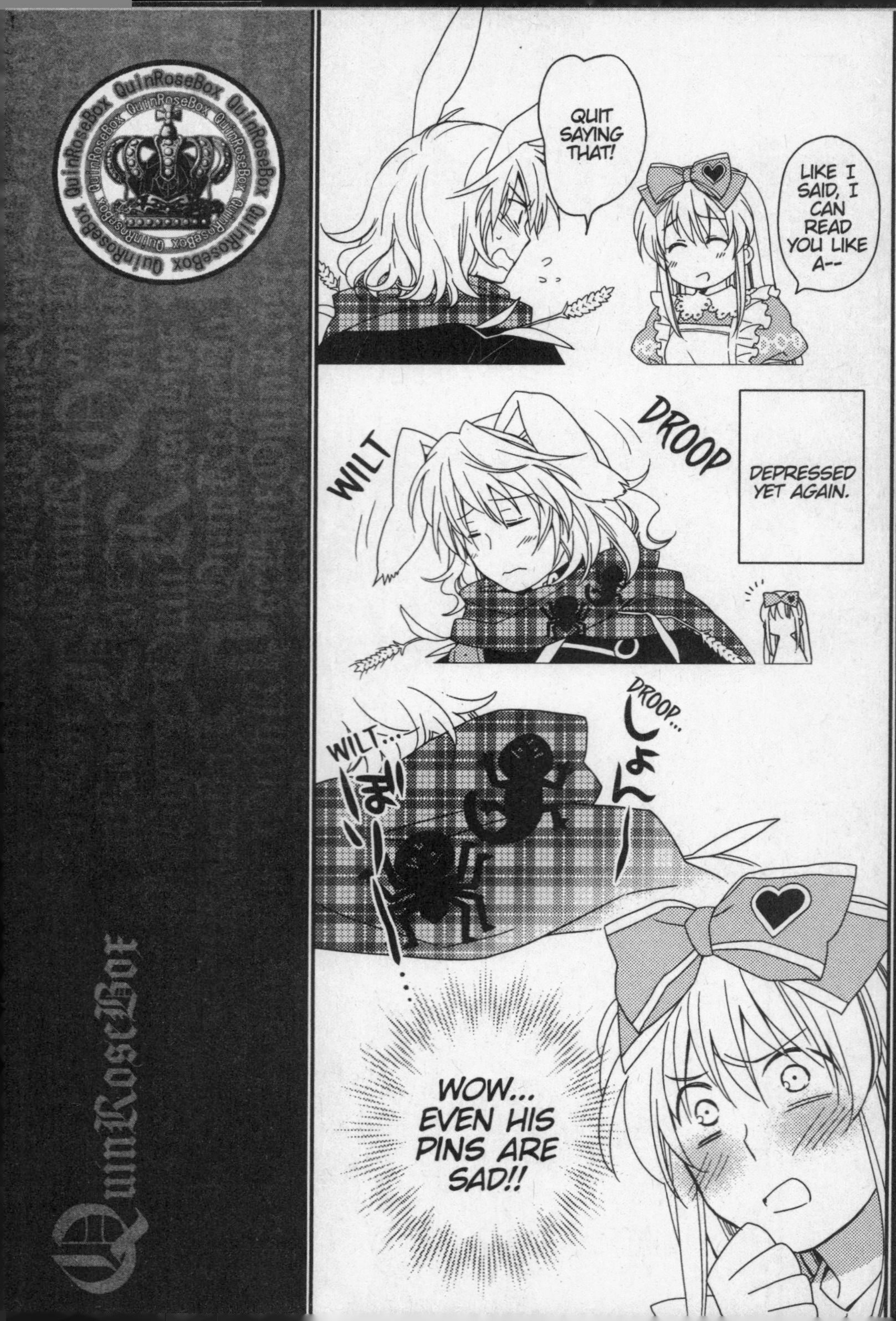
LIKE I SAID, I CAN READ YOU LIKE A--
QUIT SAYING THAT!
DEPRESSED YET AGAIN.
DROOP
WILT
DROOP...
しょん
WILT...
WOW... EVEN HIS PINS ARE SAD!!

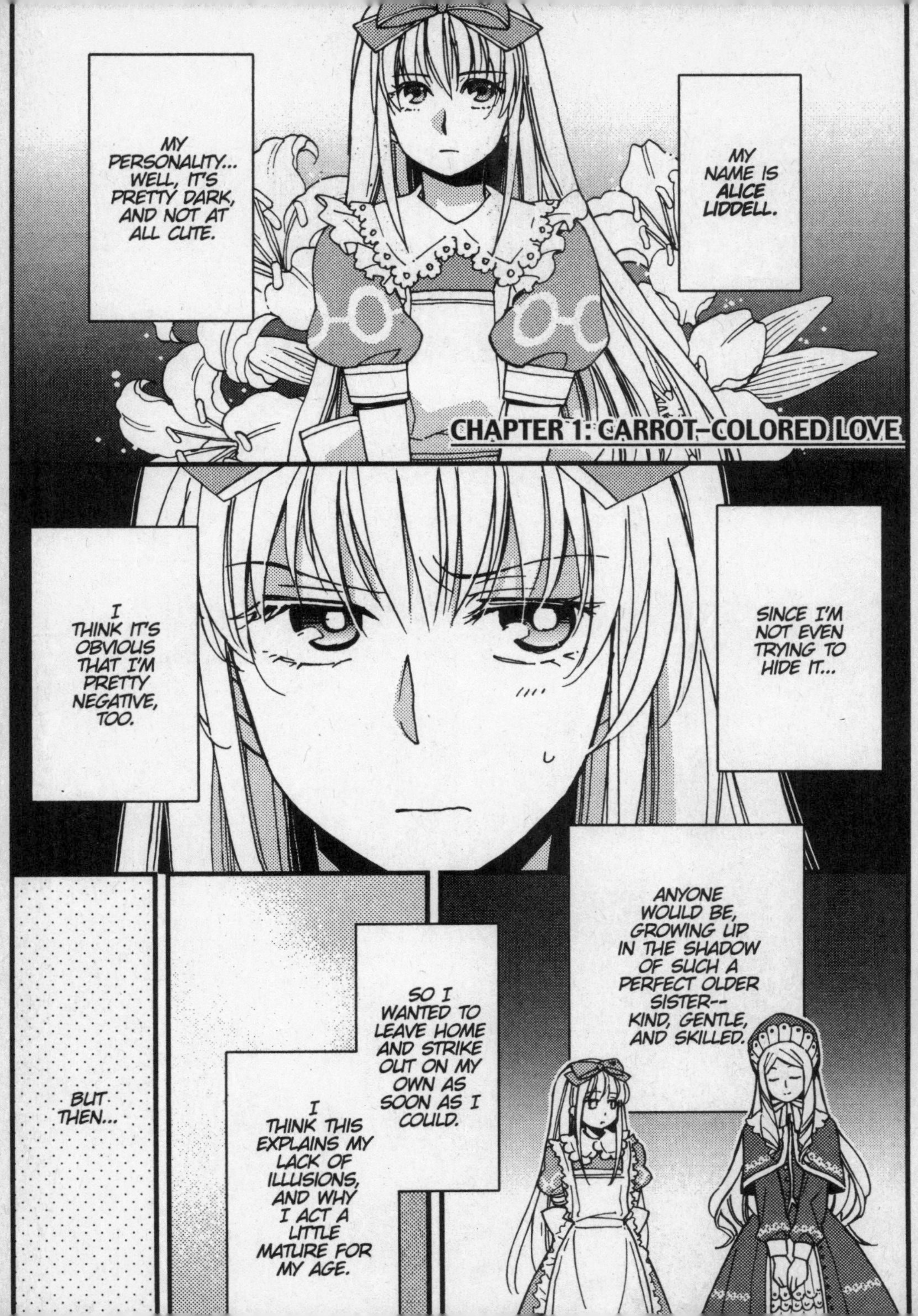
MY NAME IS ALICE LIDDELL.
MY PERSONALITY... WELL, IT'S PRETTY DARK, AND NOT AT ALL CUTE.
CHAPTER 1: CARROT-COLORED LOVE
SINCE I'M NOT EVEN TRYING TO HIDE IT...
I THINK IT'S OBVIOUS THAT I'M PRETTY NEGATIVE, TOO.
ANYONE WOULD BE, GROWING UP IN THE SHADOW OF SUCH A PERFECT OLDER SISTER-- KIND, GENTLE, AND SKILLED.
SO I WANTED TO LEAVE HOME AND STRIKE OUT ON MY OWN AS SOON AS I COULD.
I THINK THIS EXPLAINS MY LACK OF ILLUSIONS, AND WHY I ACT A LITTLE MATURE FOR MY AGE.
BUT THEN...

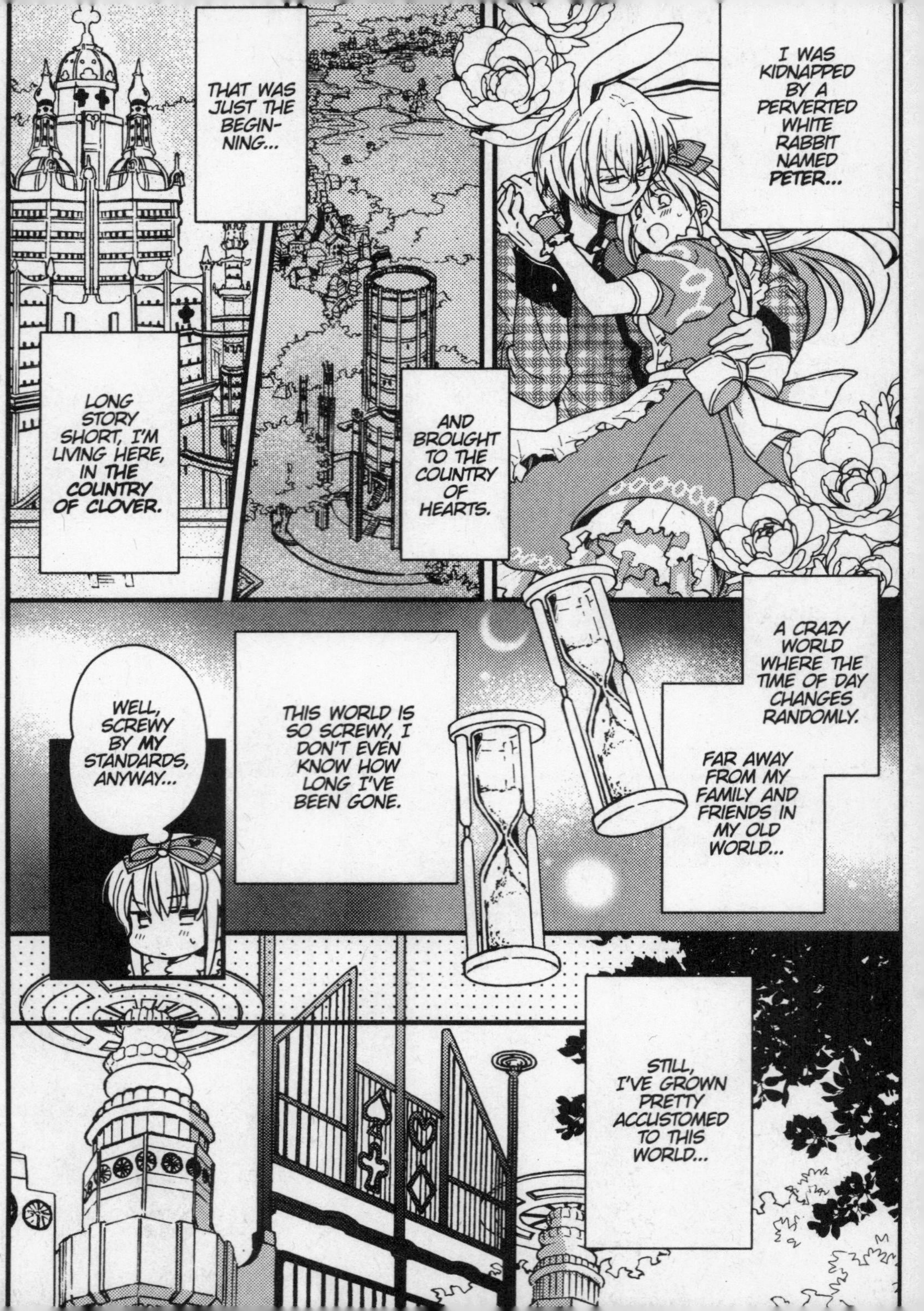
I WAS KIDNAPPED BY A PERVERTED WHITE RABBIT NAMED PETER...
AND BROUGHT TO THE COUNTRY OF HEARTS.
THAT WAS JUST THE BEGIN-NING...
LONG STORY SHORT, I'M LIVING HERE, IN THE COUNTRY OF CLOVER.
A CRAZY WORLD WHERE THE TIME OF DAY CHANGES RANDOMLY.
FAR AWAY FROM MY FAMILY AND FRIENDS IN MY OLD WORLD...
THIS WORLD IS SO SCREWY, I DON'T EVEN KNOW HOW LONG I'VE BEEN GONE.
WELL, SCREWY BY MY STANDARDS, ANYWAY...
STILL, I'VE GROWN PRETTY ACCUSTOMED TO THIS WORLD...

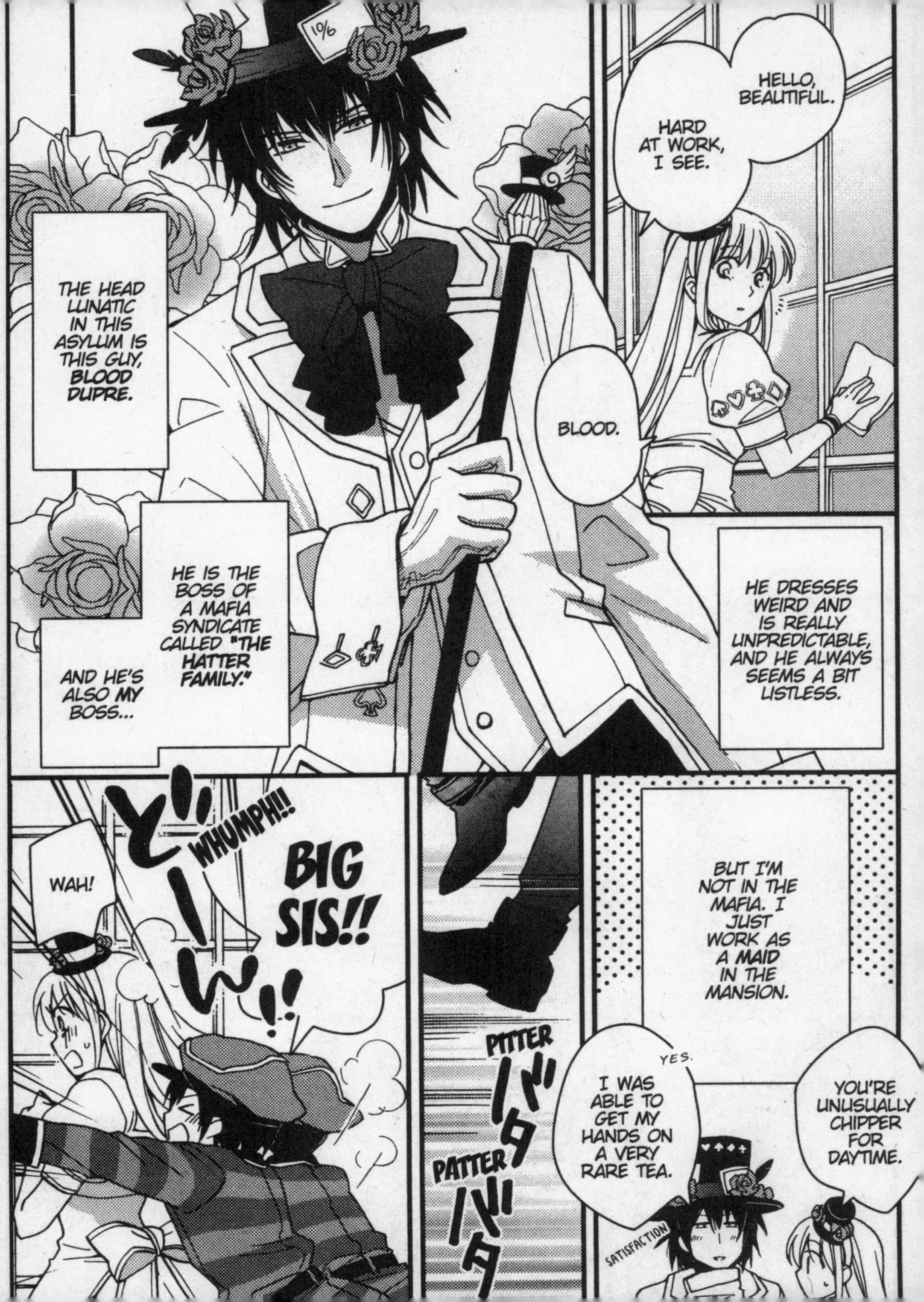
HELLO, BEAUTIFUL.
HARD AT WORK, I SEE.
BLOOD.
THE HEAD LUNATIC IN THIS ASYLUM IS THIS GUY, BLOOD DUPRE.
HE IS THE BOSS OF A MAFIA SYNDICATE CALLED "THE HATTER FAMILY."
AND HE'S ALSO MY BOSS...
HE DRESSES WEIRD AND IS REALLY UNPREDICTABLE, AND HE ALWAYS SEEMS A BIT LISTLESS.
BUT I'M NOT IN THE MAFIA. I JUST WORK AS A MAID IN THE MANSION.
YOU'RE UNUSUALLY CHIPPER FOR DAYTIME.
YES.
I WAS ABLE TO GET MY HANDS ON A VERY RARE TEA.
SATISFACTION
PITTER
PATTER
WHUMPH!!
BIG SIS!!
WAH!

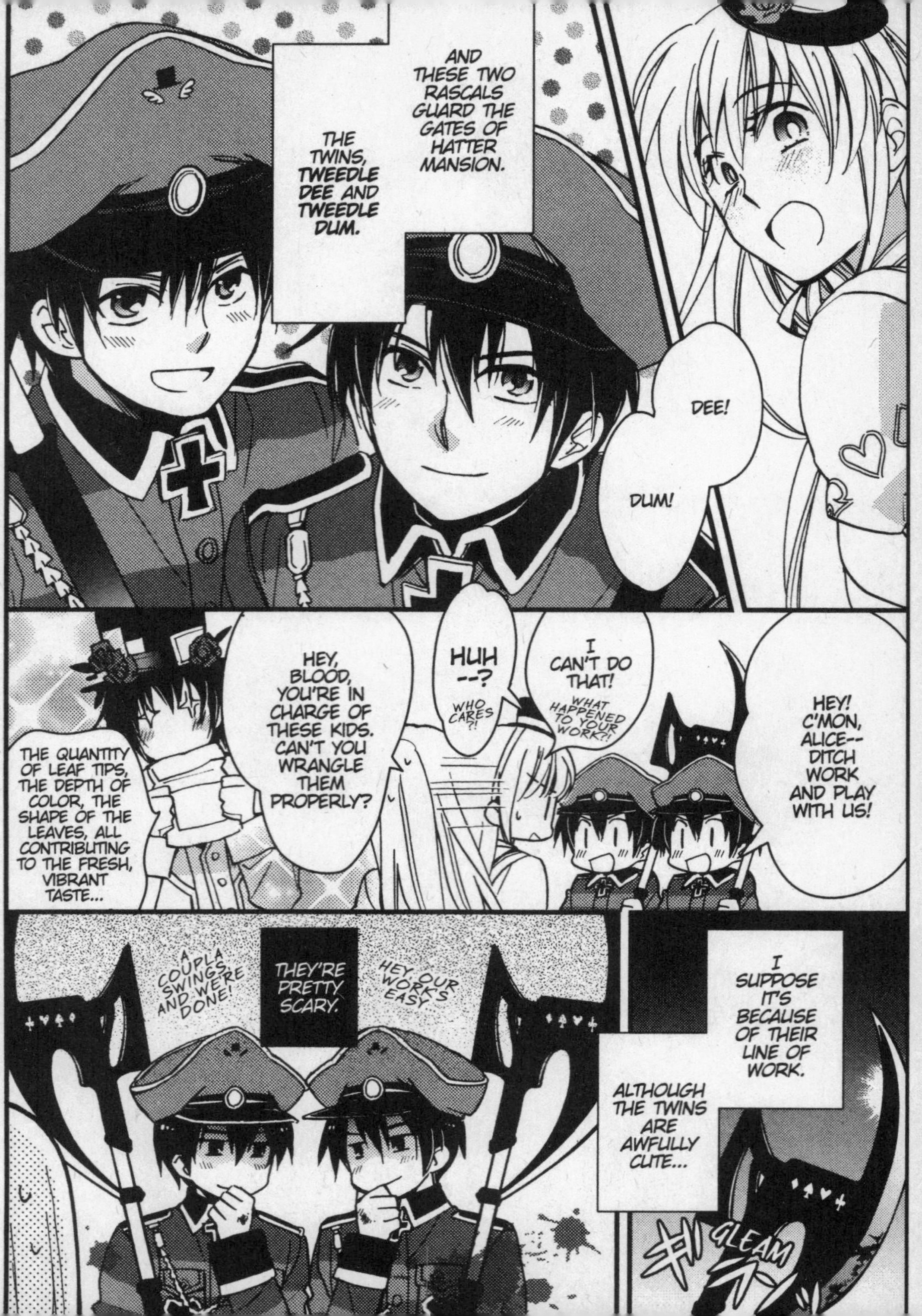
DEE!
DUM!
THE TWINS, TWEEDLE DEE AND TWEEDLE DUM.
AND THESE TWO RASCALS GUARD THE GATES OF HATTER MANSION.
HEY! C'MON, ALICE-- DITCH WORK AND PLAY WITH US!
I CAN'T DO THAT!
WHAT HAPPENED TO YOUR WORK?!
HUH --?
WHO CARES?!
HEY, BLOOD, YOU'RE IN CHARGE OF THESE KIDS. CAN'T YOU WRANGLE THEM PROPERLY?
THE QUANTITY OF LEAF TIPS, THE DEPTH OF COLOR, THE SHAPE OF THE LEAVES, ALL CONTRIBUTING TO THE FRESH, VIBRANT TASTE...
ALTHOUGH THE TWINS ARE AWFULLY CUTE...
HEY OUR WORK'S EASY
THEY'RE PRETTY SCARY.
A COUPLA SWINGS AND WE'RE DONE!
I SUPPOSE IT'S BECAUSE OF THEIR LINE OF WORK.
GLEAM

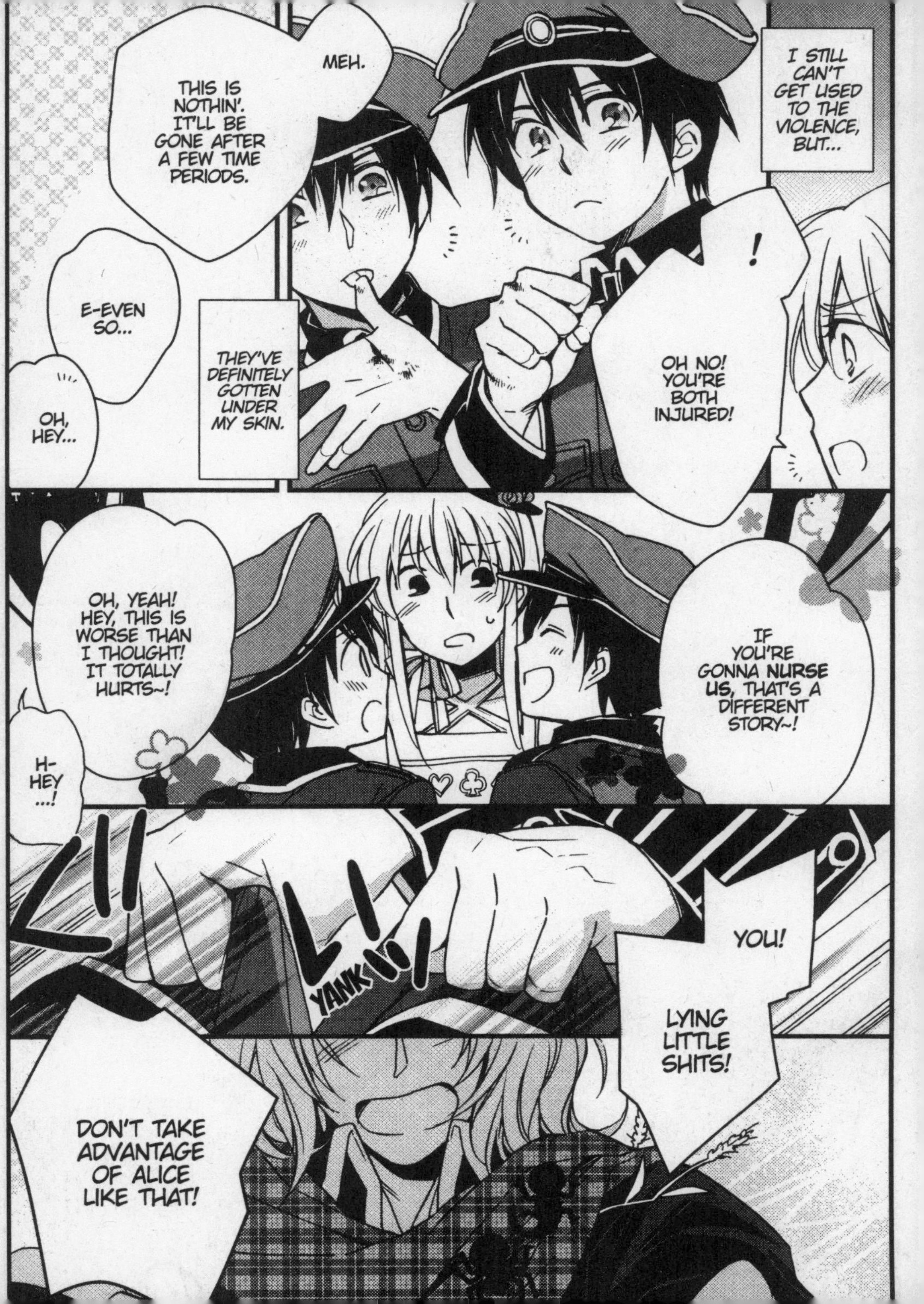
I STILL CAN'T GET USED TO THE VIOLENCE, BUT...
MEH.
THIS IS NOTHIN'. IT'LL BE GONE AFTER A FEW TIME PERIODS.
!
OH NO! YOU'RE BOTH INJURED!
THEY'VE DEFINITELY GOTTEN UNDER MY SKIN.
E-EVEN SO...
OH, HEY...
IF YOU'RE GONNA NURSE US, THAT'S A DIFFERENT STORY~!
OH, YEAH! HEY, THIS IS WORSE THAN I THOUGHT! IT TOTALLY HURTS~!
H-HEY ...!
YANK
YOU!
LYING LITTLE SHITS!
DON'T TAKE ADVANTAGE OF ALICE LIKE THAT!

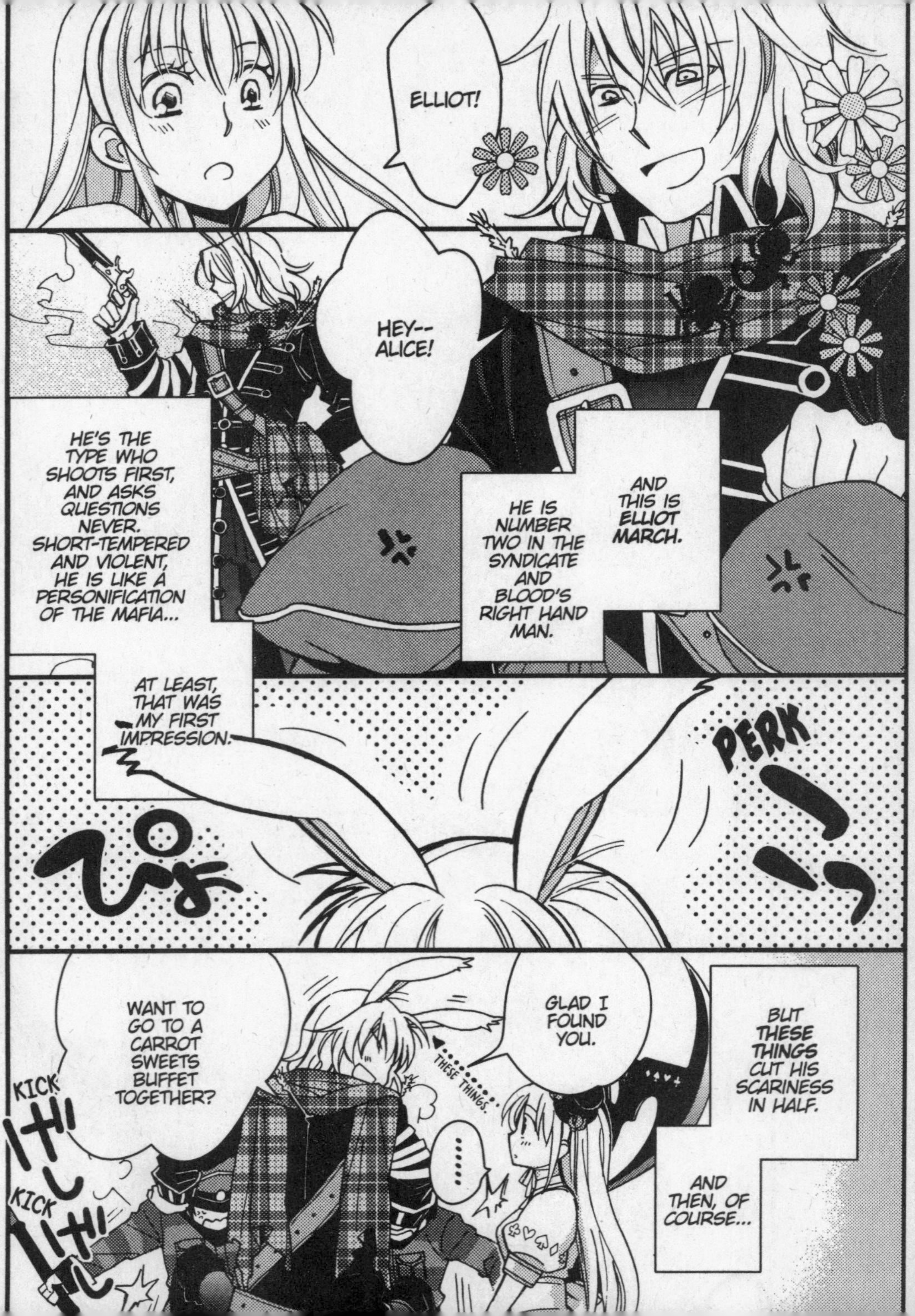
ELLIOT!
HEY-- ALICE!
AND THIS IS ELLIOT MARCH.
HE IS NUMBER TWO IN THE SYNDICATE AND BLOOD'S RIGHT HAND MAN.
HE'S THE TYPE WHO SHOOTS FIRST, AND ASKS QUESTIONS NEVER. SHORT-TEMPERED AND VIOLENT, HE IS LIKE A PERSONIFICATION OF THE MAFIA...
AT LEAST, THAT WAS MY FIRST IMPRESSION.
PERK
ぴょ
BUT THESE THINGS CUT HIS SCARINESS IN HALF.
GLAD I FOUND YOU.
THESE THINGS.
WANT TO GO TO A CARROT SWEETS BUFFET TOGETHER?
......
KICK
KICK
AND THEN, OF COURSE...

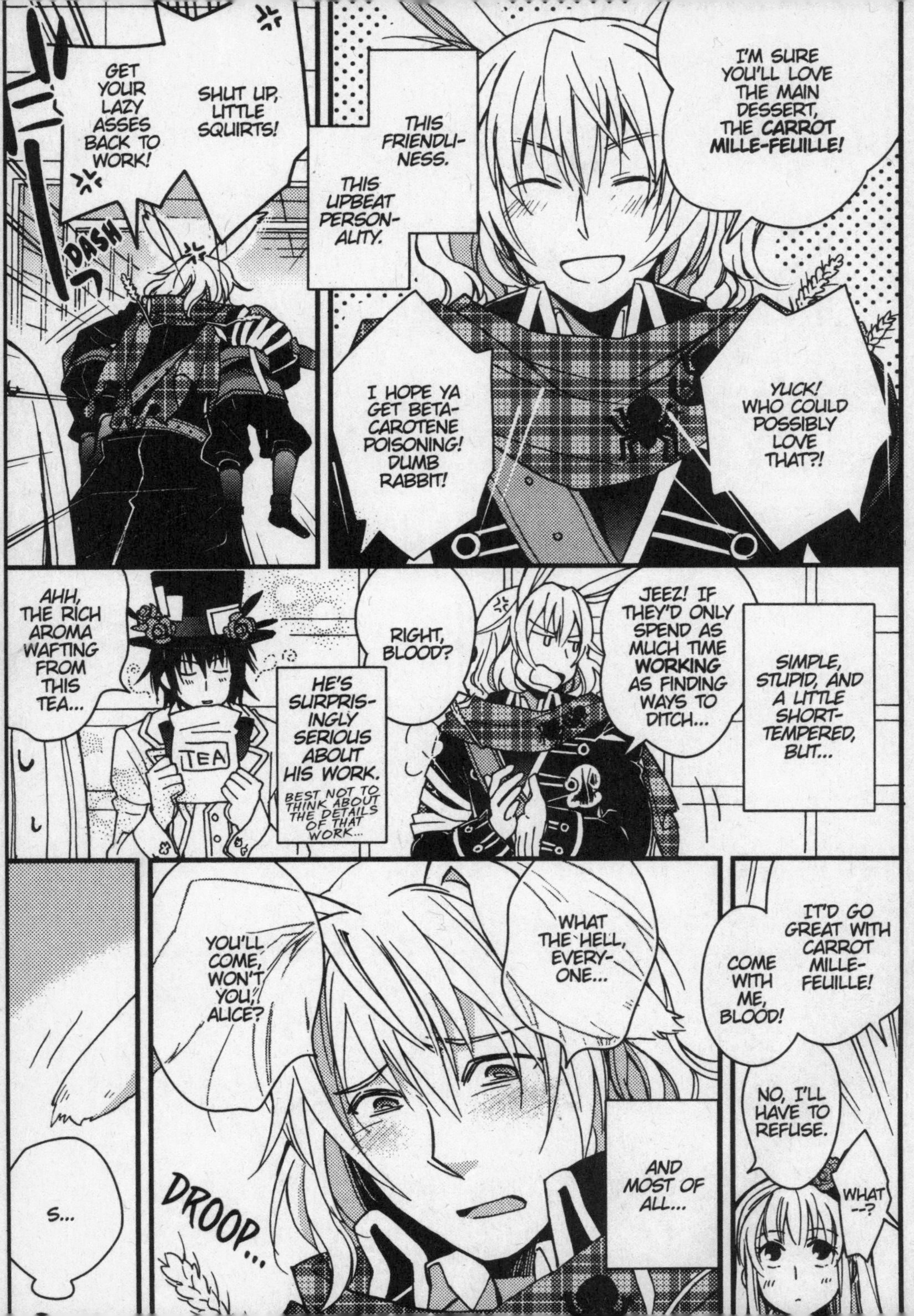
I'M SURE YOU'LL LOVE THE MAIN DESSERT, THE CARROT MILLE-FEUILLE!
THIS FRIENDLI-NESS.
THIS UPBEAT PERSON-ALITY.
YUCK! WHO COULD POSSIBLY LOVE THAT?!
I HOPE YA GET BETA-CAROTENE POISONING! DUMB RABBIT!
SHUT UP, LITTLE SQUIRTS!
GET YOUR LAZY ASSES BACK TO WORK!
DASH
SIMPLE, STUPID, AND A LITTLE SHORT-TEMPERED, BUT...
JEEZ! IF THEY'D ONLY SPEND AS MUCH TIME WORKING AS FINDING WAYS TO DITCH...
RIGHT, BLOOD?
HE'S SURPRIS-INGLY SERIOUS ABOUT HIS WORK.
BEST NOT TO THINK ABOUT THE DETAILS OF THAT WORK...
AHH, THE RICH AROMA WAFTING FROM THIS TEA...
TEA
IT'D GO GREAT WITH CARROT MILLE-FEUILLE!
COME WITH ME, BLOOD!
NO, I'LL HAVE TO REFUSE.
WHAT --?
WHAT THE HELL, EVERY-ONE...
YOU'LL COME, WON'T YOU, ALICE?
AND MOST OF ALL...
DROOP...
S...

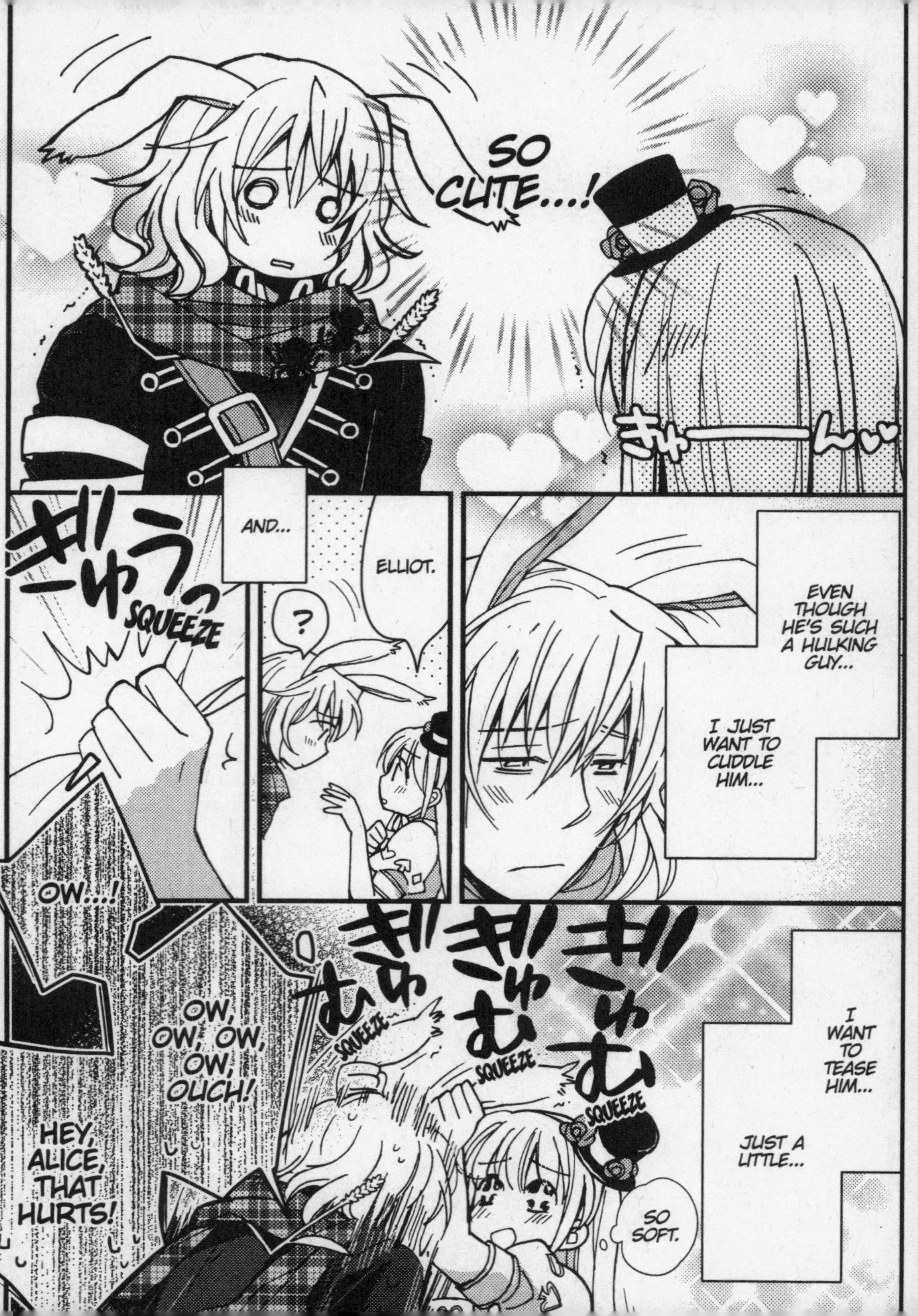

SO CUTE...!
きゅーーん~♡
EVEN THOUGH HE'S SUCH A HULKING GUY...
I JUST WANT TO CUDDLE HIM...
AND...
ELLIOT.
?
ぎゅうっ
SQUEEZE
OW...!
I WANT TO TEASE HIM...
JUST A LITTLE...
ぎゅむ
SQUEEZE
ぎゅむ
SQUEEZE
ぎゅむ
SQUEEZE
SO SOFT.
OW, OW, OW, OW, OUCH!
HEY, ALICE, THAT HURTS!

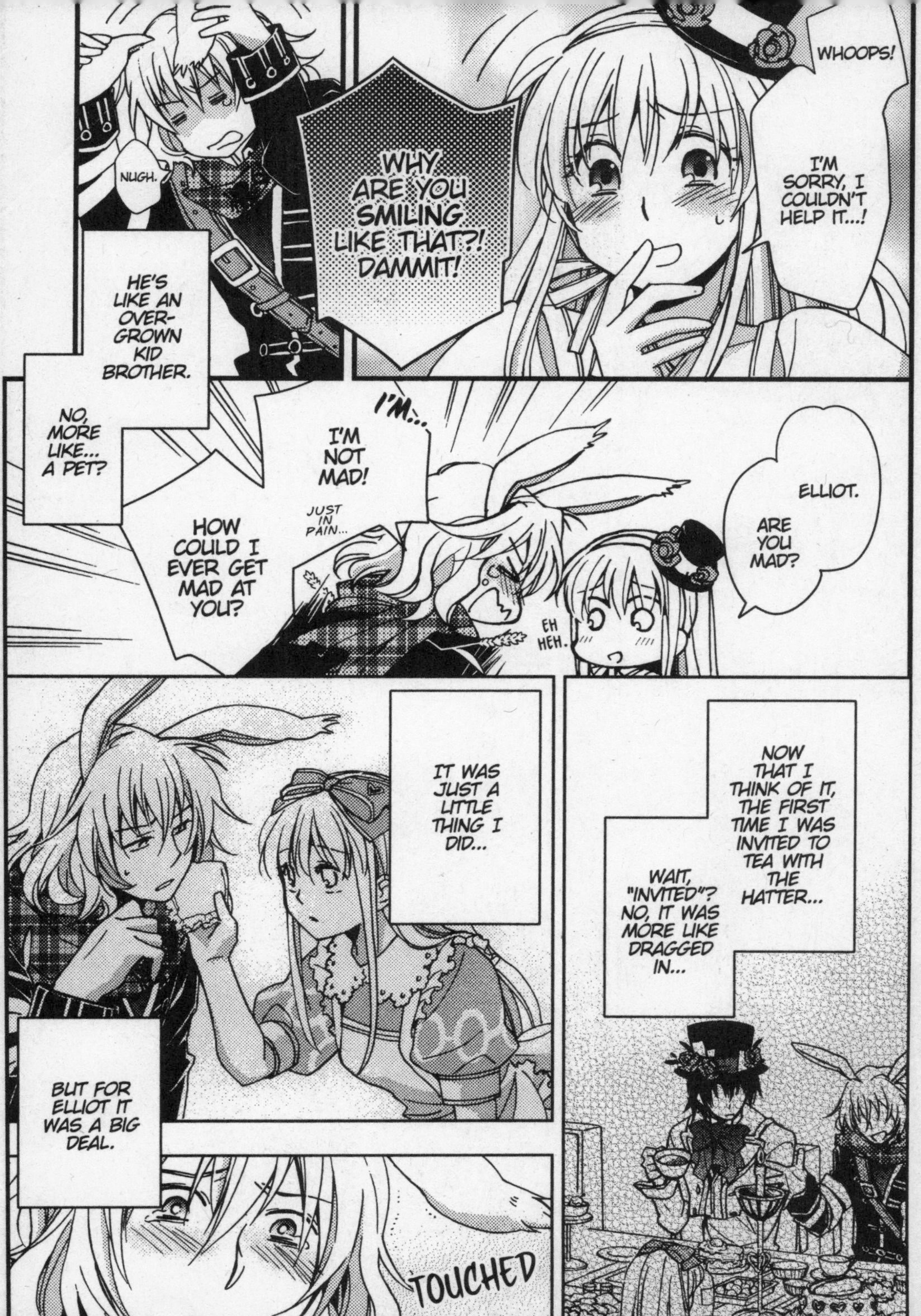
WHOOPS!
I'M SORRY, I COULDN'T HELP IT...!
WHY ARE YOU SMILING LIKE THAT?! DAMMIT!
NUGH.
HE'S LIKE AN OVER-GROWN KID BROTHER.
ELLIOT.
ARE YOU MAD?
EH HEH.
I'M...
I'M NOT MAD!
JUST IN PAIN...
HOW COULD I EVER GET MAD AT YOU?
NO, MORE LIKE... A PET?
NOW THAT I THINK OF IT, THE FIRST TIME I WAS INVITED TO TEA WITH THE HATTER...
WAIT, "INVITED"? NO, IT WAS MORE LIKE DRAGGED IN...
IT WAS JUST A LITTLE THING I DID...
BUT FOR ELLIOT IT WAS A BIG DEAL.
TOUCHED

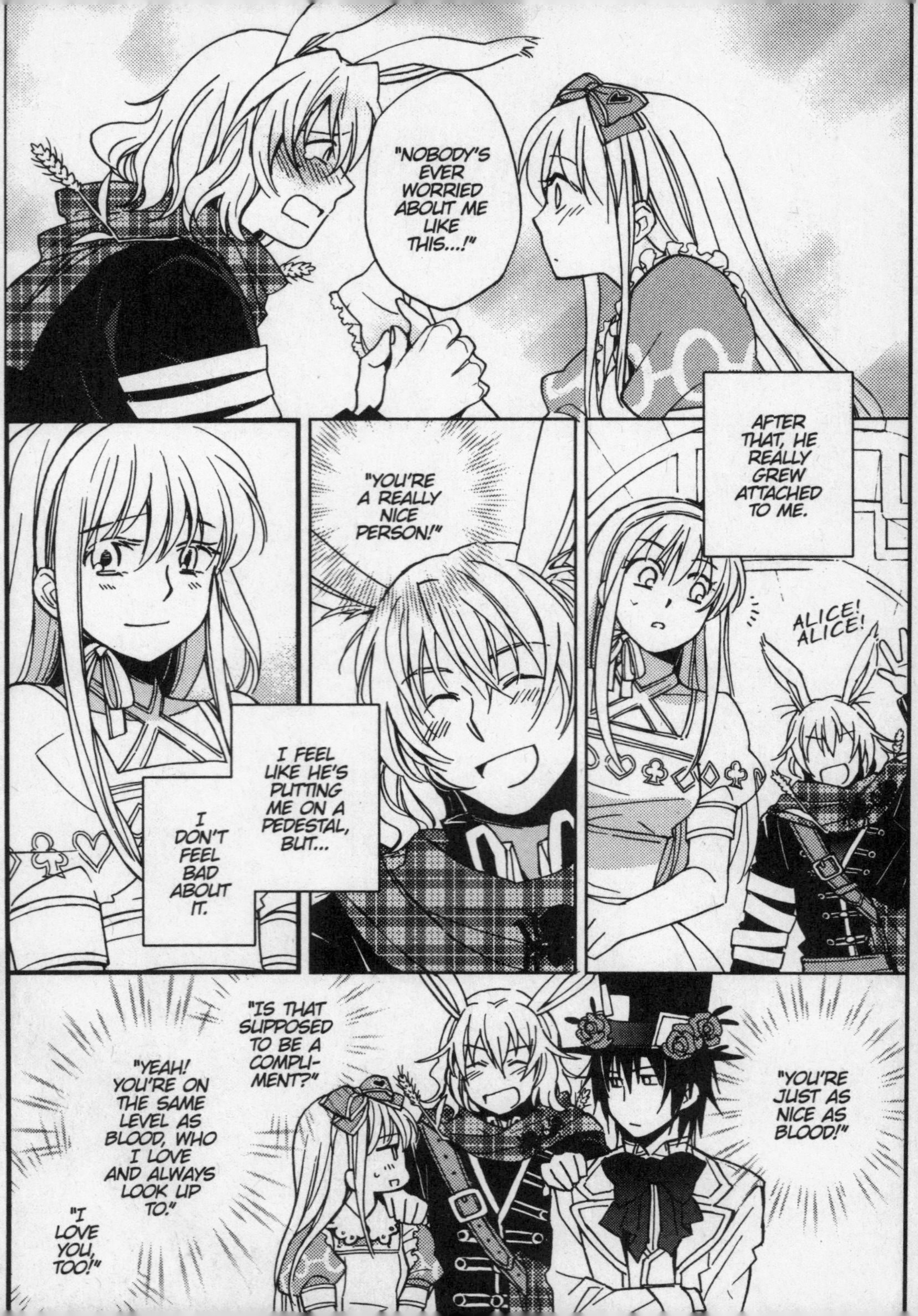
"NOBODY'S EVER WORRIED ABOUT ME LIKE THIS...!"
AFTER THAT, HE REALLY GREW ATTACHED TO ME.
ALICE! ALICE!
"YOU'RE A REALLY NICE PERSON!"
I FEEL LIKE HE'S PUTTING ME ON A PEDESTAL, BUT...
I DON'T FEEL BAD ABOUT IT.
"YOU'RE JUST AS NICE AS BLOOD!"
"IS THAT SUPPOSED TO BE A COMPLIMENT?"
"YEAH! YOU'RE ON THE SAME LEVEL AS BLOOD, WHO I LOVE AND ALWAYS LOOK UP TO."
"I LOVE YOU, TOO!"

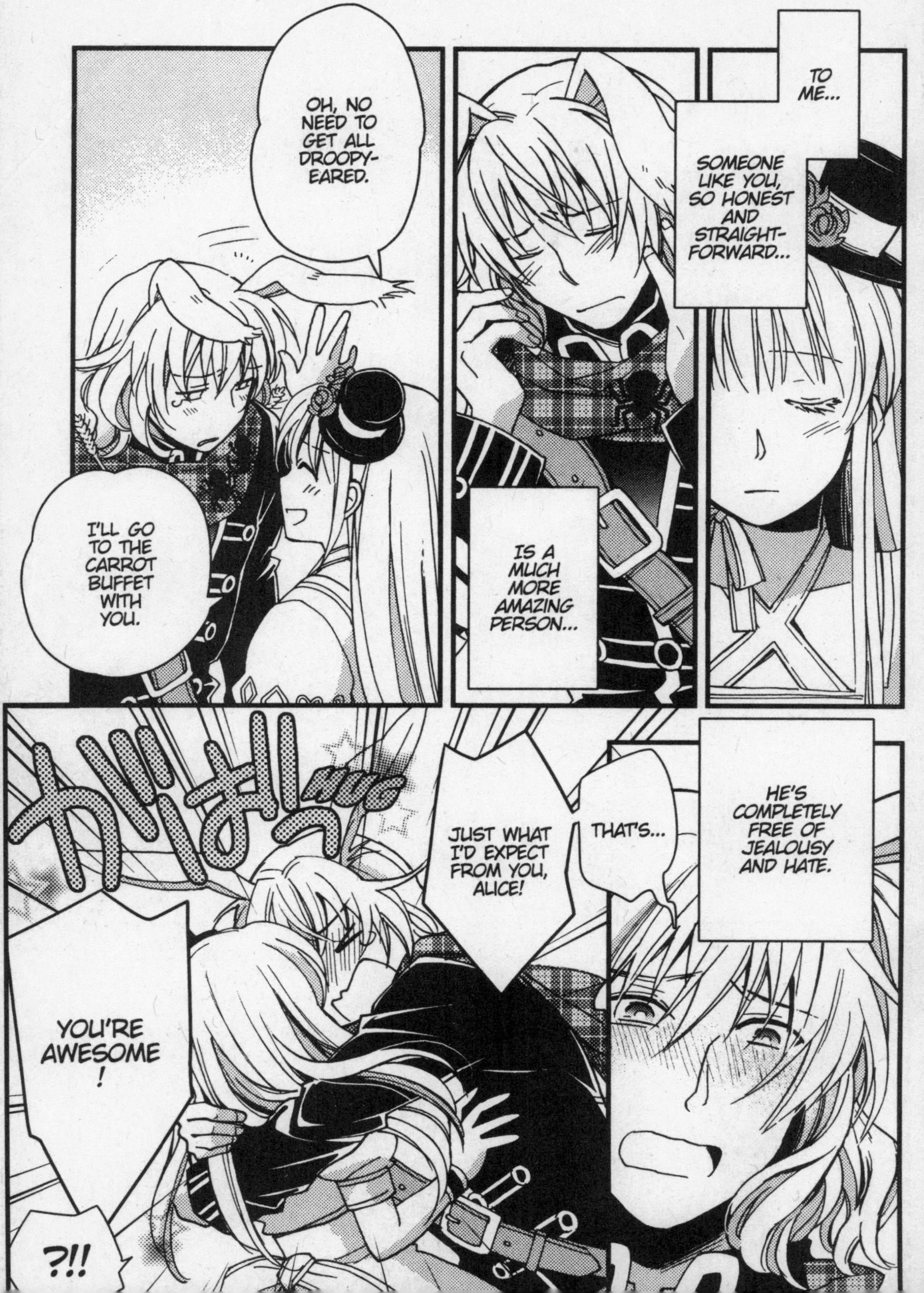
TO ME...
SOMEONE LIKE YOU, SO HONEST AND STRAIGHT-FORWARD...
IS A MUCH MORE AMAZING PERSON...
OH, NO NEED TO GET ALL DROOPY-EARED.
I'LL GO TO THE CARROT BUFFET WITH YOU.
HE'S COMPLETELY FREE OF JEALOUSY AND HATE.
THAT'S...
JUST WHAT I'D EXPECT FROM YOU, ALICE!
がばっ
HUG
YOU'RE AWESOME!
?!!

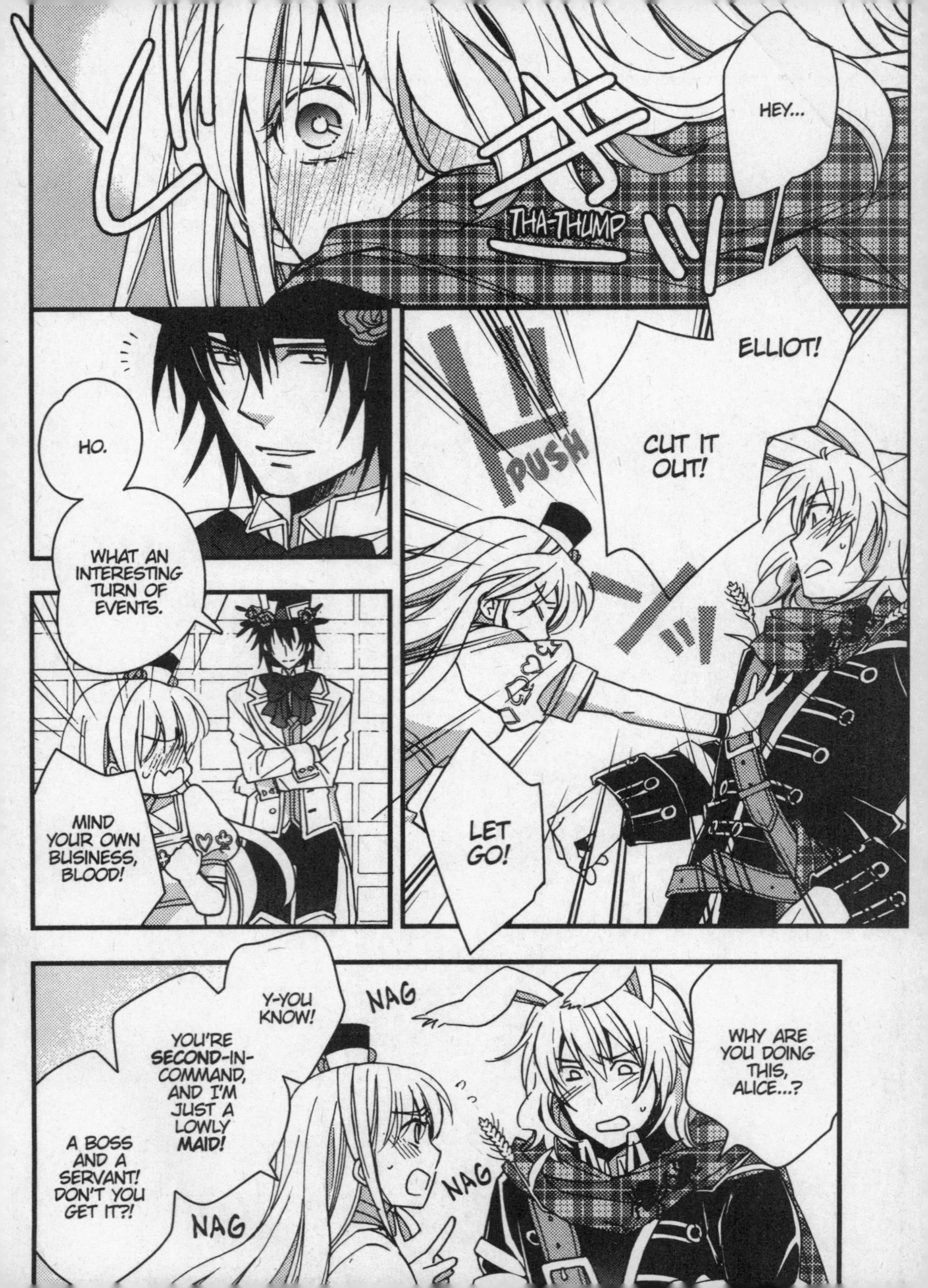
HEY...
THA-THUMP
ELLIOT!
PUSH
CUT IT OUT!
LET GO!
HO.
WHAT AN INTERESTING TURN OF EVENTS.
MIND YOUR OWN BUSINESS, BLOOD!
WHY ARE YOU DOING THIS, ALICE...?
NAG
Y-YOU KNOW!
YOU'RE SECOND-IN-COMMAND, AND I'M JUST A LOWLY MAID!
NAG
A BOSS AND A SERVANT! DON'T YOU GET IT?!
NAG

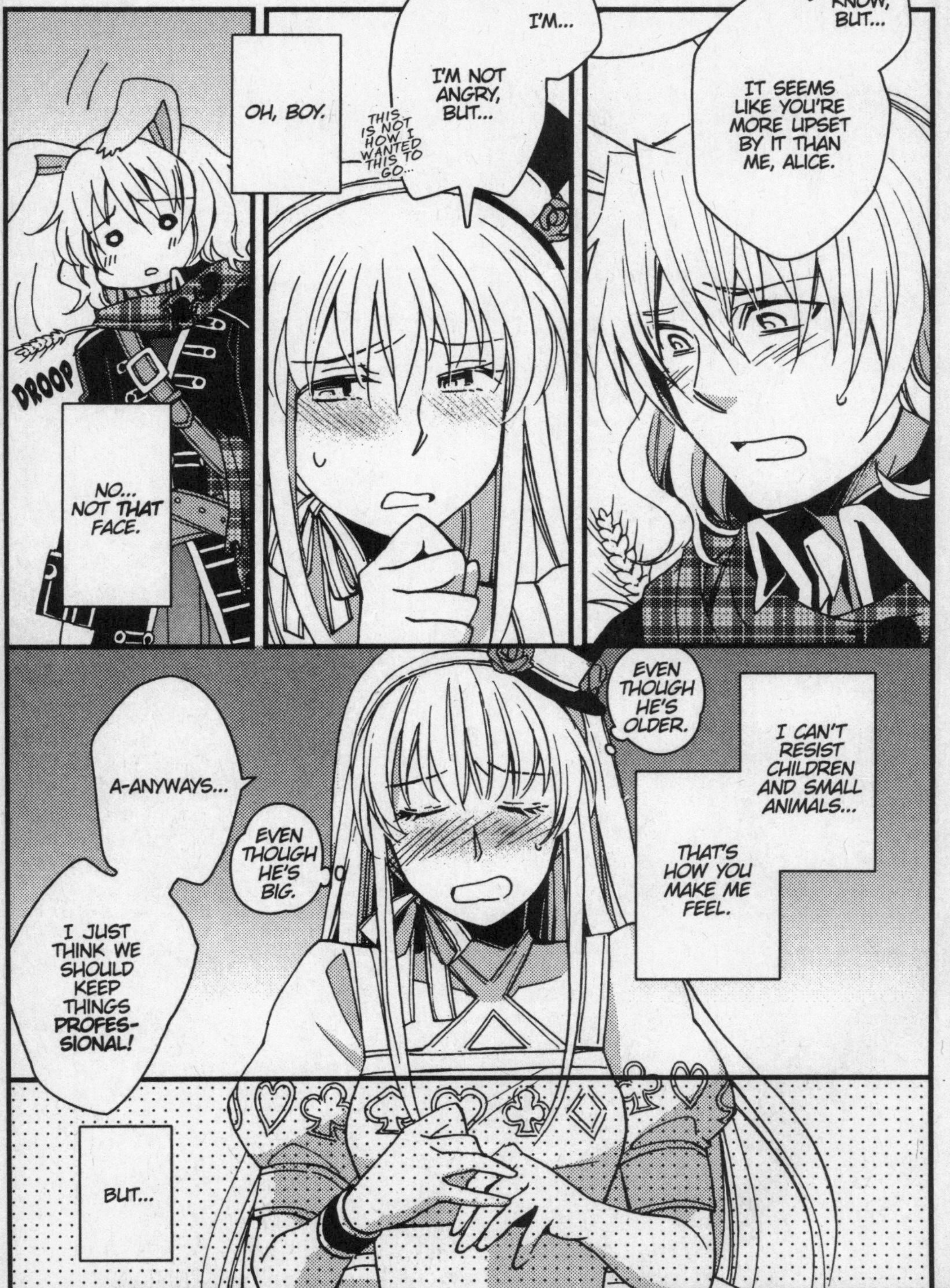
I KNOW, BUT...
IT SEEMS LIKE YOU'RE MORE UPSET BY IT THAN ME, ALICE.
I'M...
I'M NOT ANGRY, BUT...
THIS IS NOT HOW I WANTED THIS TO GO...
OH, BOY.
DROOP
NO... NOT THAT FACE.
EVEN THOUGH HE'S OLDER.
I CAN'T RESIST CHILDREN AND SMALL ANIMALS...
THAT'S HOW YOU MAKE ME FEEL.
A-ANYWAYS...
EVEN THOUGH HE'S BIG.
I JUST THINK WE SHOULD KEEP THINGS PROFES-SIONAL!
BUT...

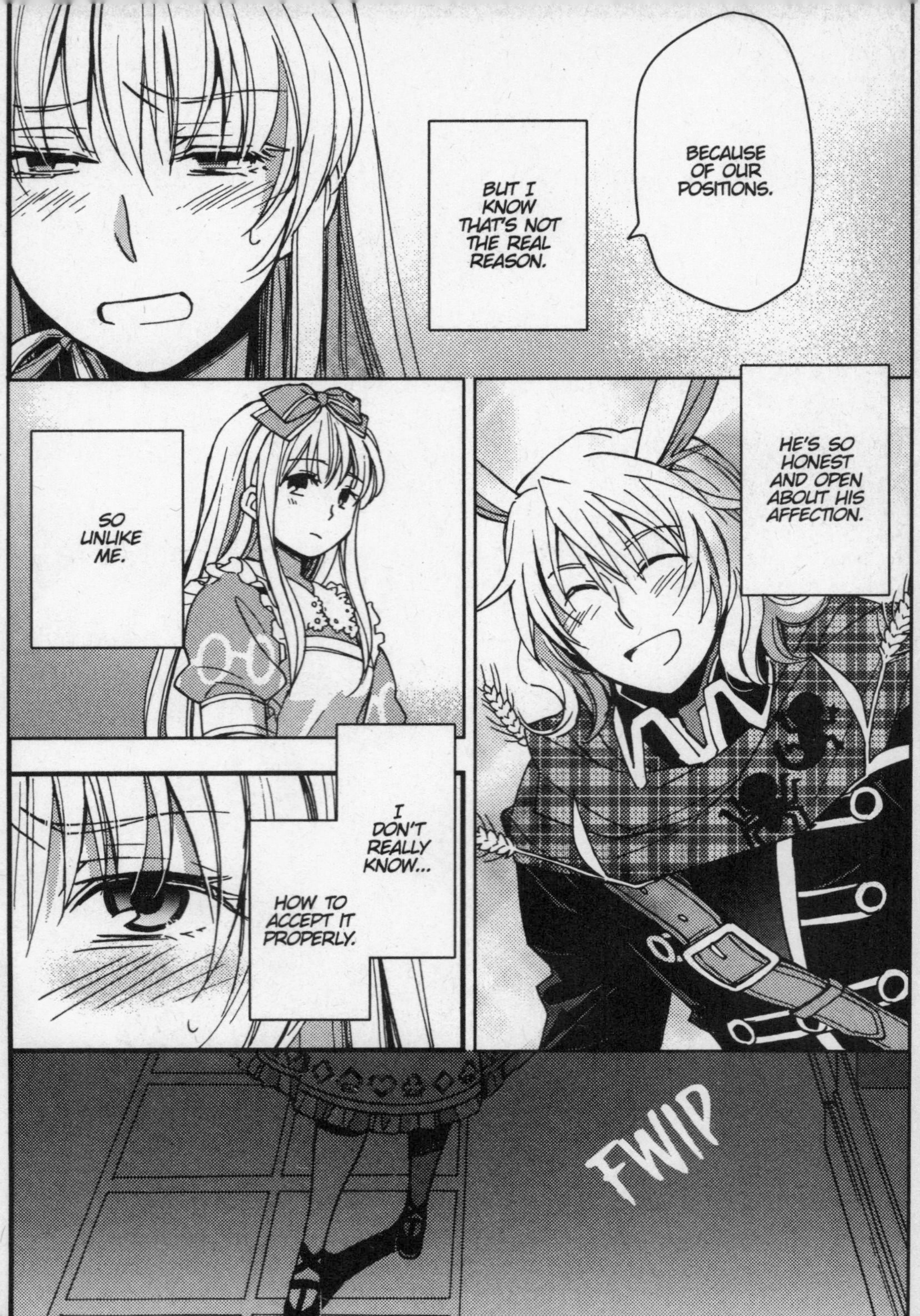

BECAUSE OF OUR POSITIONS.
BUT I KNOW THAT'S NOT THE REAL REASON.
HE'S SO HONEST AND OPEN ABOUT HIS AFFECTION.
SO UNLIKE ME.
I DON'T REALLY KNOW...
HOW TO ACCEPT IT PROPERLY.
FWIP

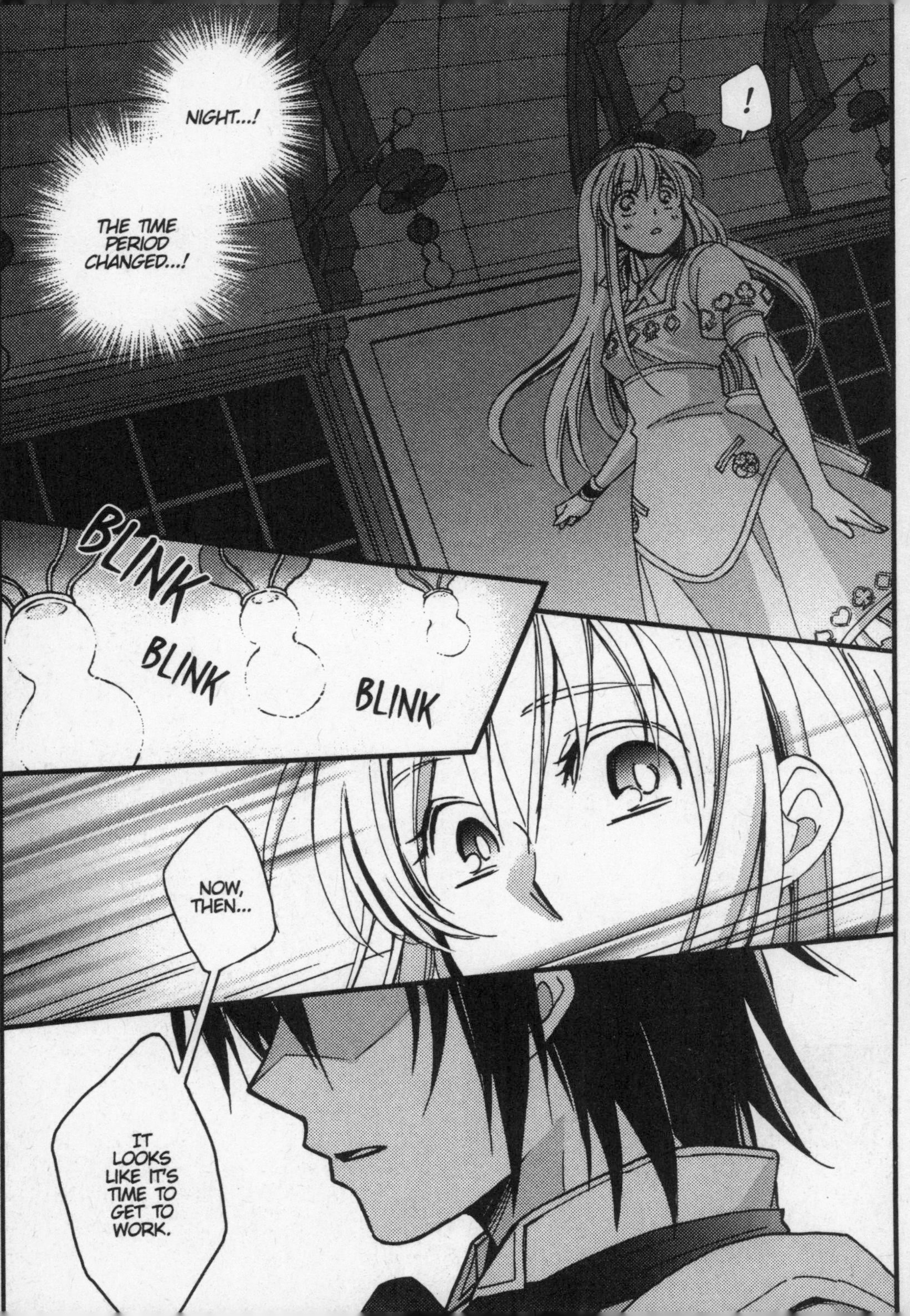
!
NIGHT...!
THE TIME PERIOD CHANGED...!
BLINK
BLINK
BLINK
NOW, THEN...
IT LOOKS LIKE IT'S TIME TO GET TO WORK.

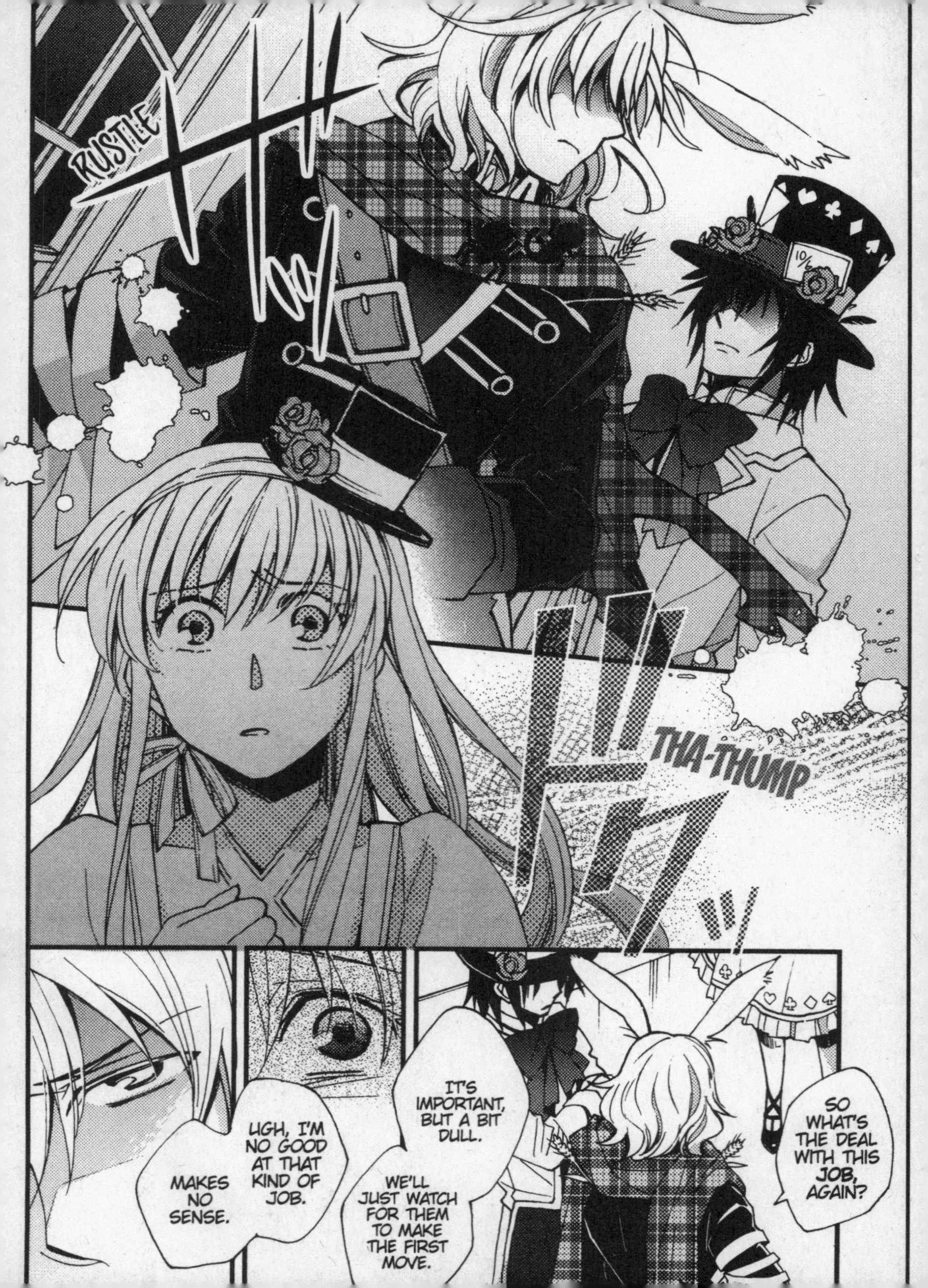
RUSTLE
THA-THUMP
SO WHAT'S THE DEAL WITH THIS JOB, AGAIN?
IT'S IMPORTANT, BUT A BIT DULL.
WE'LL JUST WATCH FOR THEM TO MAKE THE FIRST MOVE.
UGH, I'M NO GOOD AT THAT KIND OF JOB.
MAKES NO SENSE.

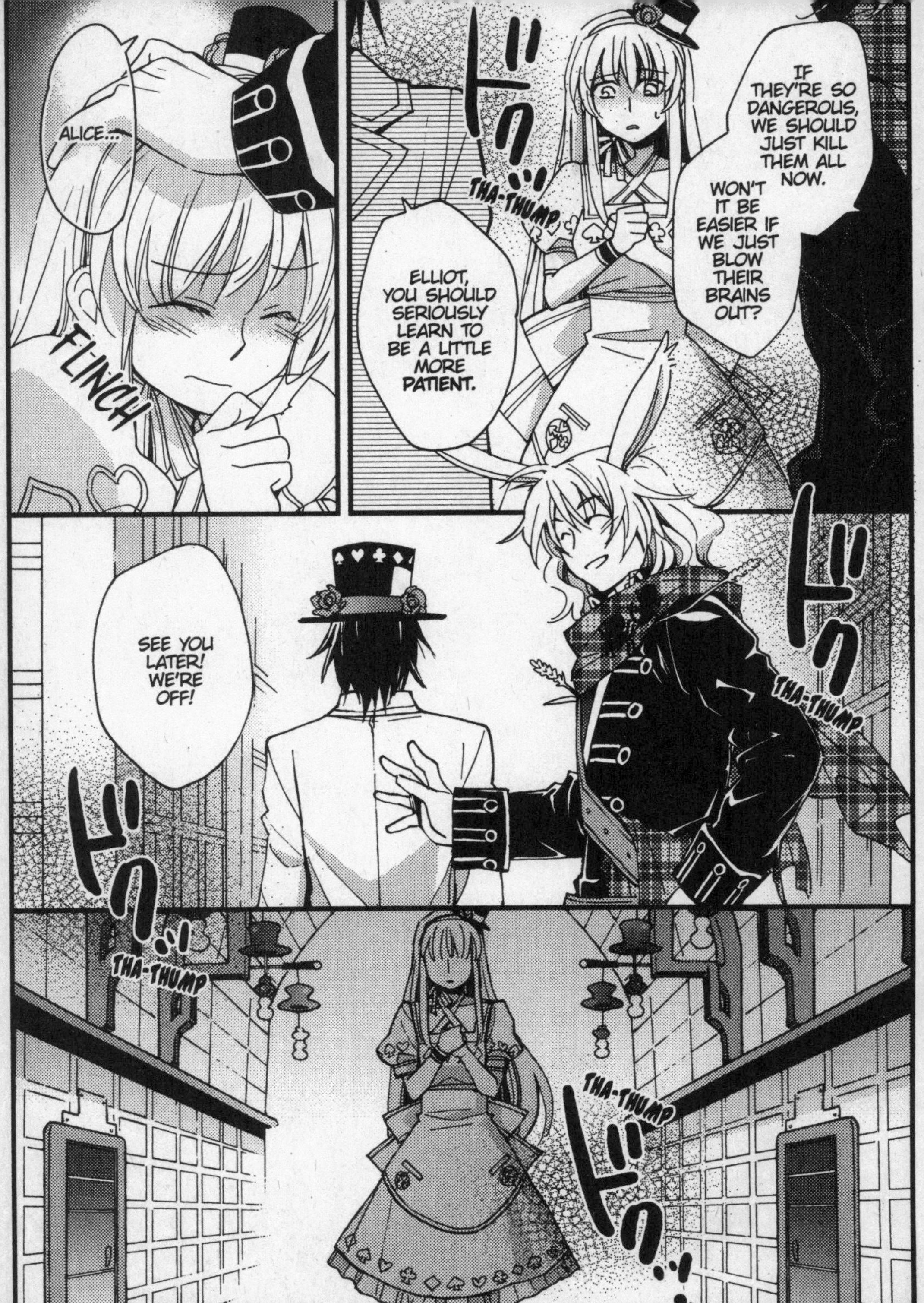

IF THEY'RE SO DANGEROUS, WE SHOULD JUST KILL THEM ALL NOW.
WON'T IT BE EASIER IF WE JUST BLOW THEIR BRAINS OUT?
ドクッ
THA-THUMP
ELLIOT, YOU SHOULD SERIOUSLY LEARN TO BE A LITTLE MORE PATIENT.
ALICE...
FLINCH
ドクッ
THA-THUMP
SEE YOU LATER! WE'RE OFF!
ドクッ
THA-THUMP
ドクッ
THA-THUMP
ドクッ
THA-THUMP

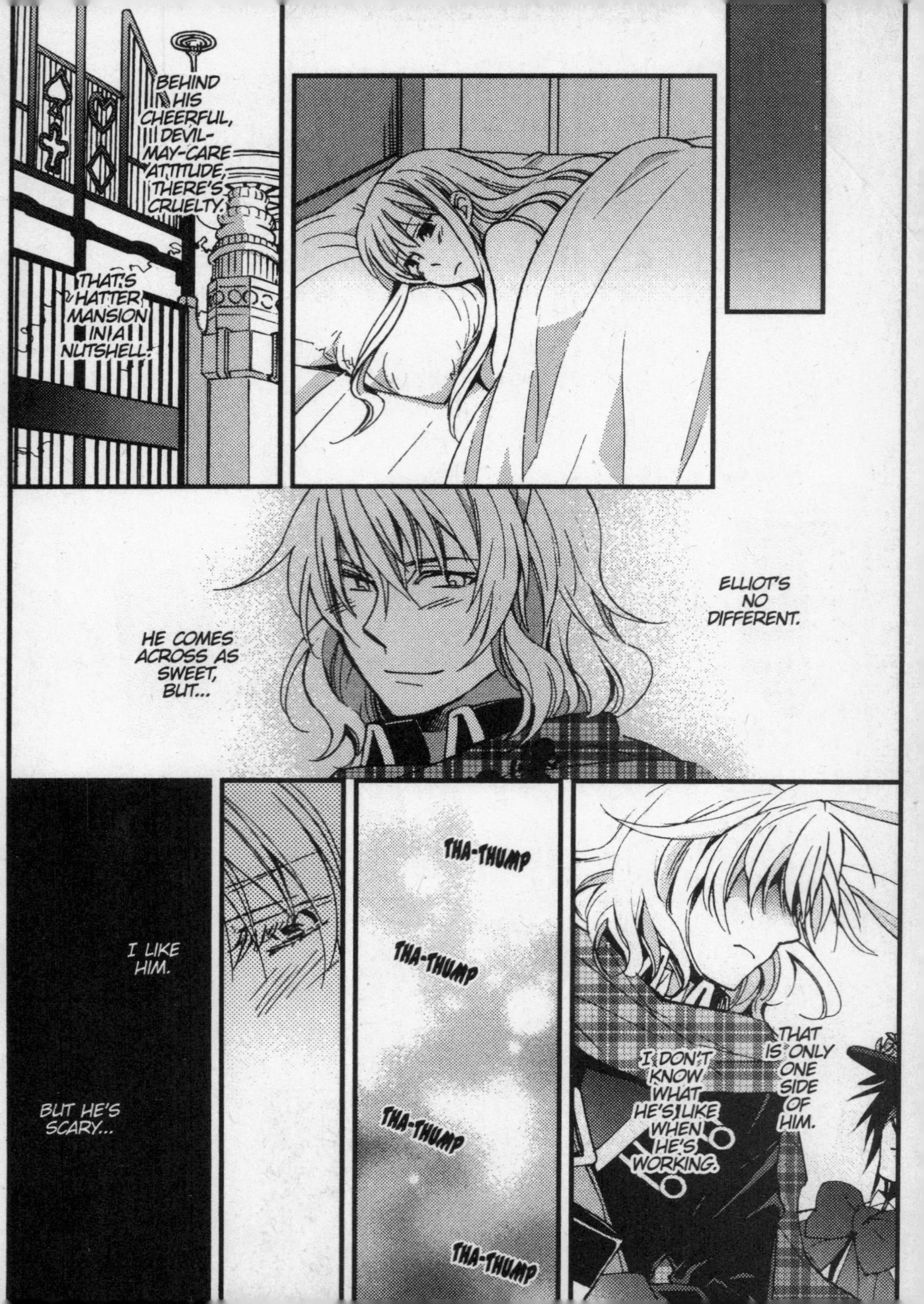
BEHIND HIS CHEERFUL, DEVIL-MAY-CARE ATTITUDE, THERE'S CRUELTY.
THAT'S HATTER MANSION IN A NUTSHELL.
ELLIOT'S NO DIFFERENT.
HE COMES ACROSS AS SWEET, BUT...
THAT IS ONLY ONE SIDE OF HIM.
I DON'T KNOW WHAT HE'S LIKE WHEN HE'S WORKING.
THA-THUMP
THA-THUMP
THA-THUMP
THA-THUMP
I LIKE HIM.
BUT HE'S SCARY...

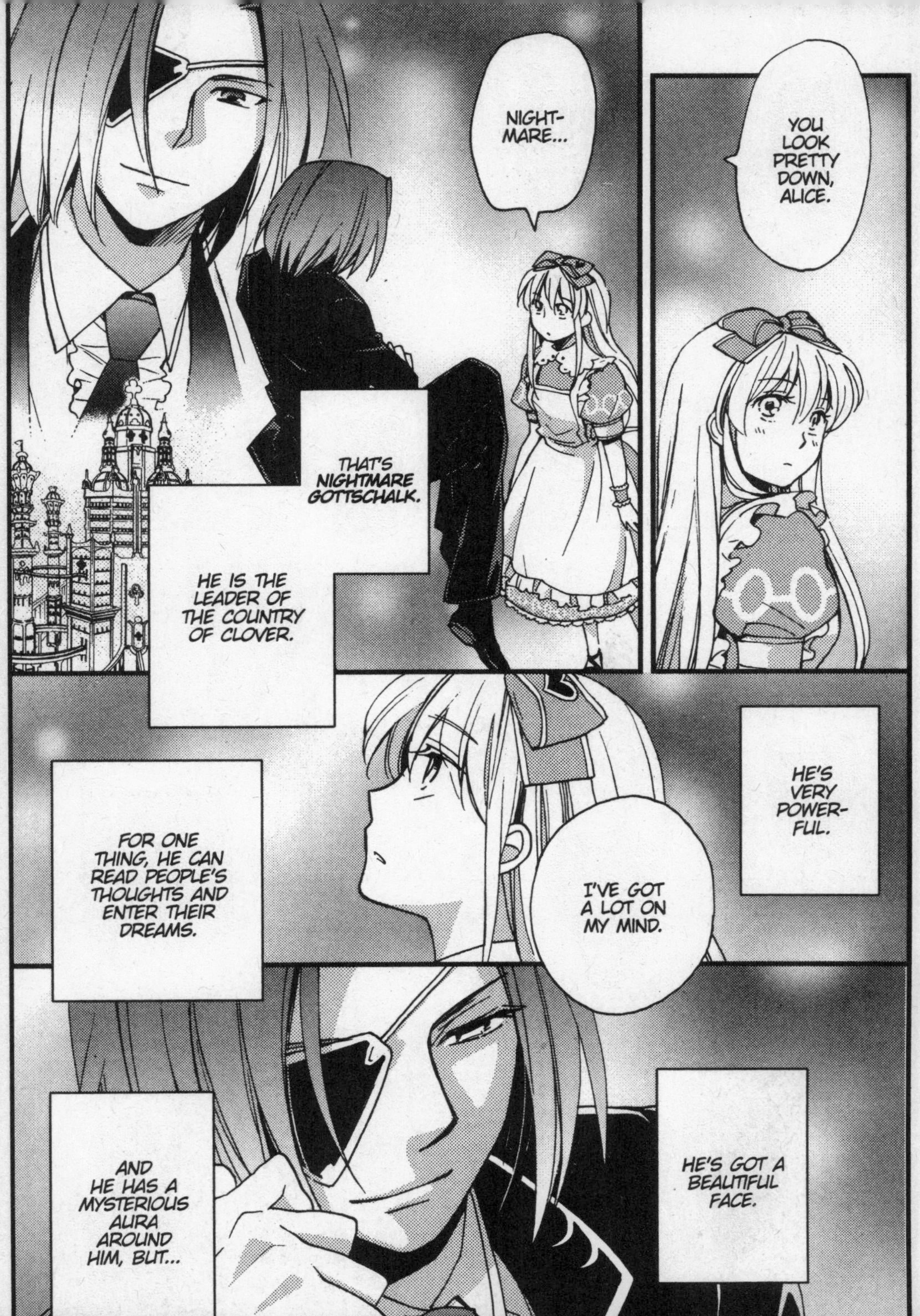
YOU LOOK PRETTY DOWN, ALICE.
NIGHT-MARE...
THAT'S NIGHTMARE GOTTSCHALK.
HE IS THE LEADER OF THE COUNTRY OF CLOVER.
HE'S VERY POWER-FUL.
I'VE GOT A LOT ON MY MIND.
FOR ONE THING, HE CAN READ PEOPLE'S THOUGHTS AND ENTER THEIR DREAMS.
HE'S GOT A BEAUTIFUL FACE.
AND HE HAS A MYSTERIOUS AURA AROUND HIM, BUT...

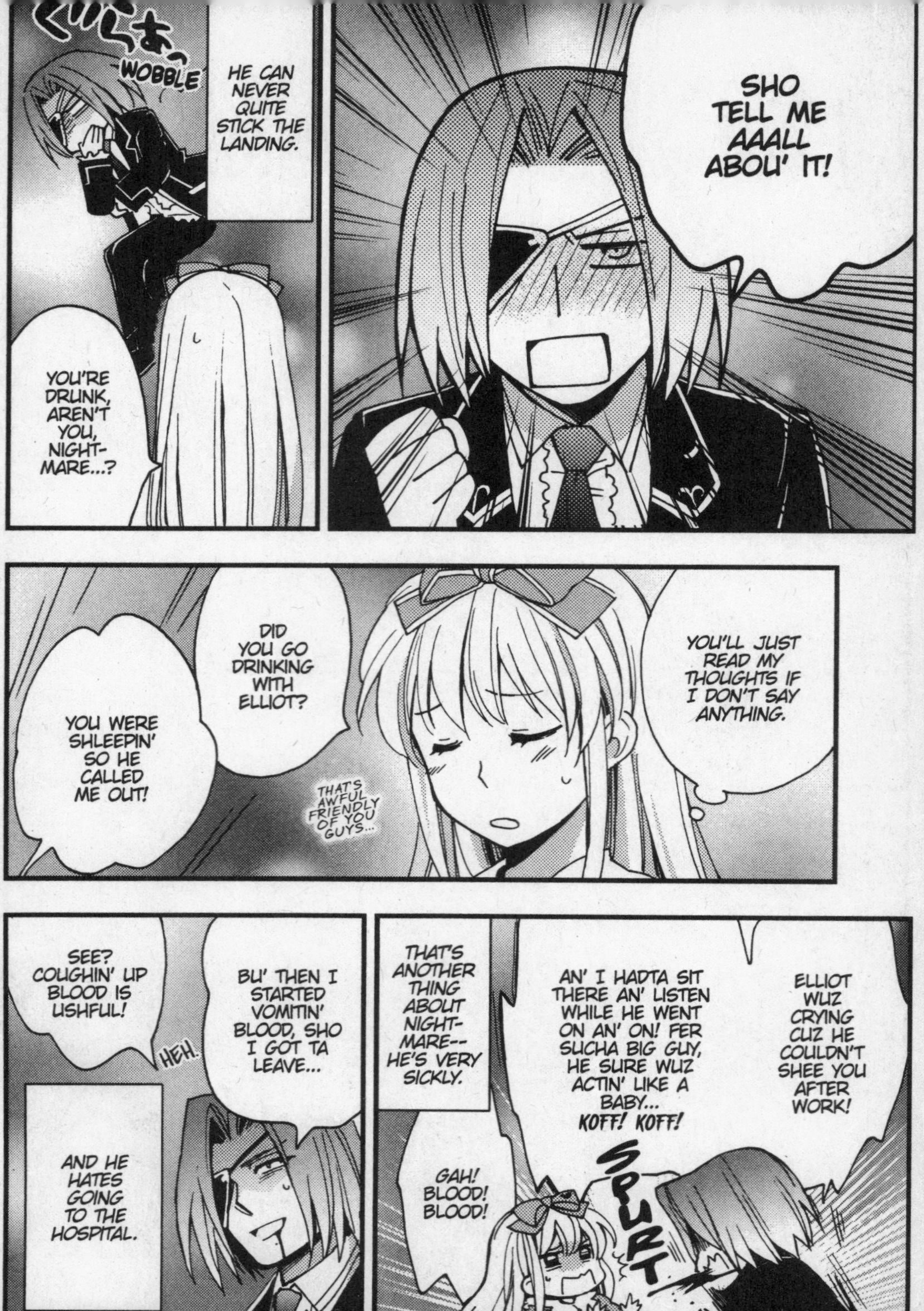
SHO TELL ME AAALL ABOU' IT!
WOBBLE
HE CAN NEVER QUITE STICK THE LANDING.
YOU'RE DRUNK, AREN'T YOU, NIGHTMARE...?
YOU'LL JUST READ MY THOUGHTS IF I DON'T SAY ANYTHING.
DID YOU GO DRINKING WITH ELLIOT?
YOU WERE SHLEEPIN' SO HE CALLED ME OUT!
THAT'S AWFUL FRIENDLY OF YOU GUYS...
ELLIOT WUZ CRYING CUZ HE COULDN'T SHEE YOU AFTER WORK!
AN' I HADTA SIT THERE AN' LISTEN WHILE HE WENT ON AN' ON! FER SUCHA BIG GUY, HE SURE WUZ ACTIN' LIKE A BABY... KOFF! KOFF!
THAT'S ANOTHER THING ABOUT NIGHTMARE-- HE'S VERY SICKLY.
SPURT
GAH! BLOOD! BLOOD!
BU' THEN I STARTED VOMITIN' BLOOD, SHO I GOT TA LEAVE...
SEE? COUGHIN' UP BLOOD IS USHFUL!
HEH.
AND HE HATES GOING TO THE HOSPITAL.

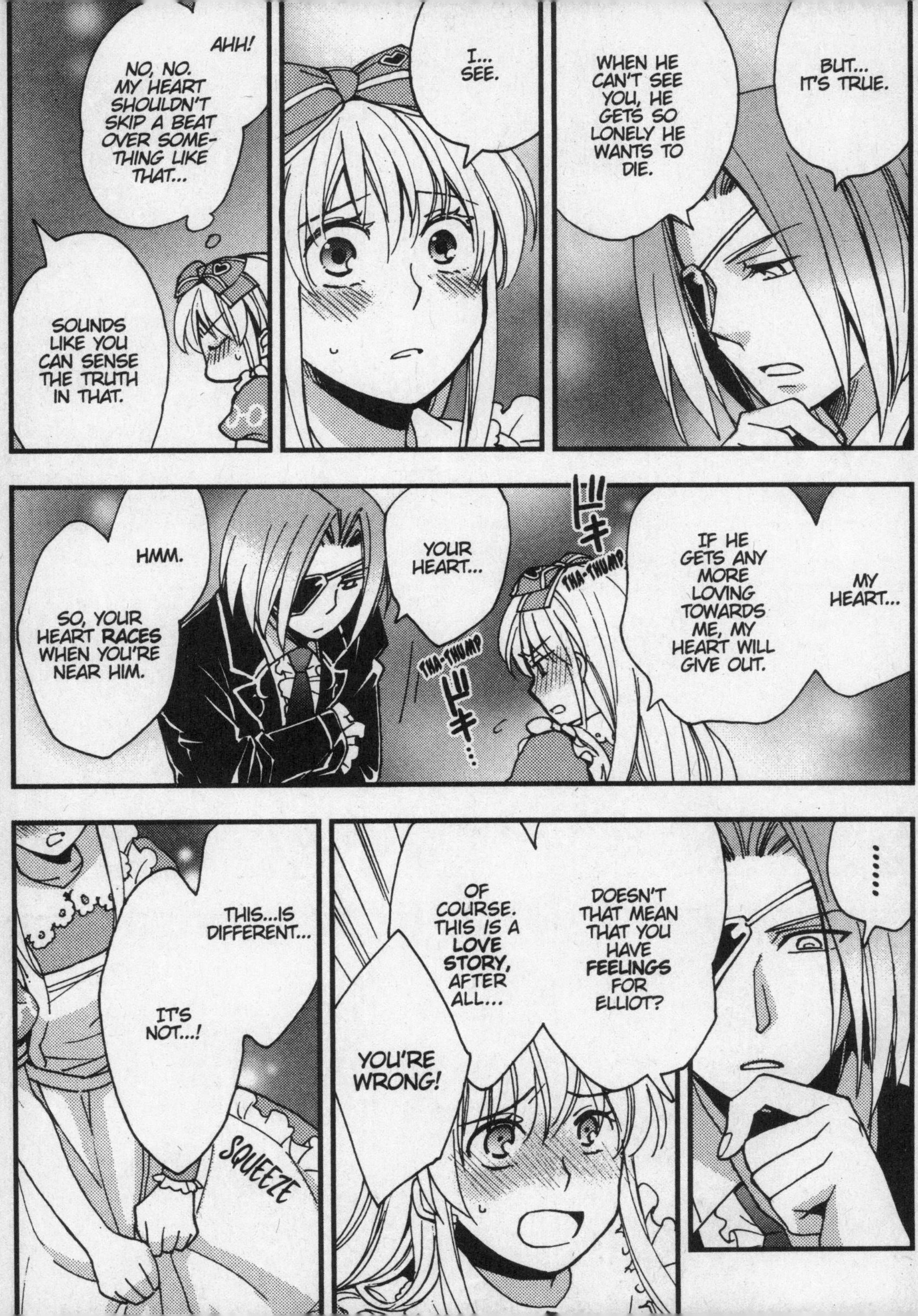
BUT... IT'S TRUE.
WHEN HE CAN'T SEE YOU, HE GETS SO LONELY HE WANTS TO DIE.
I... SEE.
AHH!
NO, NO. MY HEART SHOULDN'T SKIP A BEAT OVER SOME-THING LIKE THAT...
SOUNDS LIKE YOU CAN SENSE THE TRUTH IN THAT.
MY HEART...
IF HE GETS ANY MORE LOVING TOWARDS ME, MY HEART WILL GIVE OUT.
ドキ
THA-THUMP
YOUR HEART...
HMM.
SO, YOUR HEART RACES WHEN YOU'RE NEAR HIM.
THA-THUMP
ドキ...
......
DOESN'T THAT MEAN THAT YOU HAVE FEELINGS FOR ELLIOT?
OF COURSE. THIS IS A LOVE STORY, AFTER ALL...
YOU'RE WRONG!
THIS...IS DIFFERENT...
IT'S NOT...!
SQUEEZE

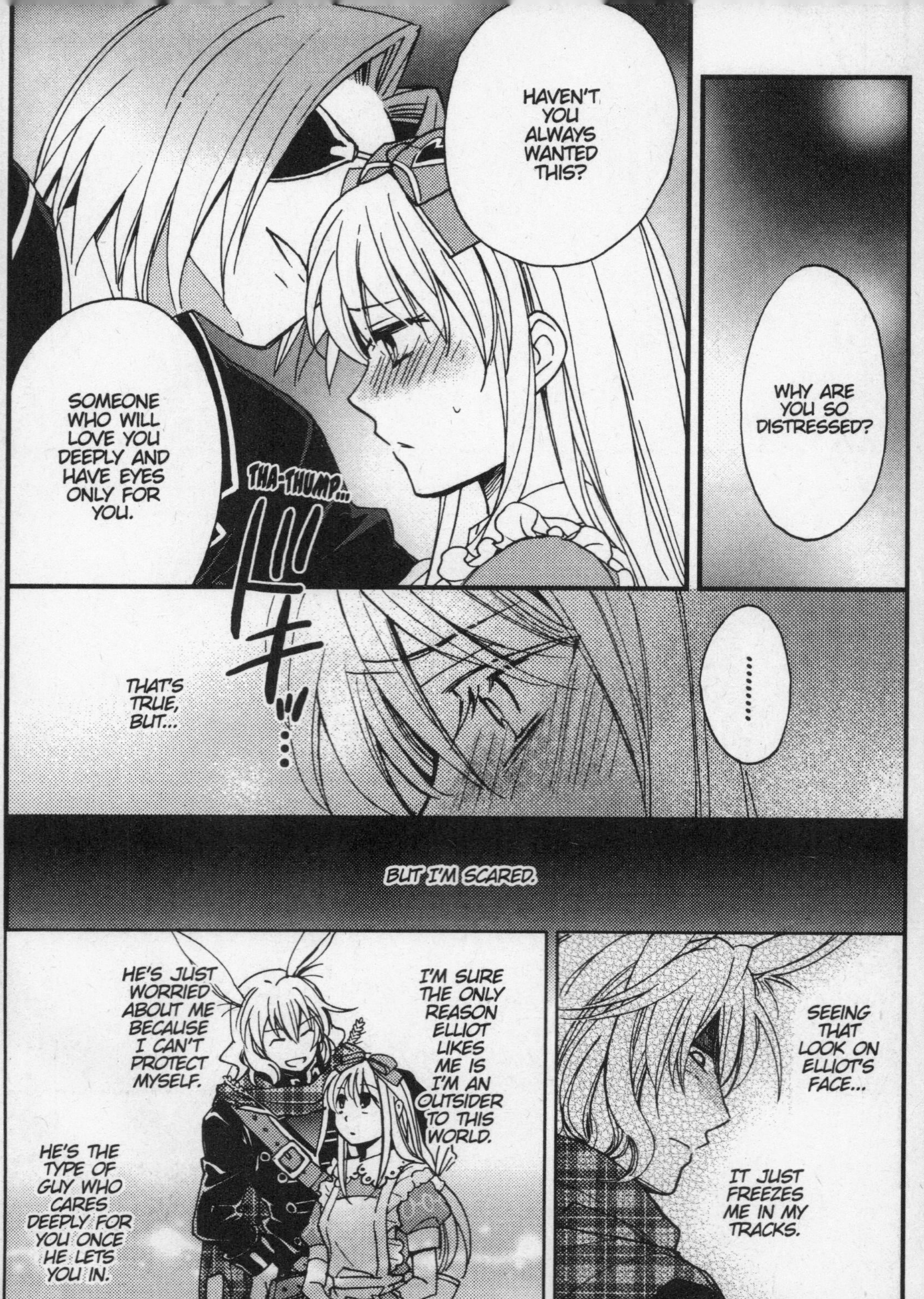

WHY ARE YOU SO DISTRESSED?
HAVEN'T YOU ALWAYS WANTED THIS?
SOMEONE WHO WILL LOVE YOU DEEPLY AND HAVE EYES ONLY FOR YOU.
THA-THUMP...
......
THAT'S TRUE, BUT...
BUT I'M SCARED.
SEEING THAT LOOK ON ELLIOT'S FACE...
IT JUST FREEZES ME IN MY TRACKS.
I'M SURE THE ONLY REASON ELLIOT LIKES ME IS I'M AN OUTSIDER TO THIS WORLD.
HE'S JUST WORRIED ABOUT ME BECAUSE I CAN'T PROTECT MYSELF.
HE'S THE TYPE OF GUY WHO CARES DEEPLY FOR YOU ONCE HE LETS YOU IN.

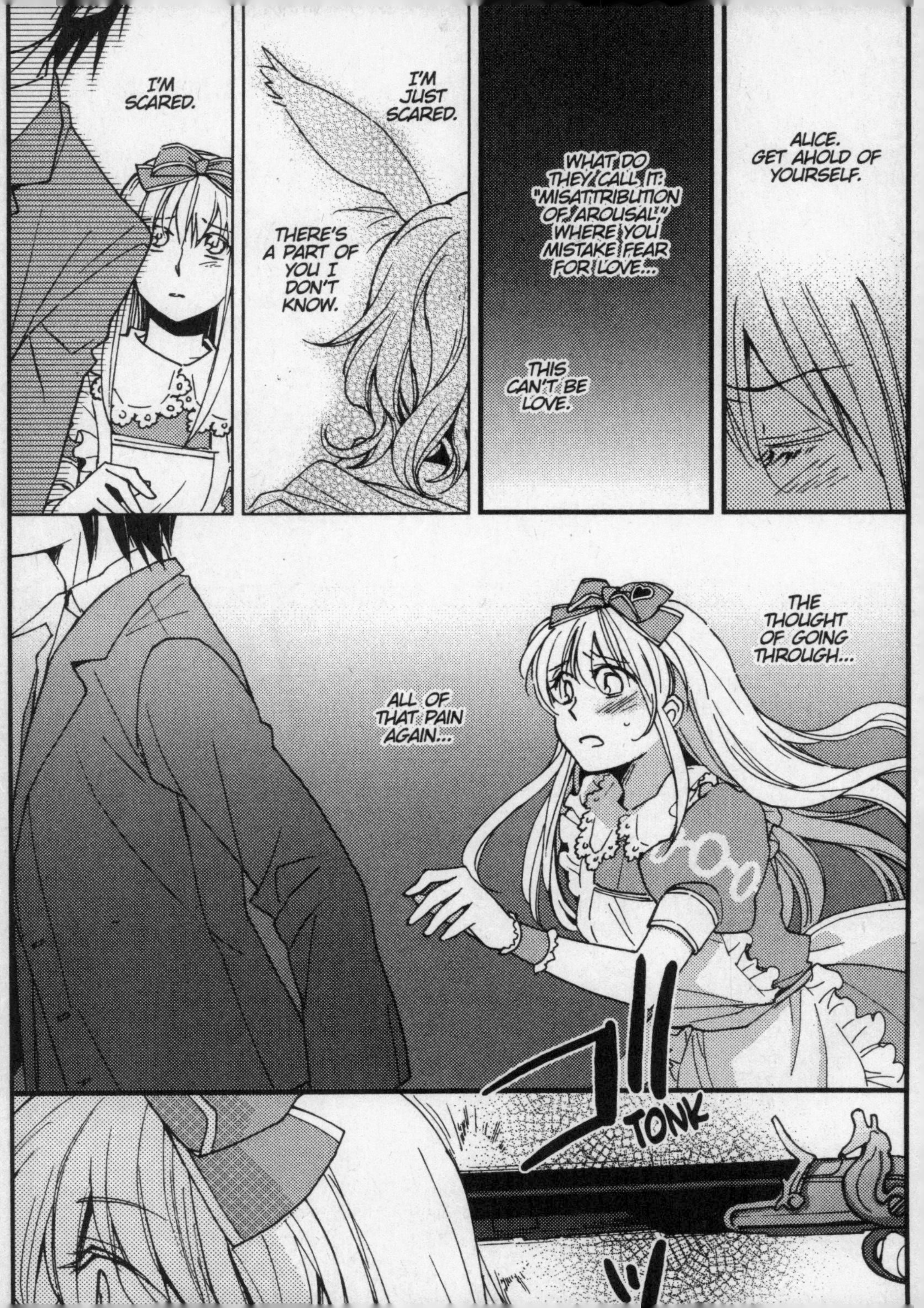
ALICE. GET AHOLD OF YOURSELF.
WHAT DO THEY CALL IT: "MISATTRIBUTION OF AROUSAL," WHERE YOU MISTAKE FEAR FOR LOVE...
THIS CAN'T BE LOVE.
I'M JUST SCARED.
THERE'S A PART OF YOU I DON'T KNOW.
I'M SCARED.
THE THOUGHT OF GOING THROUGH...
ALL OF THAT PAIN AGAIN...
TONK

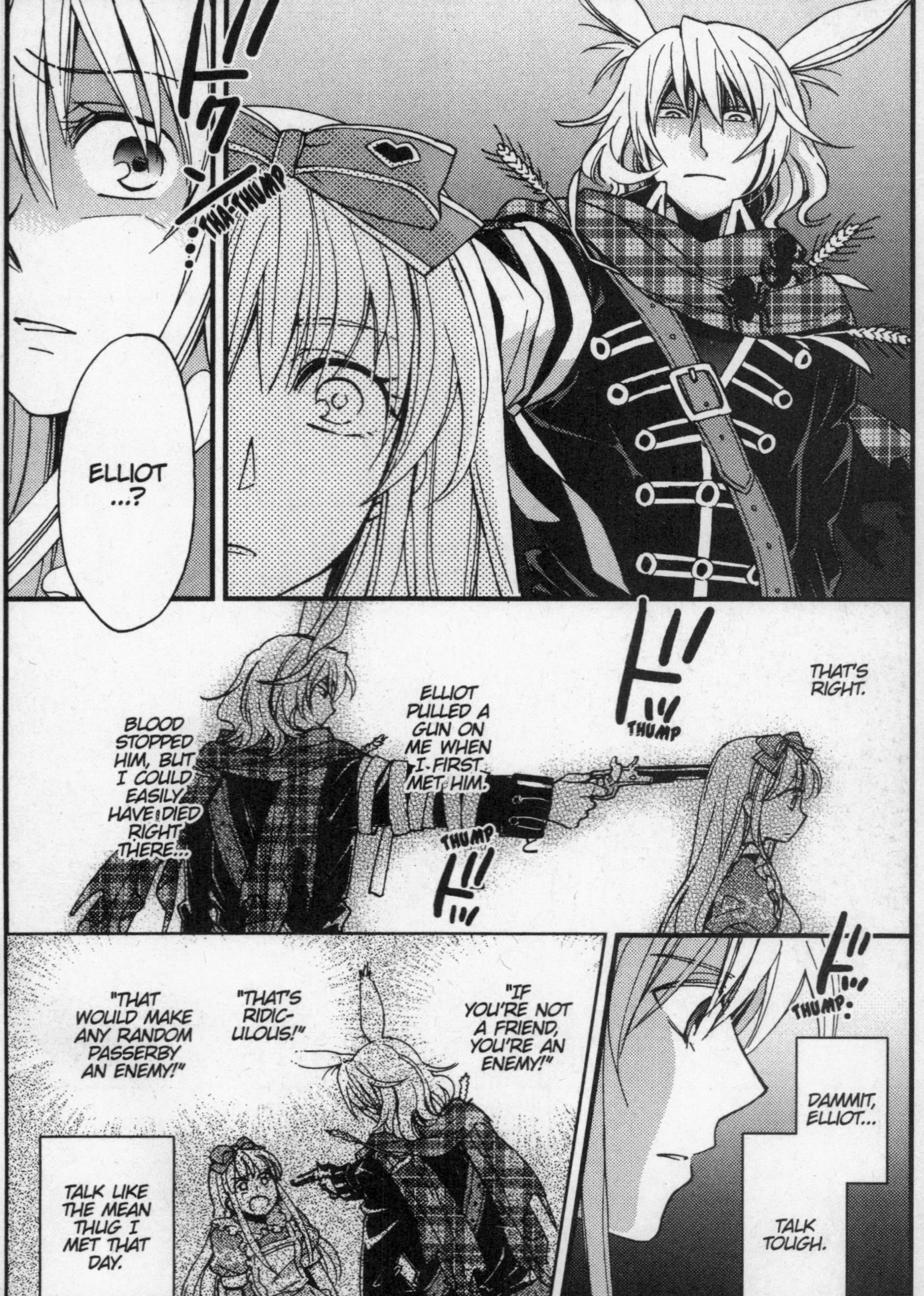
THA-THUMP
ELLIOT ...?
THAT'S RIGHT.
THUMP
ELLIOT PULLED A GUN ON ME WHEN I FIRST MET HIM.
BLOOD STOPPED HIM, BUT I COULD EASILY HAVE DIED RIGHT THERE...
THUMP
THUMP
DAMMIT, ELLIOT...
TALK TOUGH.
"IF YOU'RE NOT A FRIEND, YOU'RE AN ENEMY!"
"THAT'S RIDIC-ULOUS!"
"THAT WOULD MAKE ANY RANDOM PASSERBY AN ENEMY!"
TALK LIKE THE MEAN THUG I MET THAT DAY.

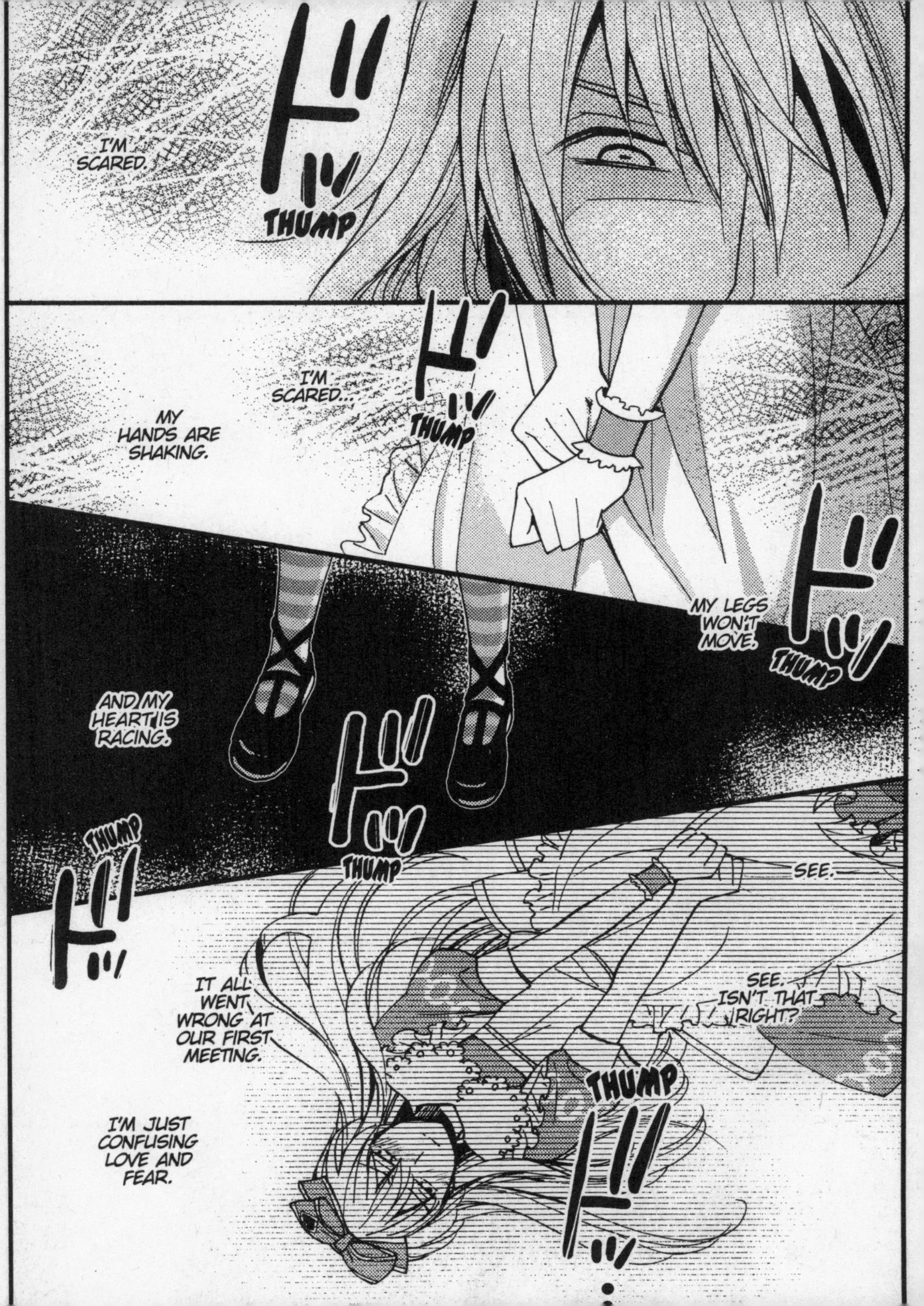

ドッ
THUMP
I'M SCARED.
ドッ
THUMP
I'M SCARED...
MY HANDS ARE SHAKING.
ドッ
THUMP
MY LEGS WON'T MOVE.
AND MY HEART IS RACING.
ドッ
THUMP
ドッ
THUMP
SEE.
SEE. ISN'T THAT RIGHT?
IT ALL WENT WRONG AT OUR FIRST MEETING.
I'M JUST CONFUSING LOVE AND FEAR.
ドッ
THUMP

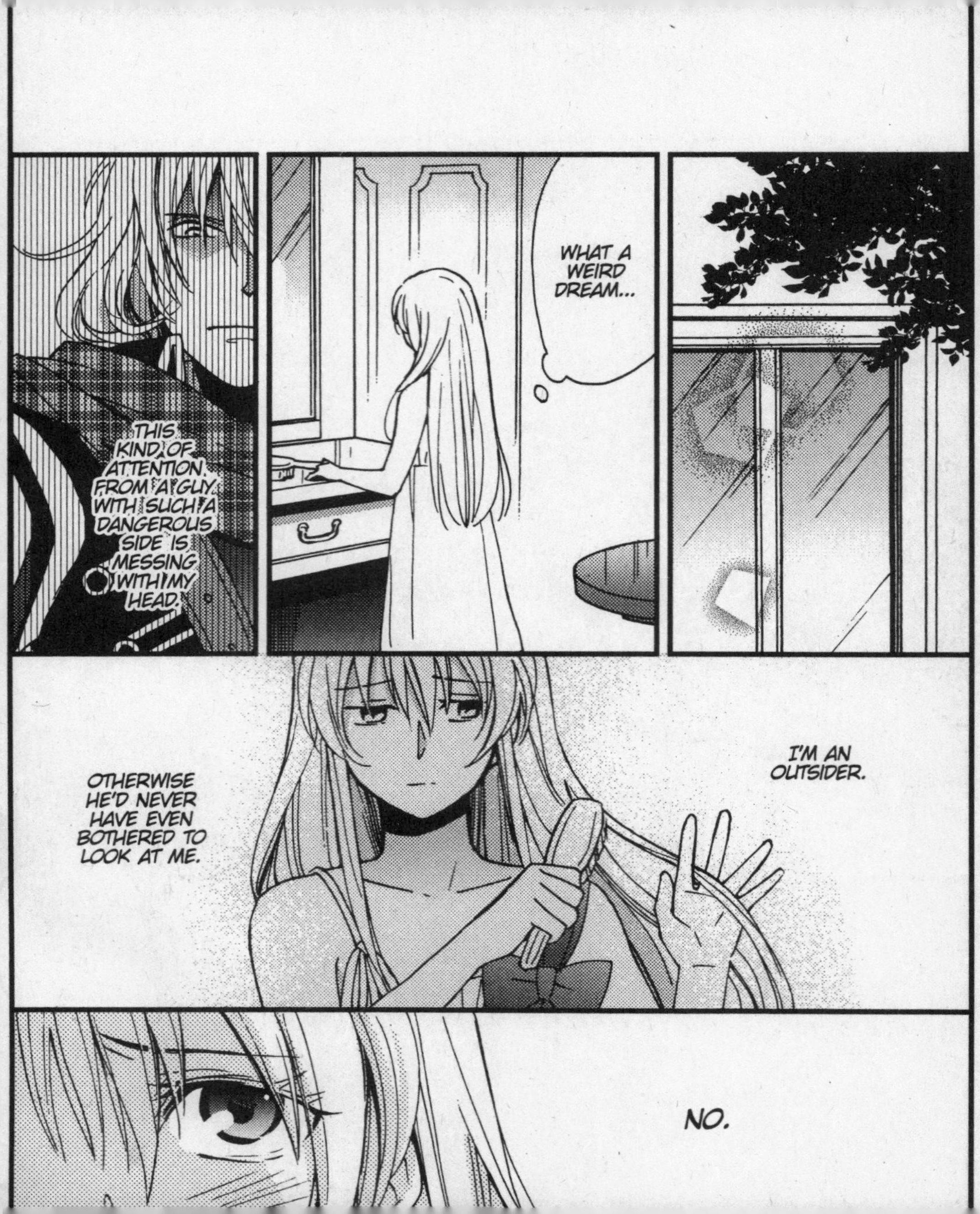
WHAT A WEIRD DREAM...
THIS KIND OF ATTENTION FROM A GUY WITH SUCH A DANGEROUS SIDE IS MESSING WITH MY HEAD.
I'M AN OUTSIDER.
OTHERWISE HE'D NEVER HAVE EVEN BOTHERED TO LOOK AT ME.
NO.

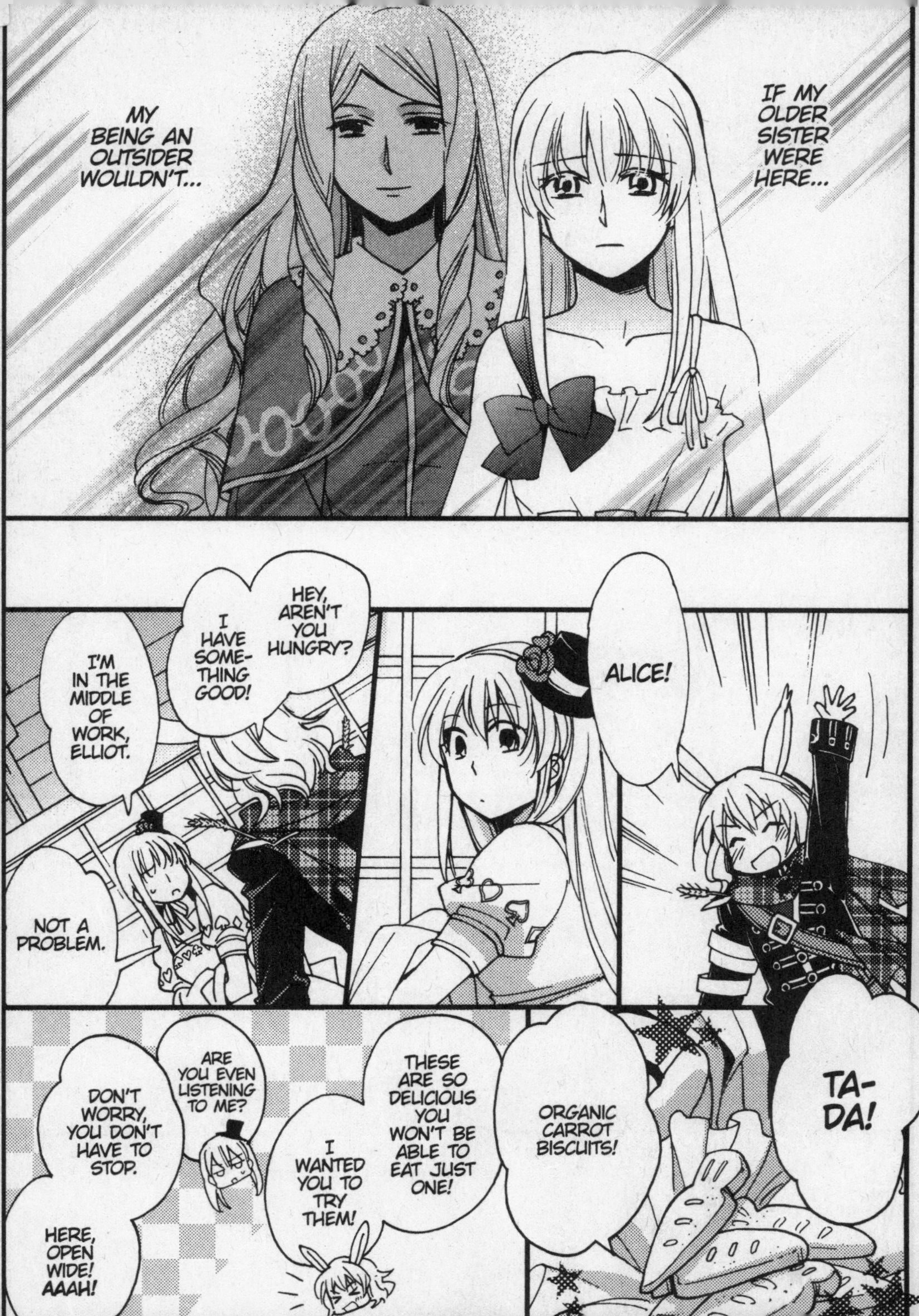
IF MY OLDER SISTER WERE HERE...
MY BEING AN OUTSIDER WOULDN'T...
ALICE!
HEY, AREN'T YOU HUNGRY?
I HAVE SOMETHING GOOD!
I'M IN THE MIDDLE OF WORK, ELLIOT.
NOT A PROBLEM.
TA-DA!
ORGANIC CARROT BISCUITS!
THESE ARE SO DELICIOUS YOU WON'T BE ABLE TO EAT JUST ONE!
I WANTED YOU TO TRY THEM!
ARE YOU EVEN LISTENING TO ME?
DON'T WORRY, YOU DON'T HAVE TO STOP.
HERE, OPEN WIDE! AAAH!

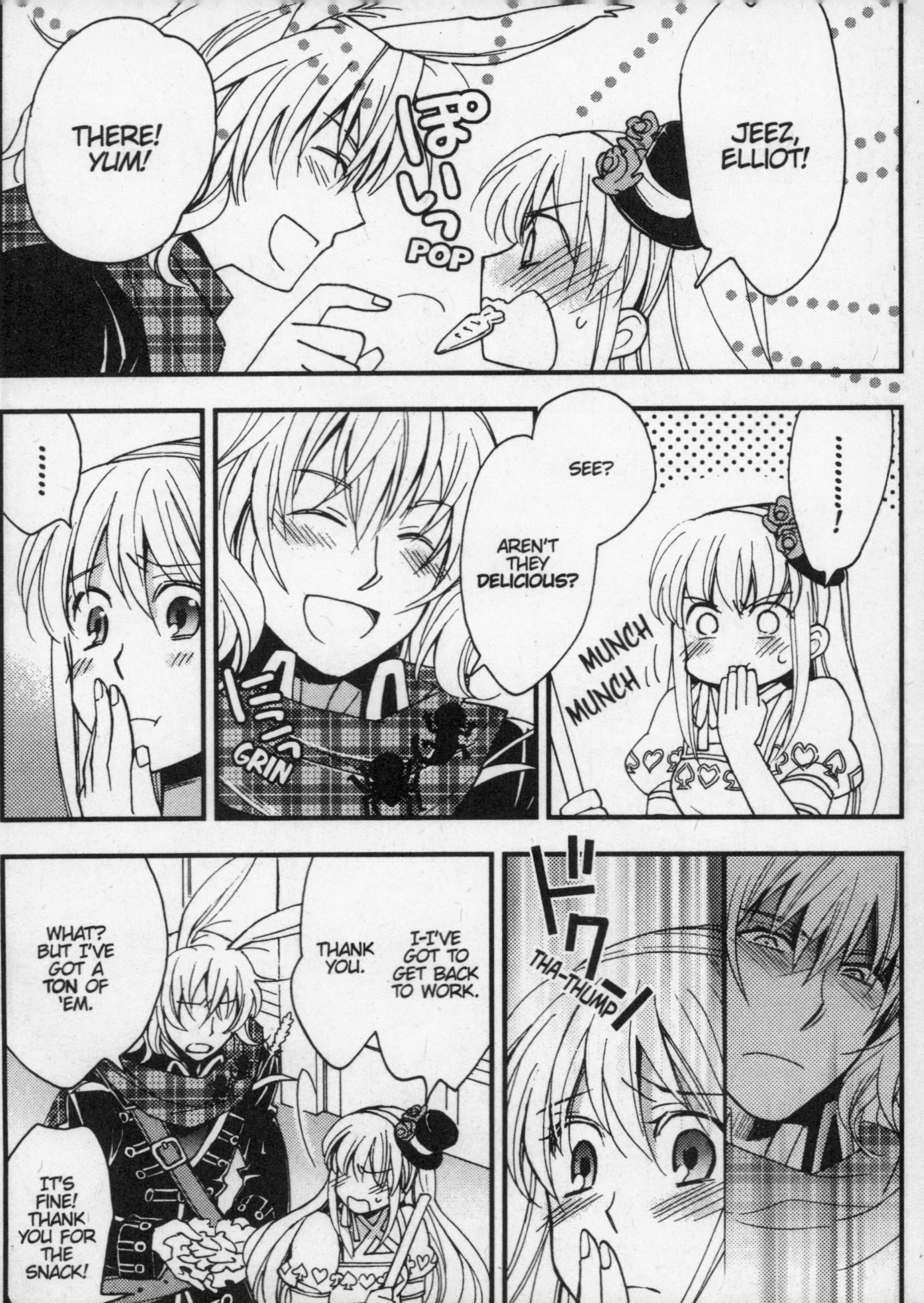
JEEZ, ELLIOT!
POP
THERE! YUM!
......!
MUNCH MUNCH
SEE?
AREN'T THEY DELICIOUS?
GRIN
......
THA-THUMP
I-I'VE GOT TO GET BACK TO WORK.
THANK YOU.
WHAT? BUT I'VE GOT A TON OF 'EM.
IT'S FINE! THANK YOU FOR THE SNACK!

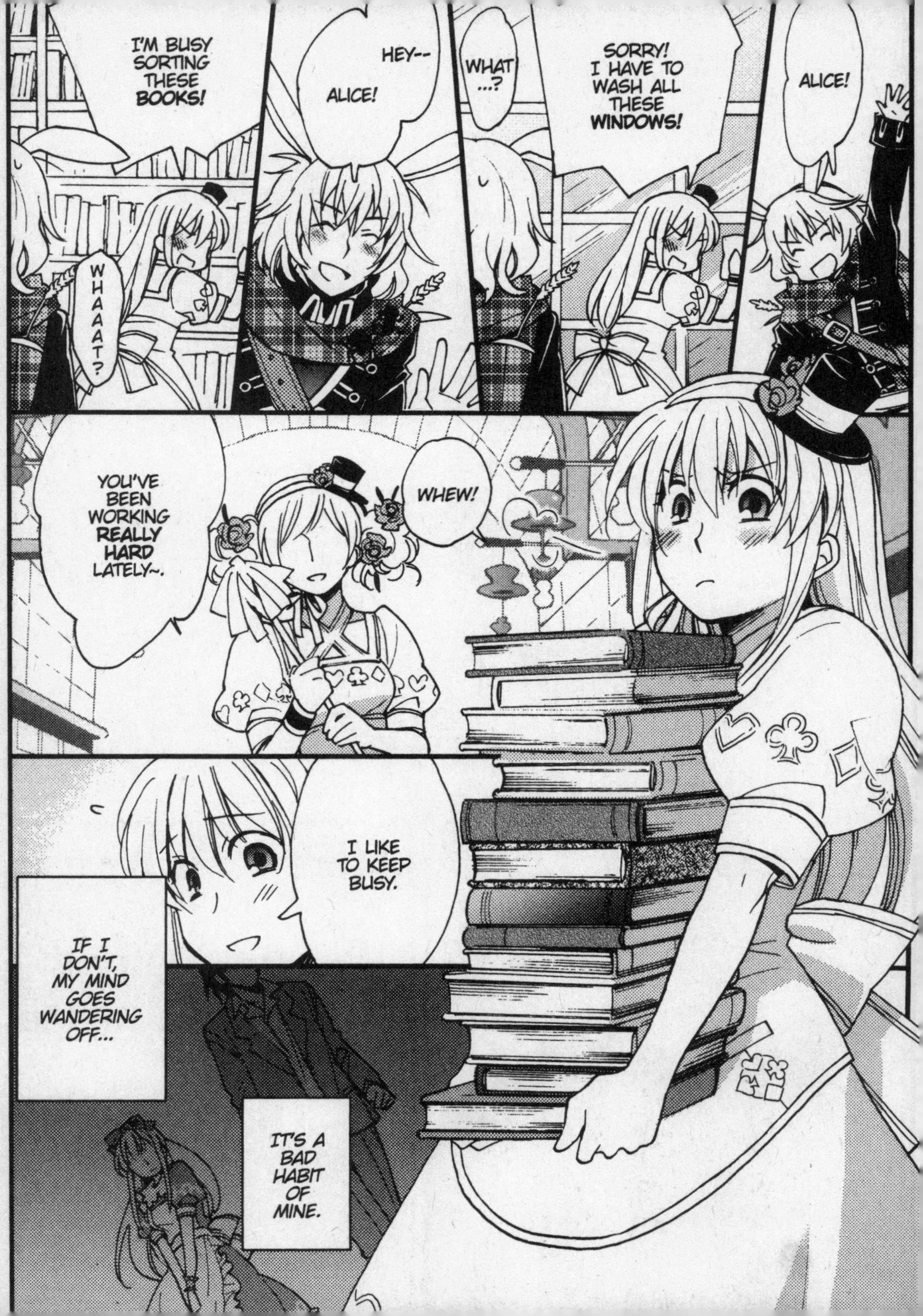
ALICE!
SORRY! I HAVE TO WASH ALL THESE WINDOWS!
WHAT ...?
HEY--
ALICE!
I'M BUSY SORTING THESE BOOKS!
WHAAAAT?
WHEW!
YOU'VE BEEN WORKING REALLY HARD LATELY~.
I LIKE TO KEEP BUSY.
IF I DON'T, MY MIND GOES WANDERING OFF...
IT'S A BAD HABIT OF MINE.

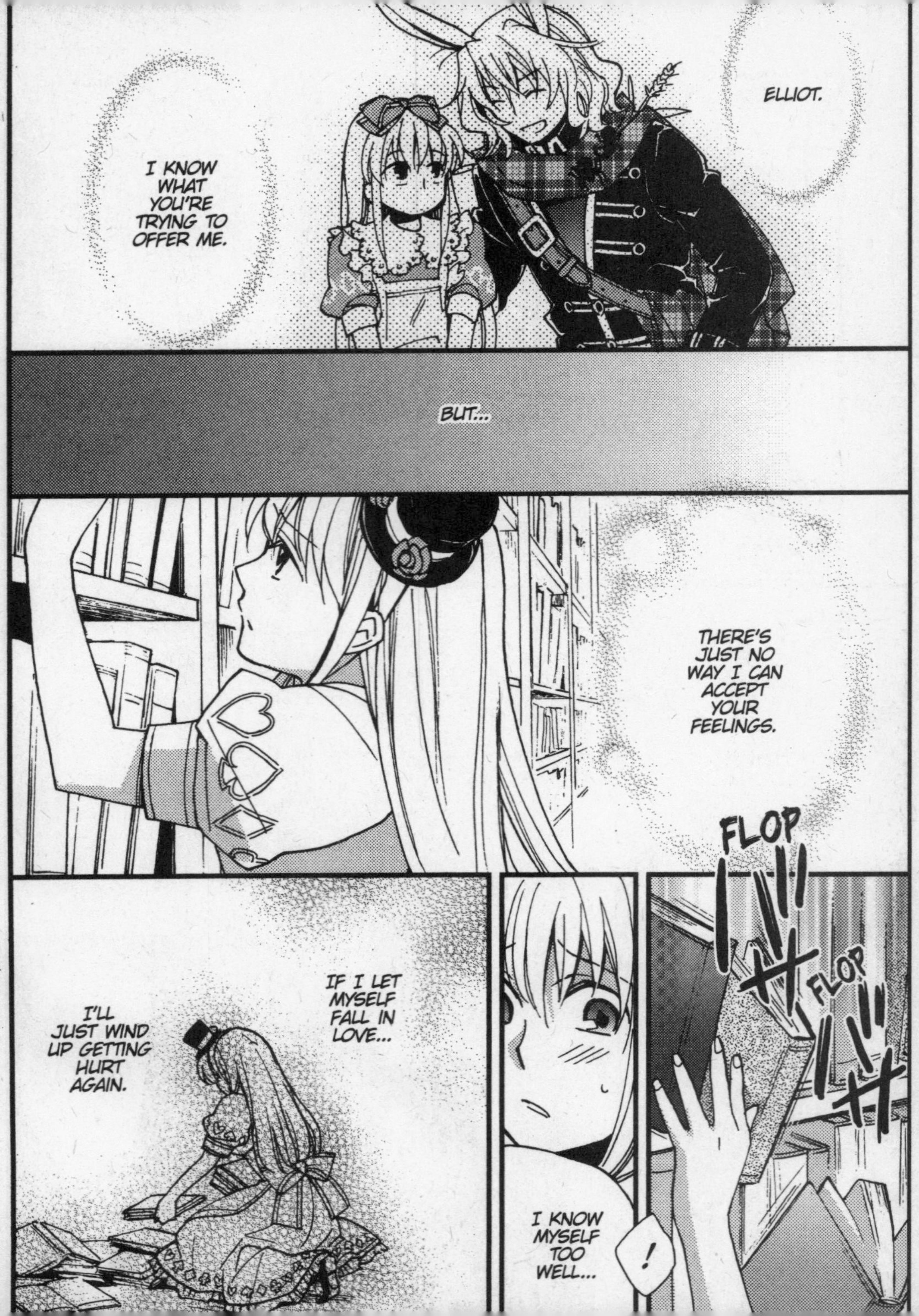
ELLIOT.
I KNOW WHAT YOU'RE TRYING TO OFFER ME.
BUT...
THERE'S JUST NO WAY I CAN ACCEPT YOUR FEELINGS.
FLOP
FLOP
!
I KNOW MYSELF TOO WELL...
IF I LET MYSELF FALL IN LOVE...
I'LL JUST WIND UP GETTING HURT AGAIN.

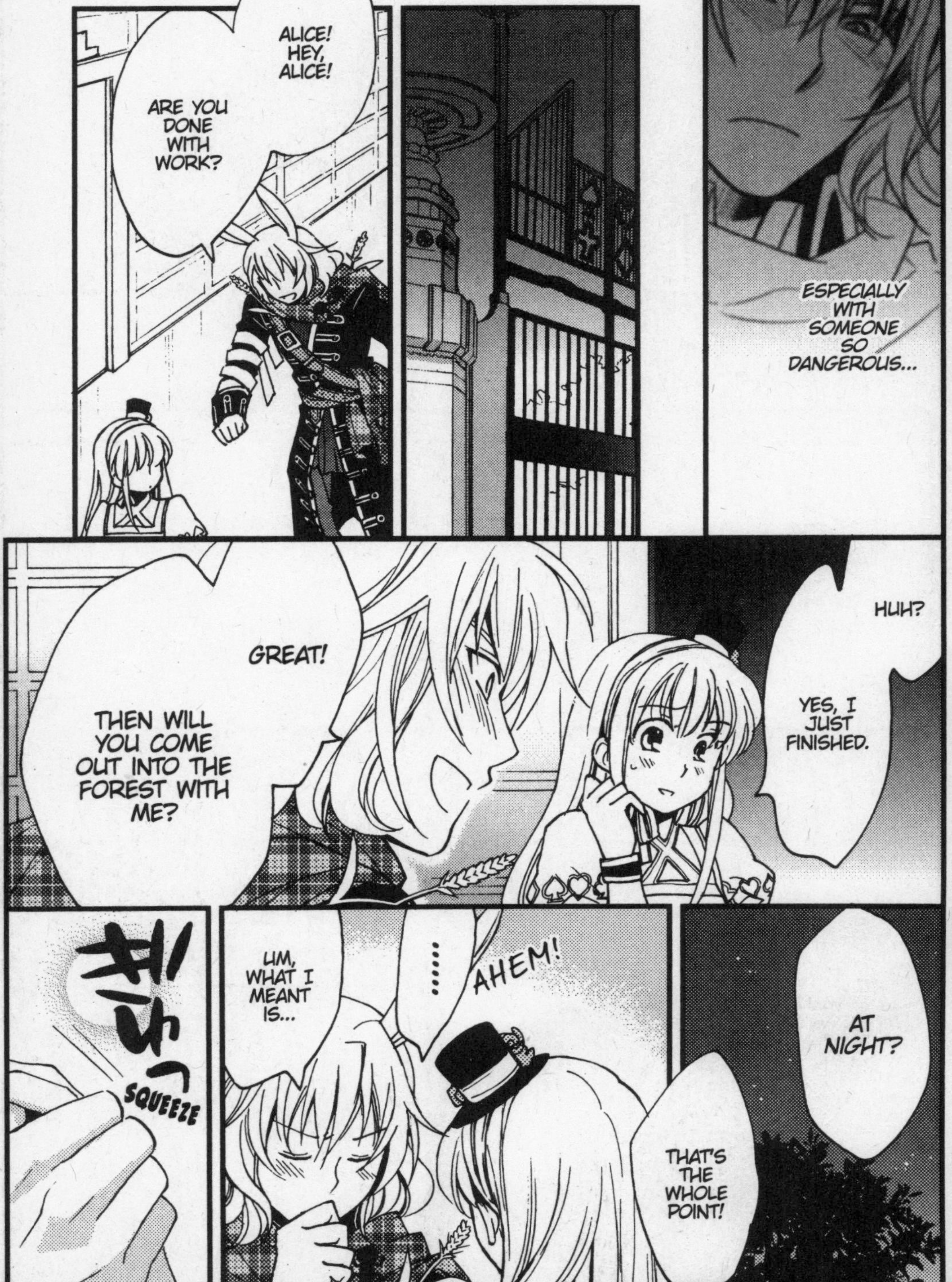
ESPECIALLY WITH SOMEONE SO DANGEROUS...
ALICE! HEY, ALICE!
ARE YOU DONE WITH WORK?
HUH?
YES, I JUST FINISHED.
GREAT!
THEN WILL YOU COME OUT INTO THE FOREST WITH ME?
AT NIGHT?
THAT'S THE WHOLE POINT!
......
AHEM!
UM, WHAT I MEANT IS...
ぎゅっ
SQUEEZE

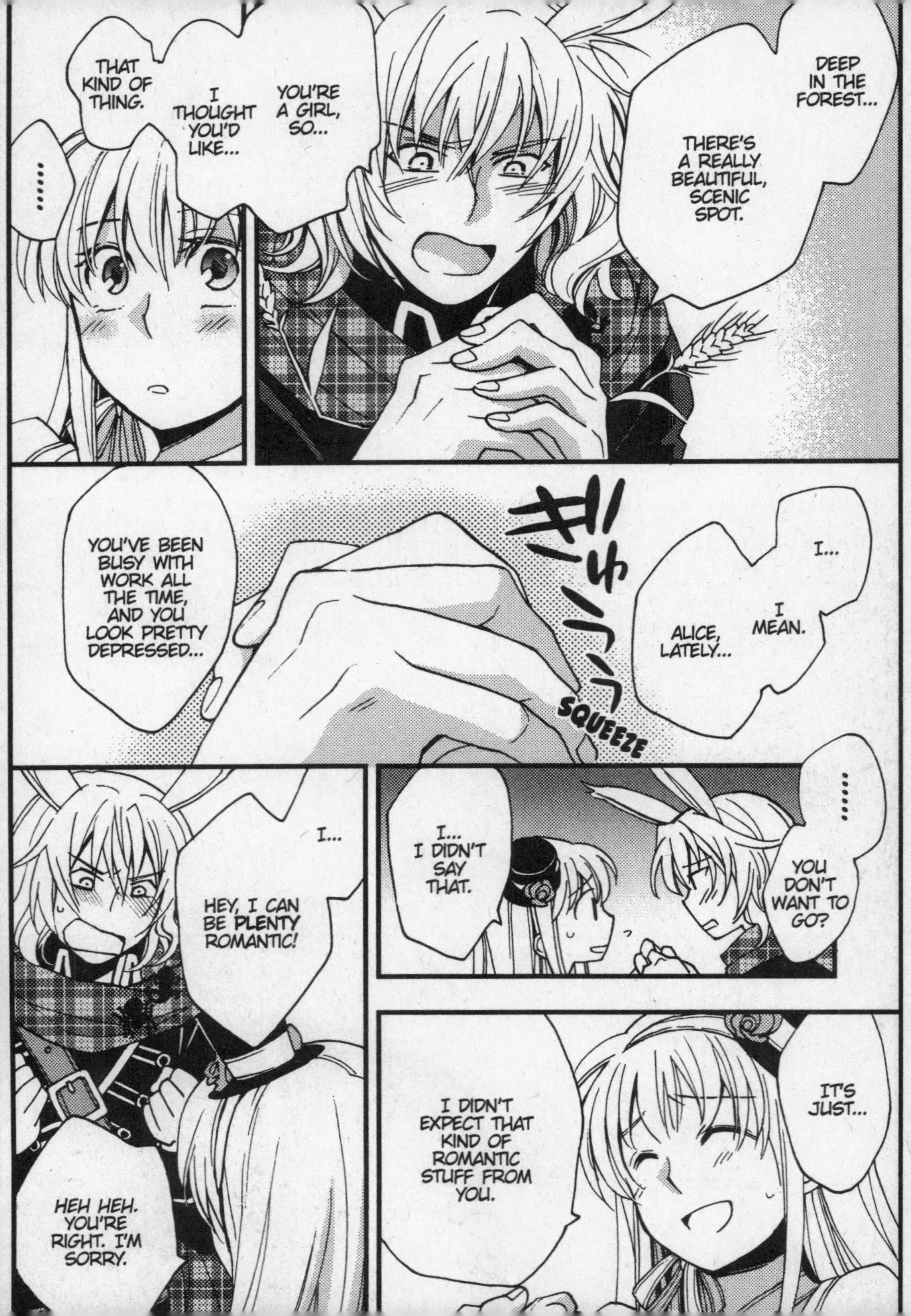
DEEP IN THE FOREST...
THERE'S A REALLY BEAUTIFUL, SCENIC SPOT.
YOU'RE A GIRL, SO...
I THOUGHT YOU'D LIKE...
THAT KIND OF THING.
......
I...
I MEAN.
ALICE, LATELY...
YOU'VE BEEN BUSY WITH WORK ALL THE TIME, AND YOU LOOK PRETTY DEPRESSED...
SQUEEZE
......
YOU DON'T WANT TO GO?
I... I DIDN'T SAY THAT.
IT'S JUST...
I DIDN'T EXPECT THAT KIND OF ROMANTIC STUFF FROM YOU.
I...
HEY, I CAN BE PLENTY ROMANTIC!
HEH HEH. YOU'RE RIGHT. I'M SORRY.

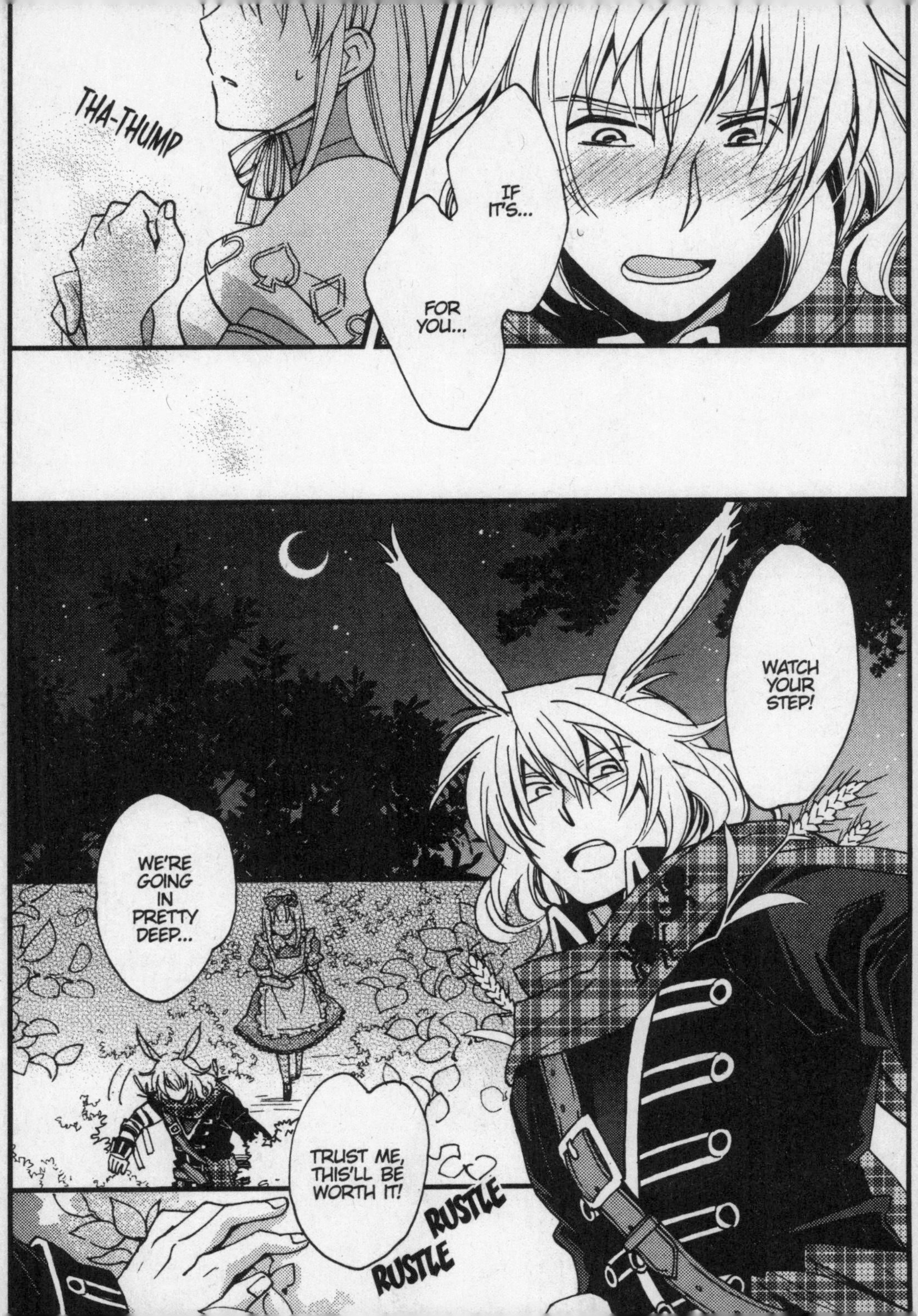
IF IT'S...
FOR YOU...
THA-THUMP
WATCH YOUR STEP!
WE'RE GOING IN PRETTY DEEP...
TRUST ME, THIS'LL BE WORTH IT!
RUSTLE
RUSTLE

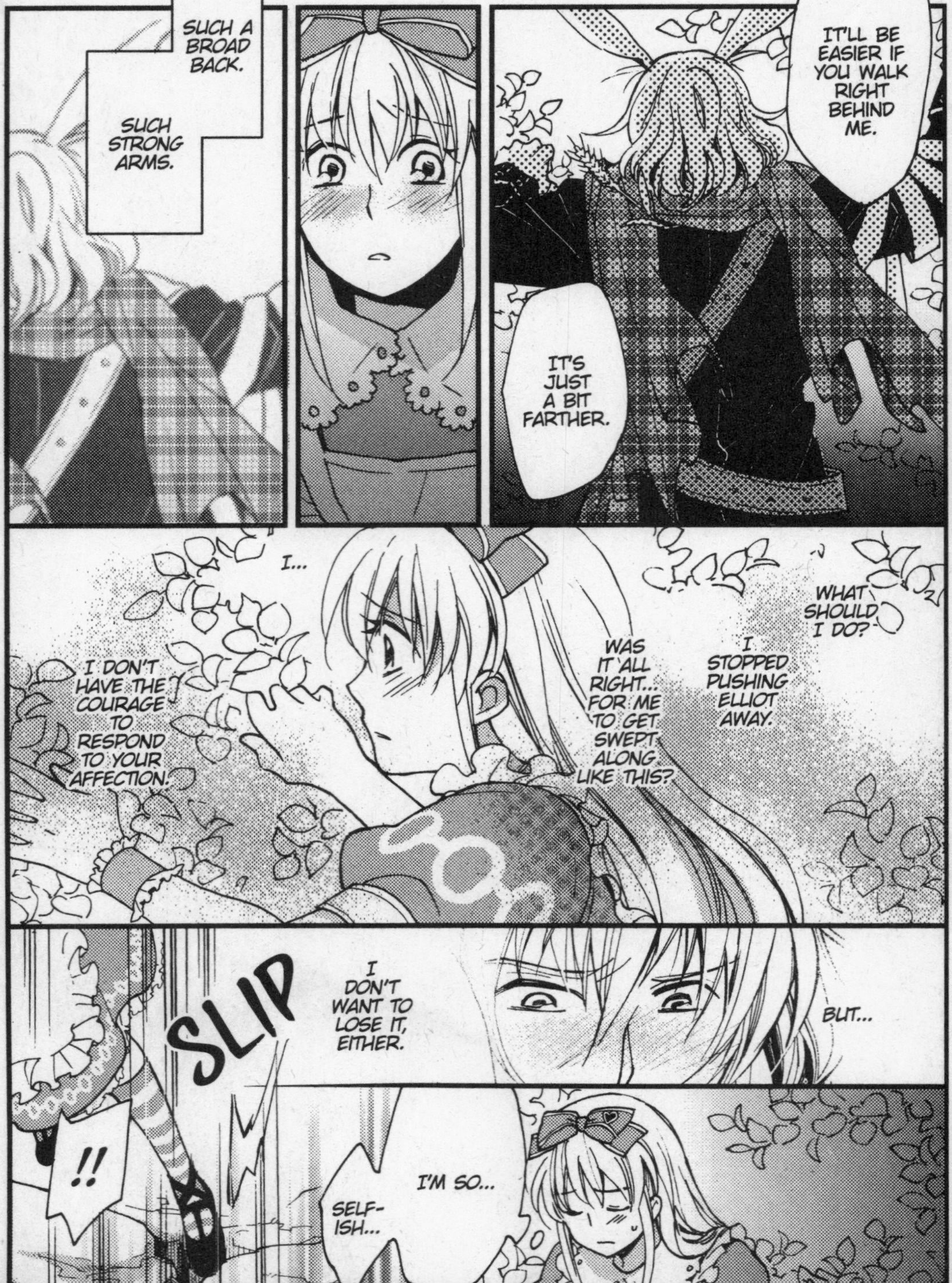
IT'LL BE EASIER IF YOU WALK RIGHT BEHIND ME.
IT'S JUST A BIT FARTHER.
SUCH A BROAD BACK.
SUCH STRONG ARMS.
WHAT SHOULD I DO?
I STOPPED PUSHING ELLIOT AWAY.
WAS IT ALL RIGHT... FOR ME TO GET SWEPT ALONG LIKE THIS?
I...
I DON'T HAVE THE COURAGE TO RESPOND TO YOUR AFFECTION.
BUT...
I DON'T WANT TO LOSE IT, EITHER.
I'M SO...
SELF-ISH...
SLIP
!!

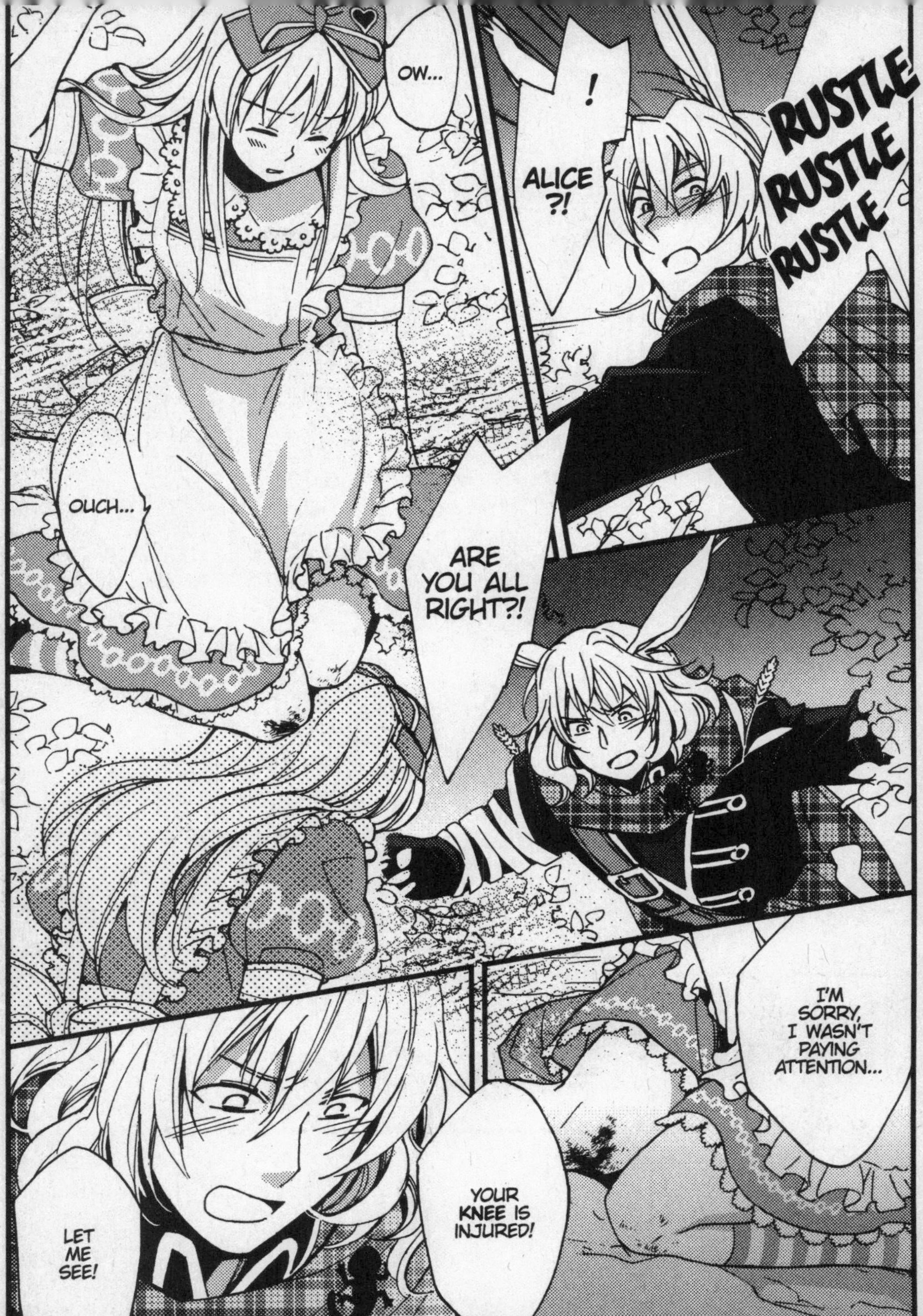
!
ALICE ?!
RUSTLE RUSTLE RUSTLE
ARE YOU ALL RIGHT?!
OW...
OUCH...
I'M SORRY, I WASN'T PAYING ATTENTION...
YOUR KNEE IS INJURED!
LET ME SEE!

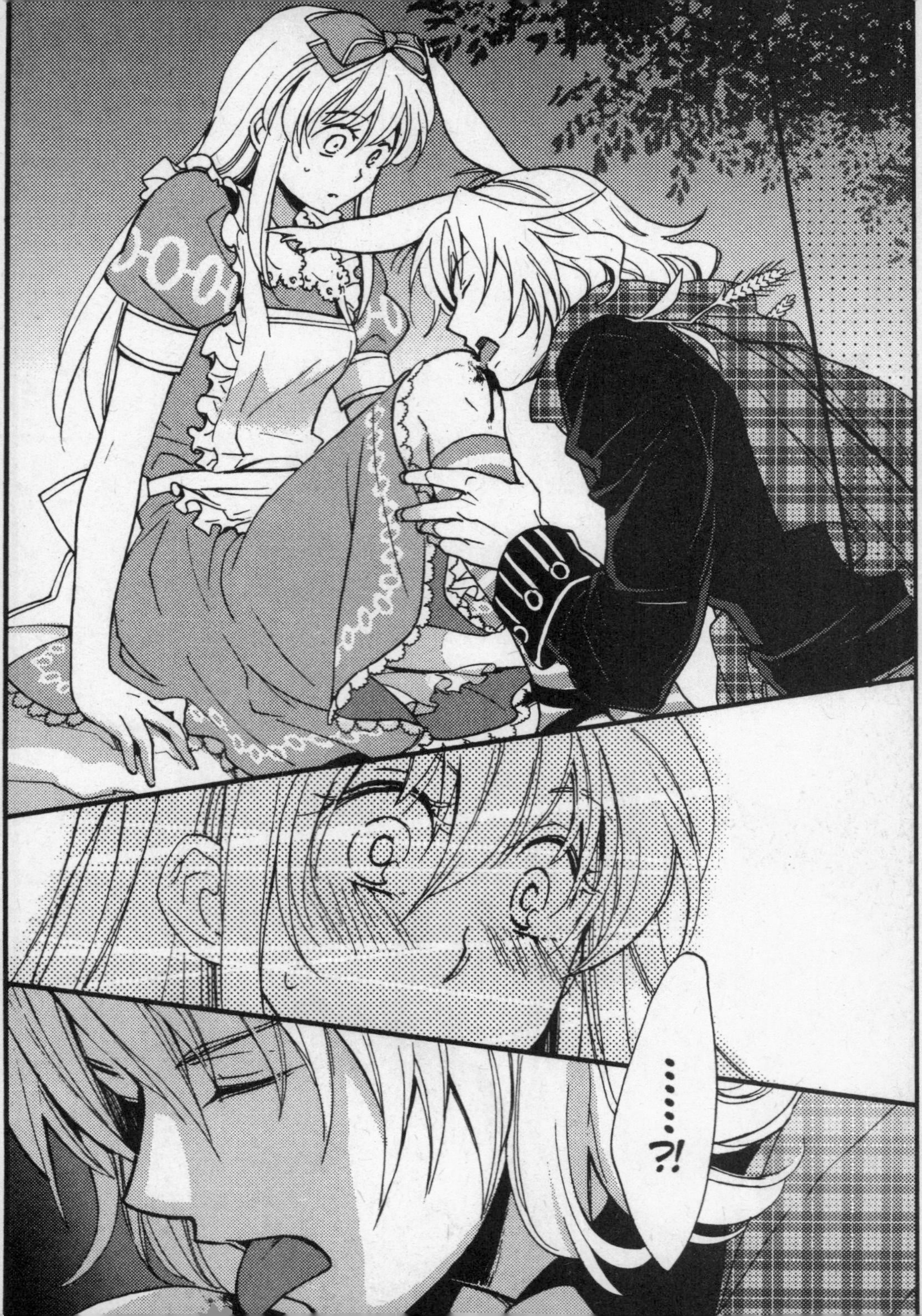
……?!

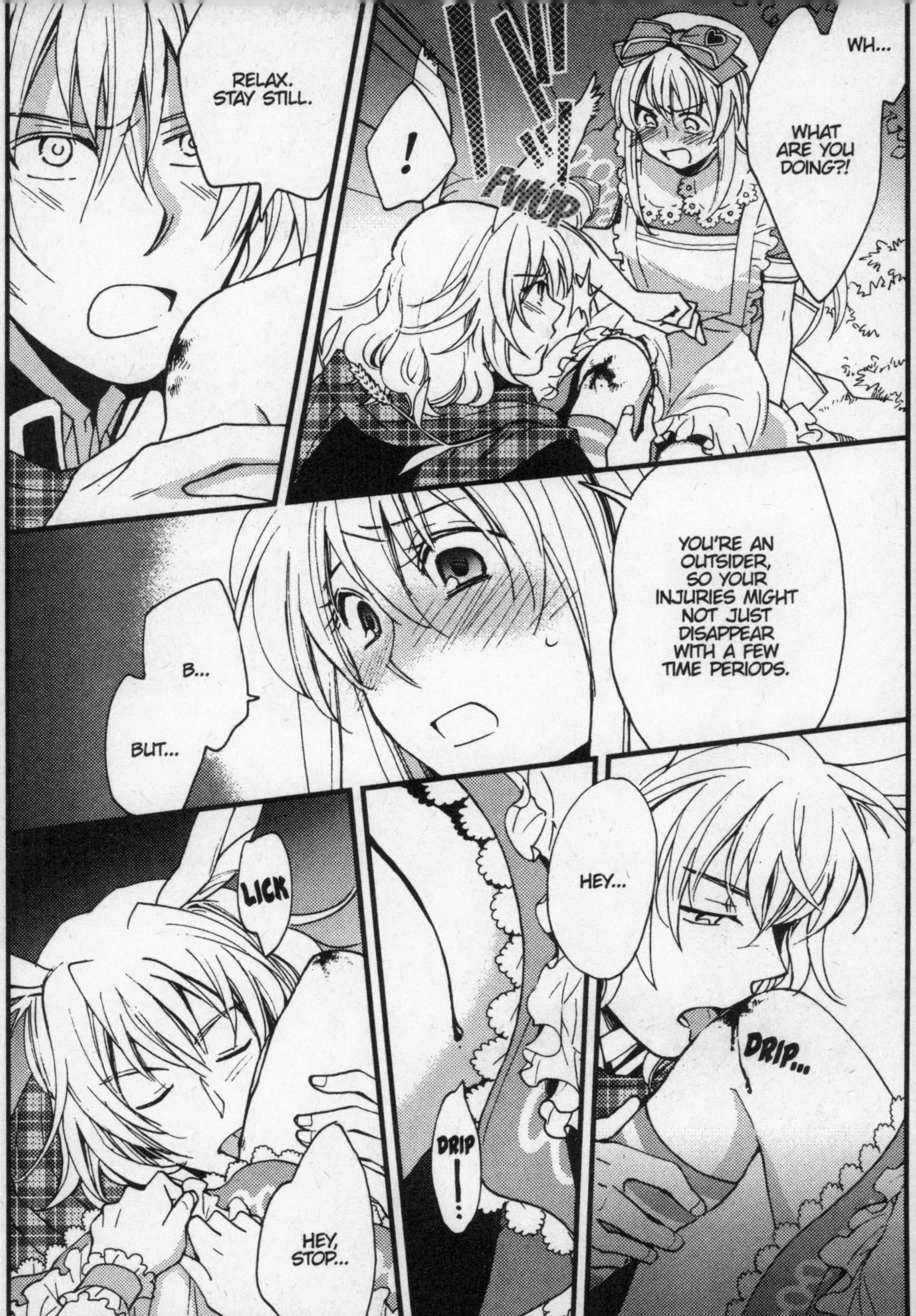
WH...
WHAT ARE YOU DOING?!
FWUP
!
RELAX. STAY STILL.
YOU'RE AN OUTSIDER, SO YOUR INJURIES MIGHT NOT JUST DISAPPEAR WITH A FEW TIME PERIODS.
B...
BUT...
HEY...
DRIP...
DRIP!
HEY, STOP...
LICK

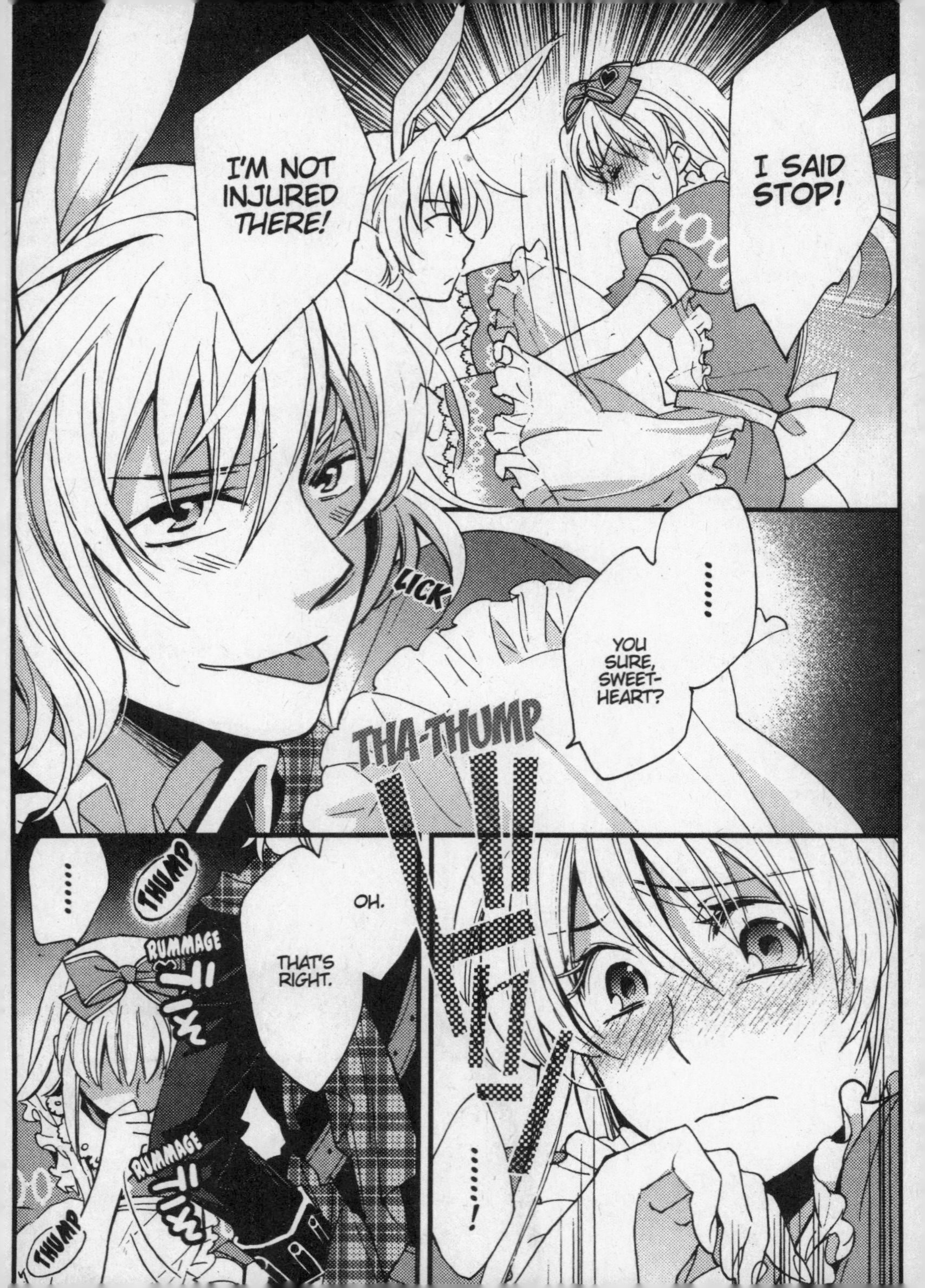
I SAID STOP!
I'M NOT INJURED THERE!
......
YOU SURE, SWEET-HEART?
LICK
THA-THUMP
......!
OH. THAT'S RIGHT.
......
THUMP
RUMMAGE
RUMMAGE
THUMP

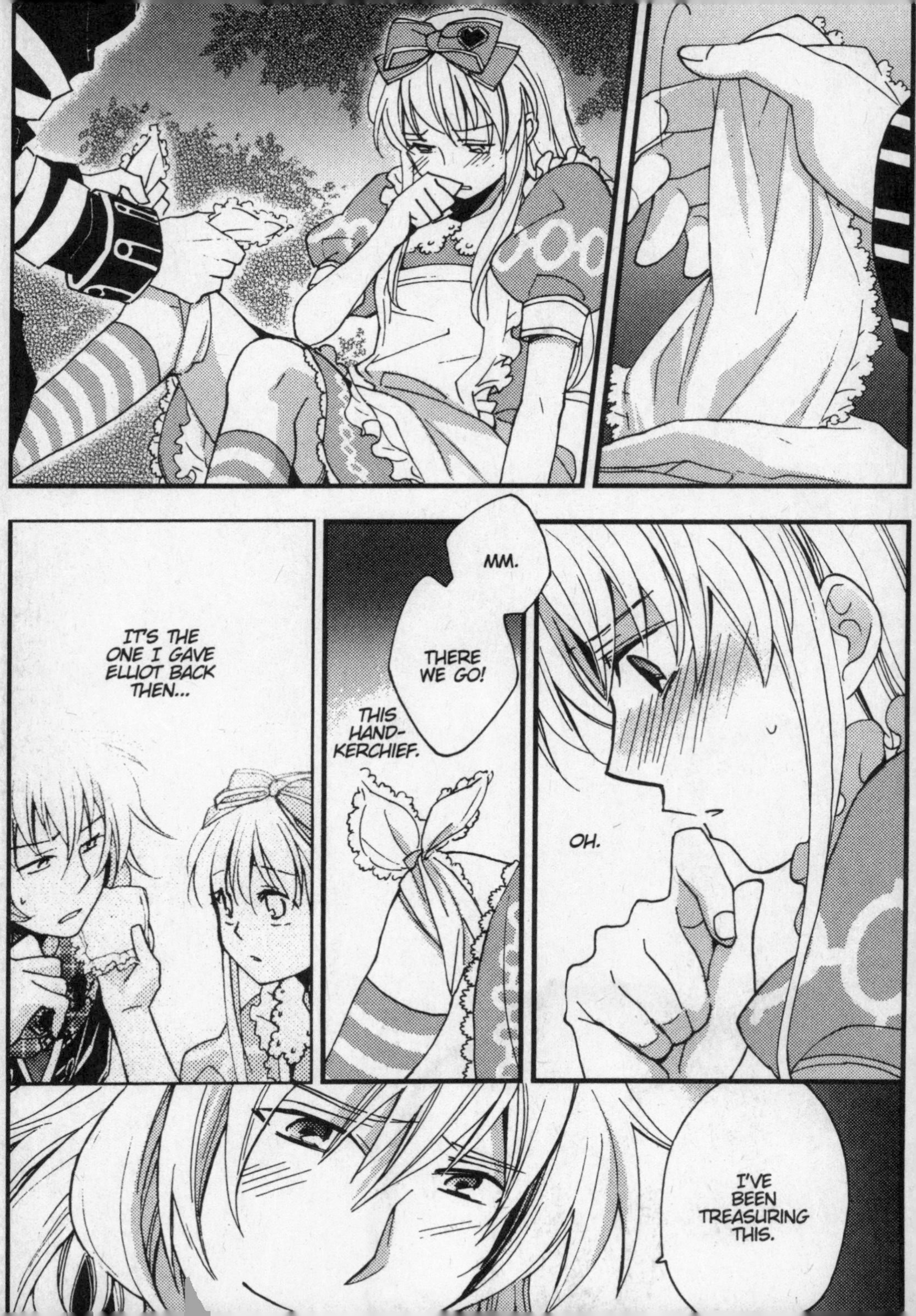
OH.
MM.
THERE WE GO!
THIS HAND-KERCHIEF.
IT'S THE ONE I GAVE ELLIOT BACK THEN...
I'VE BEEN TREASURING THIS.

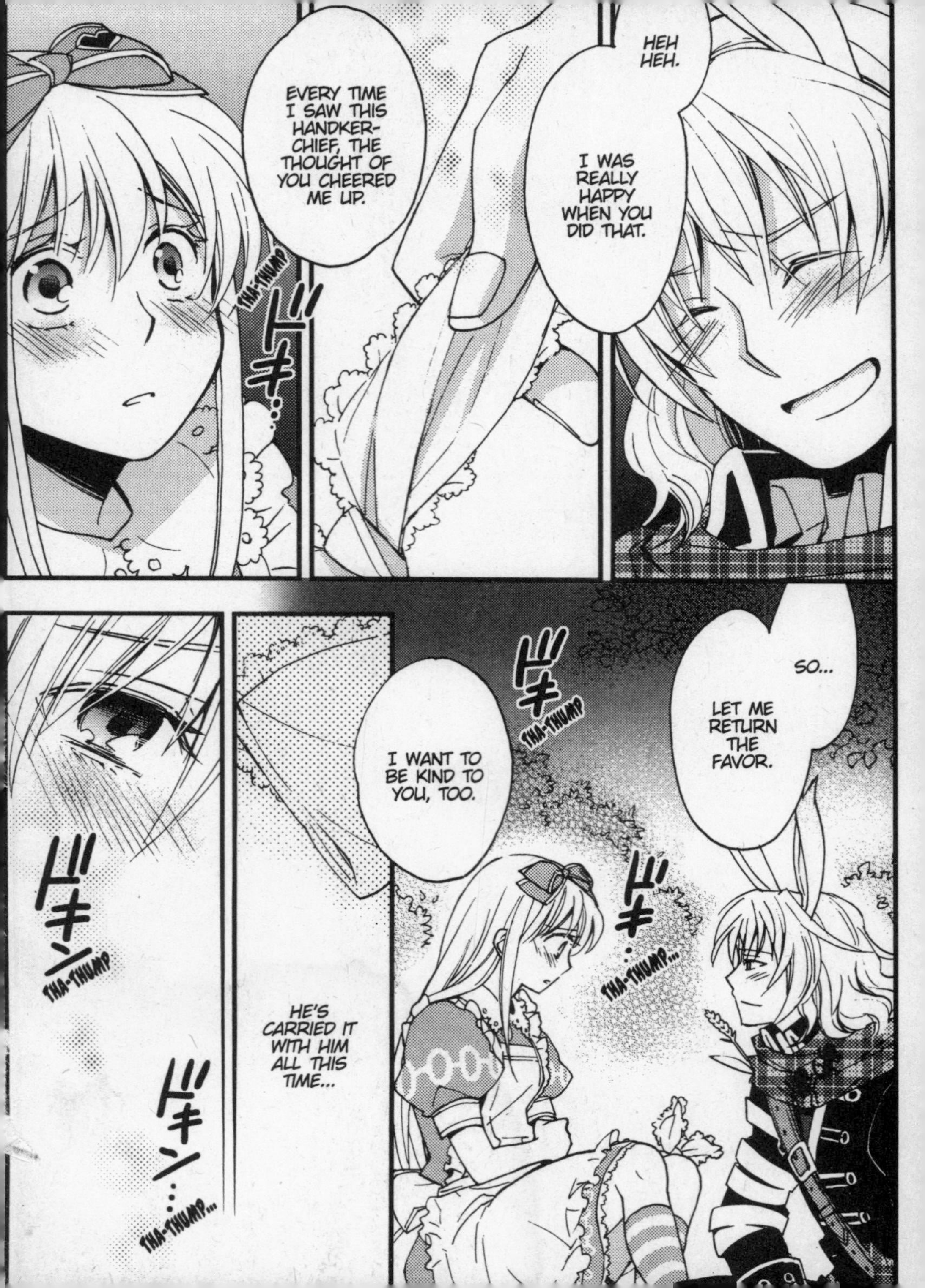
HEH HEH.
I WAS REALLY HAPPY WHEN YOU DID THAT.
EVERY TIME I SAW THIS HANDKERCHIEF, THE THOUGHT OF YOU CHEERED ME UP.
ドキ…
THA-THUMP
SO...
LET ME RETURN THE FAVOR.
I WANT TO BE KIND TO YOU, TOO.
ドキ
THA-THUMP
ドキ…
THA-THUMP...
HE'S CARRIED IT WITH HIM ALL THIS TIME...
ドキン
THA-THUMP
ドキン…
THA-THUMP...

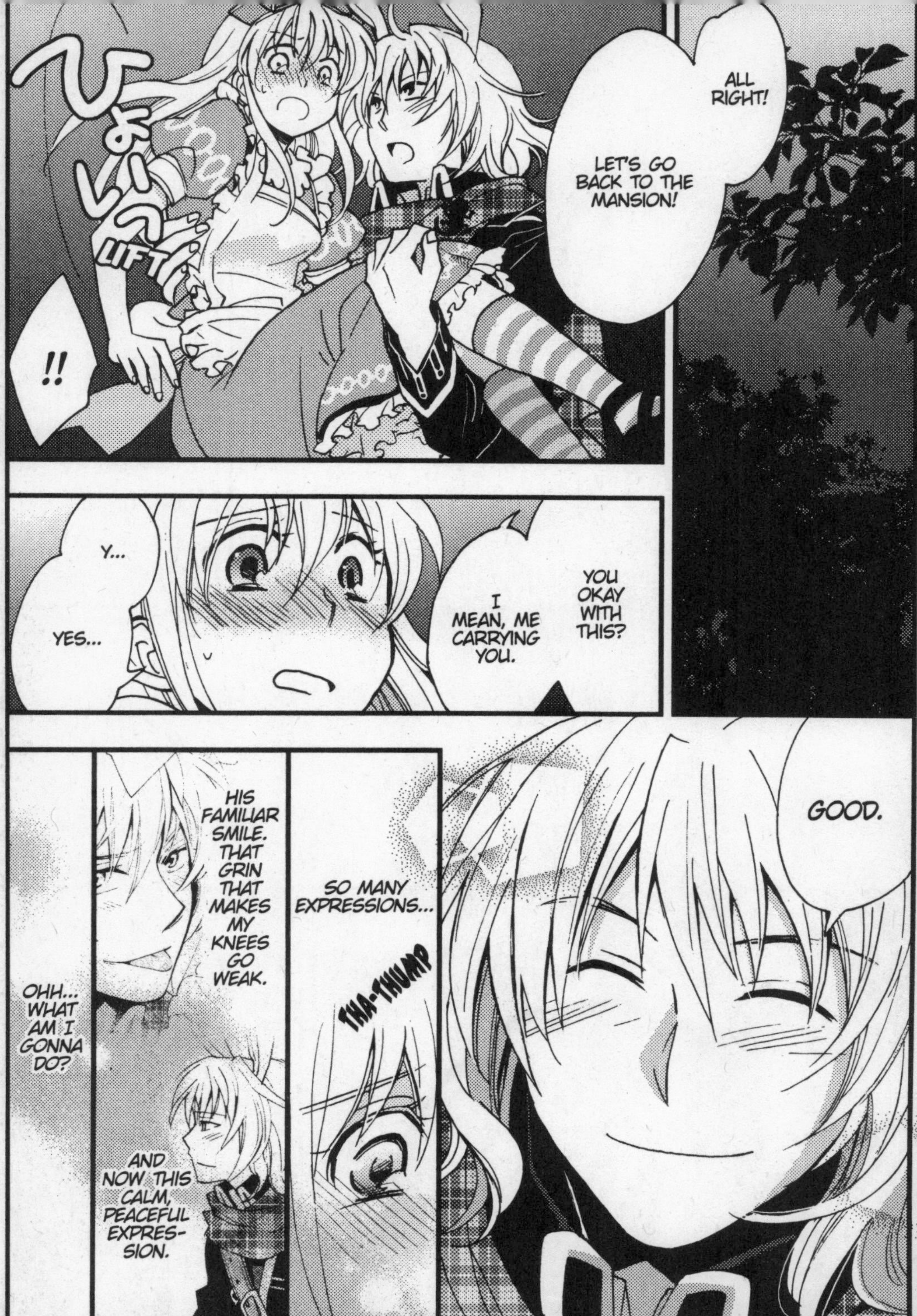
ALL RIGHT!
LET'S GO BACK TO THE MANSION!
ひょいっ
LIFT
!!
YOU OKAY WITH THIS?
I MEAN, ME CARRYING YOU.
Y...
YES...
GOOD.
THA-THUMP
SO MANY EXPRESSIONS...
HIS FAMILIAR SMILE. THAT GRIN THAT MAKES MY KNEES GO WEAK.
OHH... WHAT AM I GONNA DO?
AND NOW THIS CALM, PEACEFUL EXPRESSION.

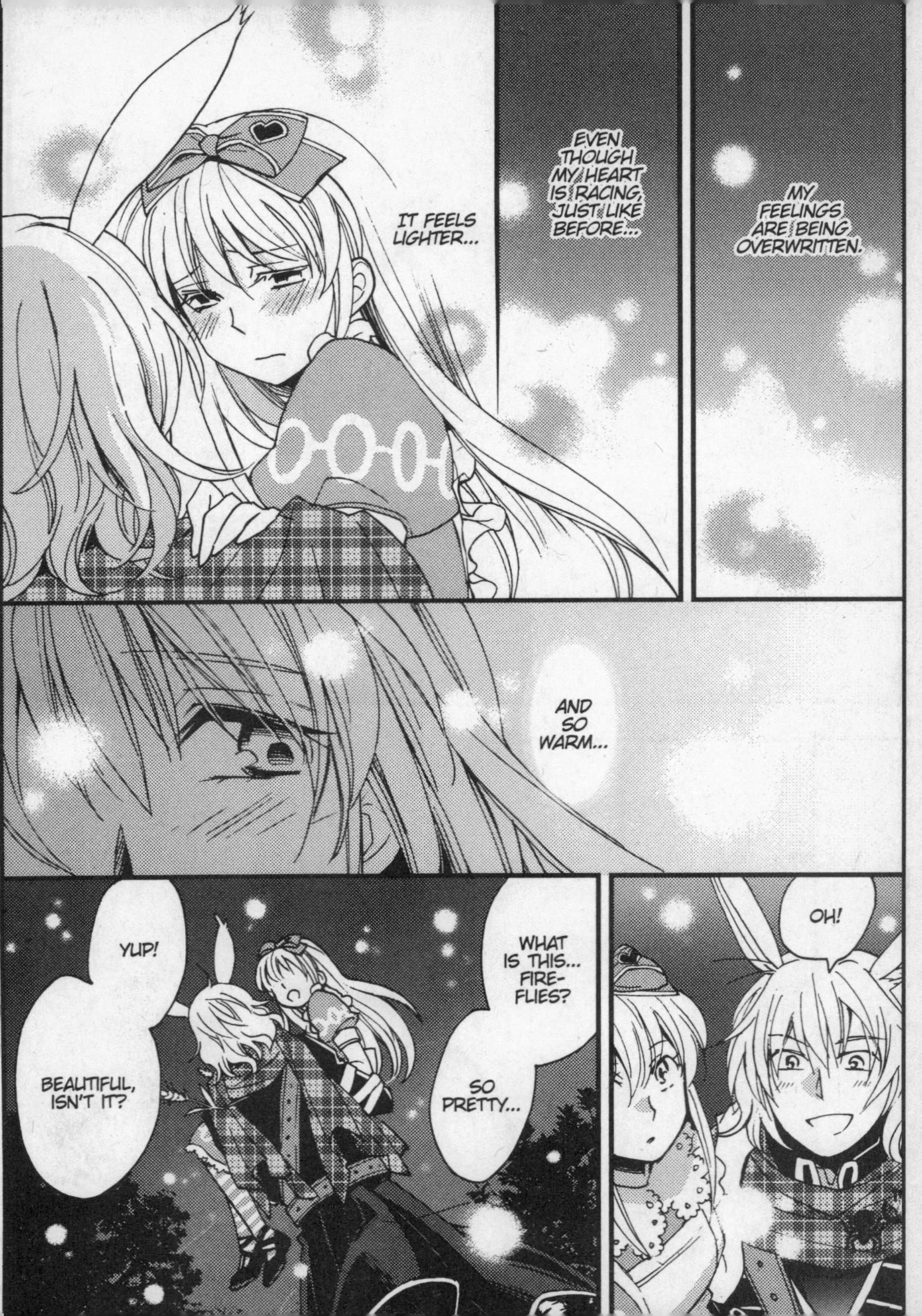
MY FEELINGS ARE BEING OVERWRITTEN.
EVEN THOUGH MY HEART IS RACING, JUST LIKE BEFORE...
IT FEELS LIGHTER...
AND SO WARM...
OH!
WHAT IS THIS... FIRE- FLIES?
YUP!
SO PRETTY...
BEAUTIFUL, ISN'T IT?

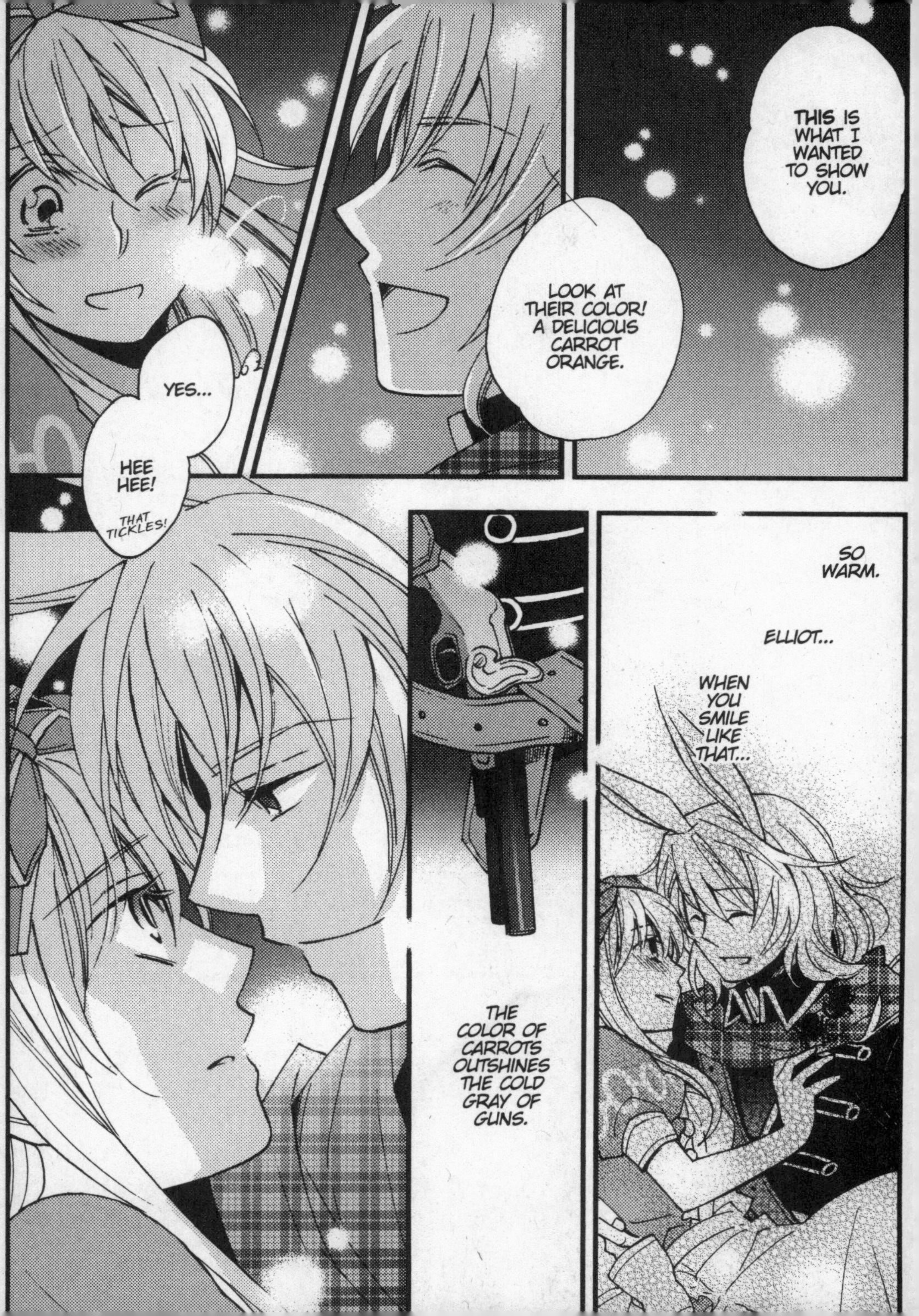
THIS IS WHAT I WANTED TO SHOW YOU.
LOOK AT THEIR COLOR! A DELICIOUS CARROT ORANGE.
YES...
HEE HEE!
THAT TICKLES!
SO WARM.
ELLIOT...
WHEN YOU SMILE LIKE THAT...
THE COLOR OF CARROTS OUTSHINES THE COLD GRAY OF GUNS.

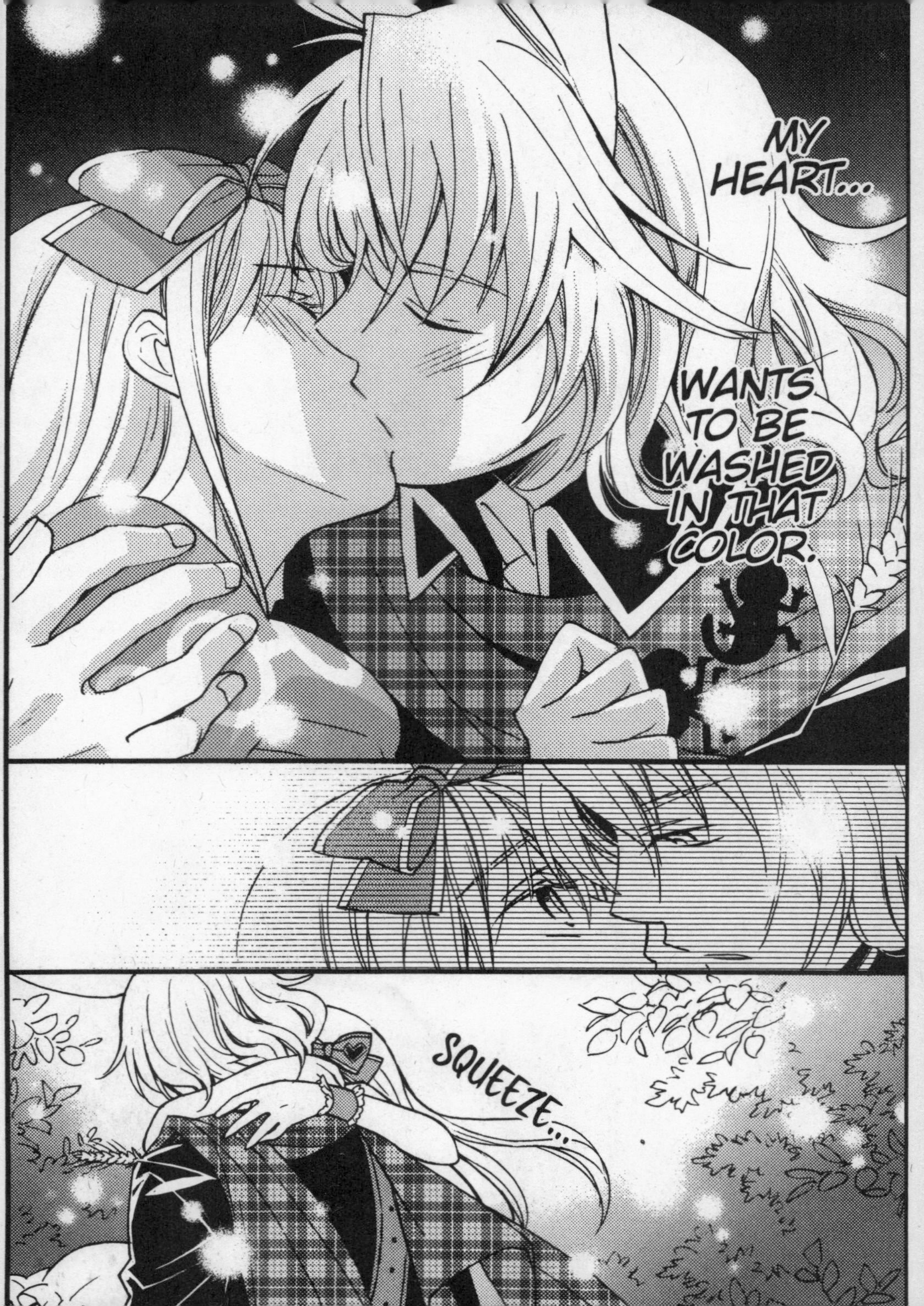
MY HEART...
WANTS TO BE WASHED IN THAT COLOR.
SQUEEZE...

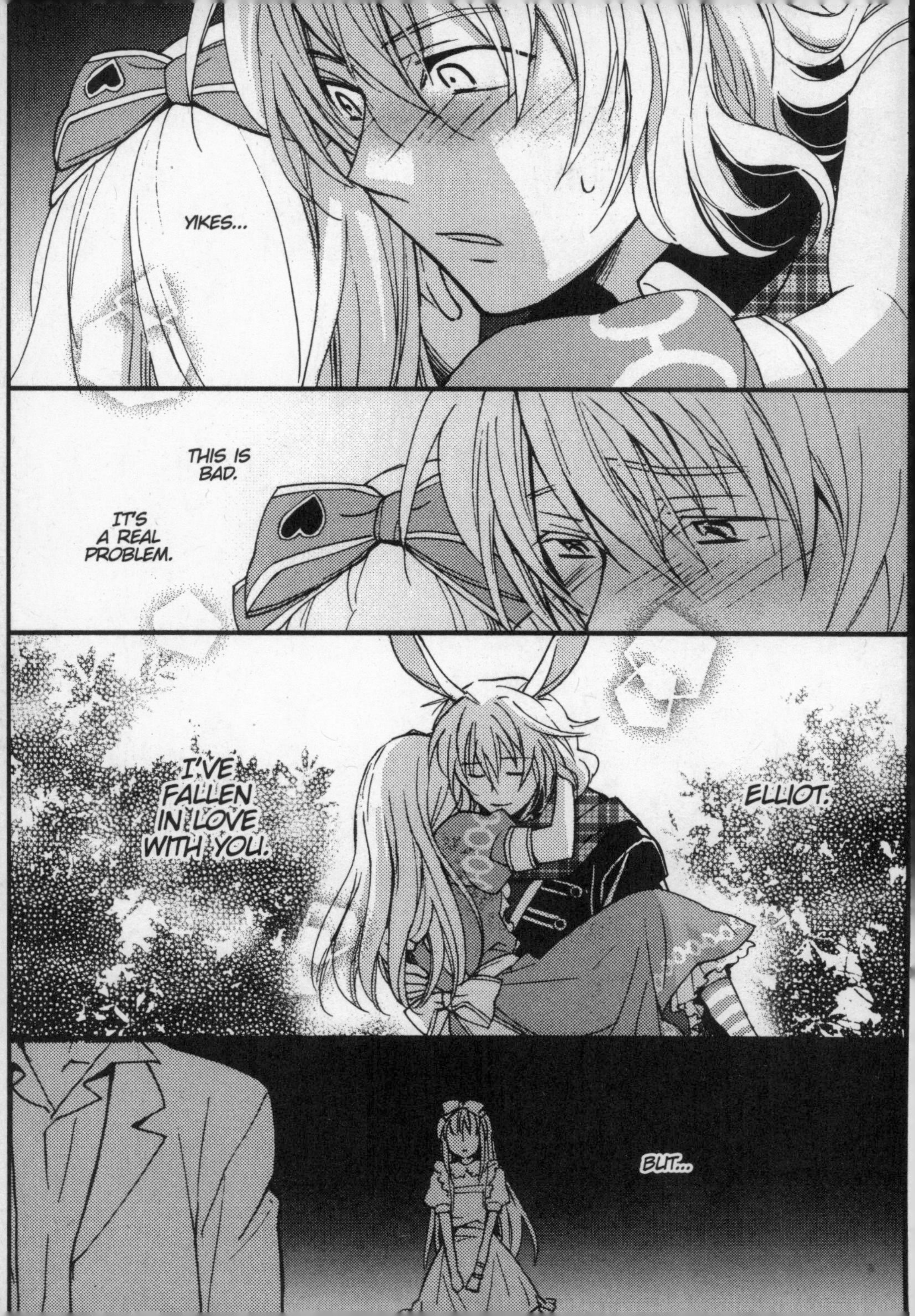
YIKES...
THIS IS BAD.
IT'S A REAL PROBLEM.
ELLIOT.
I'VE FALLEN IN LOVE WITH YOU.
BUT...

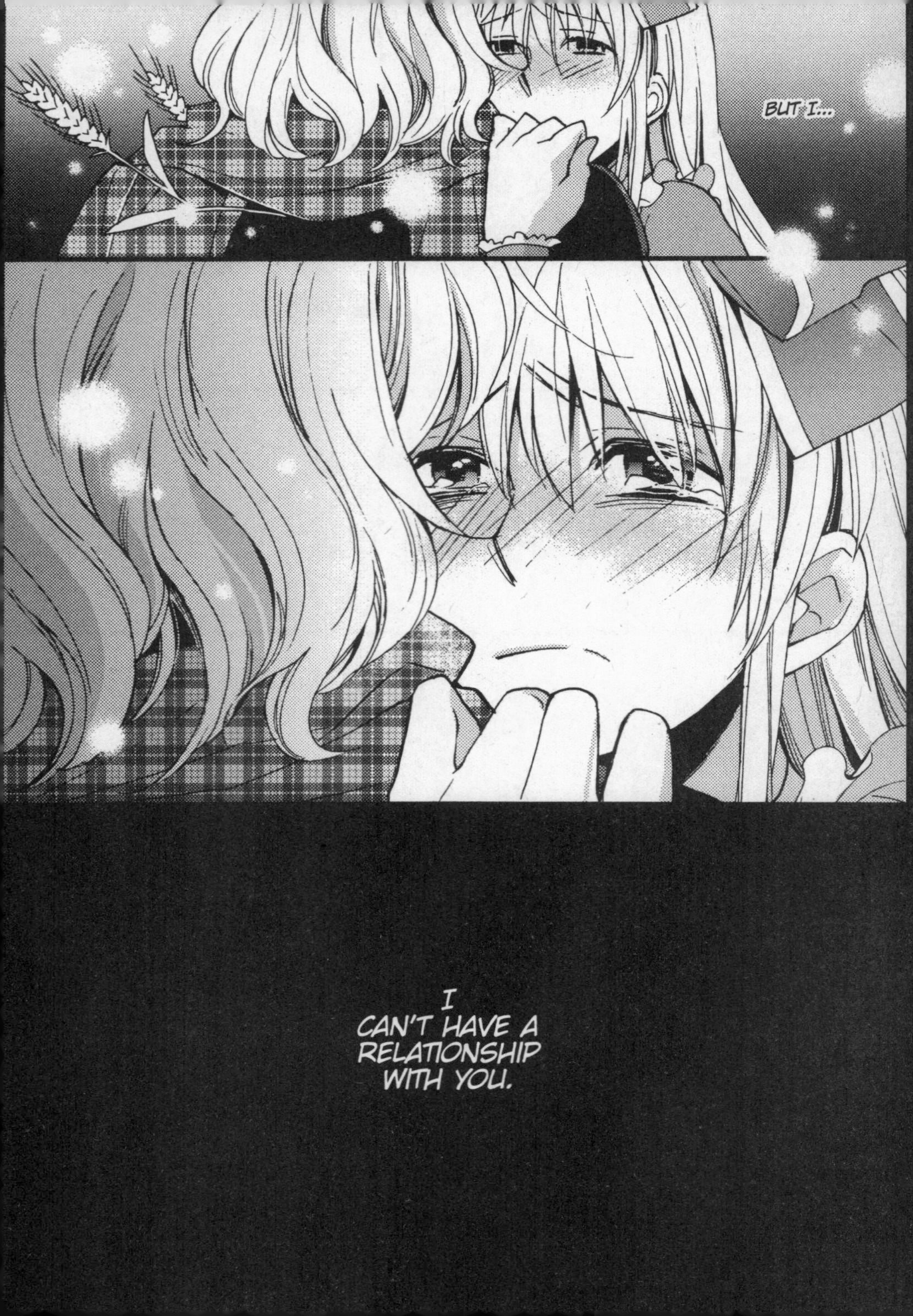
BUT I...
I CAN'T HAVE A RELATIONSHIP WITH YOU.

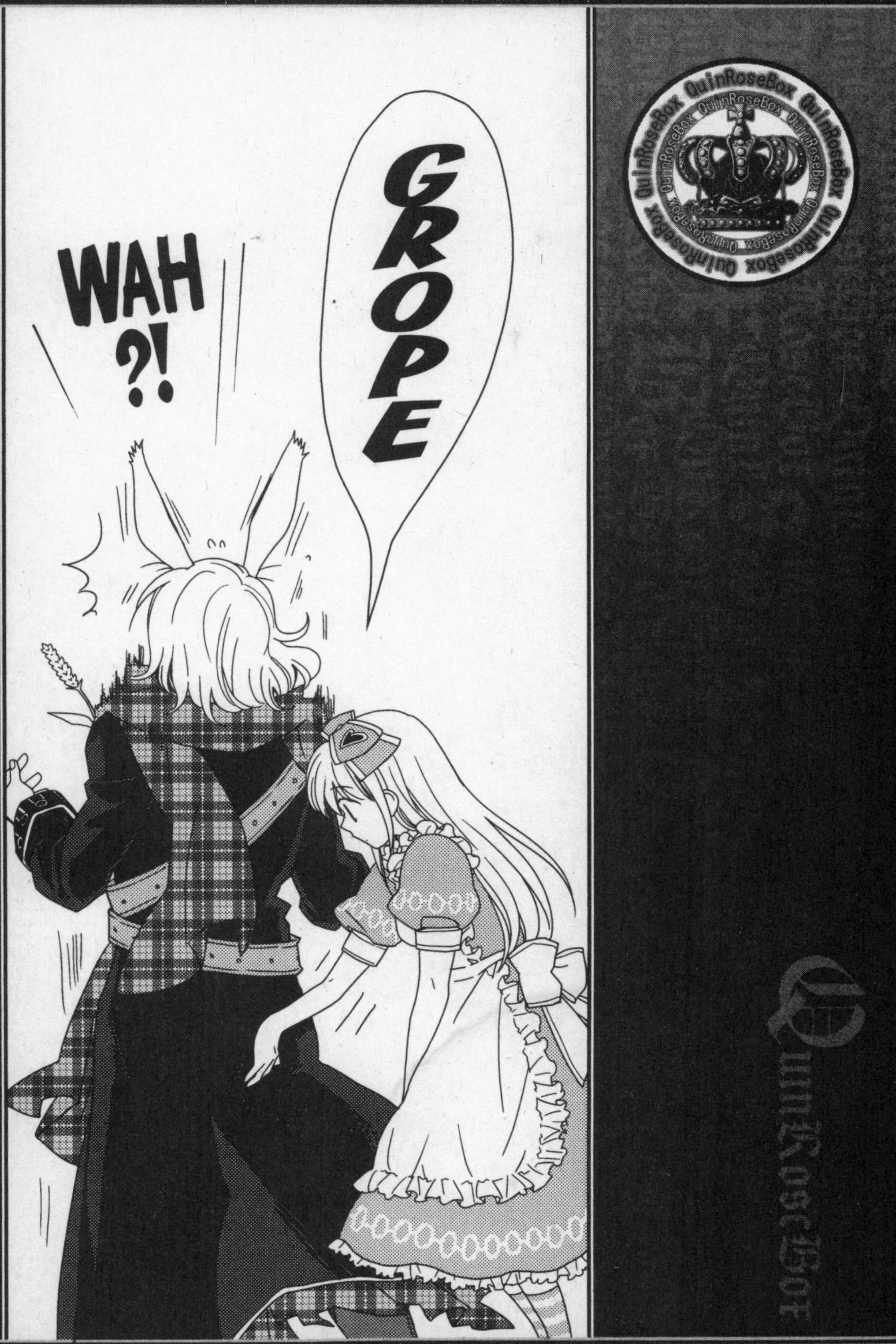

GROPE
WAH ?!

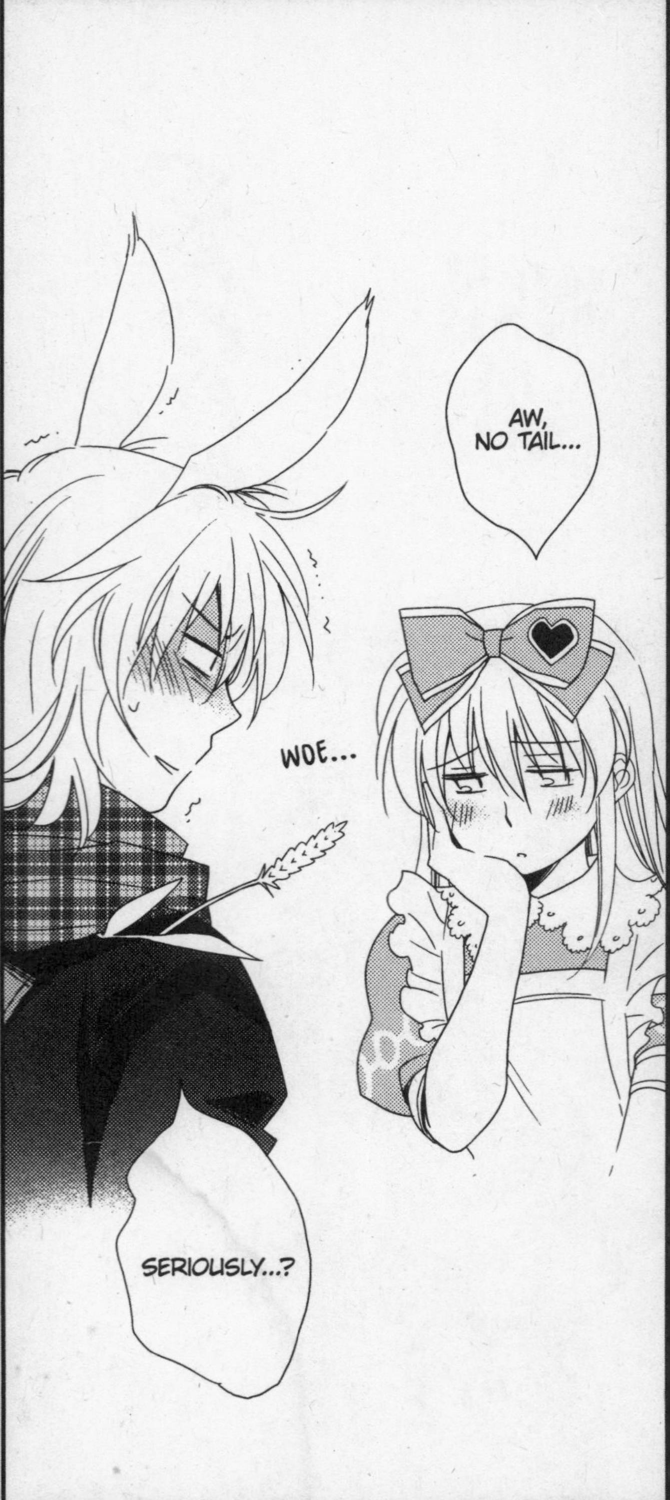
AW, NO TAIL...
WOE...
SERIOUSLY...?

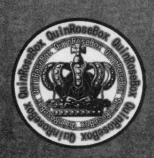

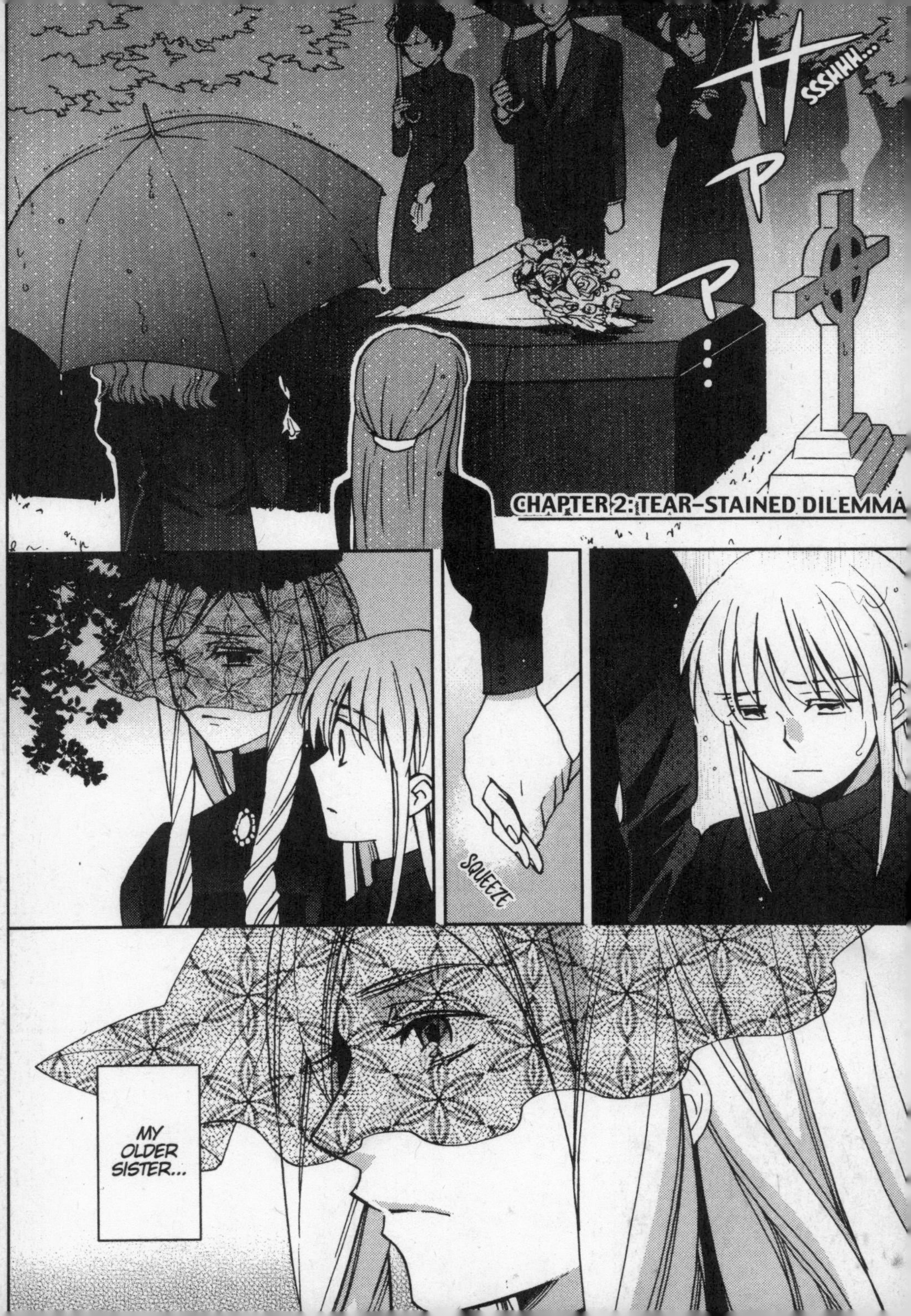
SSSHHH...
...
CHAPTER 2: TEAR-STAINED DILEMMA
SQUEEZE
MY OLDER SISTER...

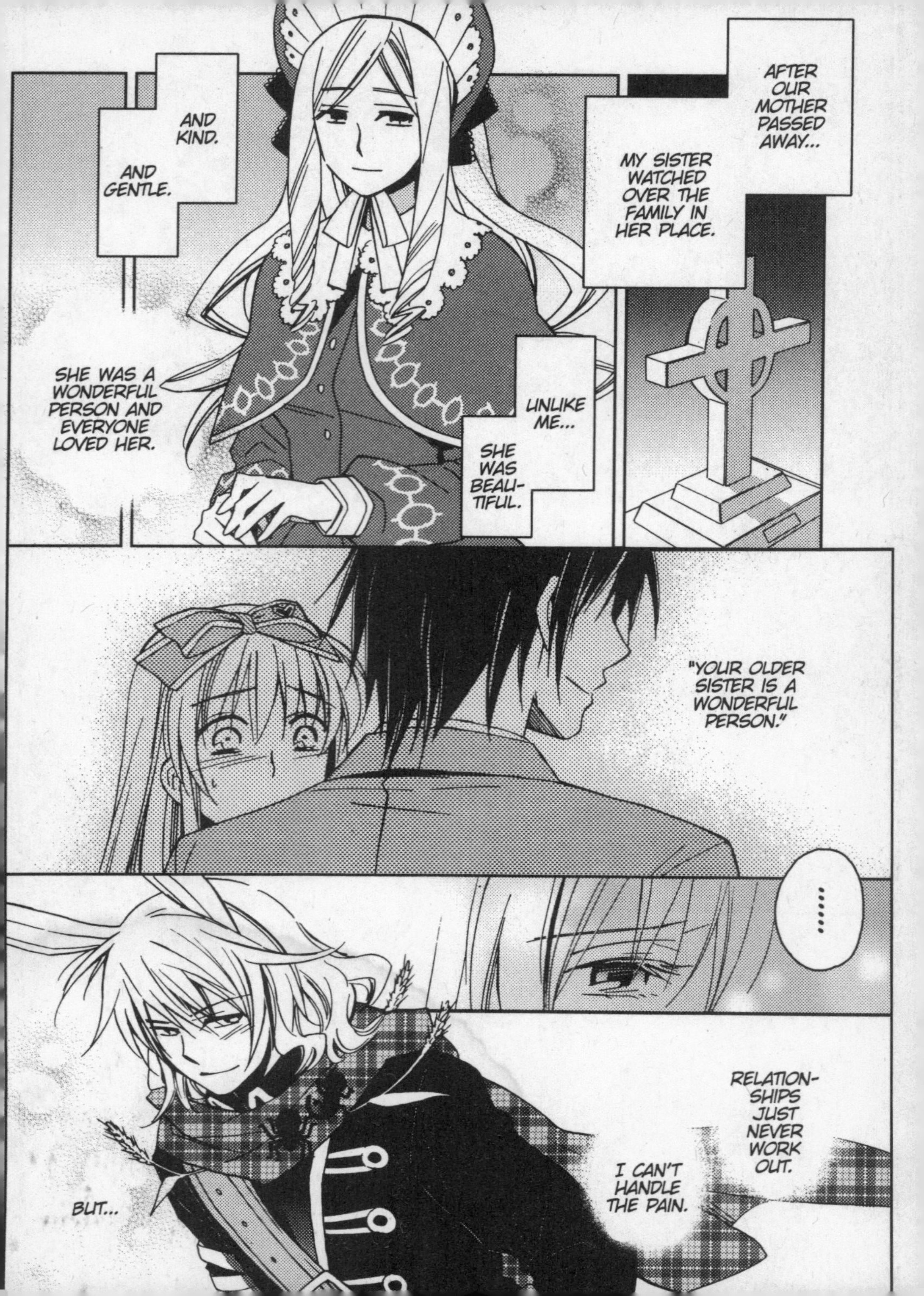
AFTER OUR MOTHER PASSED AWAY...
MY SISTER WATCHED OVER THE FAMILY IN HER PLACE.
UNLIKE ME...
SHE WAS BEAUTIFUL.
AND KIND.
AND GENTLE.
SHE WAS A WONDERFUL PERSON AND EVERYONE LOVED HER.
"YOUR OLDER SISTER IS A WONDERFUL PERSON."
......
RELATIONSHIPS JUST NEVER WORK OUT.
I CAN'T HANDLE THE PAIN.
BUT...

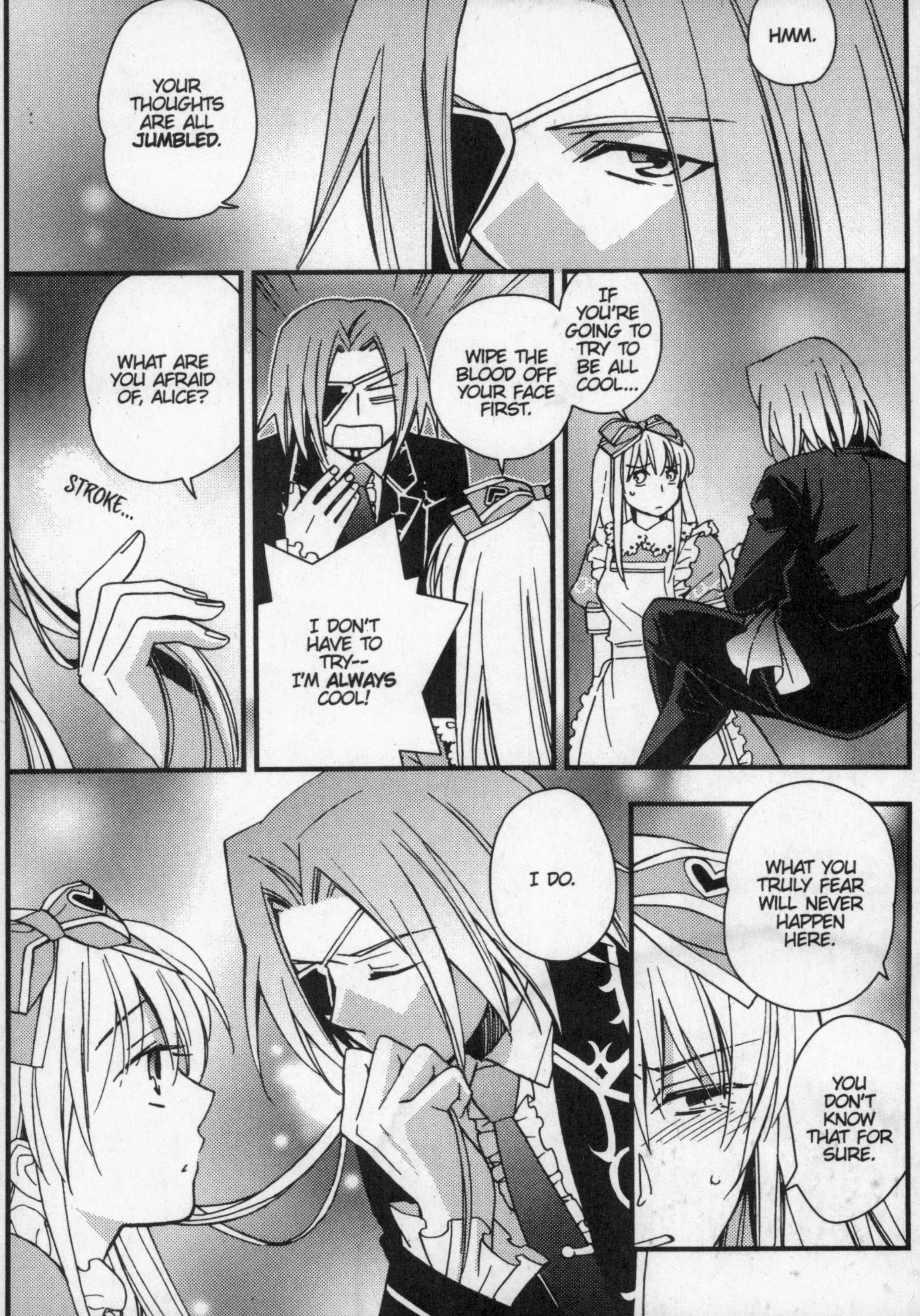
HMM.
YOUR THOUGHTS ARE ALL JUMBLED.
IF YOU'RE GOING TO TRY TO BE ALL COOL....
WIPE THE BLOOD OFF YOUR FACE FIRST.
I DON'T HAVE TO TRY-- I'M ALWAYS COOL!
WHAT ARE YOU AFRAID OF, ALICE?
STROKE...
WHAT YOU TRULY FEAR WILL NEVER HAPPEN HERE.
YOU DON'T KNOW THAT FOR SURE.
I DO.

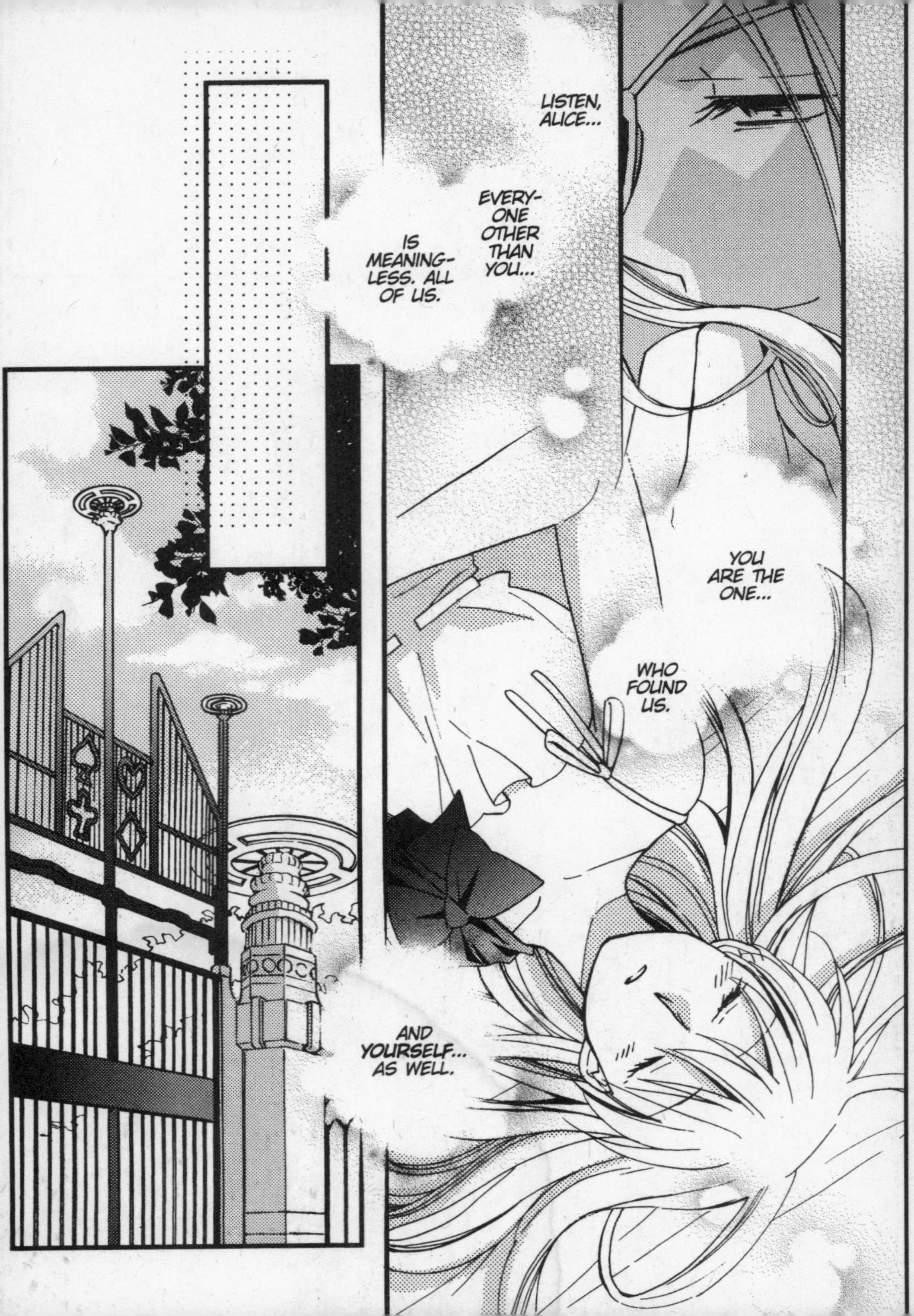
LISTEN, ALICE...
EVERY-ONE OTHER THAN YOU...
IS MEANING-LESS. ALL OF US.
YOU ARE THE ONE...
WHO FOUND US.
AND YOURSELF... AS WELL.

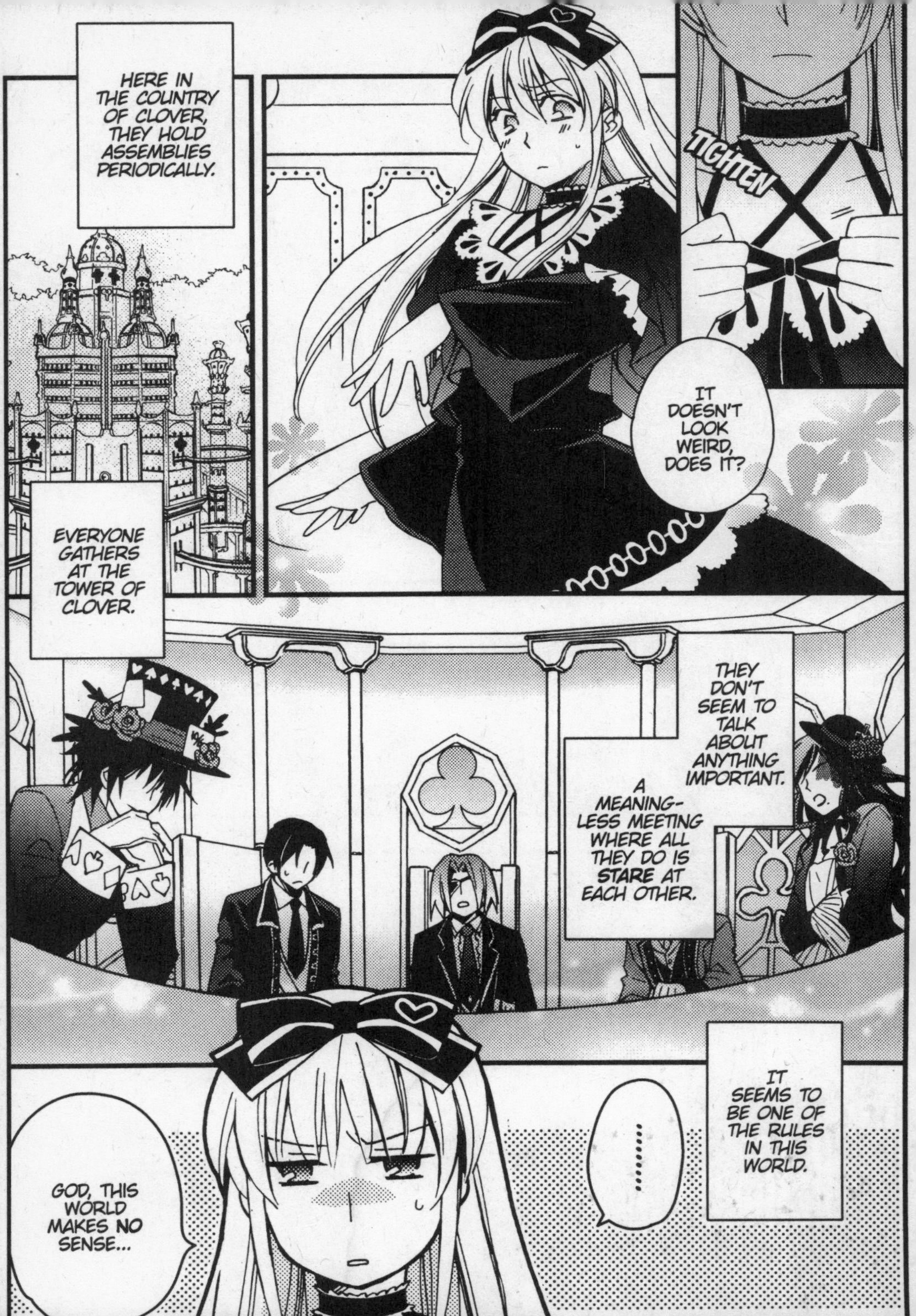
TIGHTEN
IT DOESN'T LOOK WEIRD, DOES IT?
HERE IN THE COUNTRY OF CLOVER, THEY HOLD ASSEMBLIES PERIODICALLY.
EVERYONE GATHERS AT THE TOWER OF CLOVER.
THEY DON'T SEEM TO TALK ABOUT ANYTHING IMPORTANT.
A MEANING-LESS MEETING WHERE ALL THEY DO IS STARE AT EACH OTHER.
IT SEEMS TO BE ONE OF THE RULES IN THIS WORLD.
......
GOD, THIS WORLD MAKES NO SENSE...

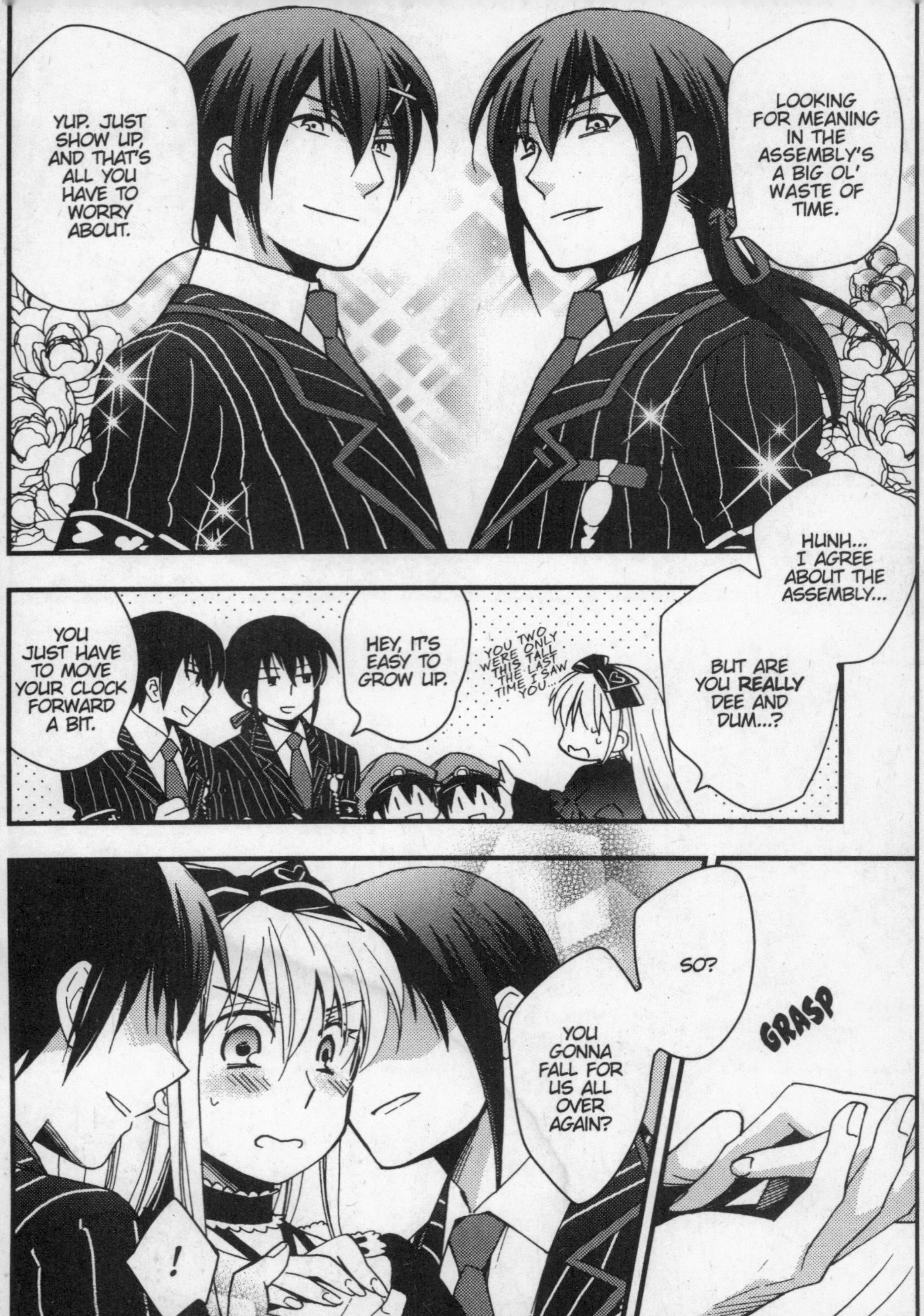
LOOKING FOR MEANING IN THE ASSEMBLY'S A BIG OL' WASTE OF TIME.
YUP. JUST SHOW UP, AND THAT'S ALL YOU HAVE TO WORRY ABOUT.
HUNH... I AGREE ABOUT THE ASSEMBLY...
BUT ARE YOU REALLY DEE AND DUM...?
YOU TWO WERE ONLY THIS TALL THE LAST TIME I SAW YOU...
HEY, IT'S EASY TO GROW UP.
YOU JUST HAVE TO MOVE YOUR CLOCK FORWARD A BIT.
GRASP
SO?
YOU GONNA FALL FOR US ALL OVER AGAIN?
!

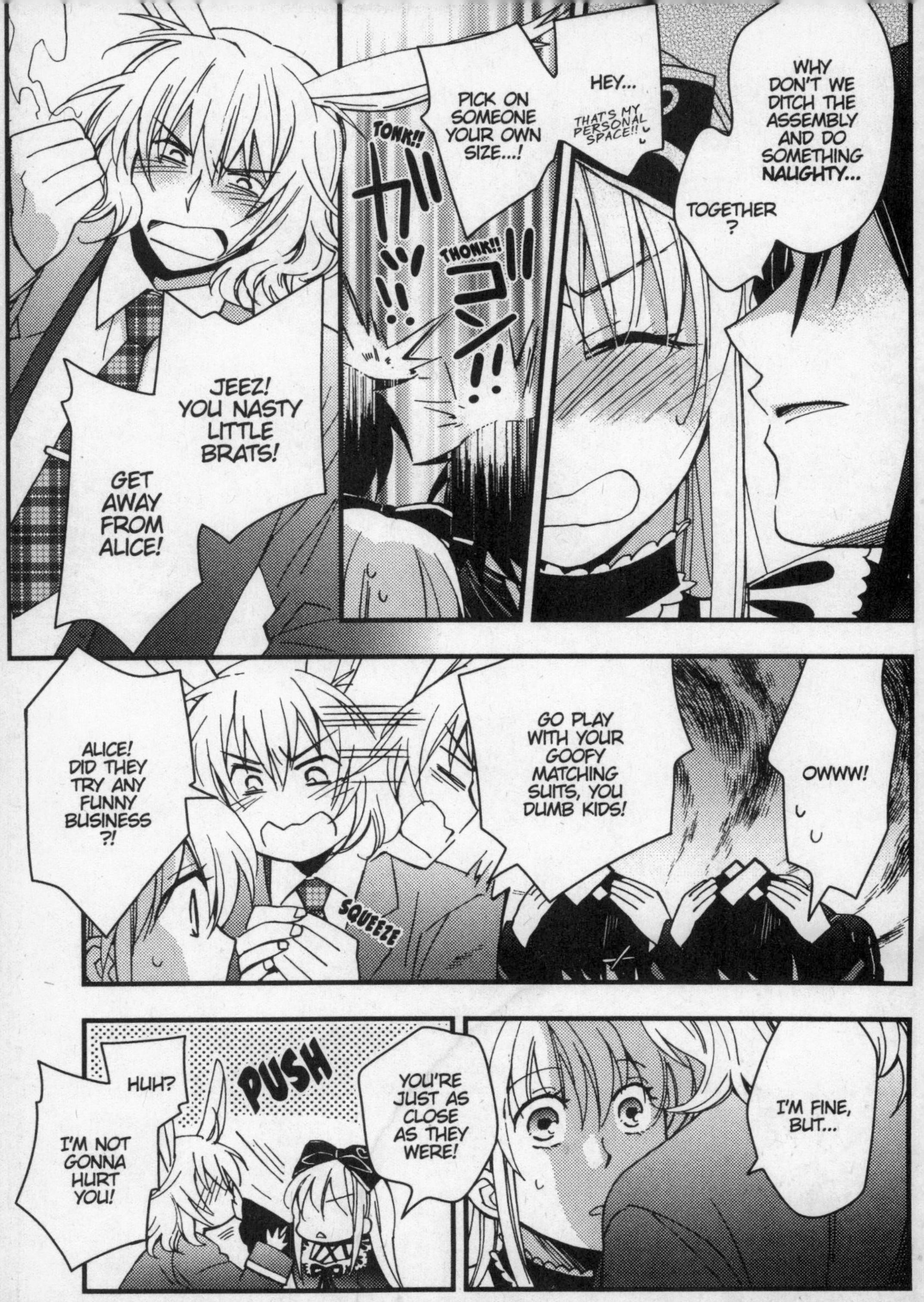
WHY DON'T WE DITCH THE ASSEMBLY AND DO SOMETHING NAUGHTY...
TOGETHER?
HEY...
THAT'S MY PERSONAL SPACE!!
PICK ON SOMEONE YOUR OWN SIZE...!
TONK!!
THONK!!
JEEZ! YOU NASTY LITTLE BRATS!
GET AWAY FROM ALICE!
OWWW!
GO PLAY WITH YOUR GOOFY MATCHING SUITS, YOU DUMB KIDS!
ALICE! DID THEY TRY ANY FUNNY BUSINESS?!
SQUEEZE
I'M FINE, BUT...
YOU'RE JUST AS CLOSE AS THEY WERE!
PUSH
HUH?
I'M NOT GONNA HURT YOU!

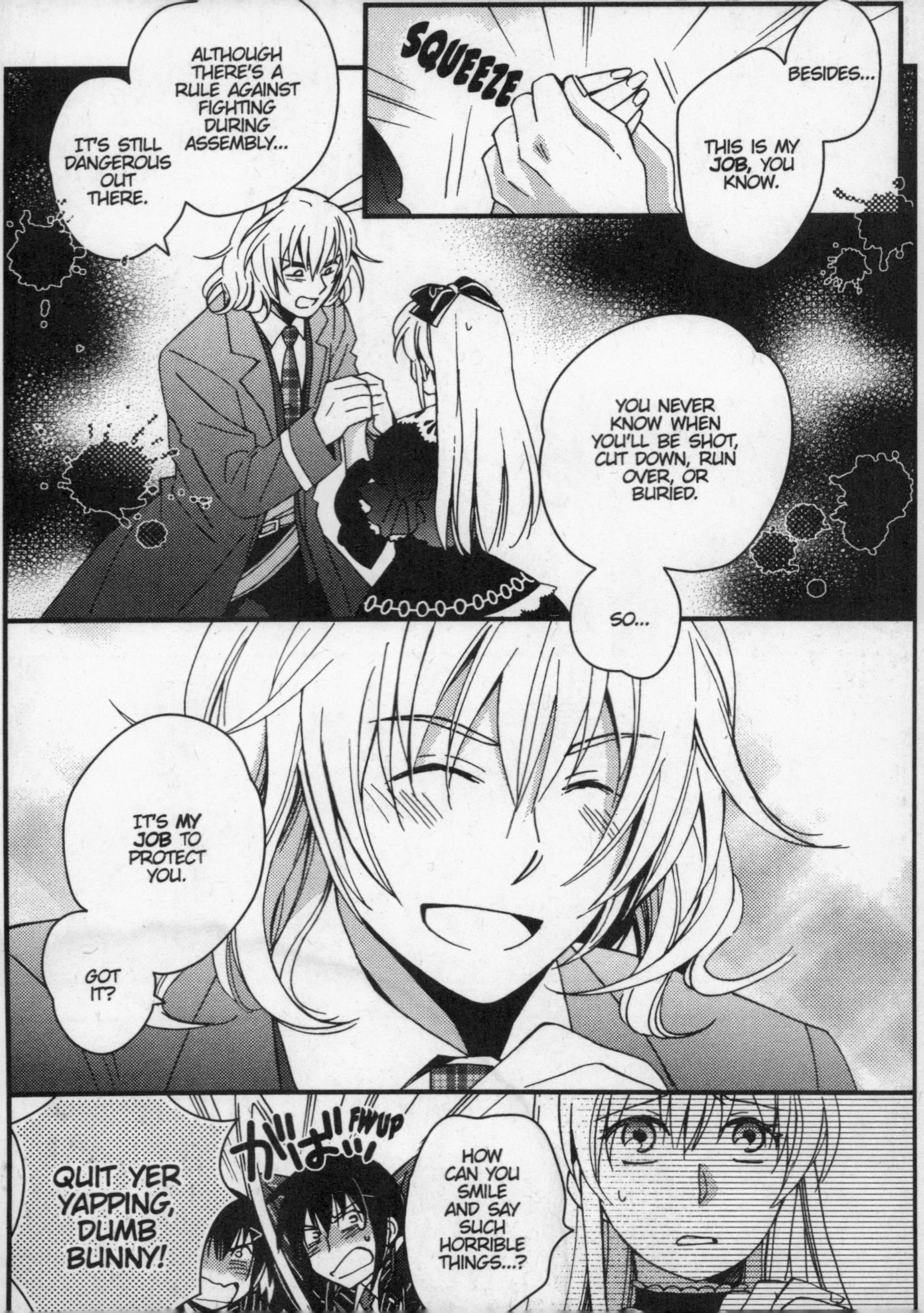
ALTHOUGH THERE'S A RULE AGAINST FIGHTING DURING ASSEMBLY...
IT'S STILL DANGEROUS OUT THERE.
SQUEEZE
BESIDES...
THIS IS MY JOB, YOU KNOW.
YOU NEVER KNOW WHEN YOU'LL BE SHOT, CUT DOWN, RUN OVER, OR BURIED.
SO...
IT'S MY JOB TO PROTECT YOU.
GOT IT?
HOW CAN YOU SMILE AND SAY SUCH HORRIBLE THINGS...?
がばっ
FWUP
QUIT YER YAPPING, DUMB BUNNY!

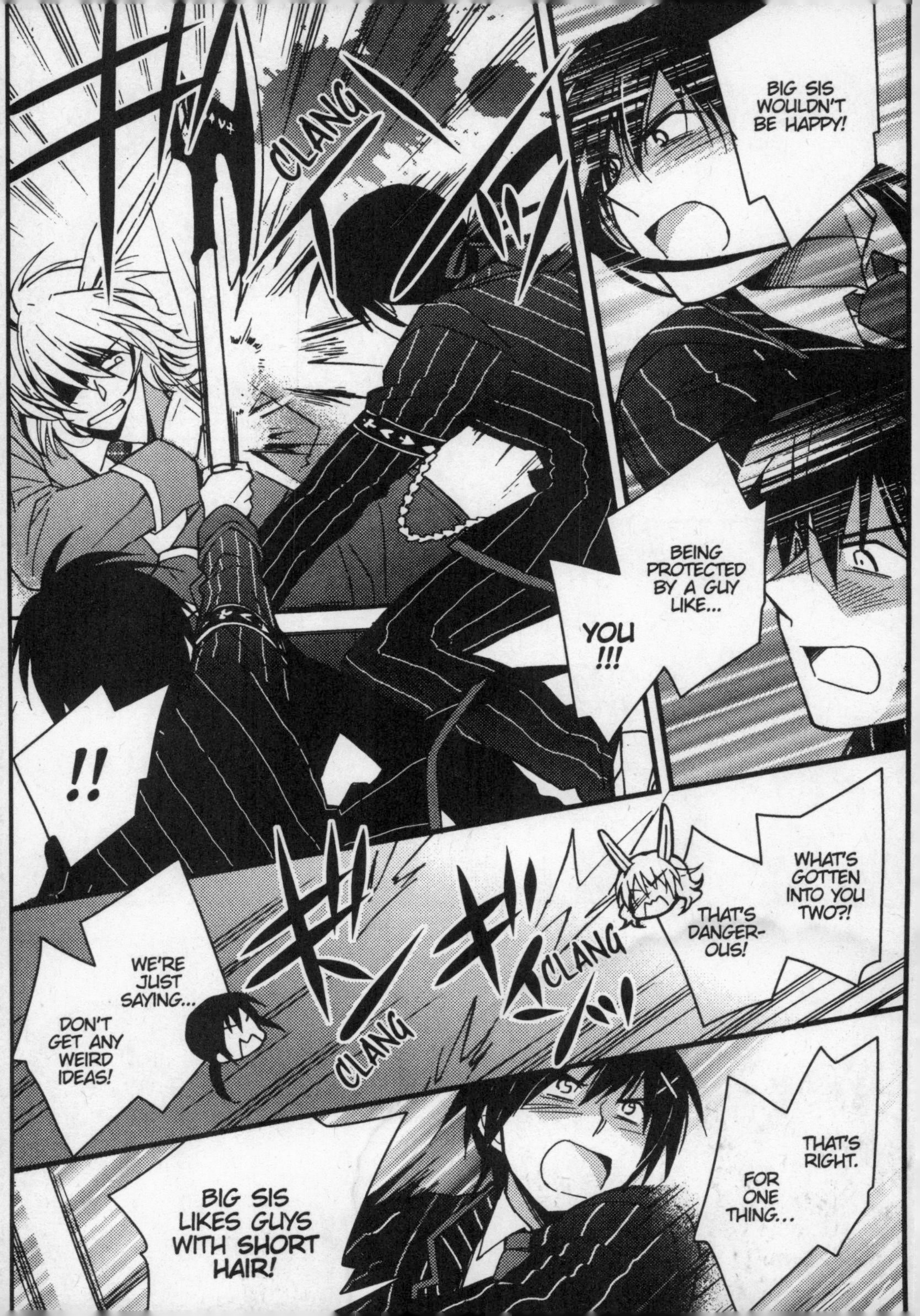
BIG SIS WOULDN'T BE HAPPY!
CLANG
BEING PROTECTED BY A GUY LIKE...
YOU !!!
!!
WHAT'S GOTTEN INTO YOU TWO?!
THAT'S DANGER-OUS!
CLANG
CLANG
WE'RE JUST SAYING...
DON'T GET ANY WEIRD IDEAS!
THAT'S RIGHT.
FOR ONE THING...
BIG SIS LIKES GUYS WITH SHORT HAIR!

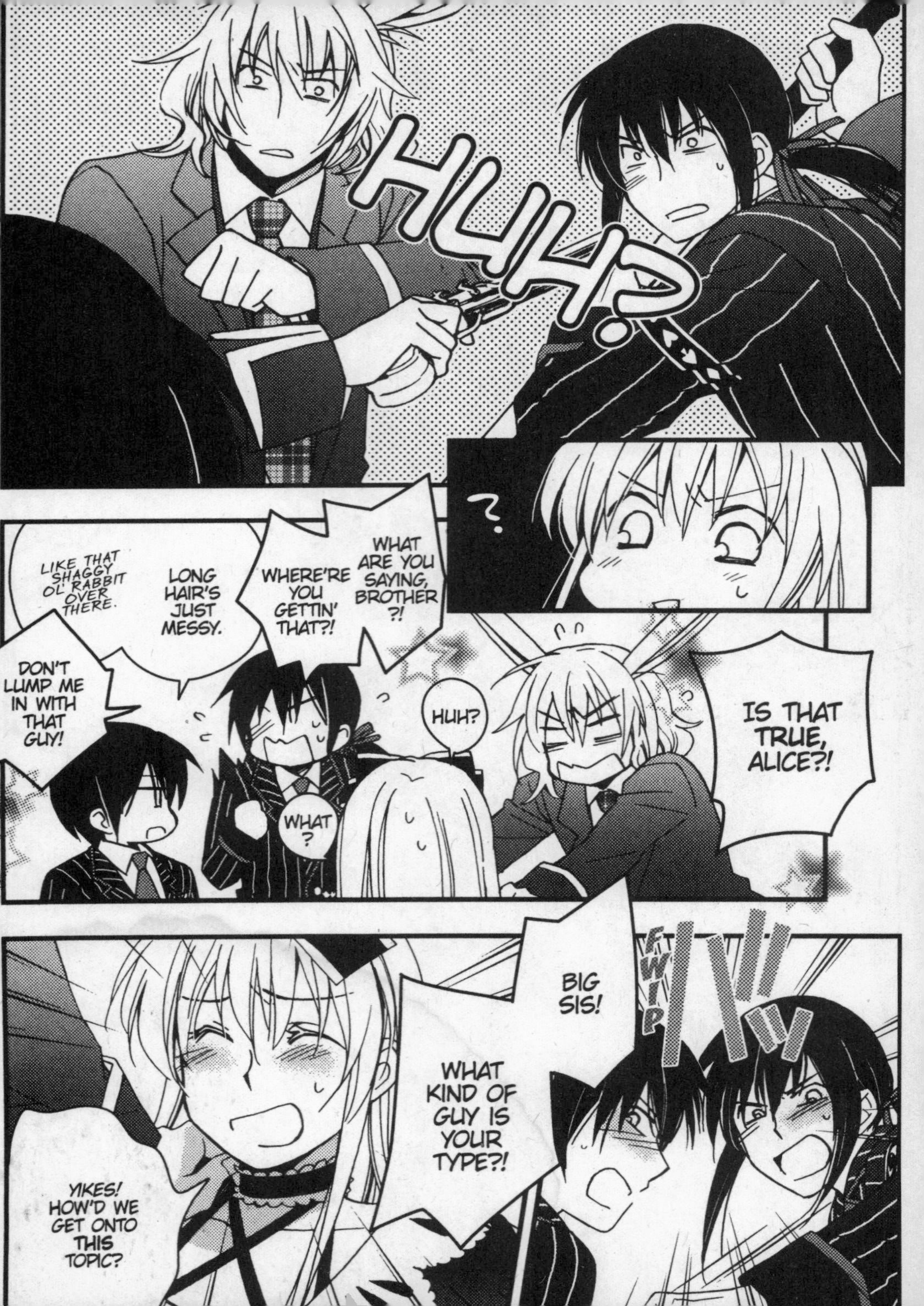
HUH?!
?
IS THAT TRUE, ALICE?!
HUH?
WHAT ARE YOU SAYING, BROTHER?!
WHERE'RE YOU GETTIN' THAT?!
LONG HAIR'S JUST MESSY.
LIKE THAT SHAGGY OL' RABBIT OVER THERE.
DON'T LUMP ME IN WITH THAT GUY!
WHAT?
FWIP
BIG SIS!
WHAT KIND OF GUY IS YOUR TYPE?!
YIKES! HOW'D WE GET ONTO THIS TOPIC?

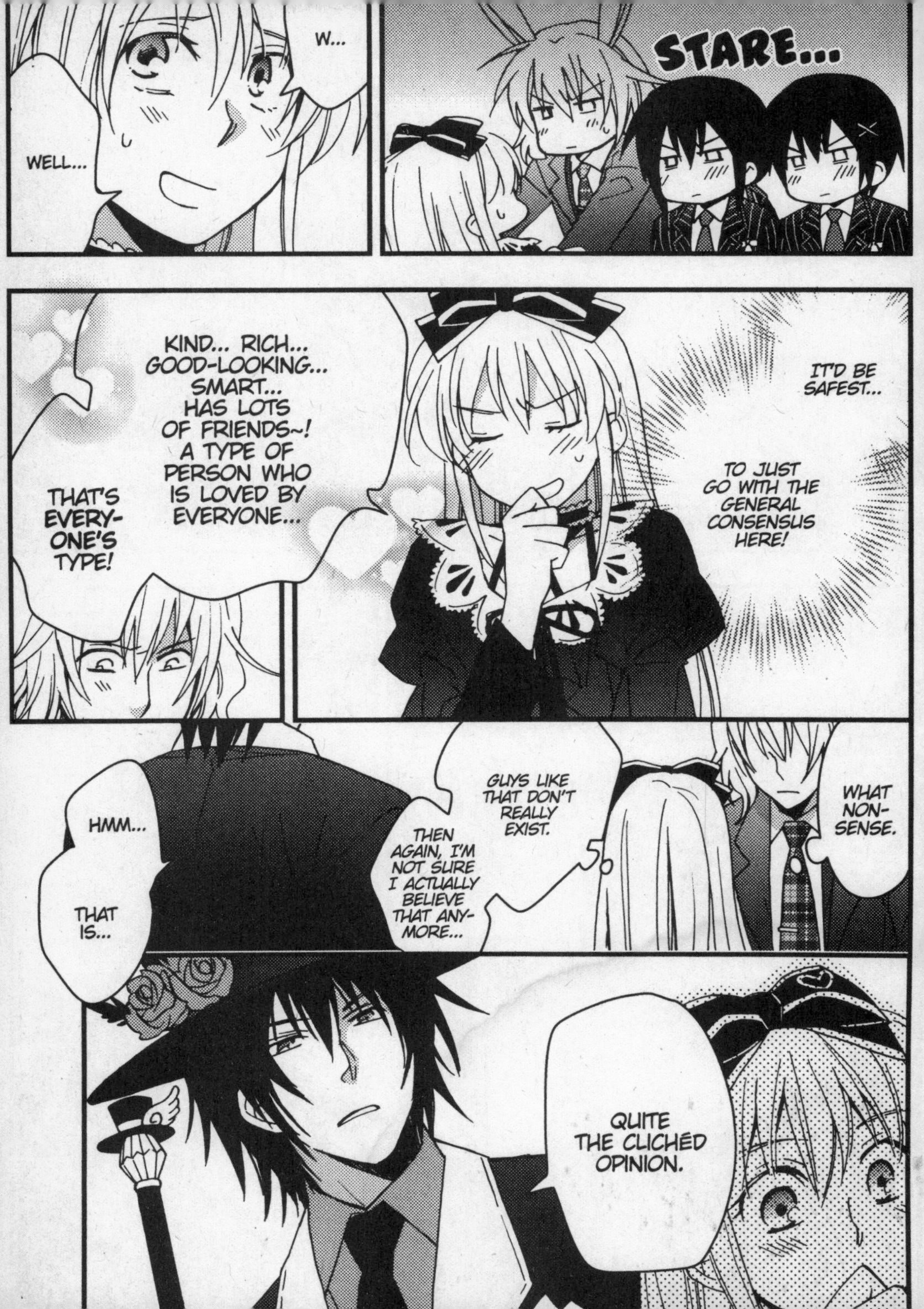
STARE...
W...
WELL...
IT'D BE SAFEST...
TO JUST GO WITH THE GENERAL CONSENSUS HERE!
KIND... RICH... GOOD-LOOKING... SMART... HAS LOTS OF FRIENDS~! A TYPE OF PERSON WHO IS LOVED BY EVERYONE...
THAT'S EVERY-ONE'S TYPE!
WHAT NON-SENSE.
GUYS LIKE THAT DON'T REALLY EXIST.
THEN AGAIN, I'M NOT SURE I ACTUALLY BELIEVE THAT ANY-MORE...
HMM...
THAT IS...
QUITE THE CLICHED OPINION.

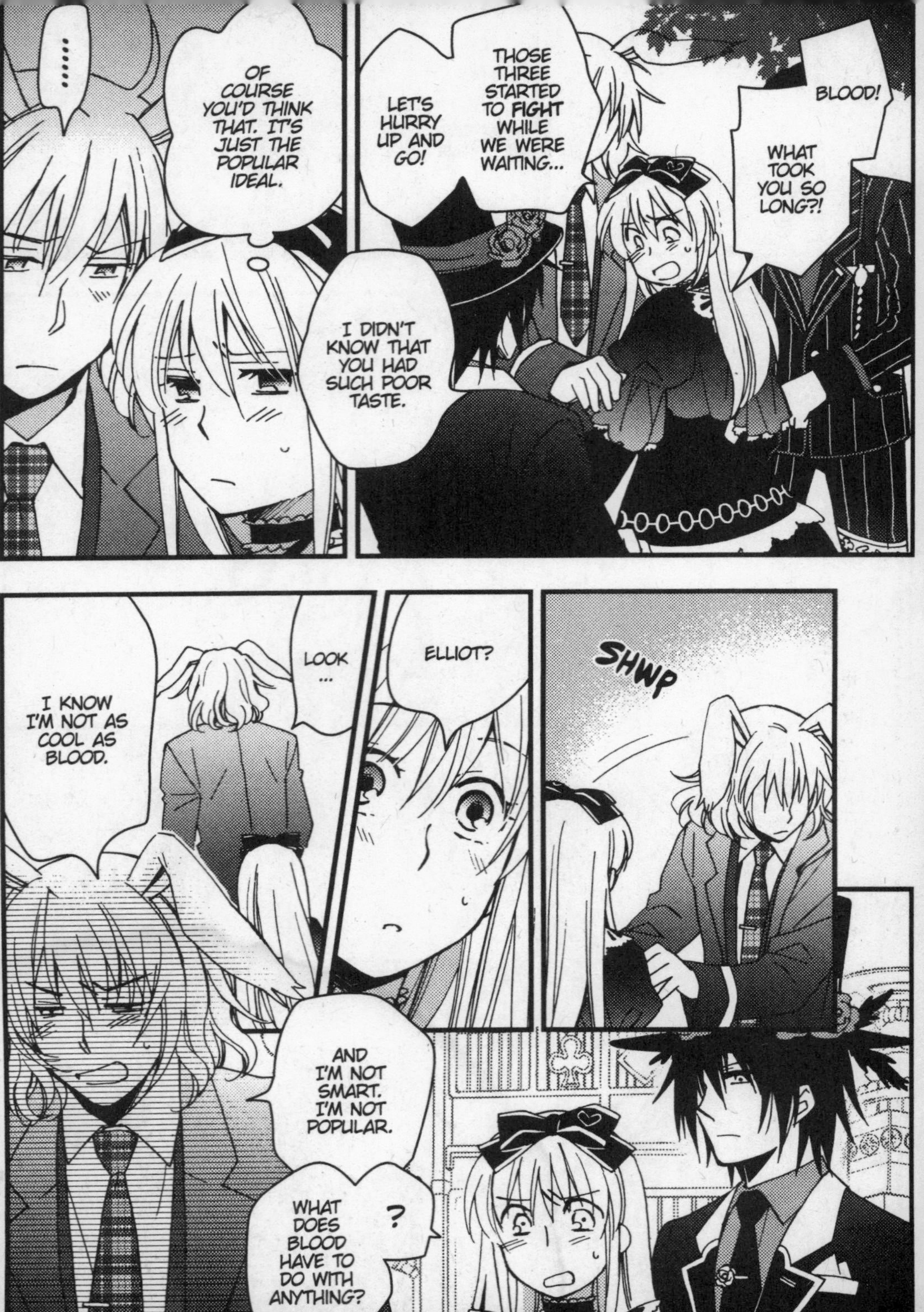
BLOOD!
WHAT TOOK YOU SO LONG?!
THOSE THREE STARTED TO FIGHT WHILE WE WERE WAITING...
LET'S HURRY UP AND GO!
I DIDN'T KNOW THAT YOU HAD SUCH POOR TASTE.
OF COURSE YOU'D THINK THAT. IT'S JUST THE POPULAR IDEAL.
......
SHWP
ELLIOT?
LOOK ...
I KNOW I'M NOT AS COOL AS BLOOD.
AND I'M NOT SMART. I'M NOT POPULAR.
?
WHAT DOES BLOOD HAVE TO DO WITH ANYTHING?

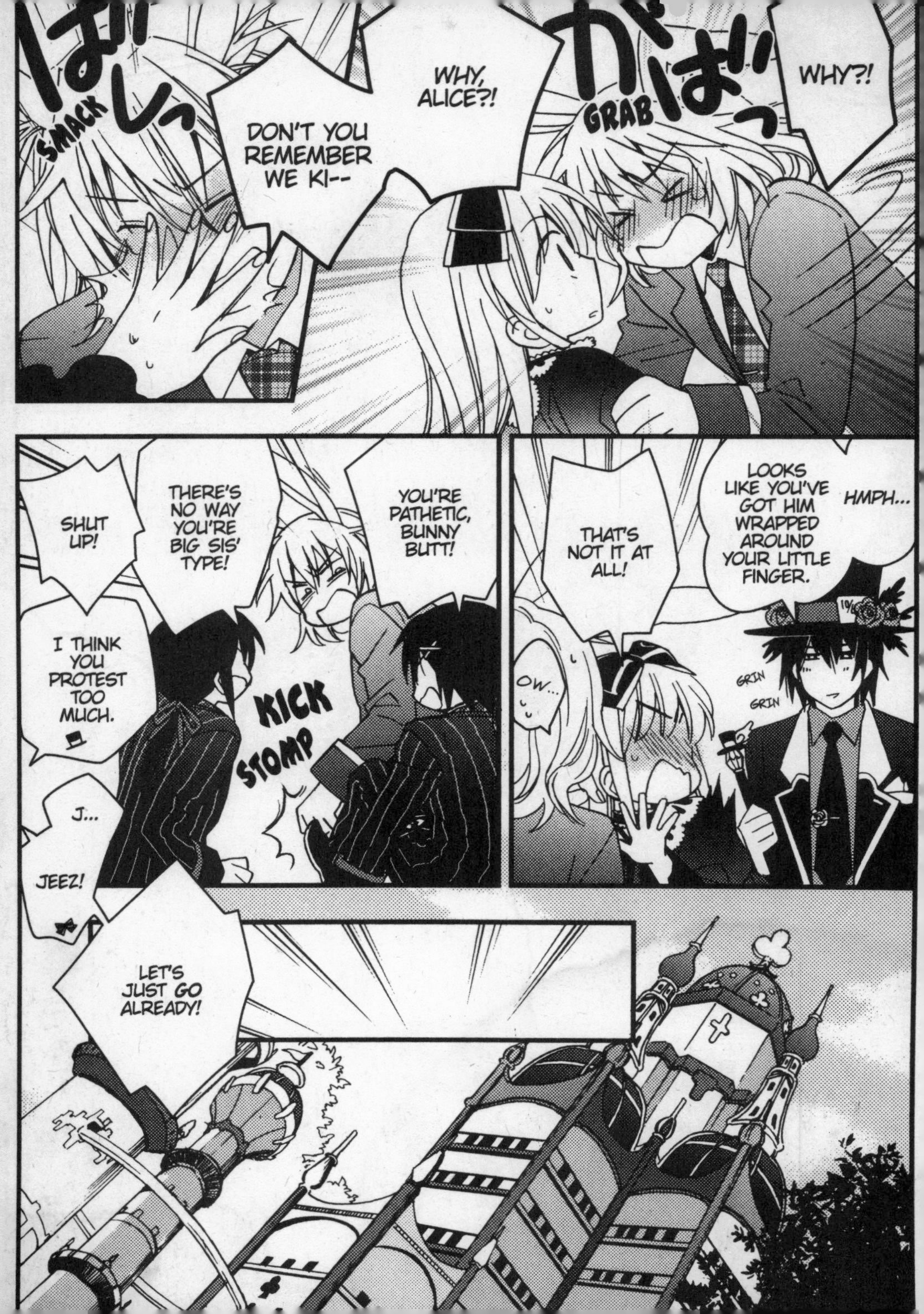

がばっ
GRAB
WHY?!
WHY, ALICE?!
DON'T YOU REMEMBER WE KI--
ばしっ
SMACK
HMPH...
LOOKS LIKE YOU'VE GOT HIM WRAPPED AROUND YOUR LITTLE FINGER.
THAT'S NOT IT AT ALL!
GRIN
GRIN
OW...
YOU'RE PATHETIC, BUNNY BUTT!
THERE'S NO WAY YOU'RE BIG SIS' TYPE!
SHUT UP!
KICK
STOMP
I THINK YOU PROTEST TOO MUCH.
J...
JEEZ!
LET'S JUST GO ALREADY!

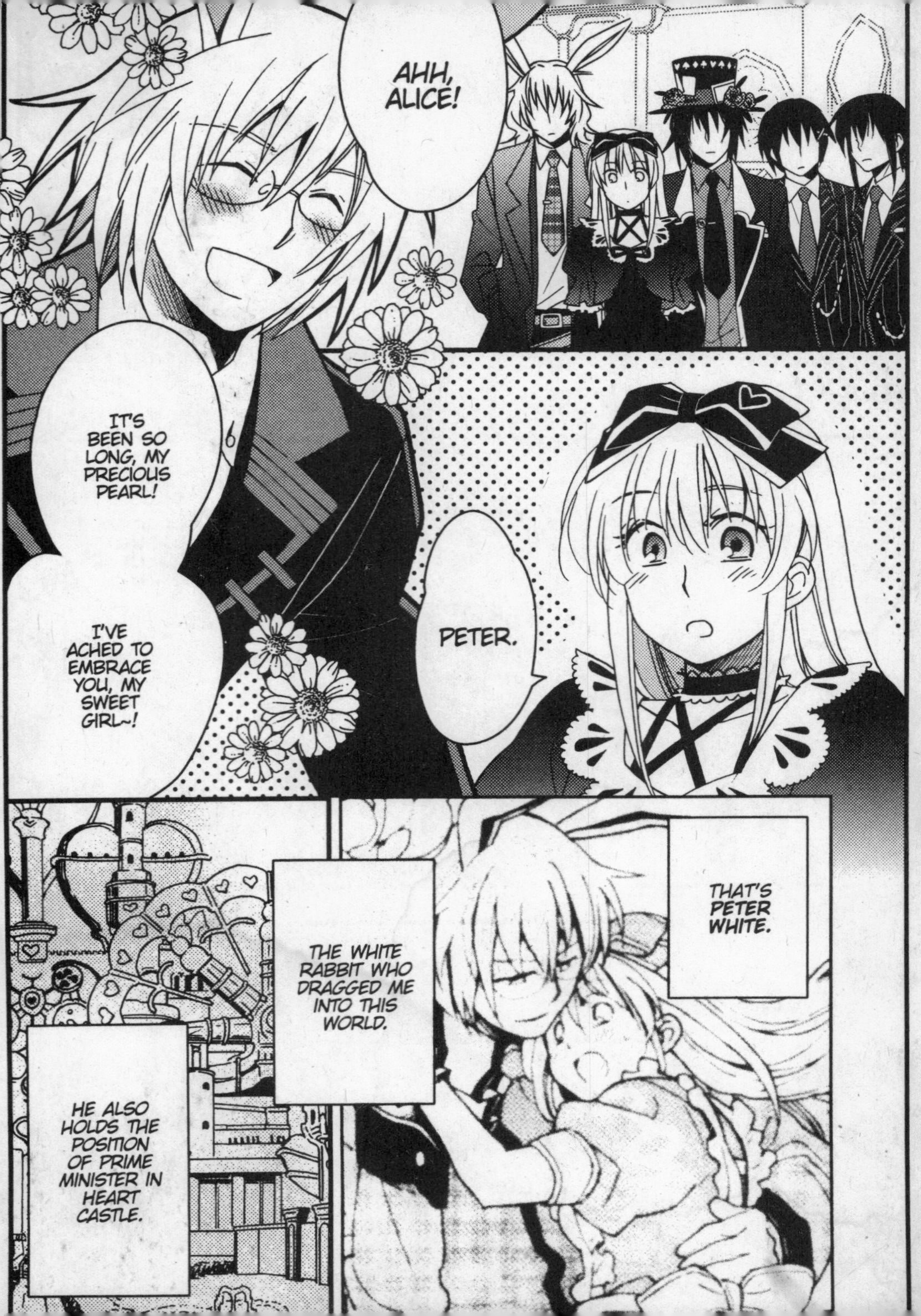
AHH, ALICE!
IT'S BEEN SO LONG, MY PRECIOUS PEARL!
I'VE ACHED TO EMBRACE YOU, MY SWEET GIRL~!
PETER.
THAT'S PETER WHITE.
THE WHITE RABBIT WHO DRAGGED ME INTO THIS WORLD.
HE ALSO HOLDS THE POSITION OF PRIME MINISTER IN HEART CASTLE.

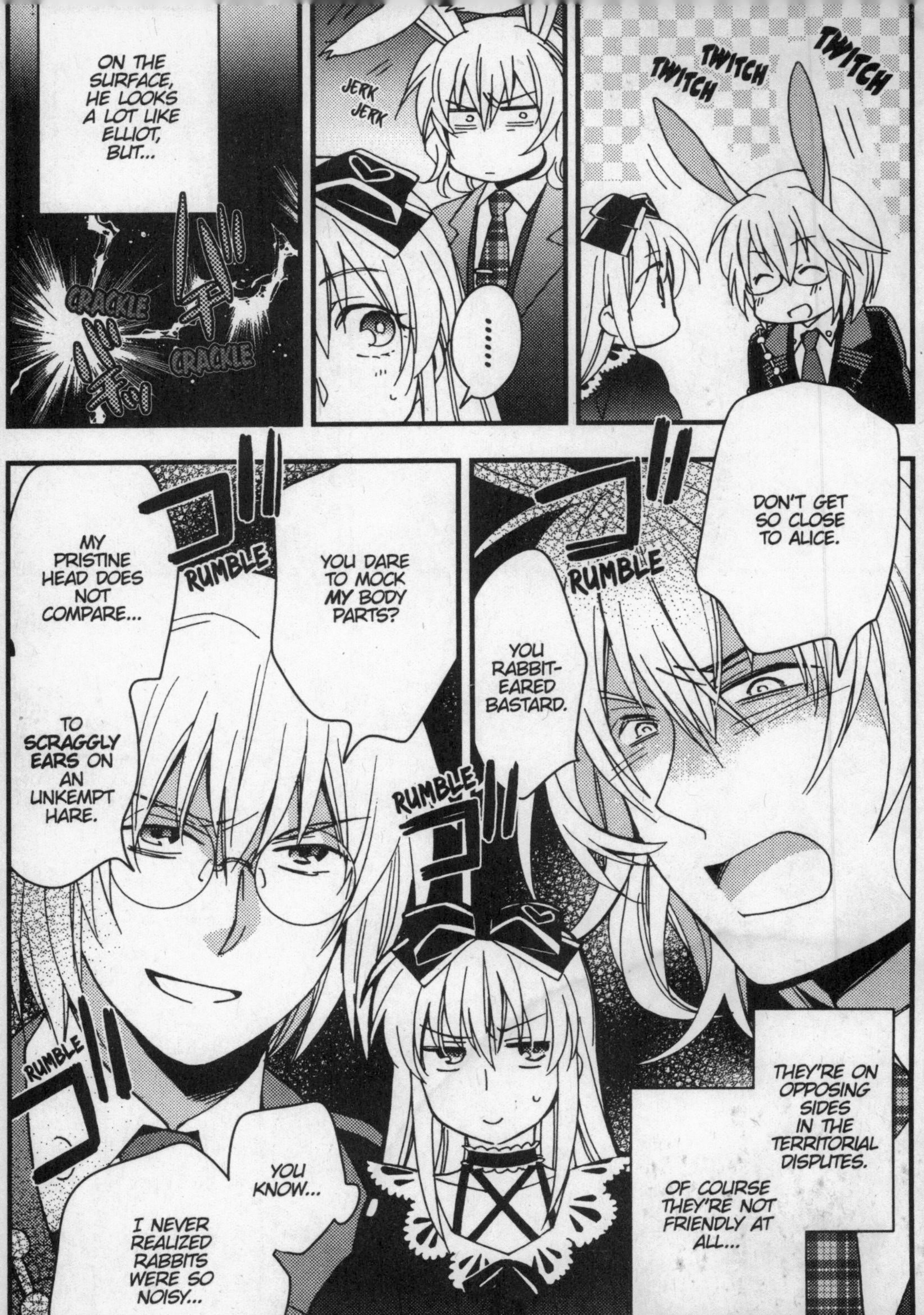
TWITCH
TWITCH
TWITCH
JERK JERK
......
ON THE SURFACE, HE LOOKS A LOT LIKE ELLIOT, BUT...
CRACKLE
CRACKLE
DON'T GET SO CLOSE TO ALICE.
RUMBLE
YOU RABBIT-EARED BASTARD.
YOU DARE TO MOCK MY BODY PARTS?
RUMBLE
MY PRISTINE HEAD DOES NOT COMPARE...
TO SCRAGGLY EARS ON AN UNKEMPT HARE.
RUMBLE
THEY'RE ON OPPOSING SIDES IN THE TERRITORIAL DISPUTES.
OF COURSE THEY'RE NOT FRIENDLY AT ALL...
YOU KNOW...
I NEVER REALIZED RABBITS WERE SO NOISY...
RUMBLE

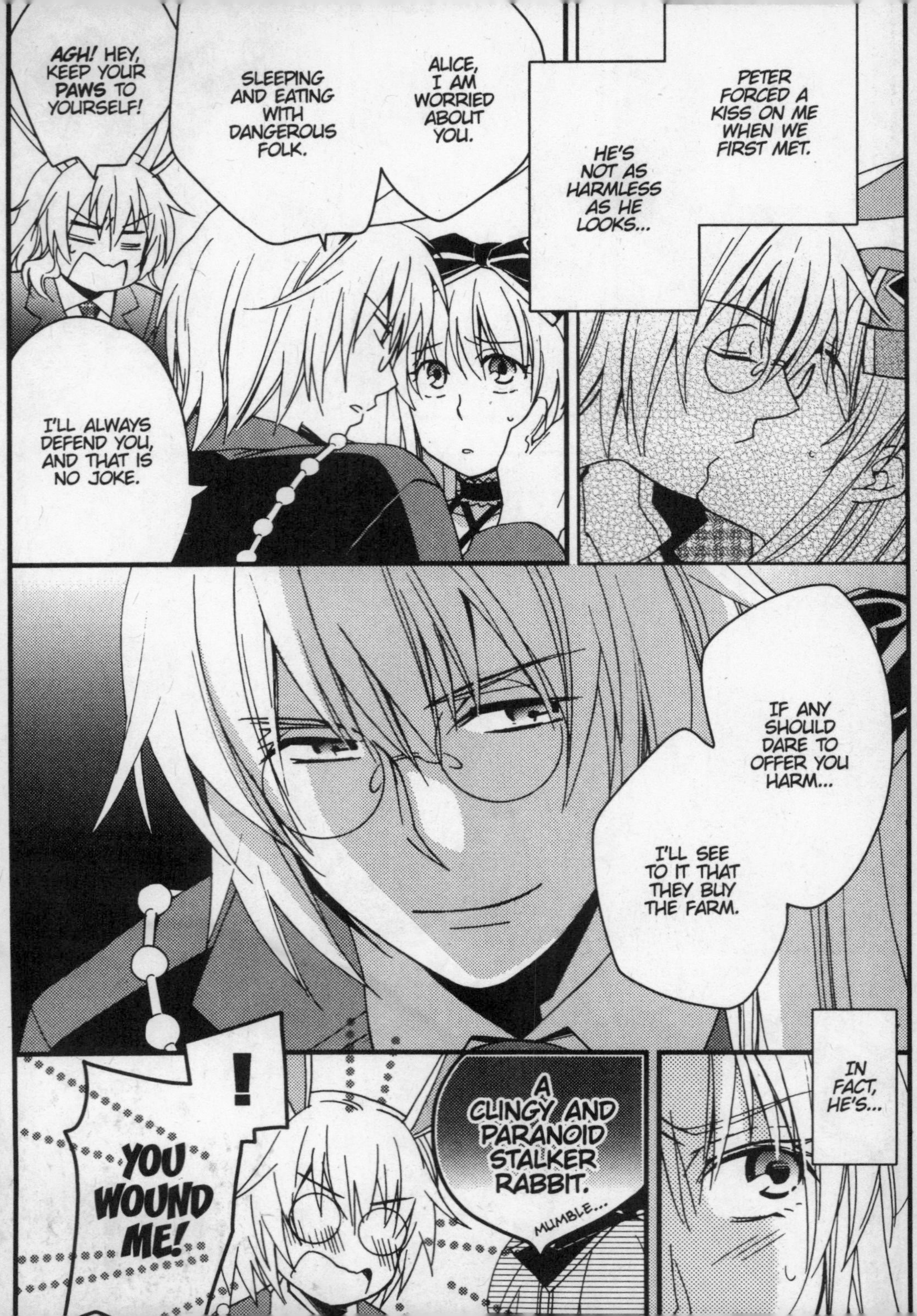
PETER FORCED A KISS ON ME WHEN WE FIRST MET.
HE'S NOT AS HARMLESS AS HE LOOKS...
ALICE, I AM WORRIED ABOUT YOU.
SLEEPING AND EATING WITH DANGEROUS FOLK.
AGH! HEY, KEEP YOUR PAWS TO YOURSELF!
I'LL ALWAYS DEFEND YOU, AND THAT IS NO JOKE.
IF ANY SHOULD DARE TO OFFER YOU HARM...
I'LL SEE TO IT THAT THEY BUY THE FARM.
IN FACT, HE'S...
A CLINGY AND PARANOID STALKER RABBIT.
MUMBLE...
!
YOU WOUND ME!

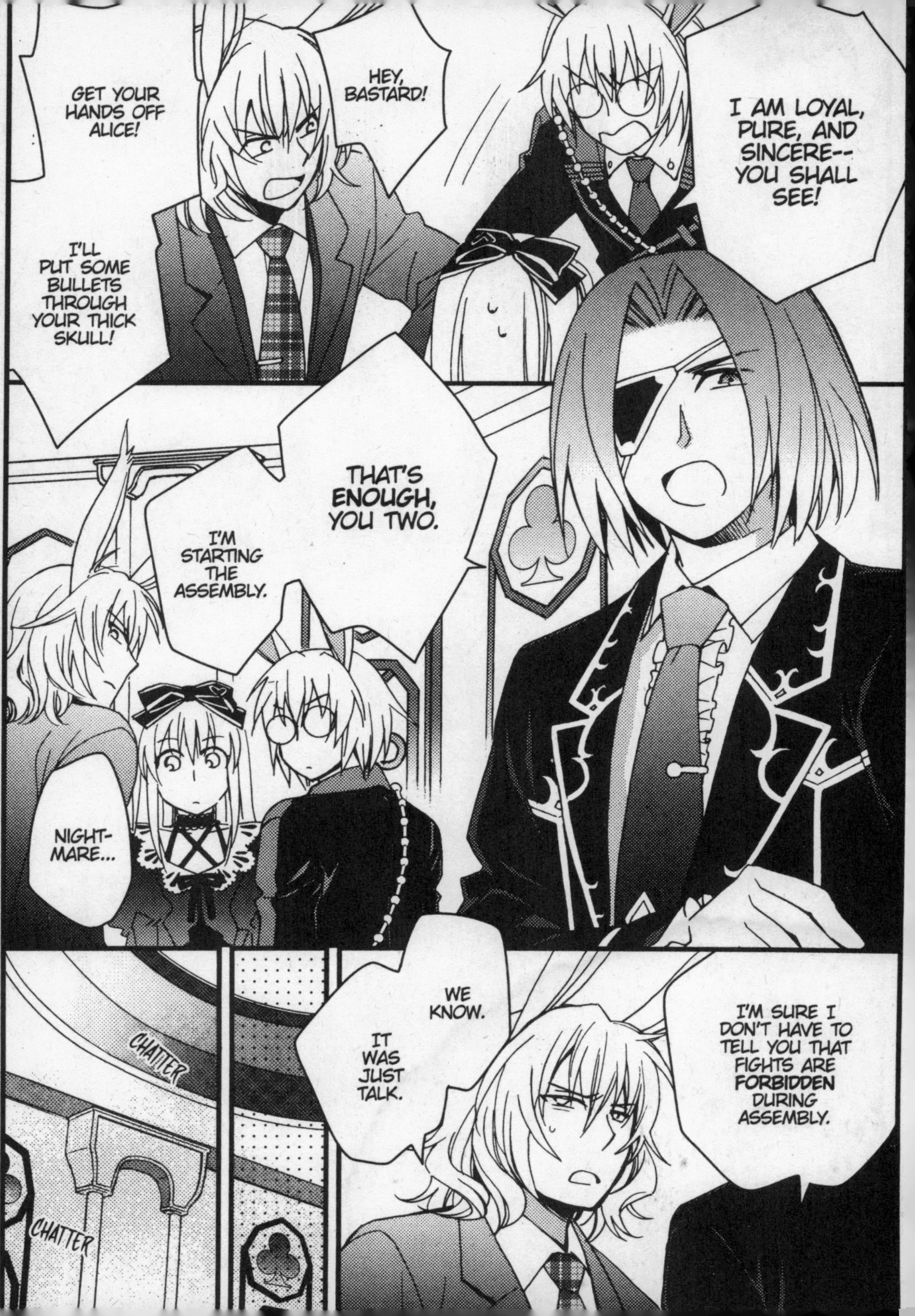
I AM LOYAL, PURE, AND SINCERE-- YOU SHALL SEE!
HEY, BASTARD!
GET YOUR HANDS OFF ALICE!
I'LL PUT SOME BULLETS THROUGH YOUR THICK SKULL!
THAT'S ENOUGH, YOU TWO.
I'M STARTING THE ASSEMBLY.
NIGHT-MARE...
I'M SURE I DON'T HAVE TO TELL YOU THAT FIGHTS ARE FORBIDDEN DURING ASSEMBLY.
WE KNOW.
IT WAS JUST TALK.
CHATTER
CHATTER

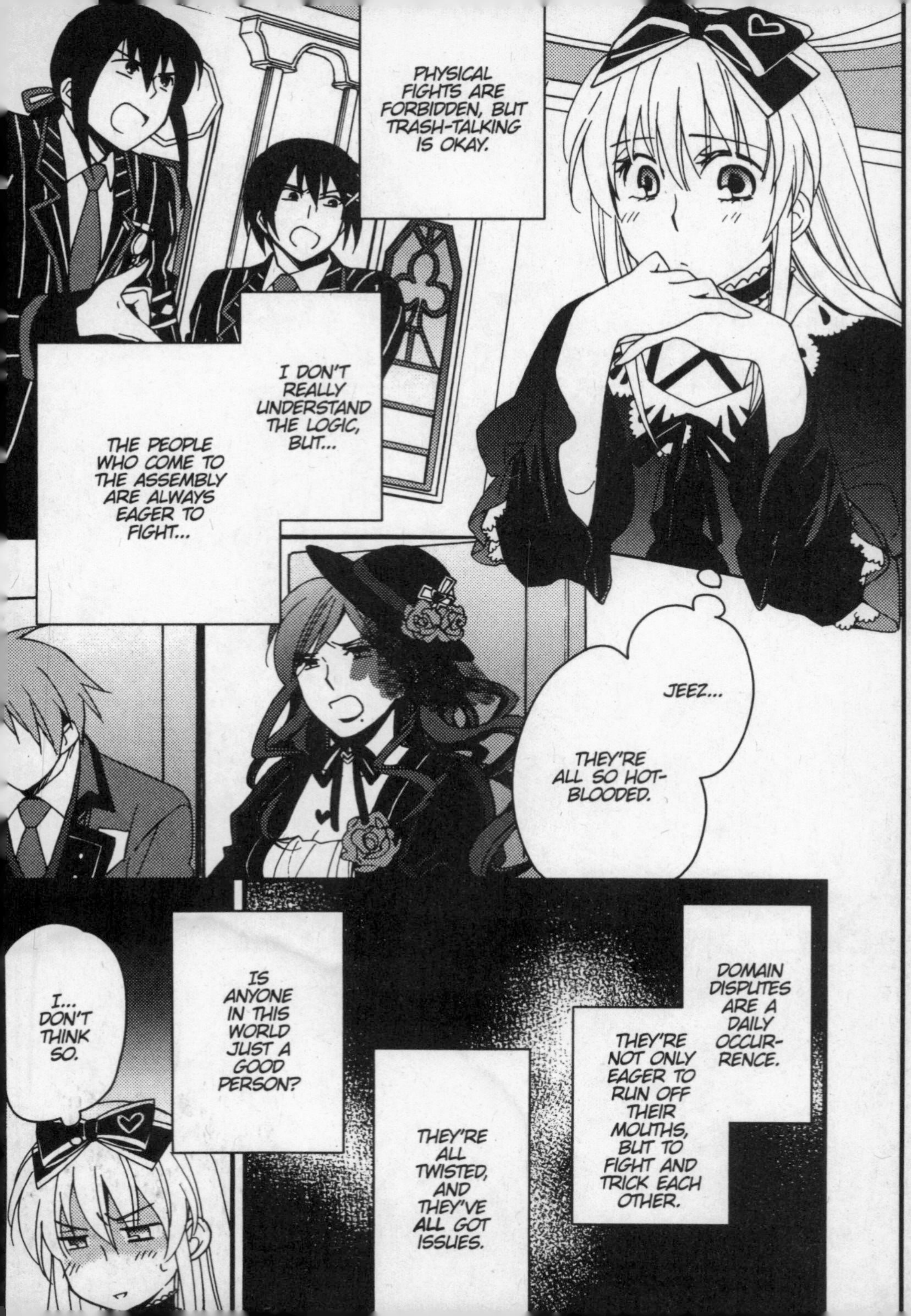
PHYSICAL FIGHTS ARE FORBIDDEN, BUT TRASH-TALKING IS OKAY.
I DON'T REALLY UNDERSTAND THE LOGIC, BUT...
THE PEOPLE WHO COME TO THE ASSEMBLY ARE ALWAYS EAGER TO FIGHT...
JEEZ...
THEY'RE ALL SO HOT-BLOODED.
DOMAIN DISPUTES ARE A DAILY OCCURRENCE.
THEY'RE NOT ONLY EAGER TO RUN OFF THEIR MOUTHS, BUT TO FIGHT AND TRICK EACH OTHER.
THEY'RE ALL TWISTED, AND THEY'VE ALL GOT ISSUES.
IS ANYONE IN THIS WORLD JUST A GOOD PERSON?
I... DON'T THINK SO.

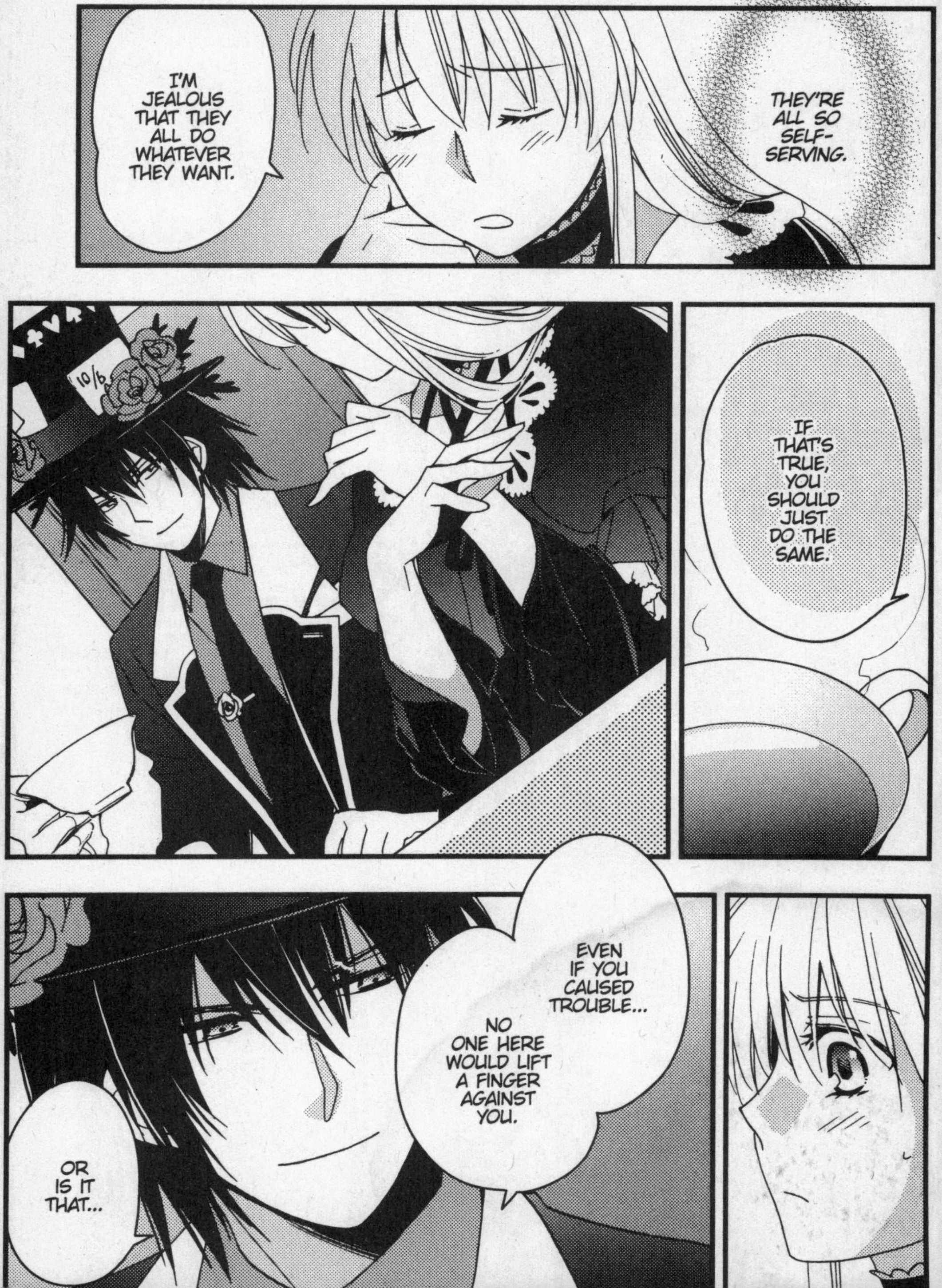
THEY'RE ALL SO SELF-SERVING.
I'M JEALOUS THAT THEY ALL DO WHATEVER THEY WANT.
IF THAT'S TRUE, YOU SHOULD JUST DO THE SAME.
EVEN IF YOU CAUSED TROUBLE...
NO ONE HERE WOULD LIFT A FINGER AGAINST YOU.
OR IS IT THAT...

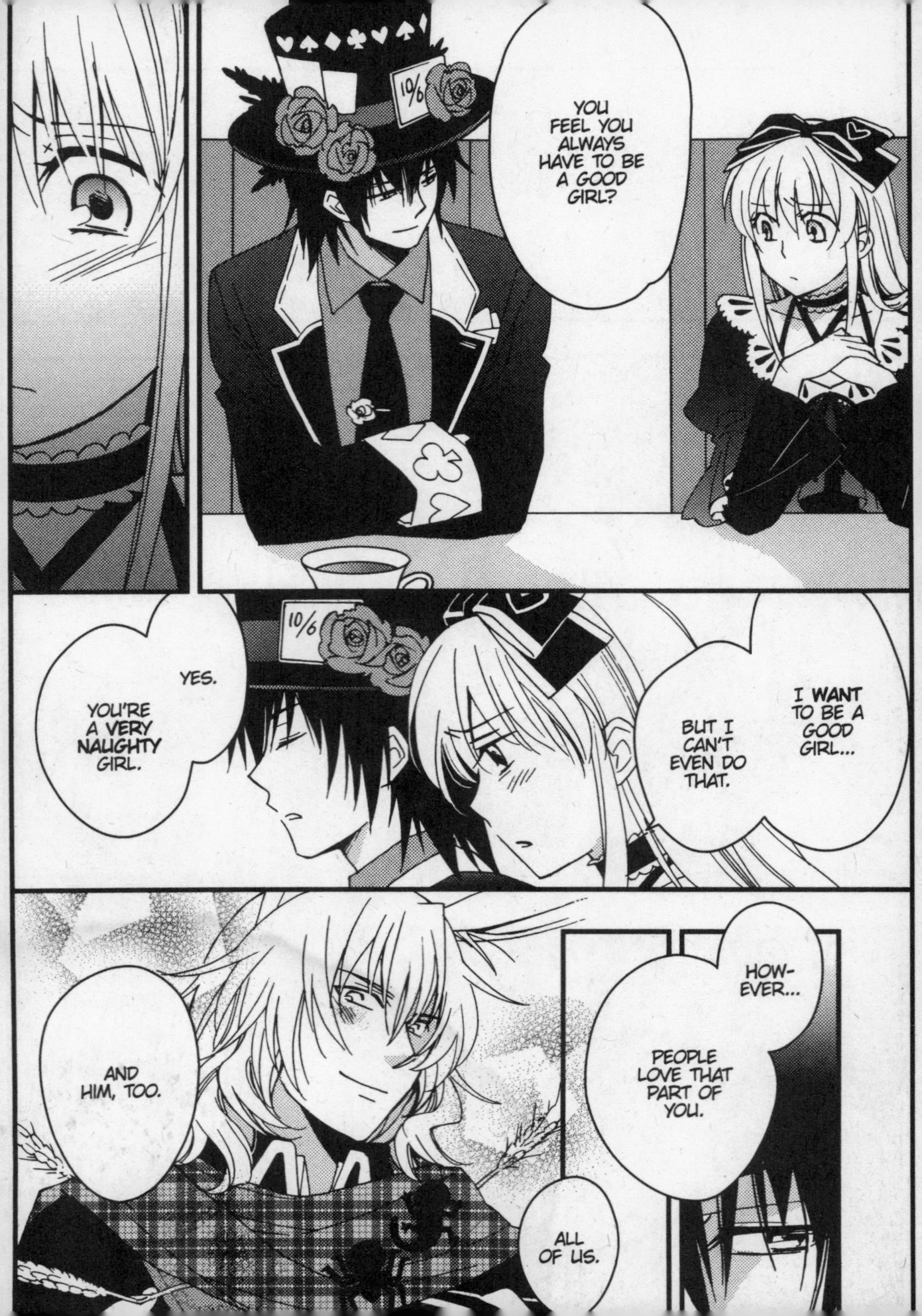
YOU FEEL YOU ALWAYS HAVE TO BE A GOOD GIRL?
I WANT TO BE A GOOD GIRL... BUT I CAN'T EVEN DO THAT.
YES. YOU'RE A VERY NAUGHTY GIRL.
HOW-EVER... PEOPLE LOVE THAT PART OF YOU.
AND HIM, TOO.
ALL OF US.

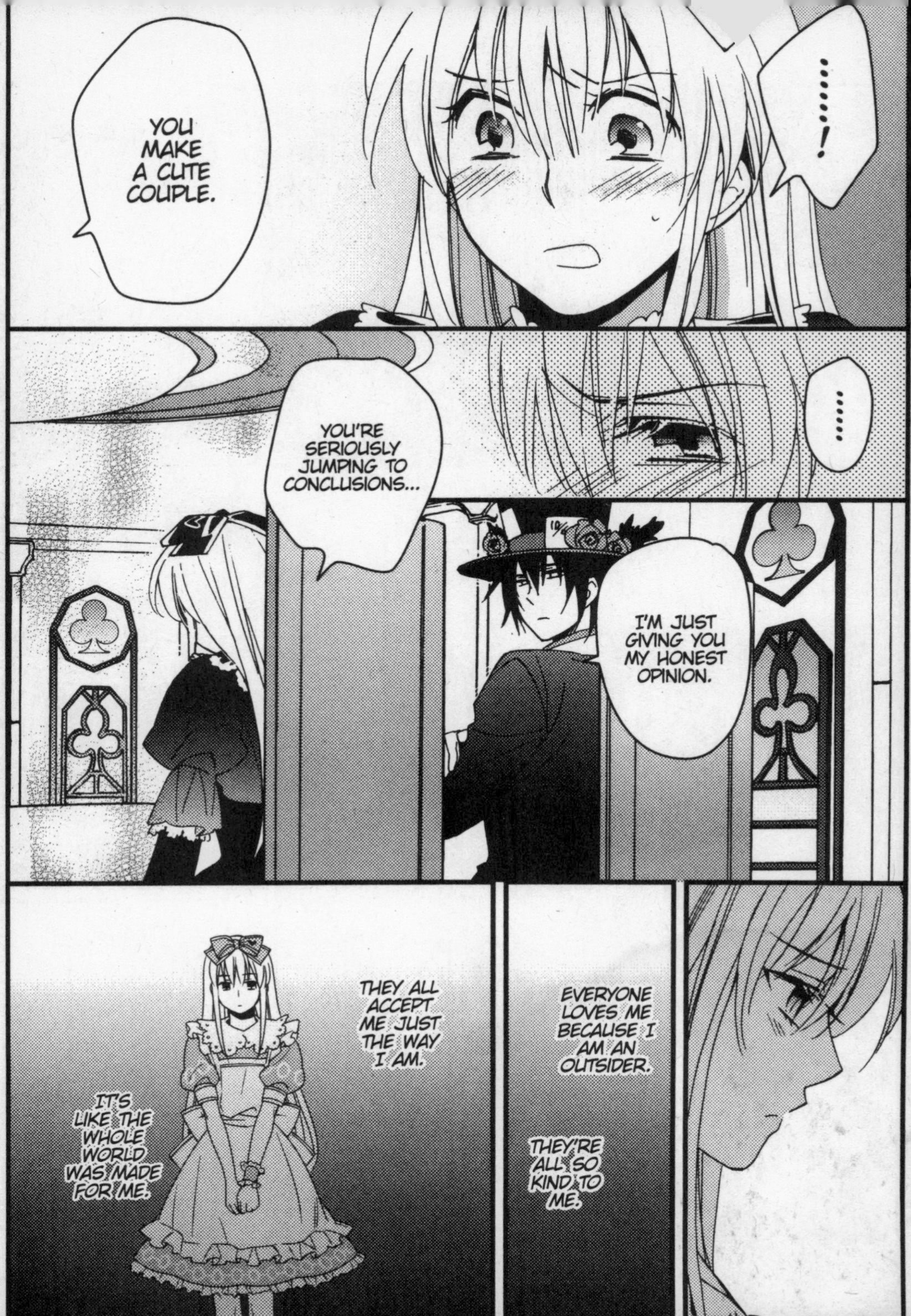
......!
YOU MAKE A CUTE COUPLE.
......
YOU'RE SERIOUSLY JUMPING TO CONCLUSIONS...
I'M JUST GIVING YOU MY HONEST OPINION.
EVERYONE LOVES ME BECAUSE I AM AN OUTSIDER.
THEY'RE ALL SO KIND TO ME.
THEY ALL ACCEPT ME JUST THE WAY I AM.
IT'S LIKE THE WHOLE WORLD WAS MADE FOR ME.

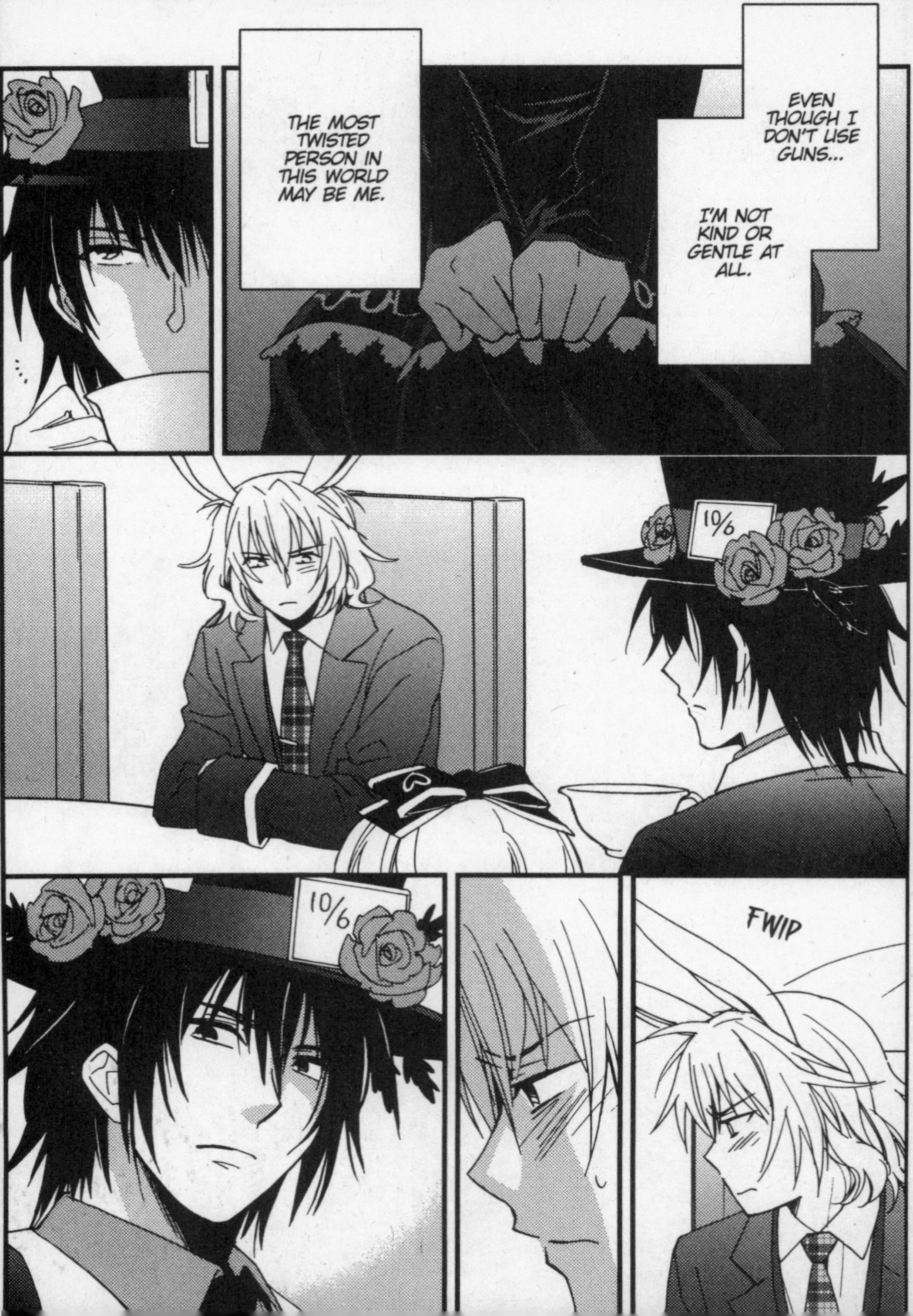
EVEN THOUGH I DON'T USE GUNS...
I'M NOT KIND OR GENTLE AT ALL.
THE MOST TWISTED PERSON IN THIS WORLD MAY BE ME.
10/6
10/6
FWIP

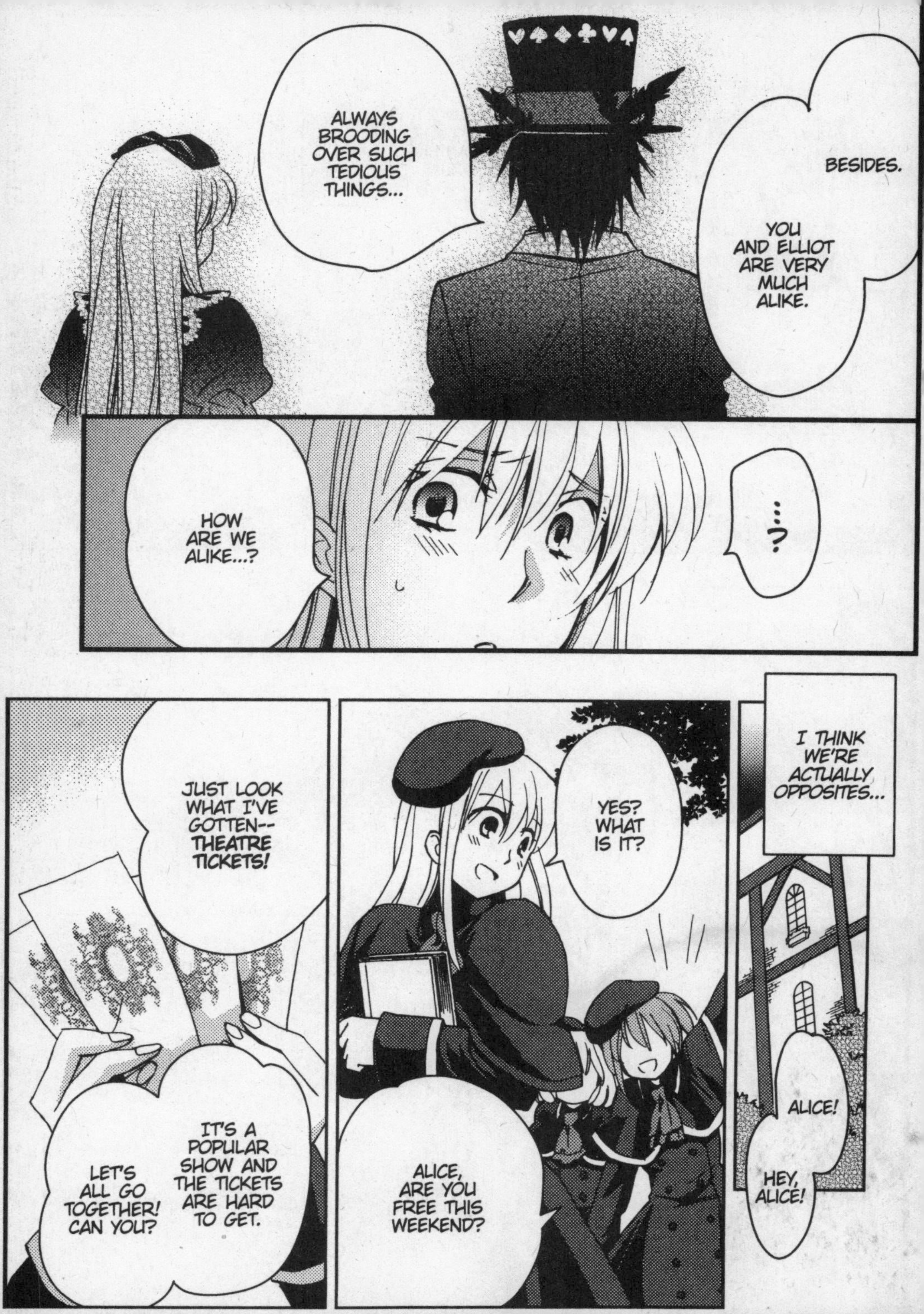
BESIDES.
YOU AND ELLIOT ARE VERY MUCH ALIKE.
ALWAYS BROODING OVER SUCH TEDIOUS THINGS...
...?
HOW ARE WE ALIKE...?
I THINK WE'RE ACTUALLY OPPOSITES...
ALICE!
HEY, ALICE!
YES? WHAT IS IT?
ALICE, ARE YOU FREE THIS WEEKEND?
JUST LOOK WHAT I'VE GOTTEN--THEATRE TICKETS!
IT'S A POPULAR SHOW AND THE TICKETS ARE HARD TO GET.
LET'S ALL GO TOGETHER! CAN YOU?

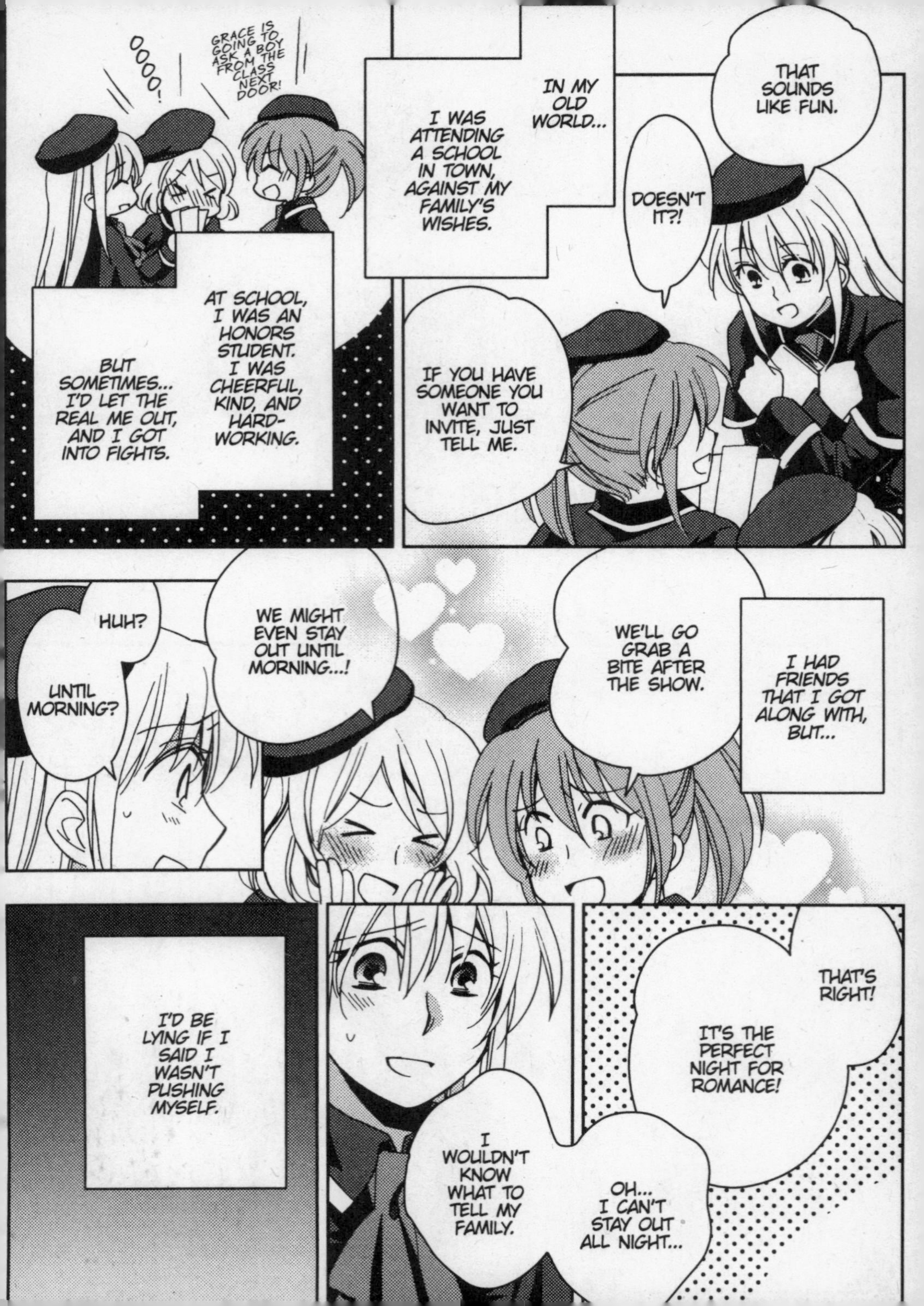
THAT SOUNDS LIKE FUN.
DOESN'T IT?!
IF YOU HAVE SOMEONE YOU WANT TO INVITE, JUST TELL ME.
IN MY OLD WORLD...
I WAS ATTENDING A SCHOOL IN TOWN, AGAINST MY FAMILY'S WISHES.
GRACE IS GOING TO ASK A BOY FROM THE CLASS NEXT DOOR!
OOOO!
AT SCHOOL, I WAS AN HONORS STUDENT. I WAS CHEERFUL, KIND, AND HARD-WORKING.
BUT SOMETIMES... I'D LET THE REAL ME OUT, AND I GOT INTO FIGHTS.
I HAD FRIENDS THAT I GOT ALONG WITH, BUT...
WE'LL GO GRAB A BITE AFTER THE SHOW.
WE MIGHT EVEN STAY OUT UNTIL MORNING...!
HUH?
UNTIL MORNING?
THAT'S RIGHT!
IT'S THE PERFECT NIGHT FOR ROMANCE!
OH... I CAN'T STAY OUT ALL NIGHT...
I WOULDN'T KNOW WHAT TO TELL MY FAMILY.
I'D BE LYING IF I SAID I WASN'T PUSHING MYSELF.

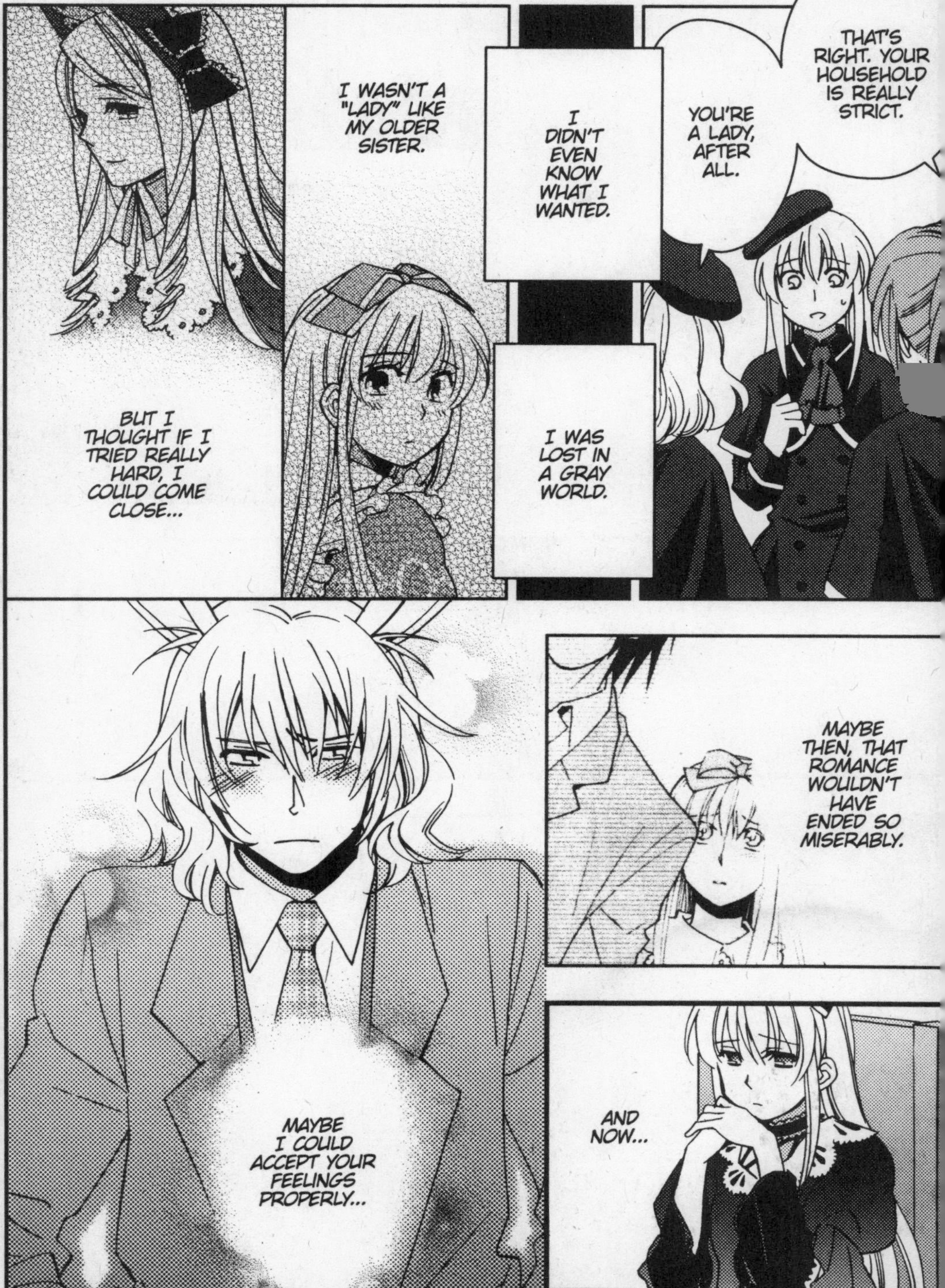
THAT'S RIGHT. YOUR HOUSEHOLD IS REALLY STRICT.
YOU'RE A LADY, AFTER ALL.
I DIDN'T EVEN KNOW WHAT I WANTED.
I WAS LOST IN A GRAY WORLD.
I WASN'T A "LADY" LIKE MY OLDER SISTER.
BUT I THOUGHT IF I TRIED REALLY HARD, I COULD COME CLOSE...
MAYBE THEN, THAT ROMANCE WOULDN'T HAVE ENDED SO MISERABLY.
AND NOW...
MAYBE I COULD ACCEPT YOUR FEELINGS PROPERLY...

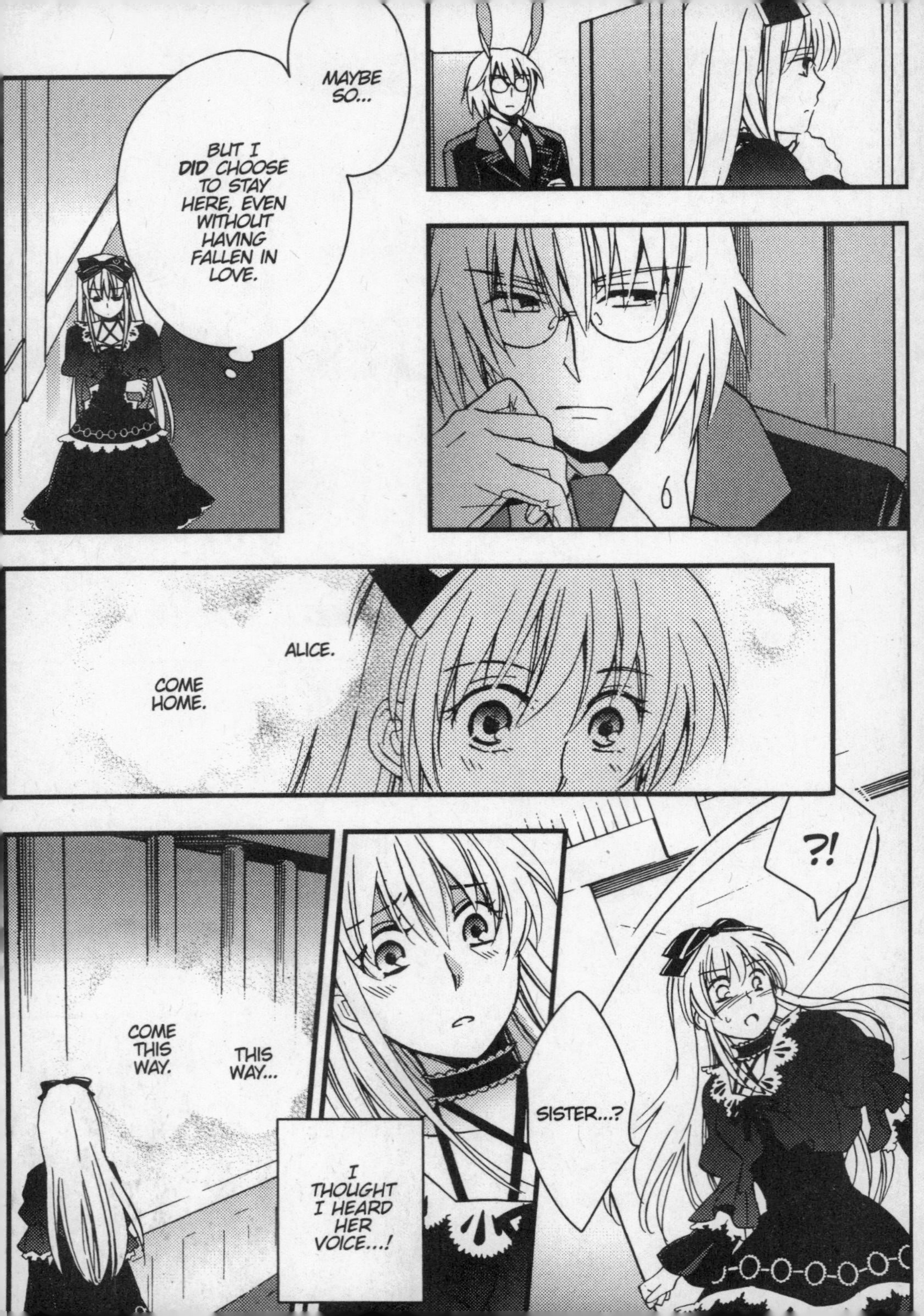
MAYBE SO...
BUT I DID CHOOSE TO STAY HERE, EVEN WITHOUT HAVING FALLEN IN LOVE.
ALICE.
COME HOME.
?!
SISTER...?
I THOUGHT I HEARD HER VOICE...!
COME THIS WAY.
THIS WAY...

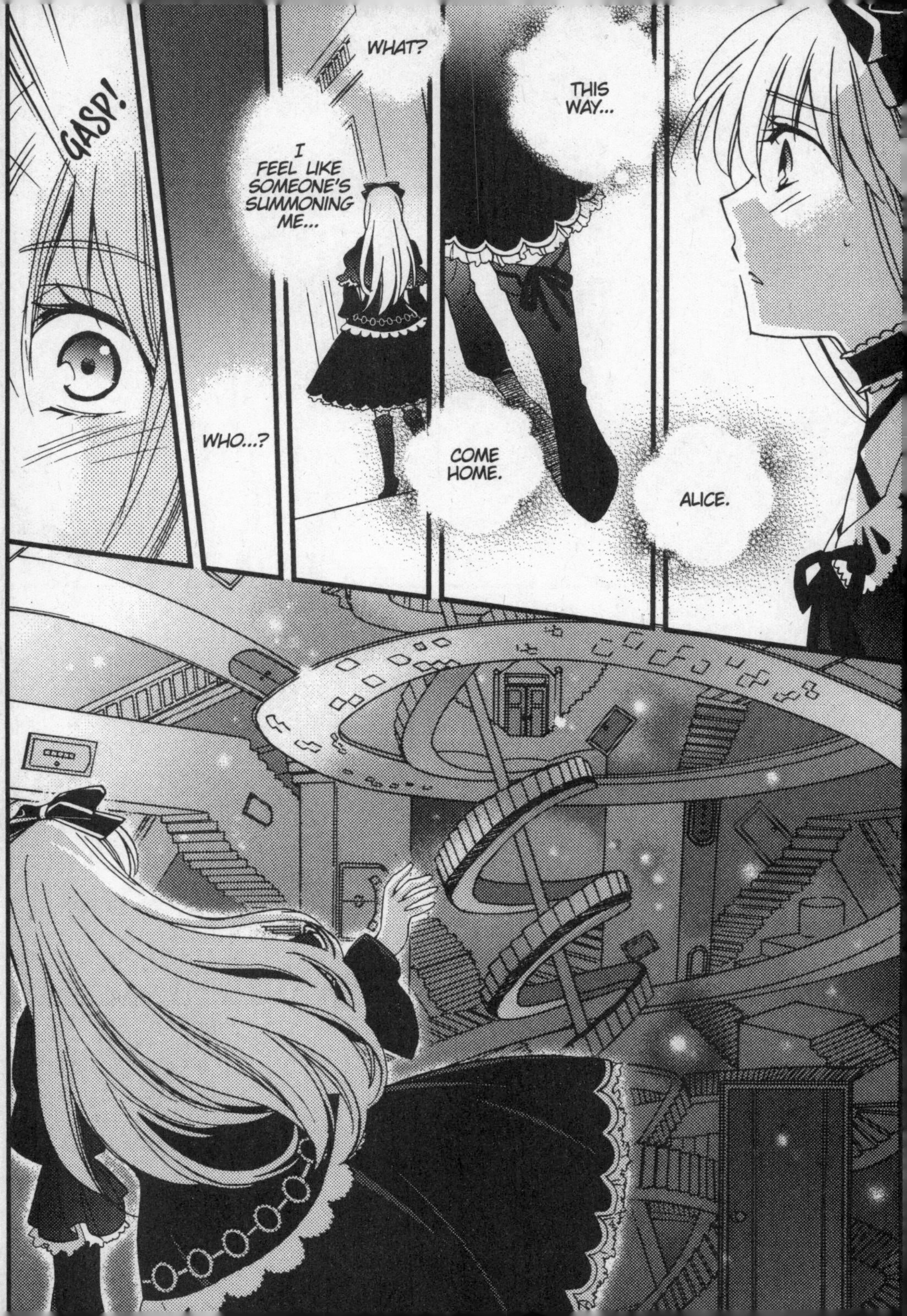
ALICE.
THIS WAY...
COME HOME.
WHAT?
I FEEL LIKE SOMEONE'S SUMMONING ME...
WHO...?
GASP!

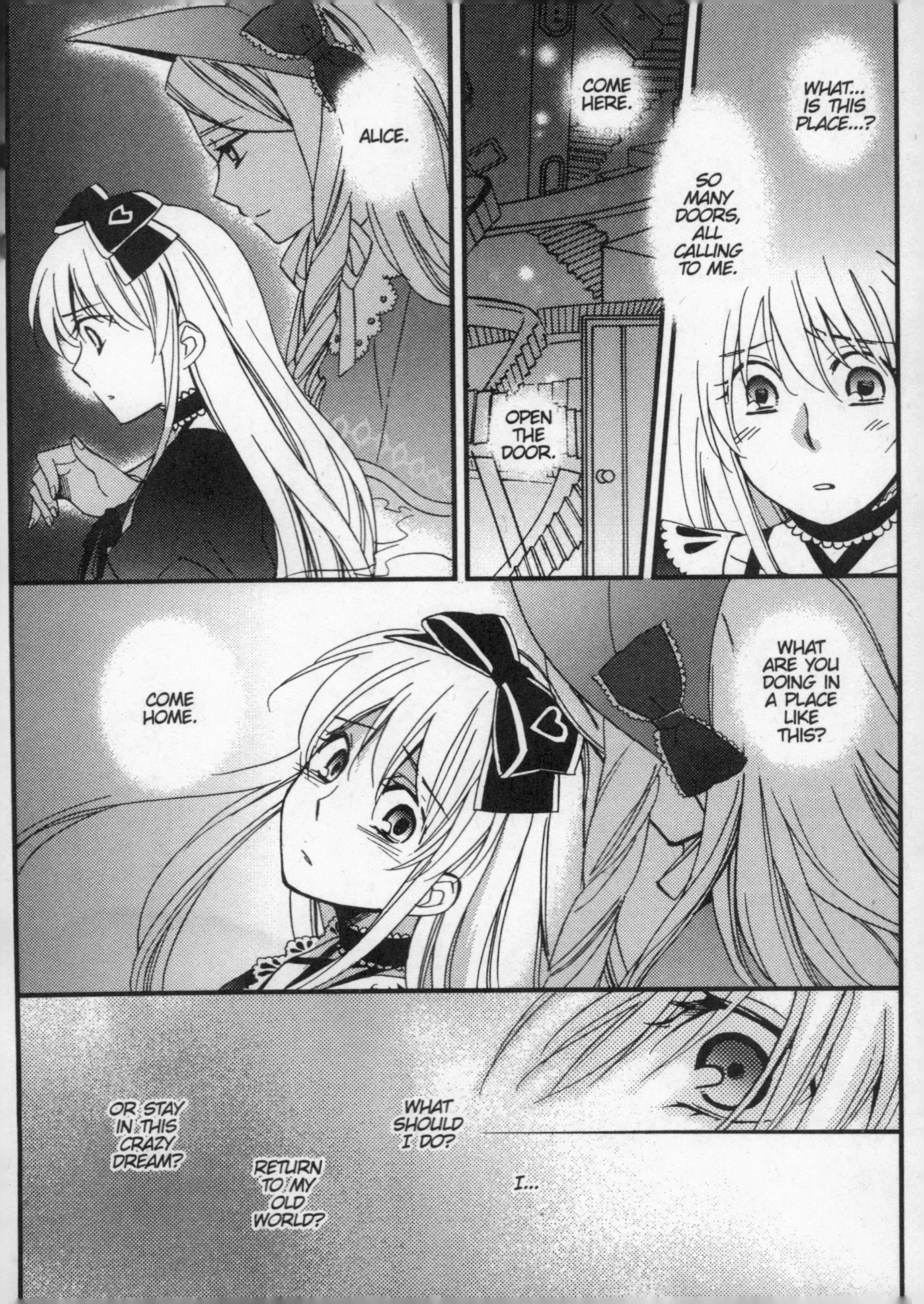

WHAT... IS THIS PLACE...?
SO MANY DOORS, ALL CALLING TO ME.
COME HERE.
OPEN THE DOOR.
ALICE.
WHAT ARE YOU DOING IN A PLACE LIKE THIS?
COME HOME.
WHAT SHOULD I DO?
RETURN TO MY OLD WORLD?
OR STAY IN THIS CRAZY DREAM?
I...

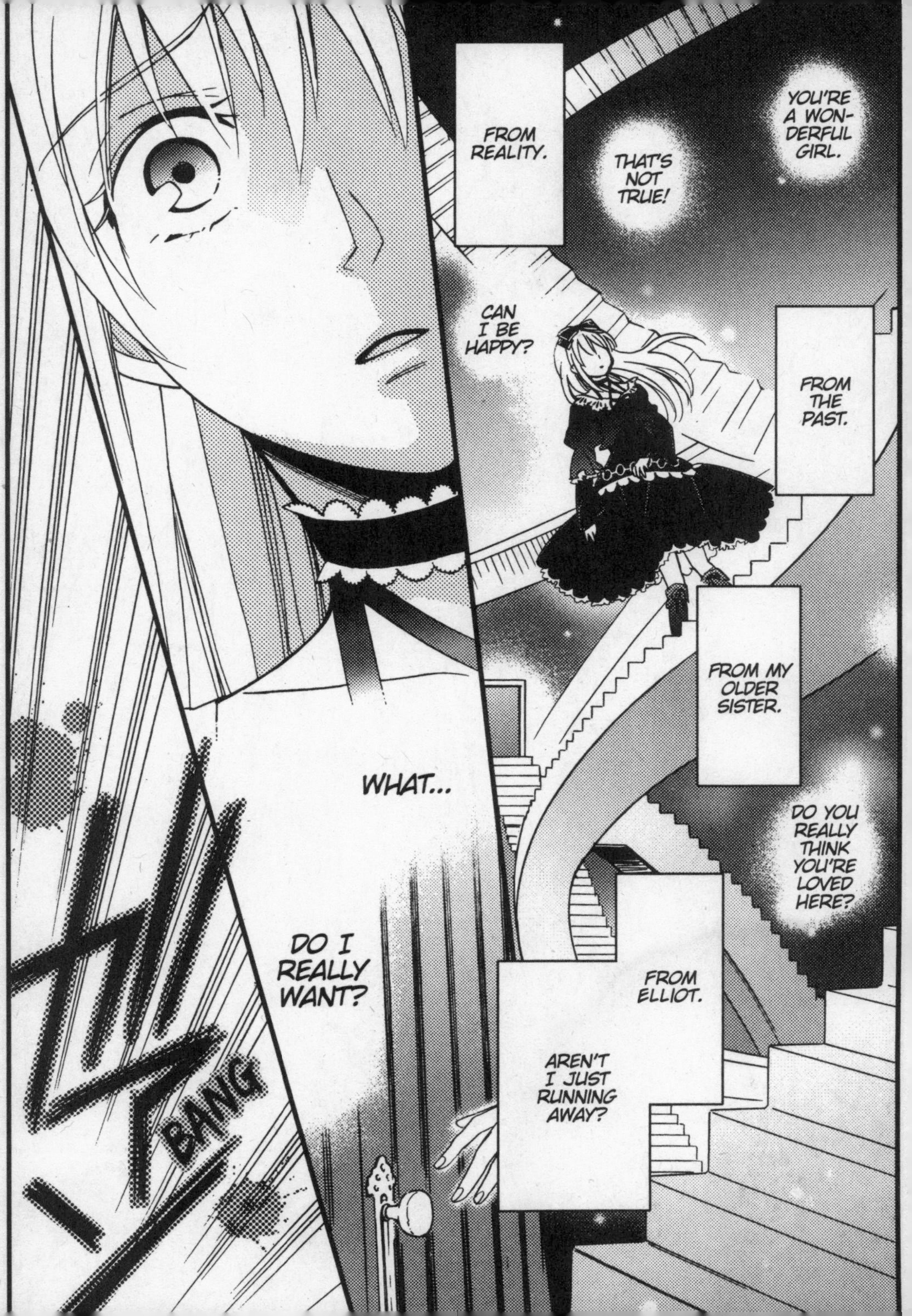
YOU'RE A WON-DERFUL GIRL.
THAT'S NOT TRUE!
FROM REALITY.
CAN I BE HAPPY?
FROM THE PAST.
FROM MY OLDER SISTER.
DO YOU REALLY THINK YOU'RE LOVED HERE?
FROM ELLIOT.
AREN'T I JUST RUNNING AWAY?
WHAT...
DO I REALLY WANT?
BANG

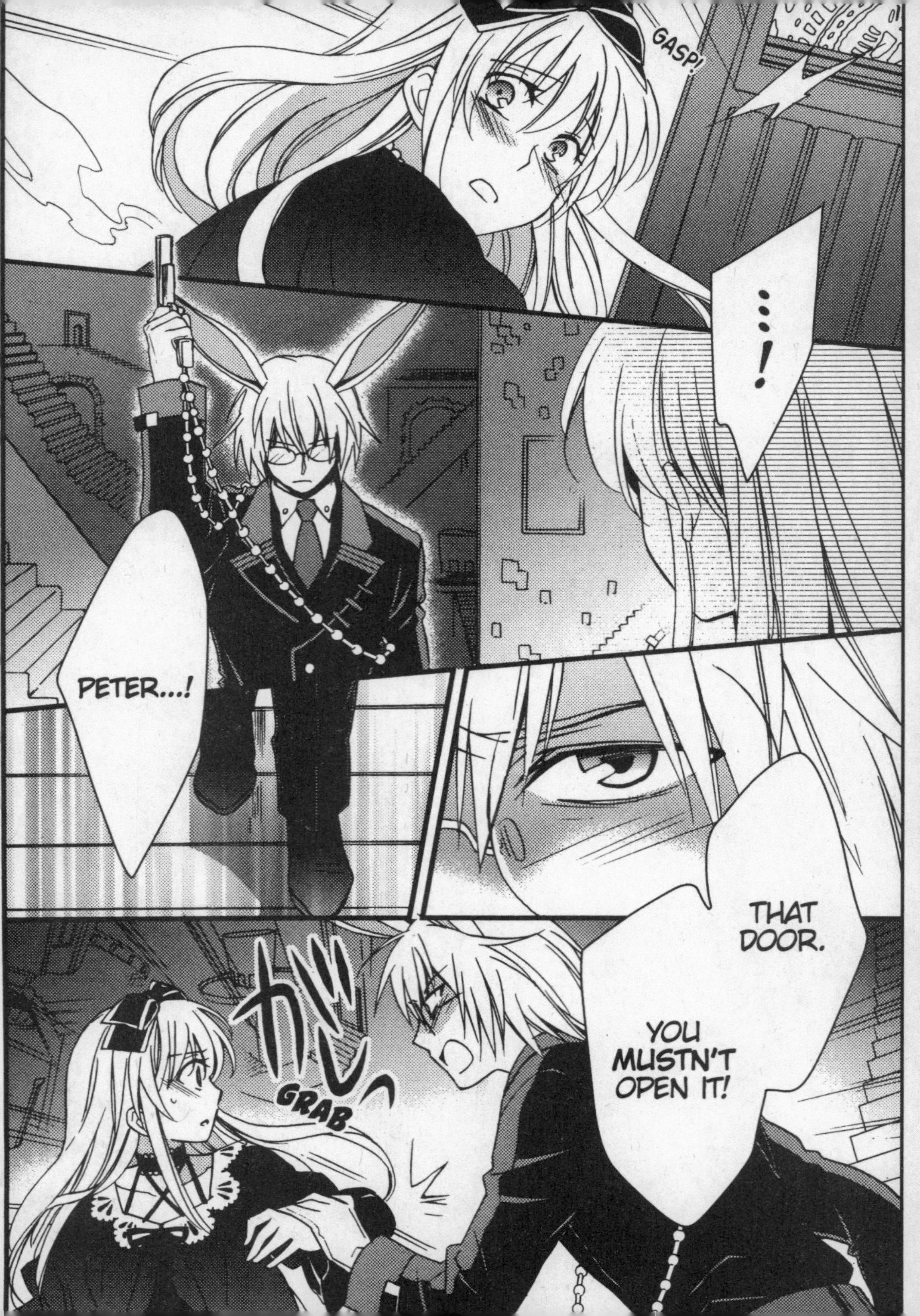
GASP!
...!
PETER...!
THAT DOOR.
YOU MUSTN'T OPEN IT!
GRAB

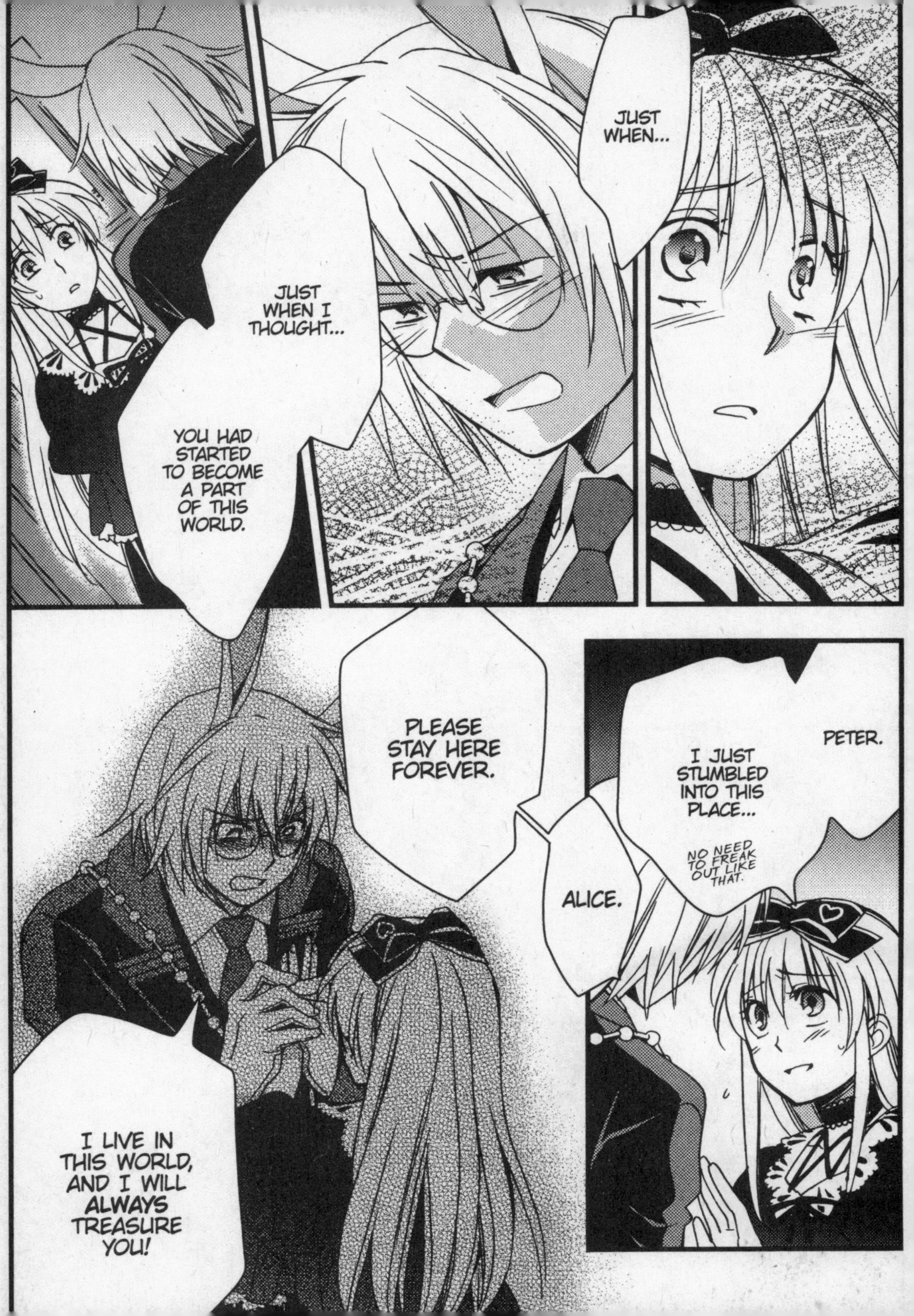
JUST WHEN...
JUST WHEN I THOUGHT...
YOU HAD STARTED TO BECOME A PART OF THIS WORLD.
PETER.
I JUST STUMBLED INTO THIS PLACE...
NO NEED TO FREAK OUT LIKE THAT.
ALICE.
PLEASE STAY HERE FOREVER.
I LIVE IN THIS WORLD, AND I WILL **ALWAYS** TREASURE YOU!

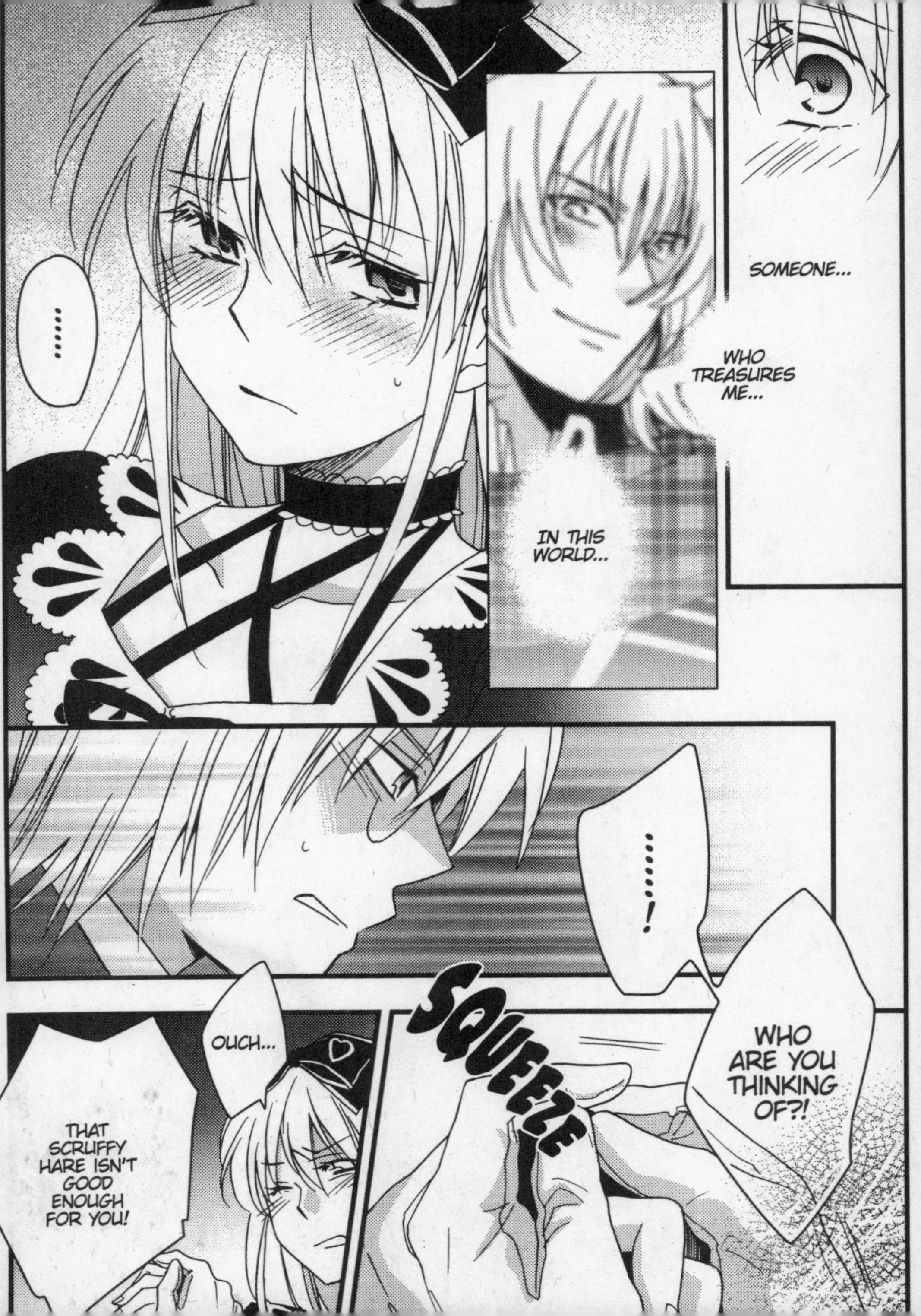
SOMEONE...
WHO TREASURES ME...
IN THIS WORLD...
......
......!
WHO ARE YOU THINKING OF?!
SQUEEZE
OUCH...
THAT SCRUFFY HARE ISN'T GOOD ENOUGH FOR YOU!

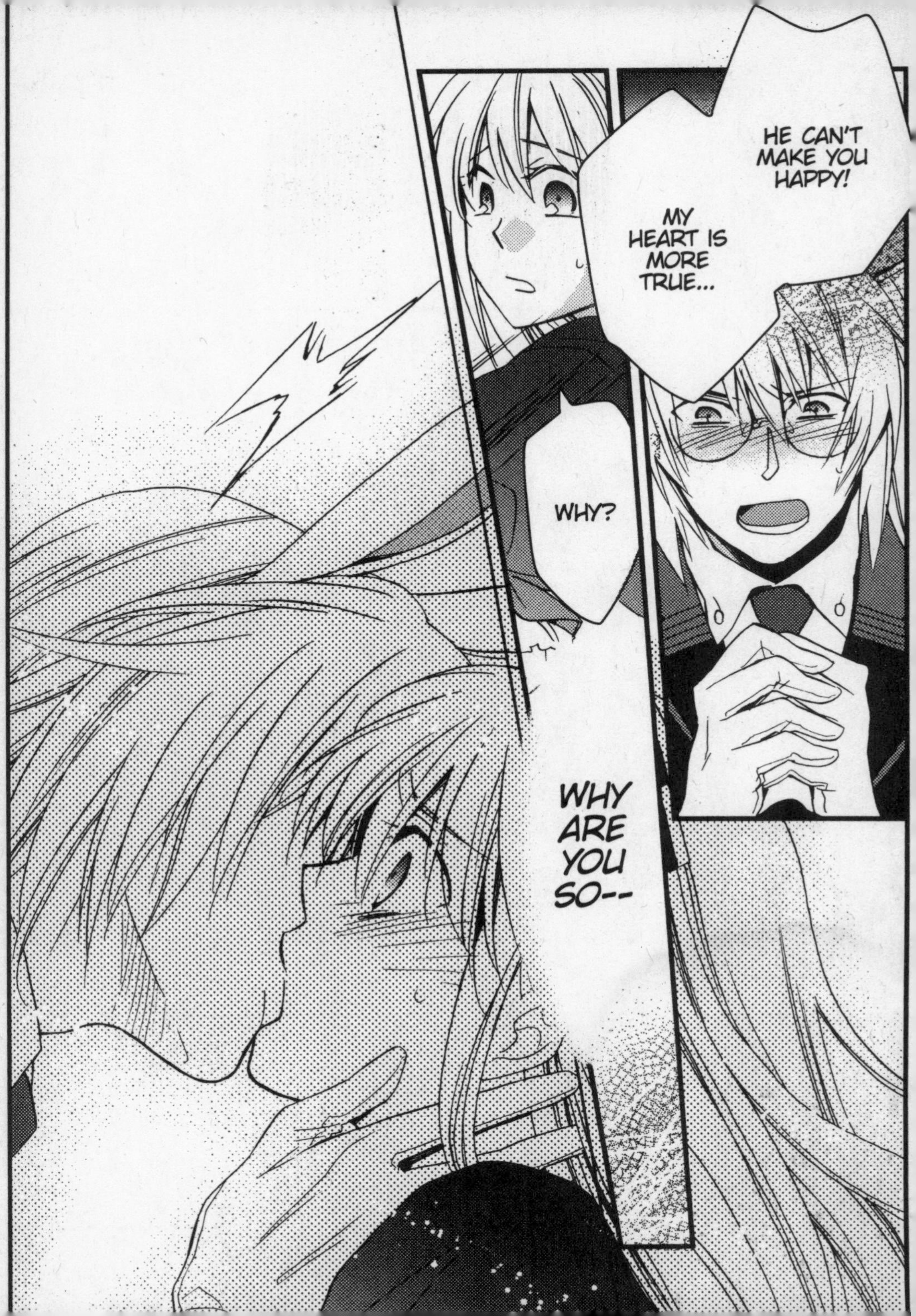
HE CAN'T MAKE YOU HAPPY!
MY HEART IS MORE TRUE...
WHY?
WHY ARE YOU SO--

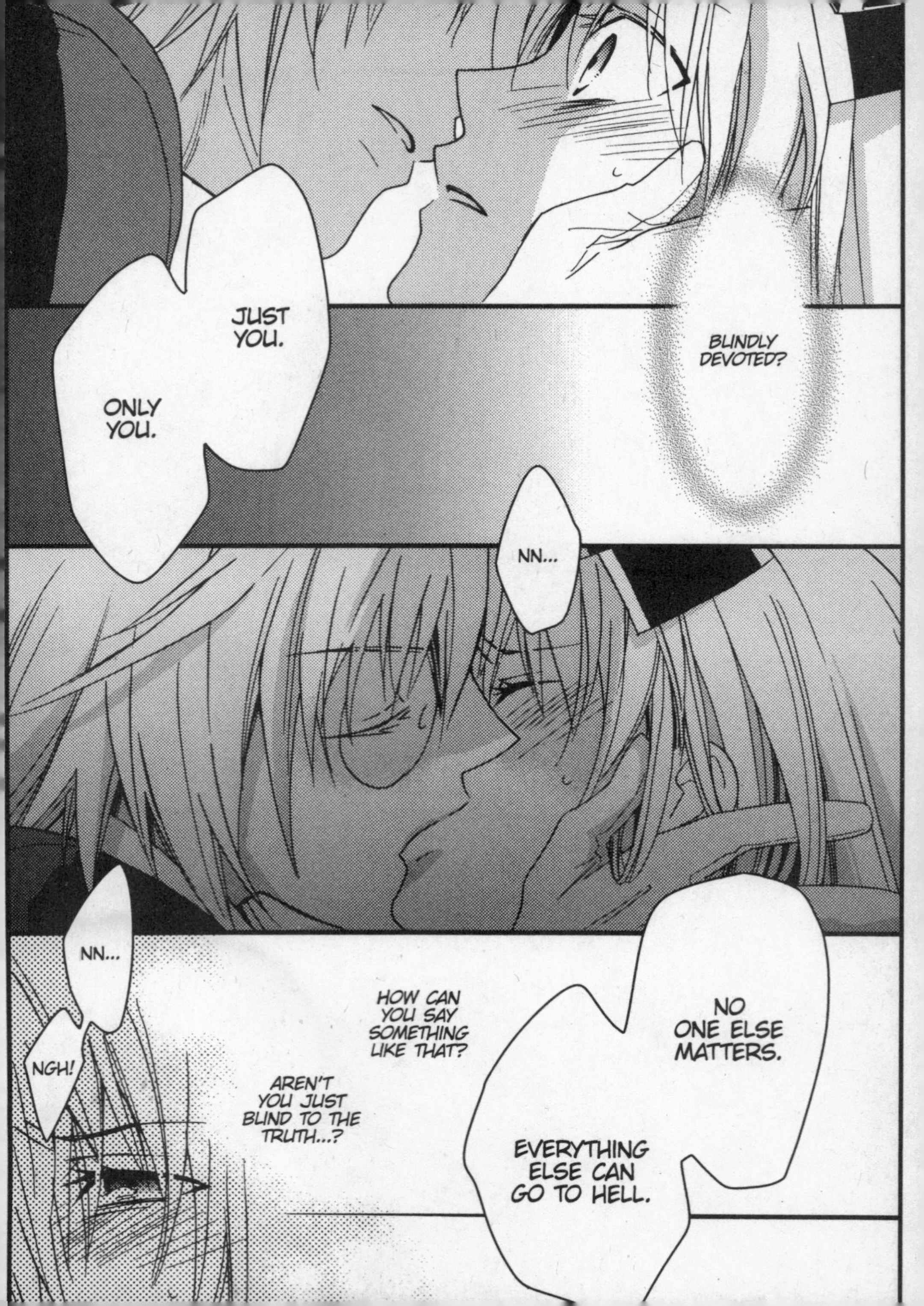
BLINDLY DEVOTED?
JUST YOU.
ONLY YOU.
NN...
NO ONE ELSE MATTERS.
EVERYTHING ELSE CAN GO TO HELL.
HOW CAN YOU SAY SOMETHING LIKE THAT?
AREN'T YOU JUST BLIND TO THE TRUTH...?
NN...
NGH!

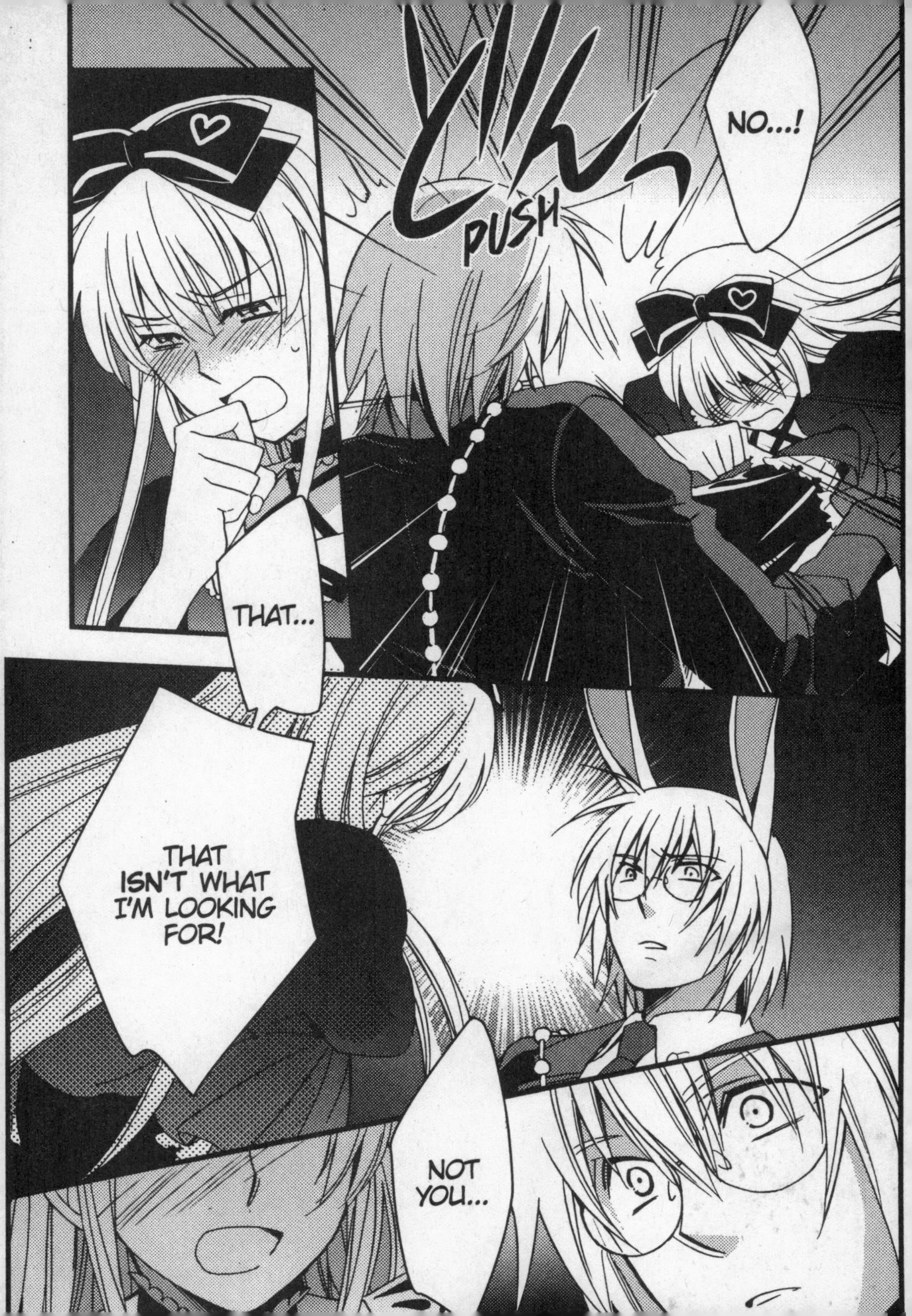

NO...!
PUSH
THAT...
THAT ISN'T WHAT I'M LOOKING FOR!
NOT YOU...

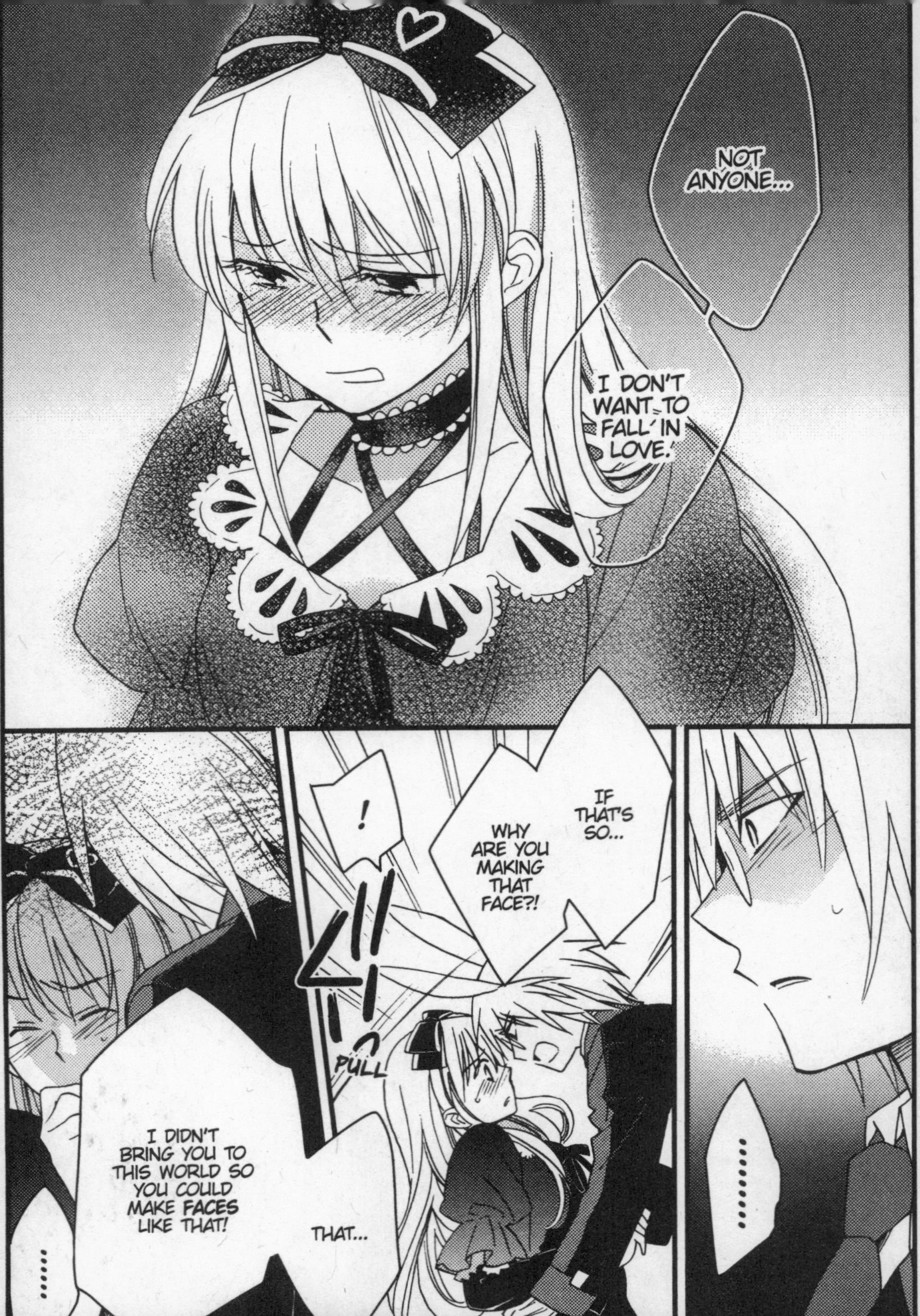
NOT ANYONE...
I DON'T WANT TO FALL IN LOVE.
......
IF THAT'S SO...
WHY ARE YOU MAKING THAT FACE?!
!
PULL
THAT...
I DIDN'T BRING YOU TO THIS WORLD SO YOU COULD MAKE FACES LIKE THAT!
......

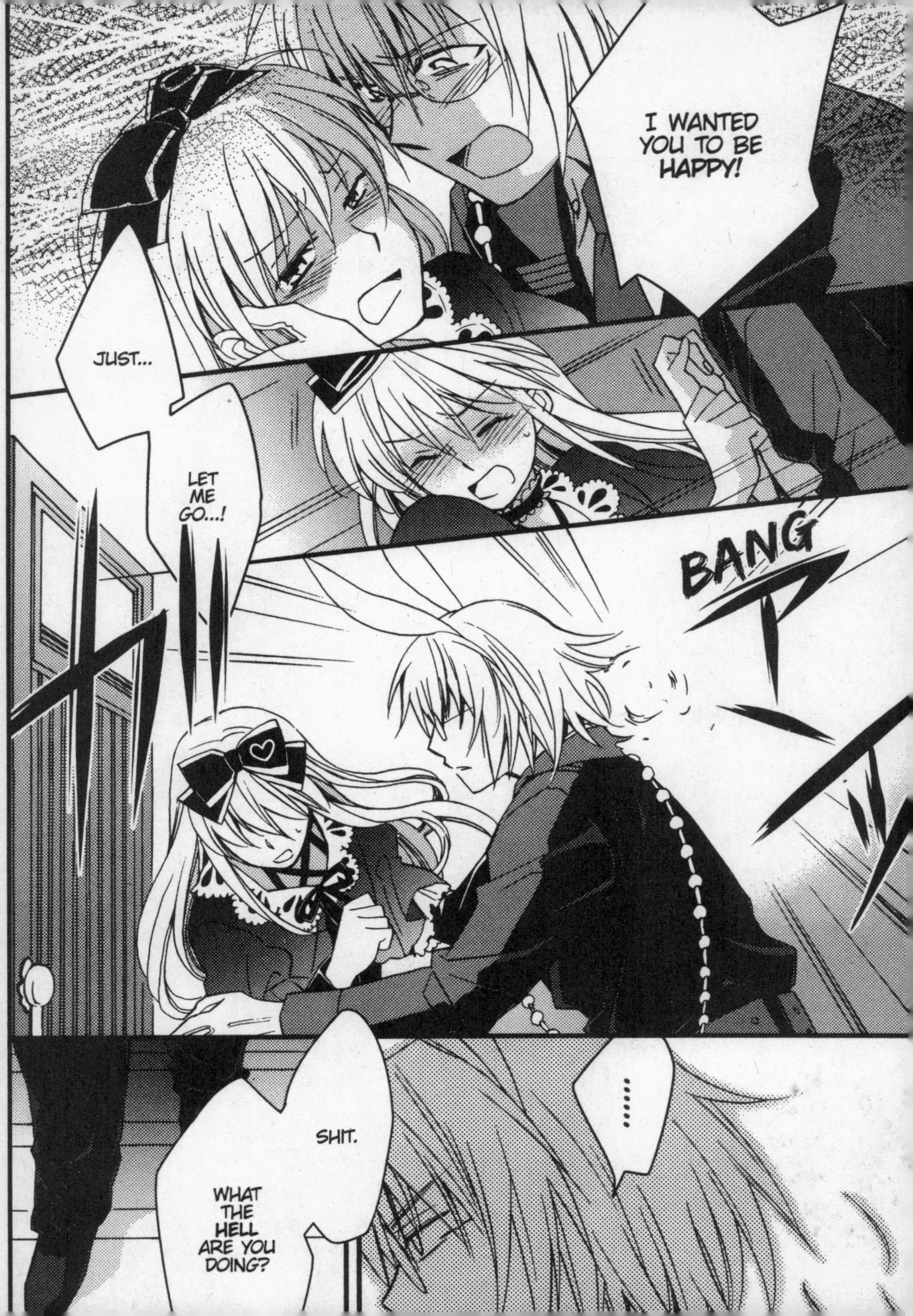
I WANTED YOU TO BE HAPPY!
JUST...
LET ME GO...!
BANG
......
SHIT.
WHAT THE HELL ARE YOU DOING?

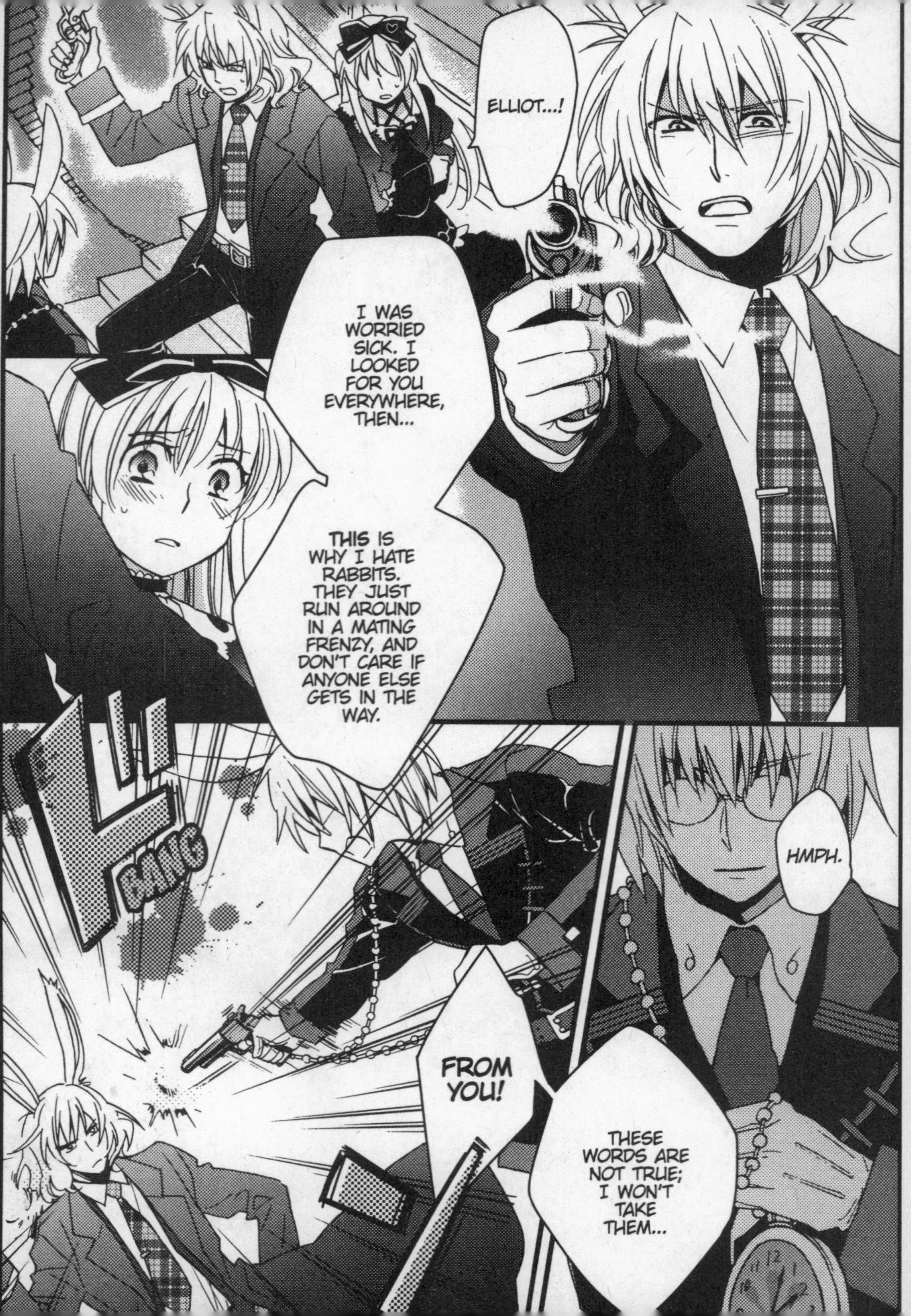
ELLIOT...!
I WAS WORRIED SICK. I LOOKED FOR YOU EVERYWHERE, THEN...
THIS IS WHY I HATE RABBITS. THEY JUST RUN AROUND IN A MATING FRENZY, AND DON'T CARE IF ANYONE ELSE GETS IN THE WAY.
HMPH.
THESE WORDS ARE NOT TRUE; I WON'T TAKE THEM...
FROM YOU!
BANG

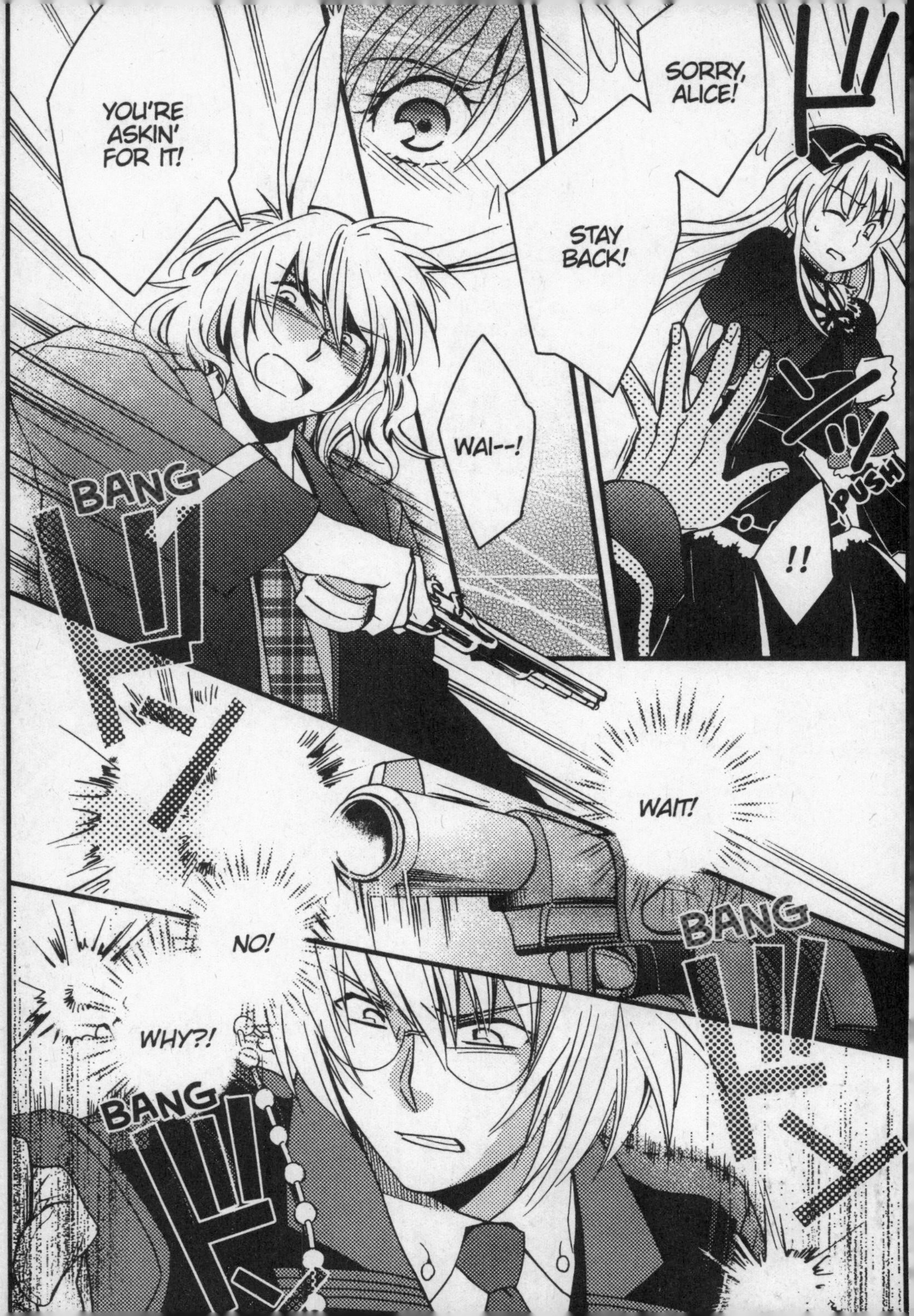
SORRY, ALICE!
STAY BACK!
PUSH
!!
WAI--!
YOU'RE ASKIN' FOR IT!
BANG
WAIT!
BANG
NO!
WHY?!
BANG

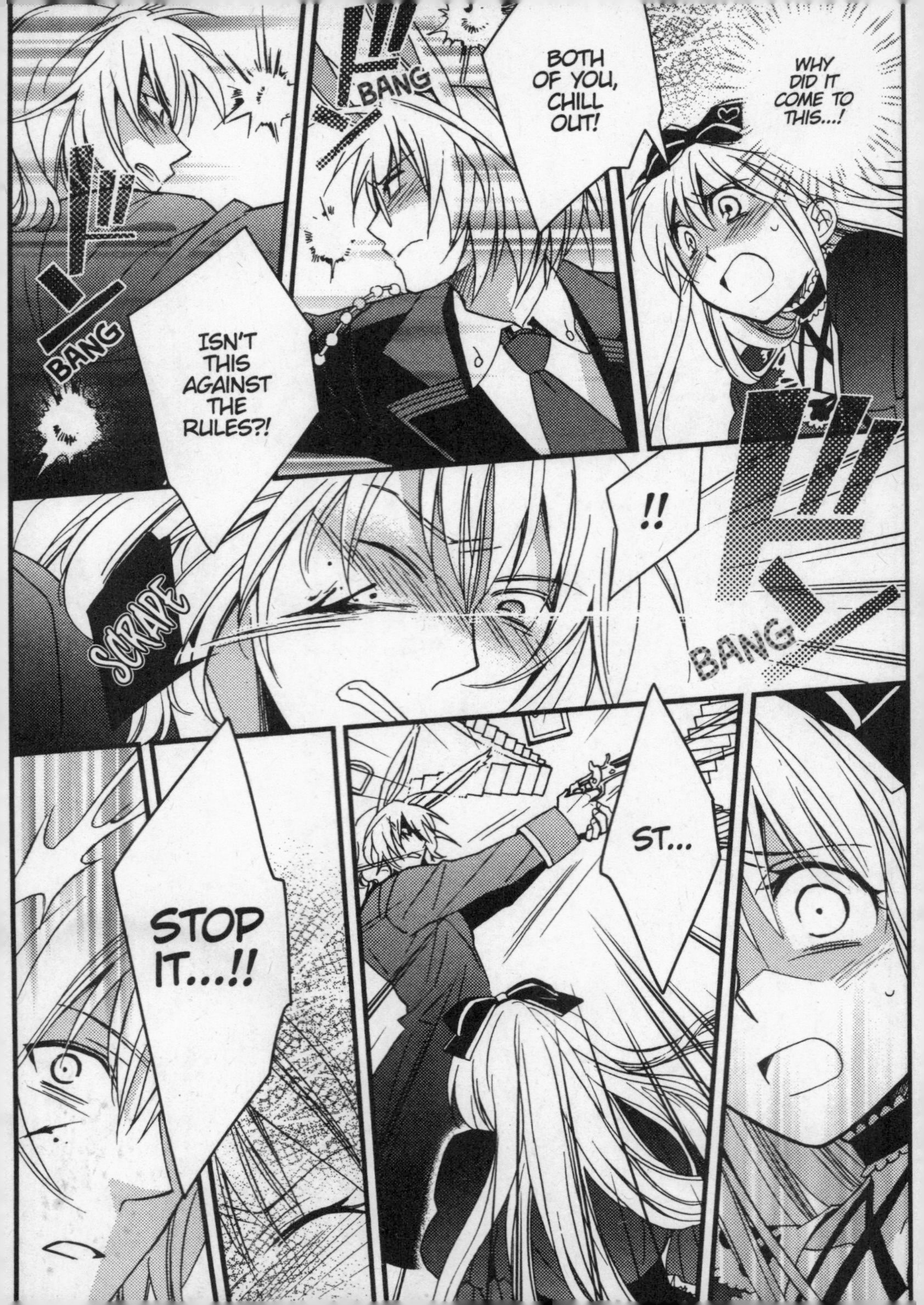

WHY DID IT COME TO THIS...!
BOTH OF YOU, CHILL OUT!
BANG
BANG
ISN'T THIS AGAINST THE RULES?!
!!
BANG
SCRAPE
ST...
STOP IT...!!

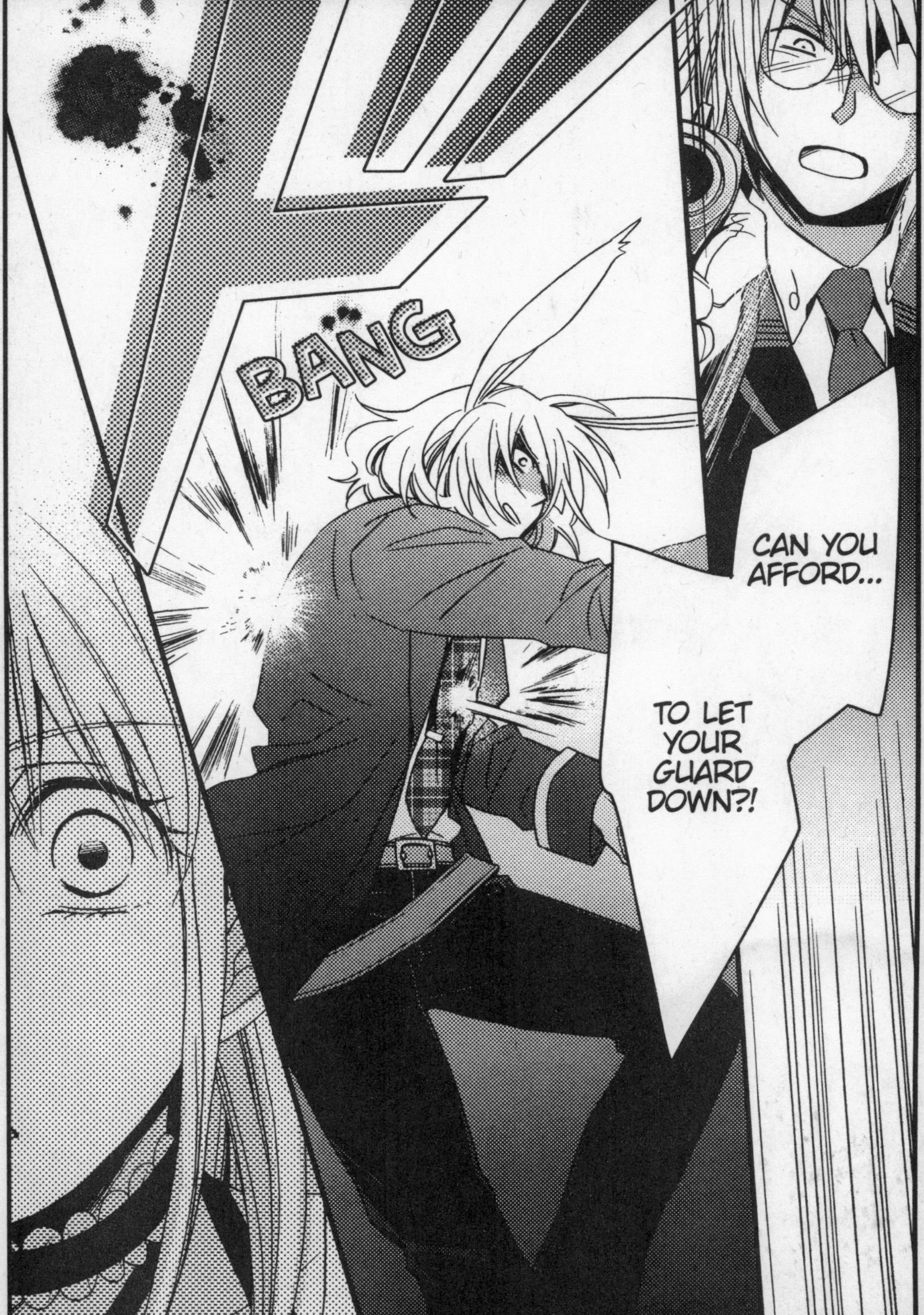
BANG
CAN YOU AFFORD...
TO LET YOUR GUARD DOWN?!

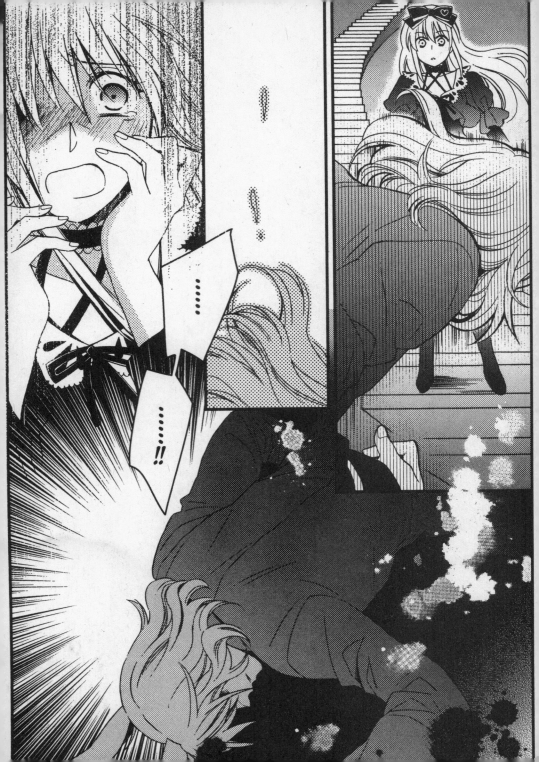

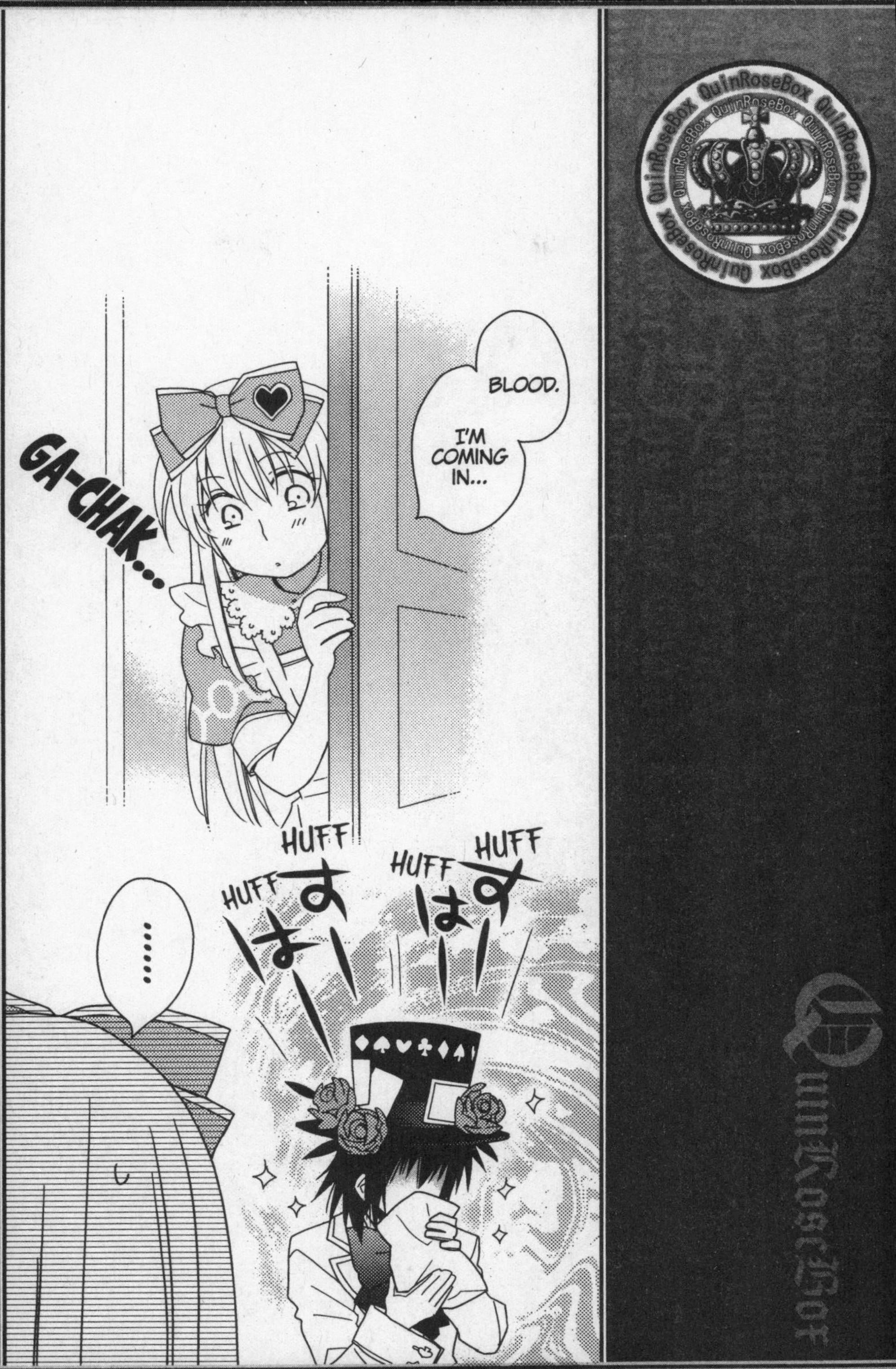
BLOOD.
I'M COMING IN...
GA-CHAK...
HUFF HUFF すは
HUFF HUFF すは
......

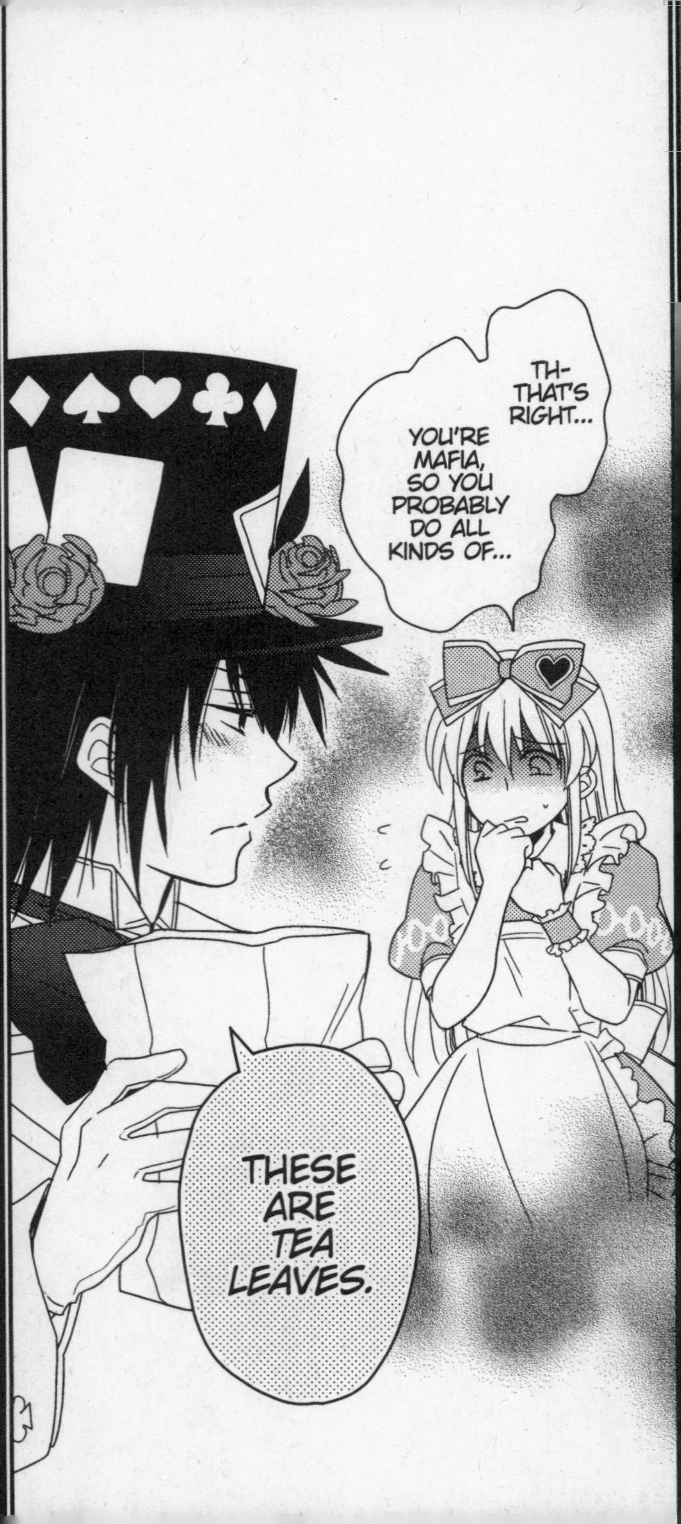
TH- THAT'S RIGHT... YOU'RE MAFIA, SO YOU PROBABLY DO ALL KINDS OF...
THESE ARE TEA LEAVES.

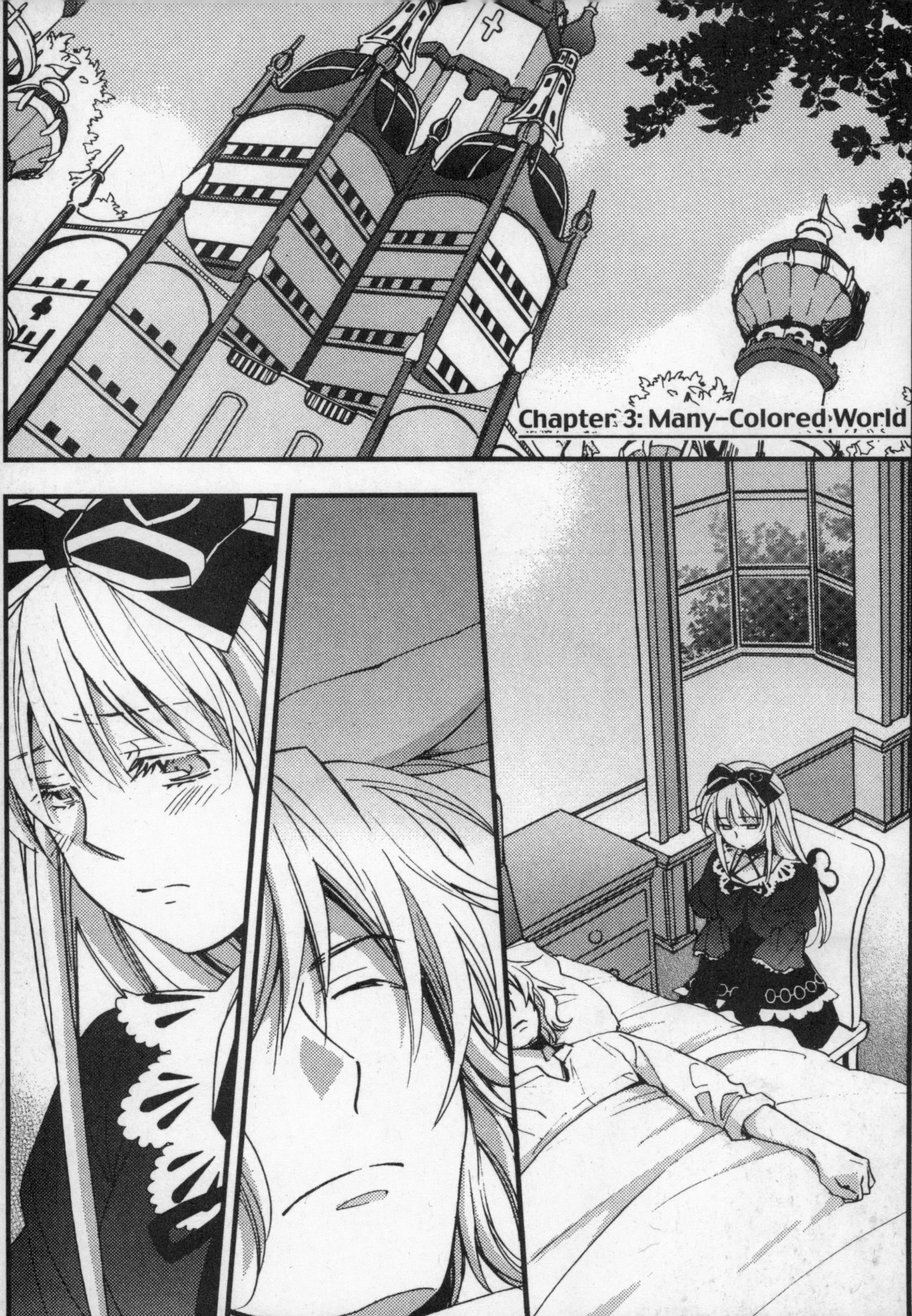
Chapter 3: Many-Colored World

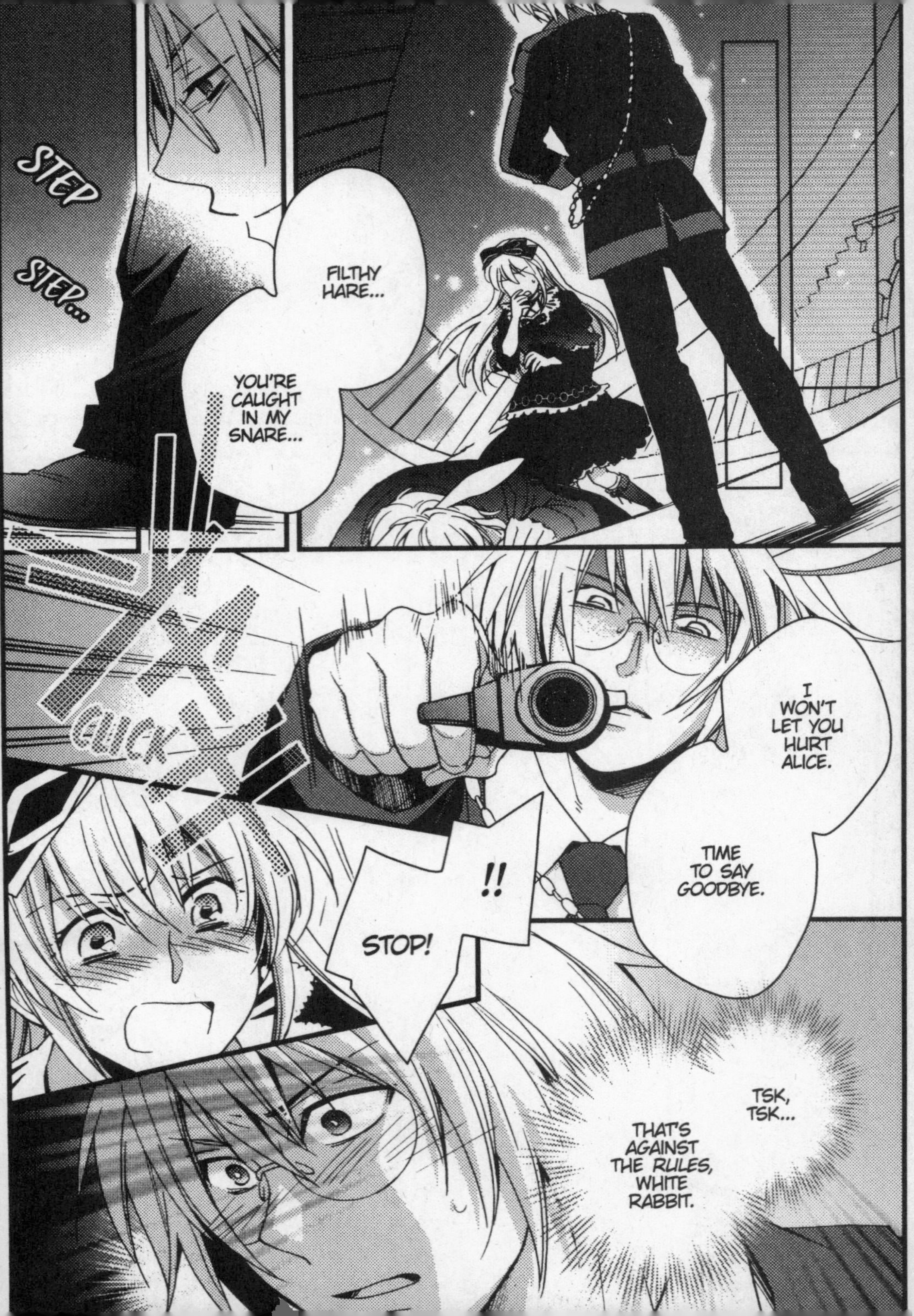
FILTHY HARE...
YOU'RE CAUGHT IN MY SNARE...
STEP
STEP...
I WON'T LET YOU HURT ALICE.
TIME TO SAY GOODBYE.
CLICK
!!
STOP!
TSK, TSK...
THAT'S AGAINST THE RULES, WHITE RABBIT.

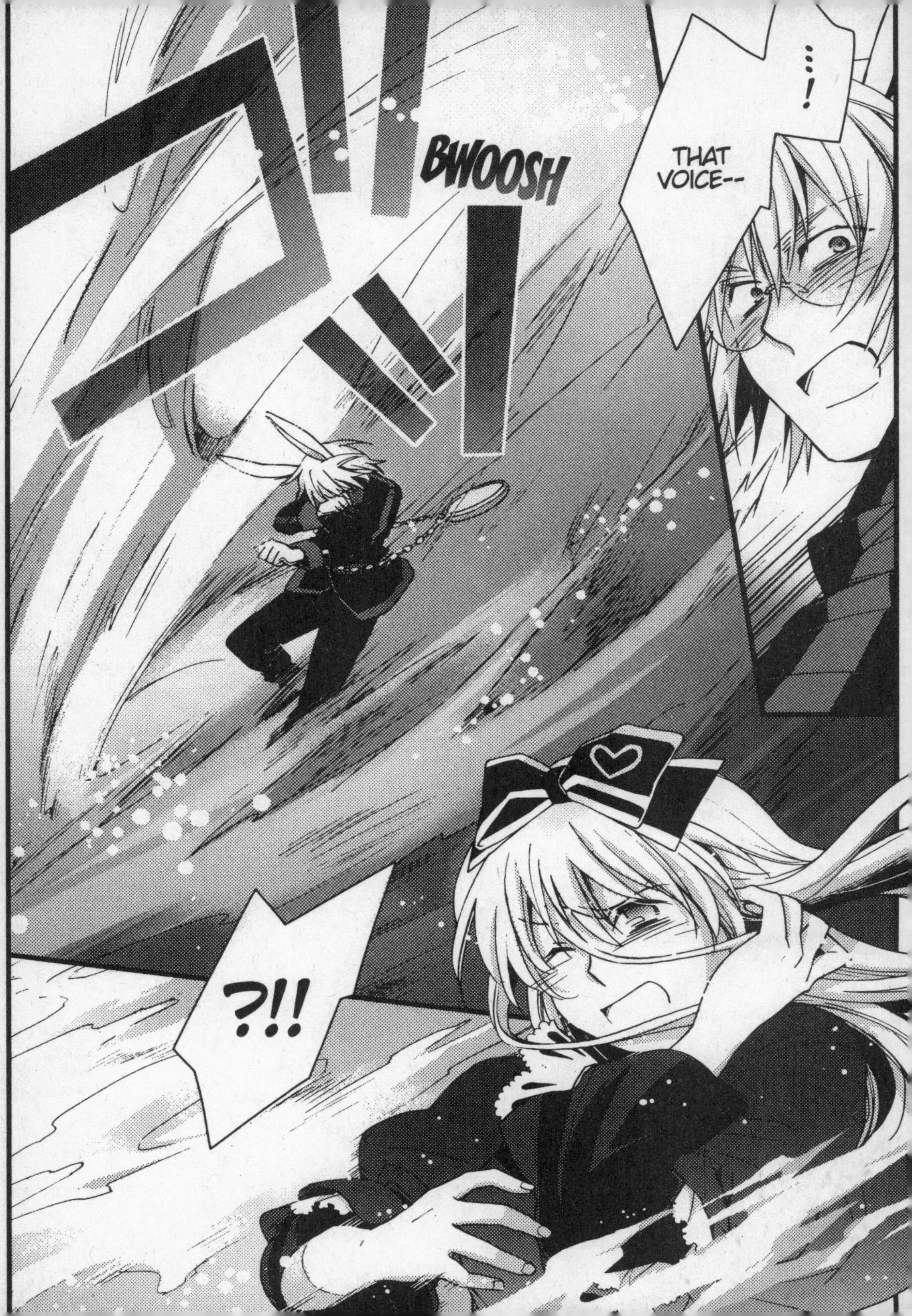
...!
THAT VOICE--
BWOOSH
?!!

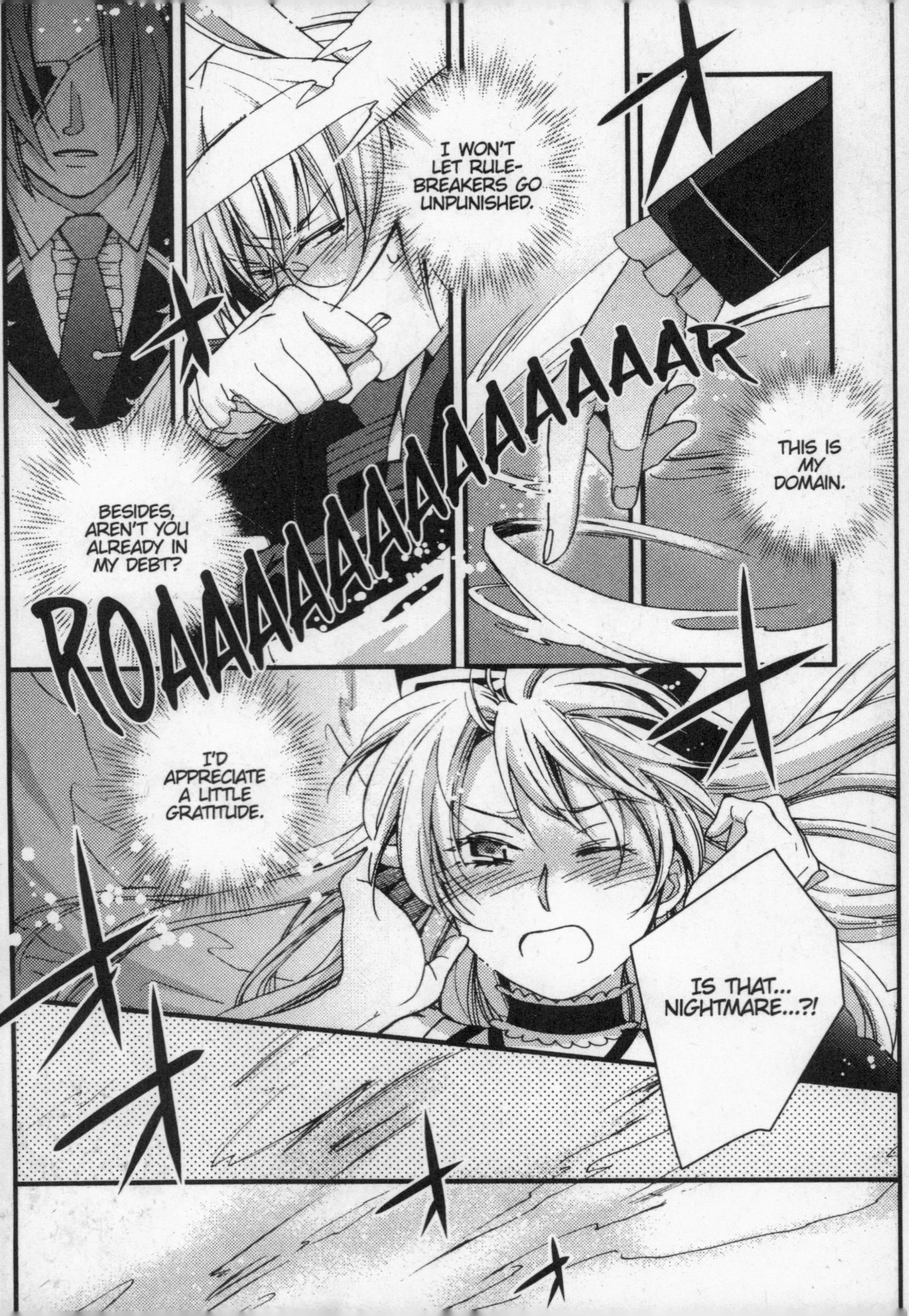
THIS IS MY DOMAIN.
I WON'T LET RULE-BREAKERS GO UNPUNISHED.
ROAAAAAAAAAAAAAAAR
BESIDES, AREN'T YOU ALREADY IN MY DEBT?
I'D APPRECIATE A LITTLE GRATITUDE.
IS THAT... NIGHTMARE...?!

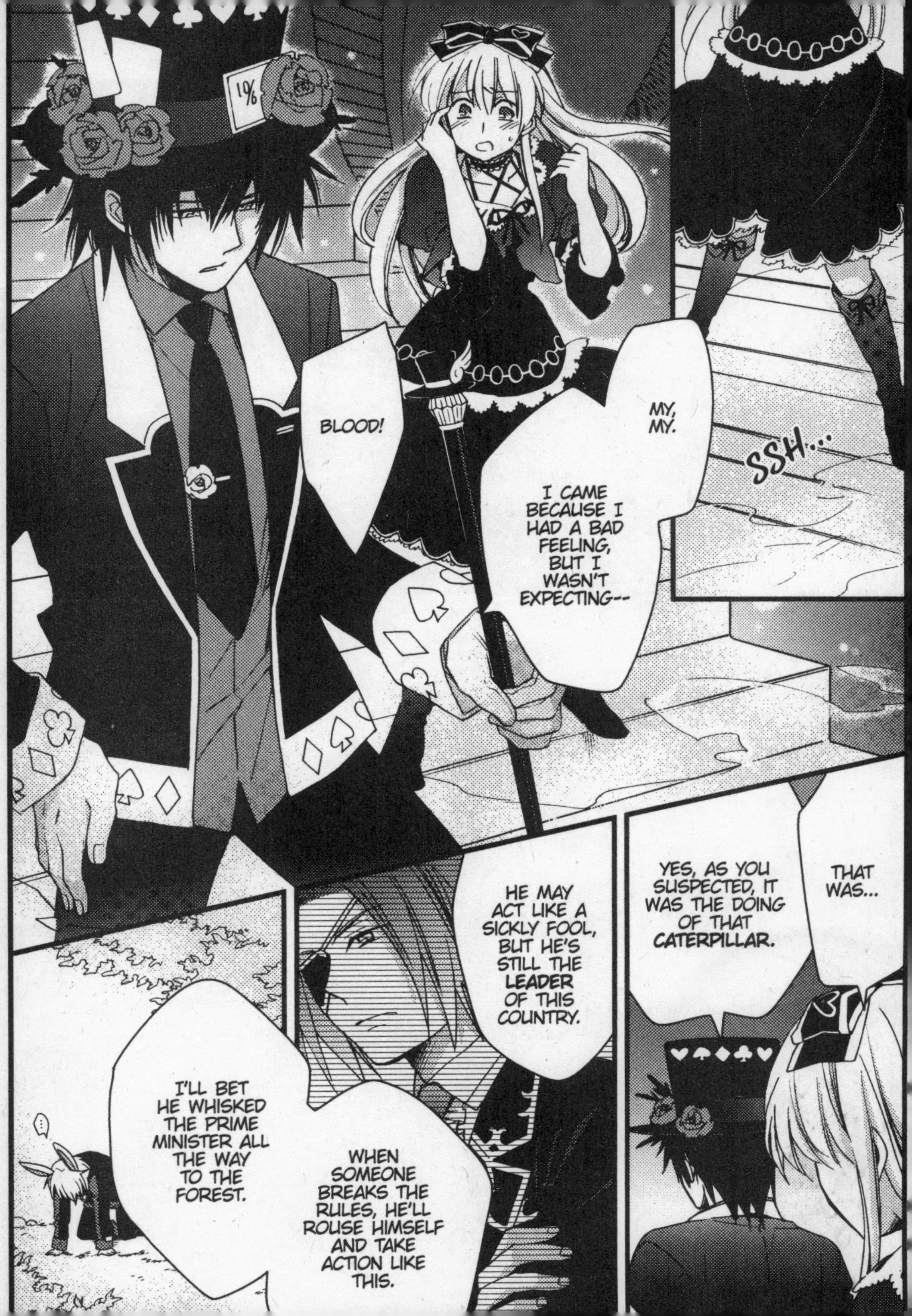
SSH...
MY, MY.
I CAME BECAUSE I HAD A BAD FEELING, BUT I WASN'T EXPECTING--
BLOOD!
THAT WAS...
YES, AS YOU SUSPECTED, IT WAS THE DOING OF THAT CATERPILLAR.
HE MAY ACT LIKE A SICKLY FOOL, BUT HE'S STILL THE LEADER OF THIS COUNTRY.
WHEN SOMEONE BREAKS THE RULES, HE'LL ROUSE HIMSELF AND TAKE ACTION LIKE THIS.
I'LL BET HE WHISKED THE PRIME MINISTER ALL THE WAY TO THE FOREST.
...

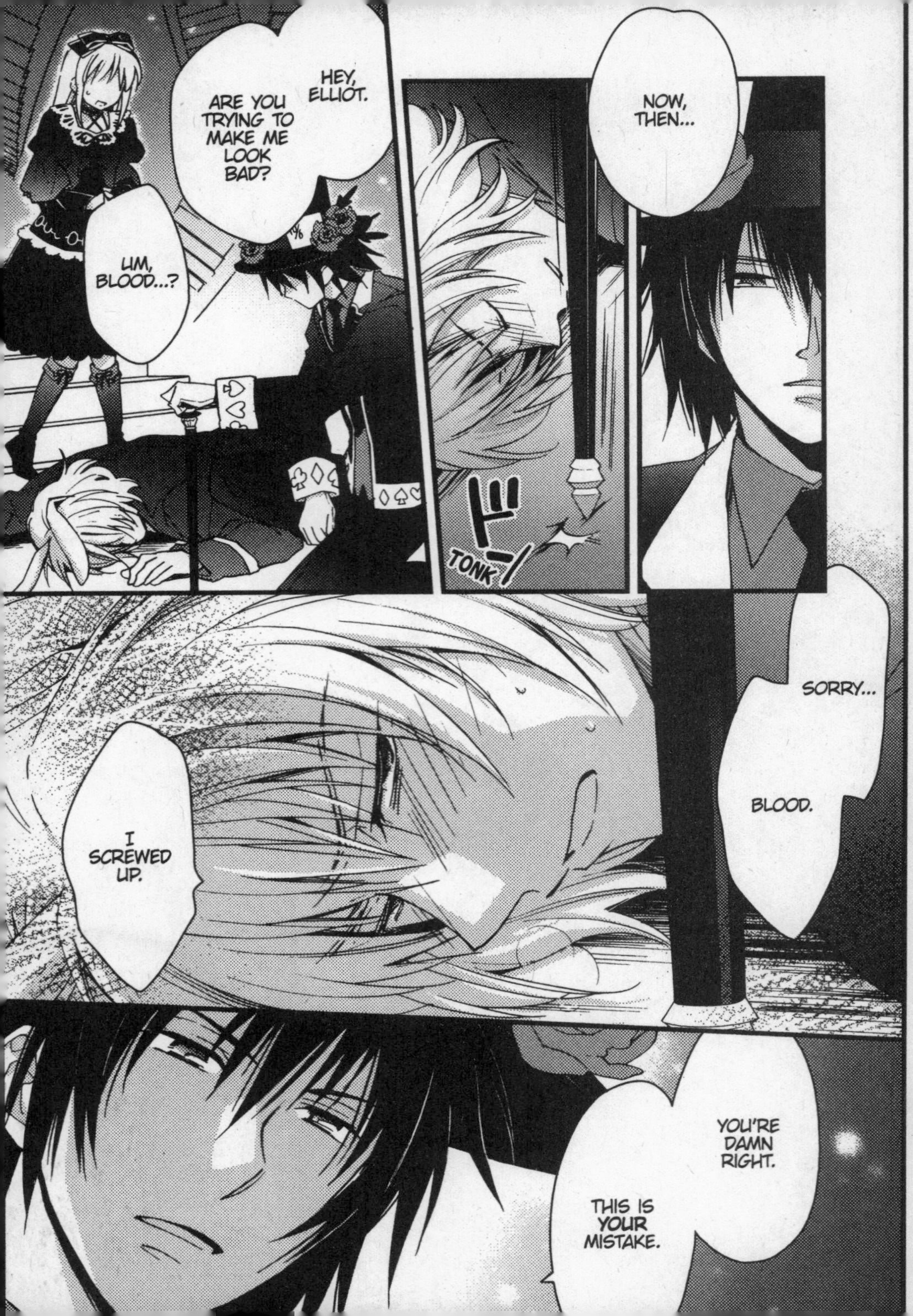

NOW, THEN...
ド
TONK
HEY, ELLIOT.
ARE YOU TRYING TO MAKE ME LOOK BAD?
UM, BLOOD...?
SORRY...
BLOOD.
I SCREWED UP.
YOU'RE DAMN RIGHT.
THIS IS YOUR MISTAKE.

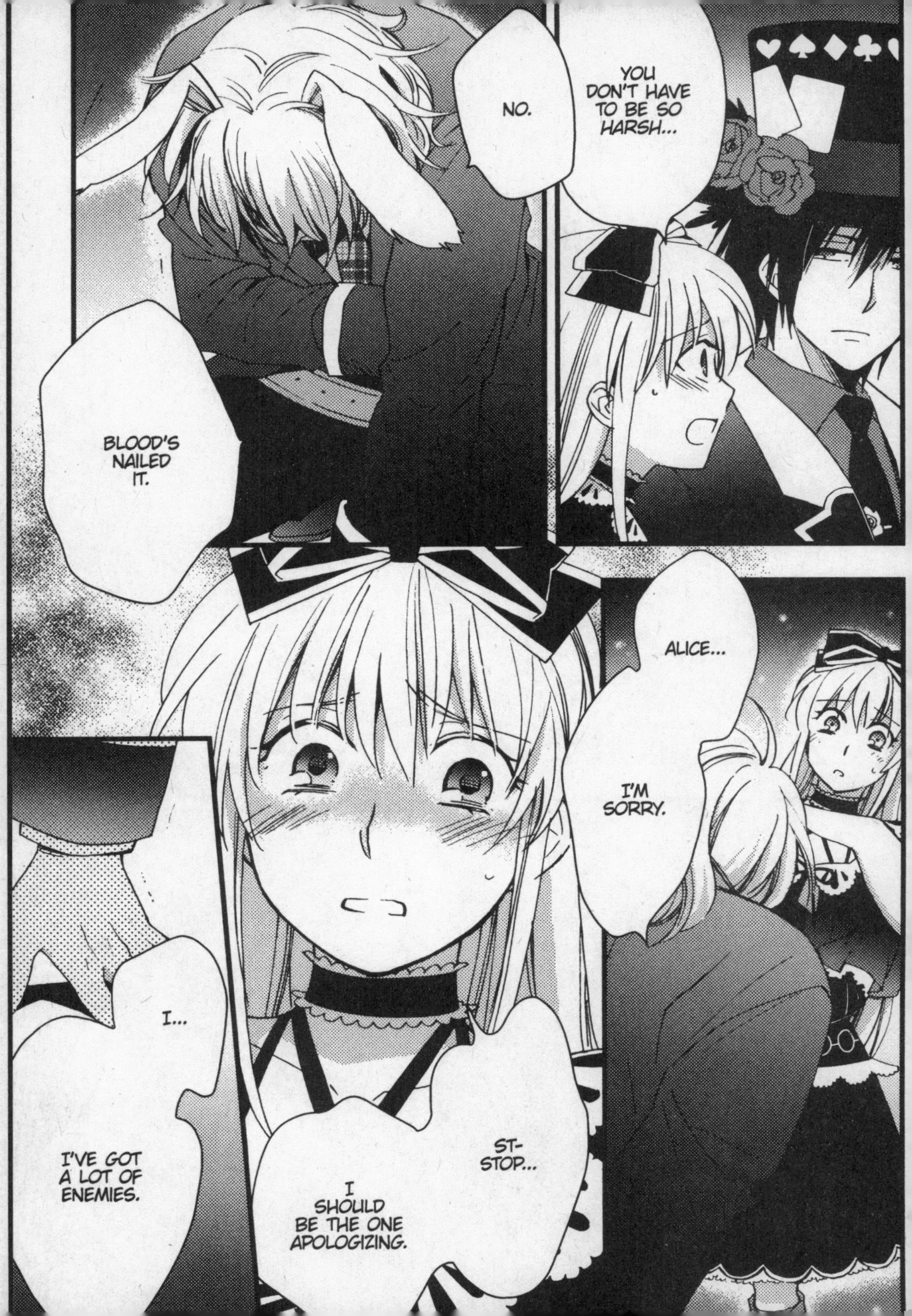
YOU DON'T HAVE TO BE SO HARSH...
NO.
BLOOD'S NAILED IT.
ALICE...
I'M SORRY.
ST- STOP...
I SHOULD BE THE ONE APOLOGIZING.
I...
I'VE GOT A LOT OF ENEMIES.

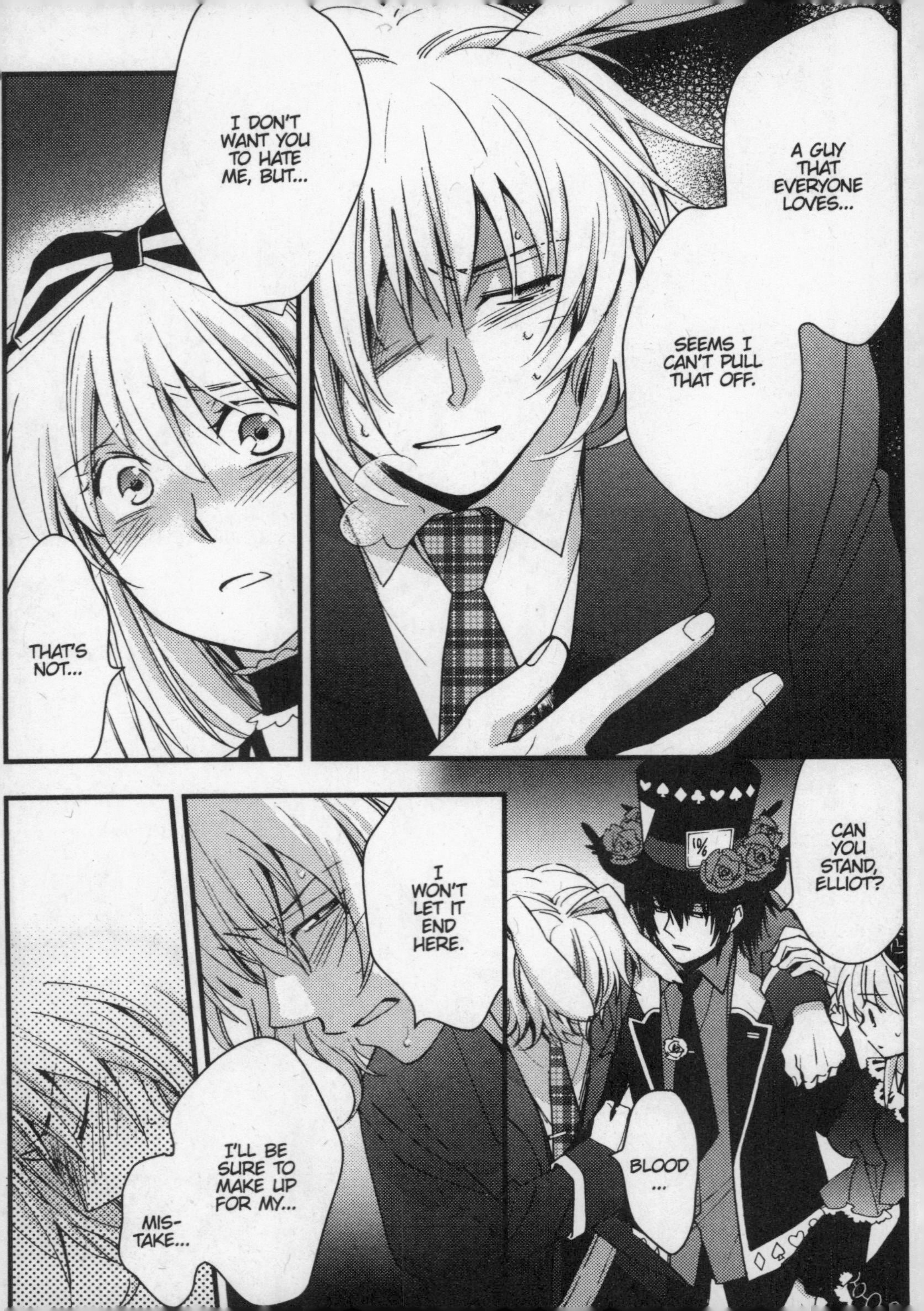
A GUY THAT EVERYONE LOVES...
SEEMS I CAN'T PULL THAT OFF.
I DON'T WANT YOU TO HATE ME, BUT...
THAT'S NOT...
CAN YOU STAND, ELLIOT?
BLOOD ...
I WON'T LET IT END HERE.
I'LL BE SURE TO MAKE UP FOR MY...
MIS-TAKE...

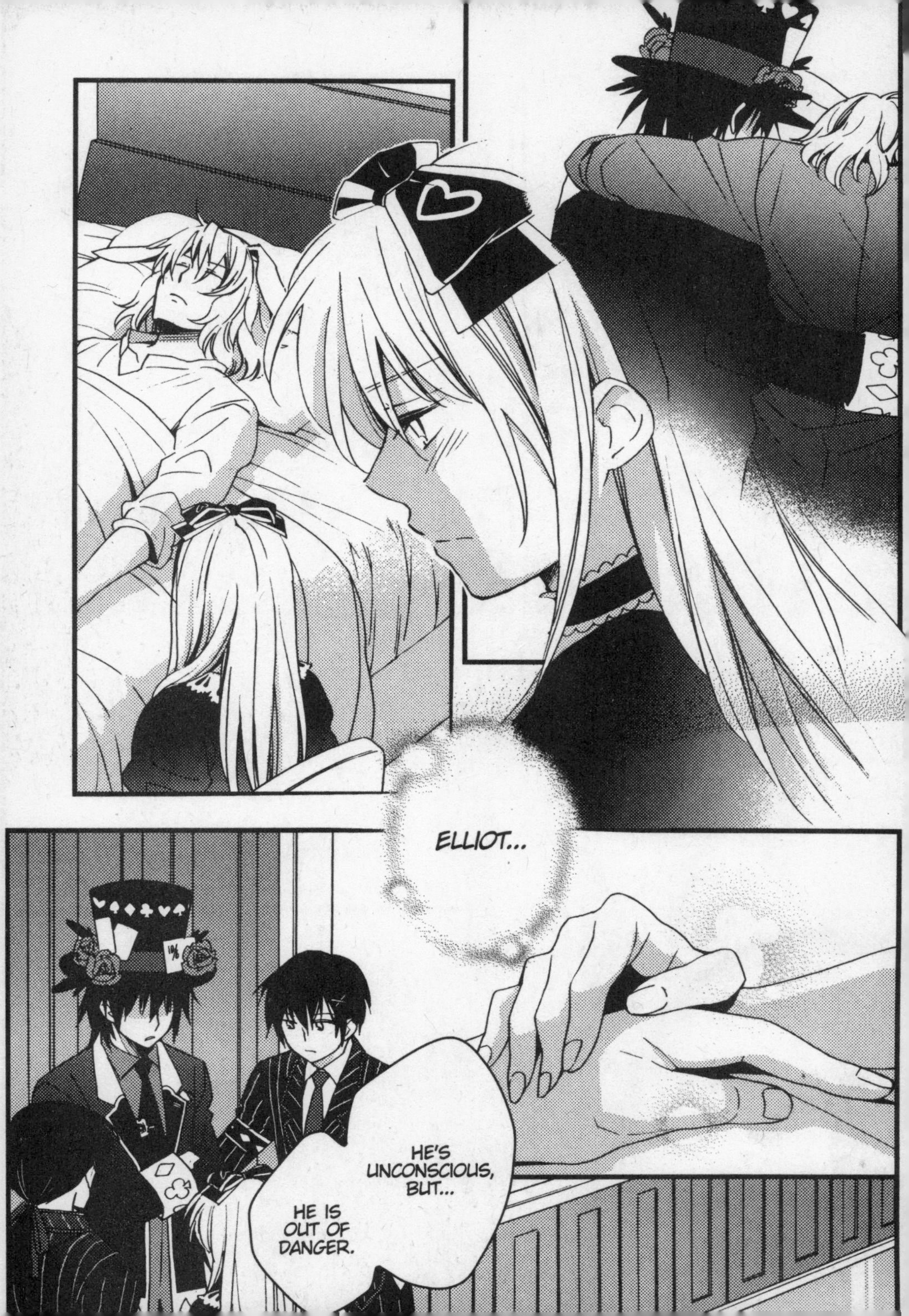
ELLIOT...
HE'S UNCONSCIOUS, BUT...
HE IS OUT OF DANGER.

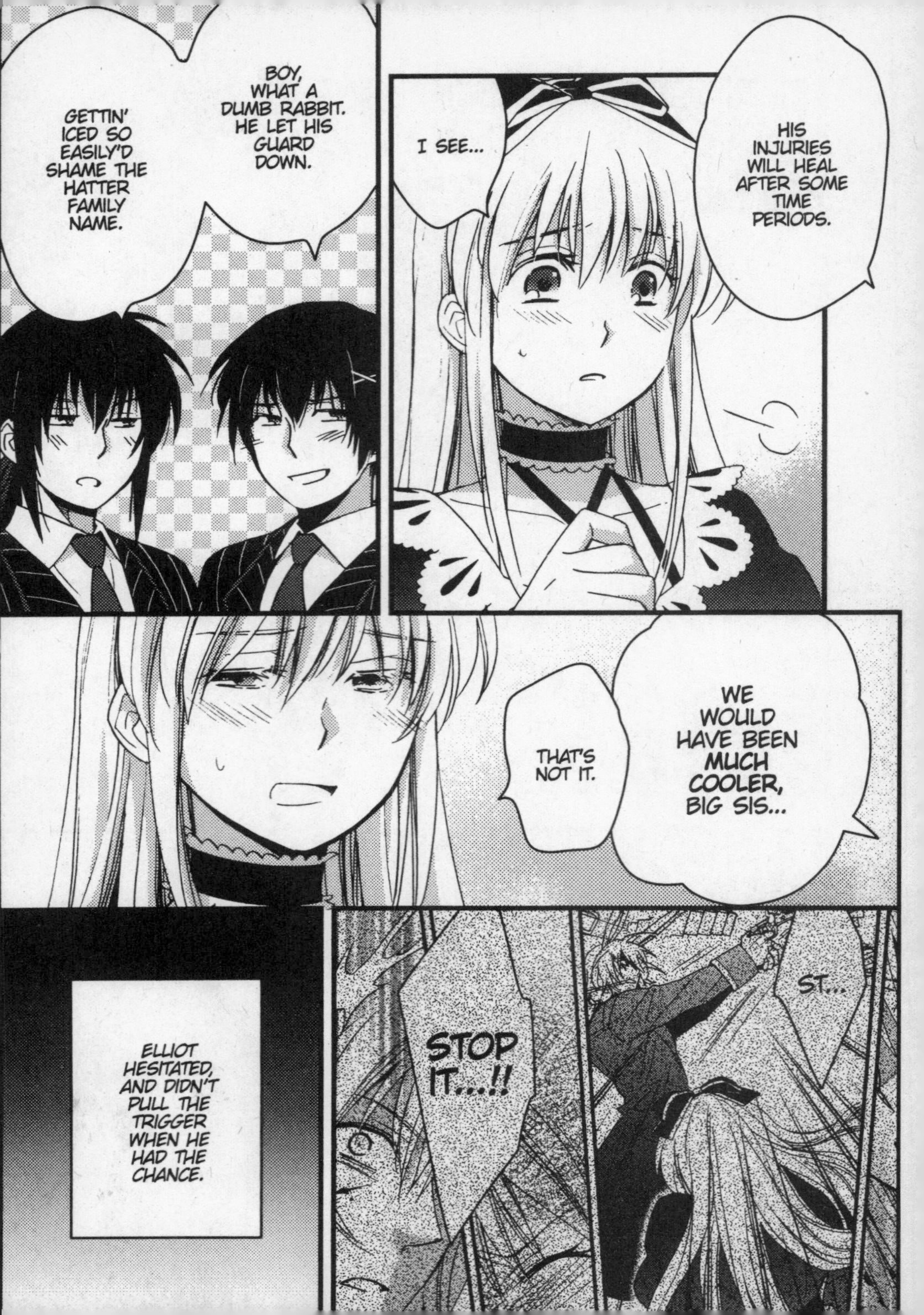
HIS INJURIES WILL HEAL AFTER SOME TIME PERIODS.
I SEE...
BOY, WHAT A DUMB RABBIT. HE LET HIS GUARD DOWN.
GETTIN' ICED SO EASILY'D SHAME THE HATTER FAMILY NAME.
WE WOULD HAVE BEEN MUCH COOLER, BIG SIS...
THAT'S NOT IT.
ST...
STOP IT...!!
ELLIOT HESITATED, AND DIDN'T PULL THE TRIGGER WHEN HE HAD THE CHANCE.

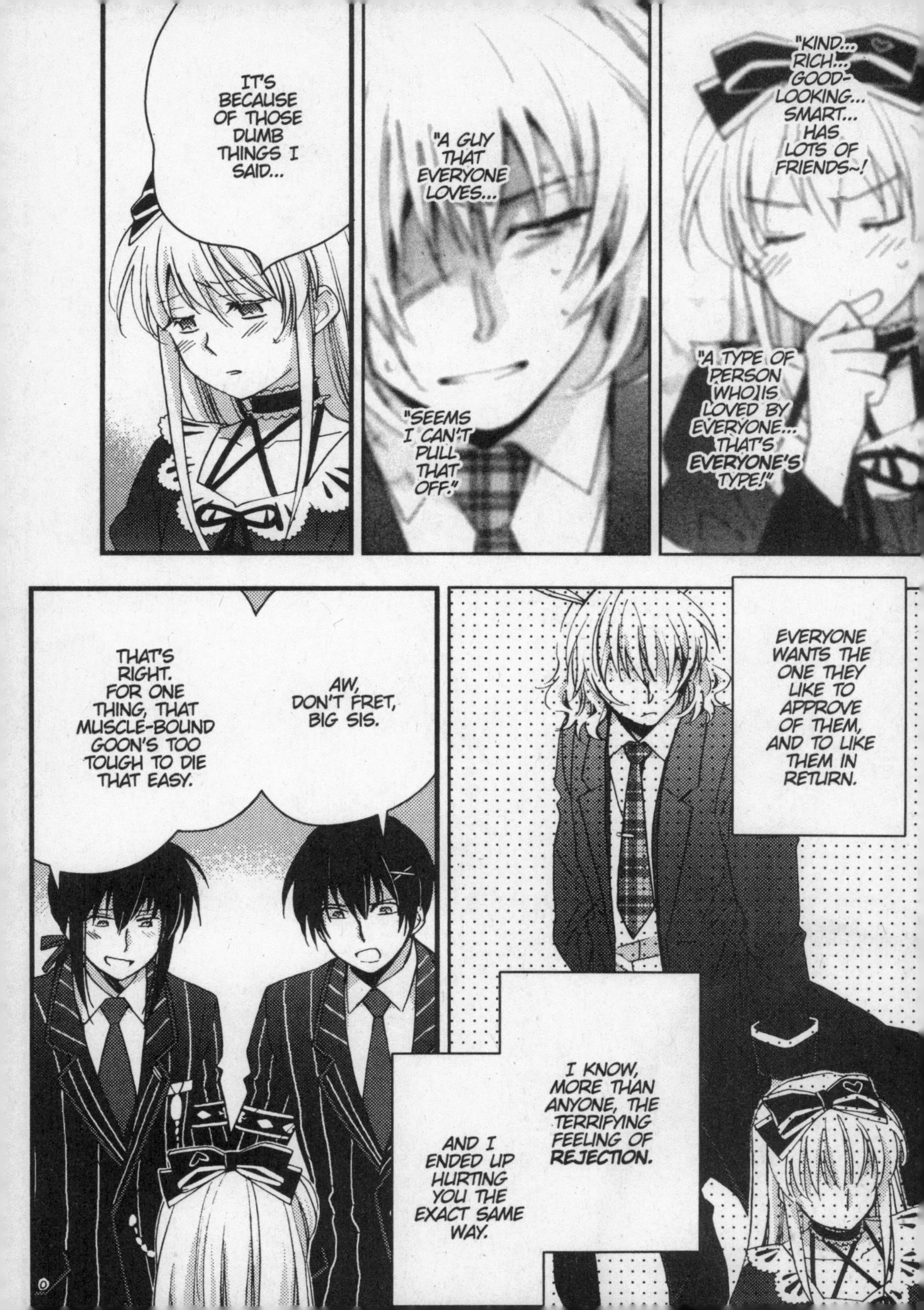
"KIND... RICH... GOOD-LOOKING... SMART... HAS LOTS OF FRIENDS~!
"A TYPE OF PERSON WHO IS LOVED BY EVERYONE... THAT'S EVERYONE'S TYPE!"
"A GUY THAT EVERYONE LOVES...
"SEEMS I CAN'T PULL THAT OFF."
IT'S BECAUSE OF THOSE DUMB THINGS I SAID...
EVERYONE WANTS THE ONE THEY LIKE TO APPROVE OF THEM, AND TO LIKE THEM IN RETURN.
I KNOW, MORE THAN ANYONE, THE TERRIFYING FEELING OF REJECTION.
AND I ENDED UP HURTING YOU THE EXACT SAME WAY.
AW, DON'T FRET, BIG SIS.
THAT'S RIGHT. FOR ONE THING, THAT MUSCLE-BOUND GOON'S TOO TOUGH TO DIE THAT EASY.

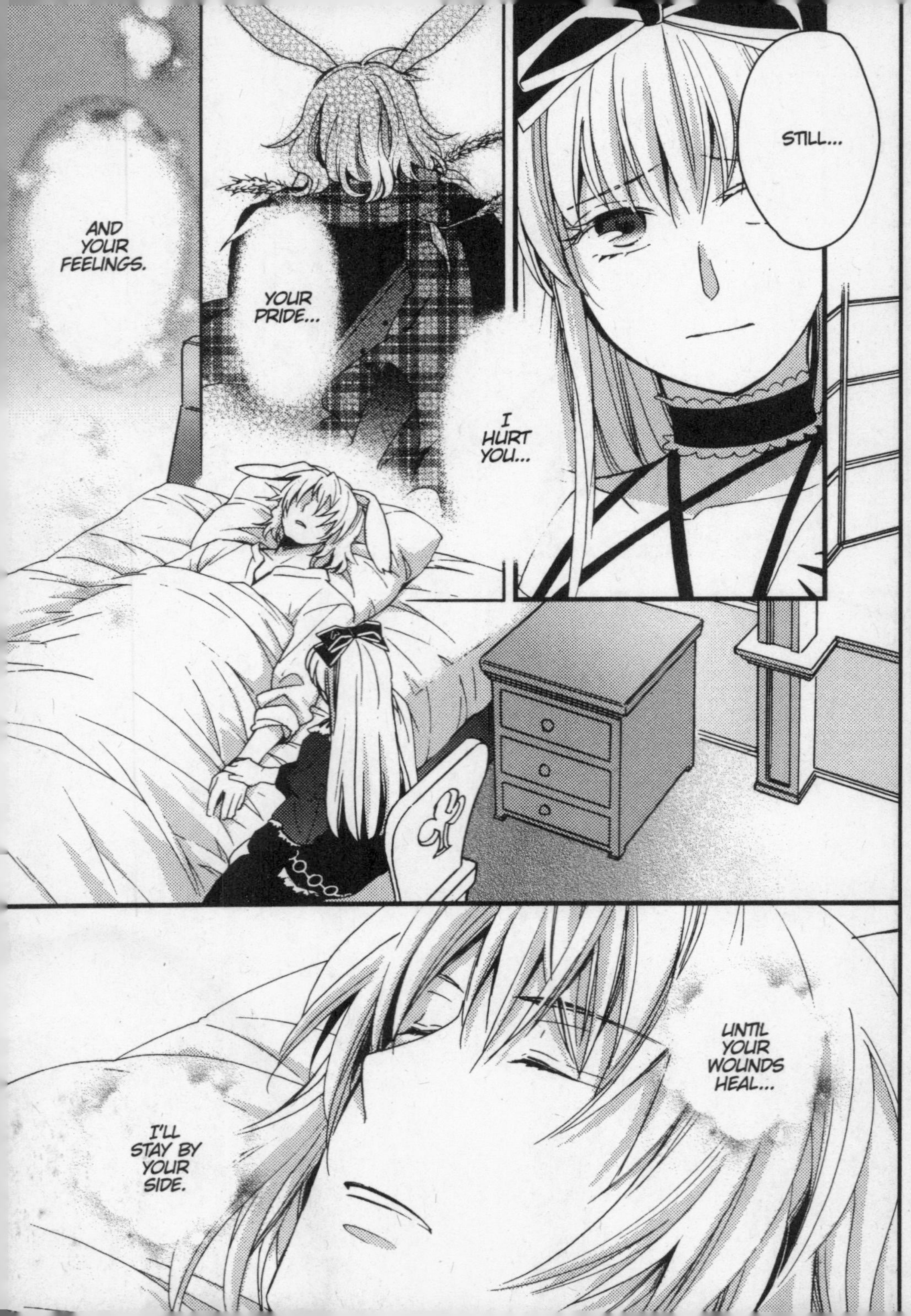
STILL...
I HURT YOU...
YOUR PRIDE...
AND YOUR FEELINGS.
UNTIL YOUR WOUNDS HEAL...
I'LL STAY BY YOUR SIDE.

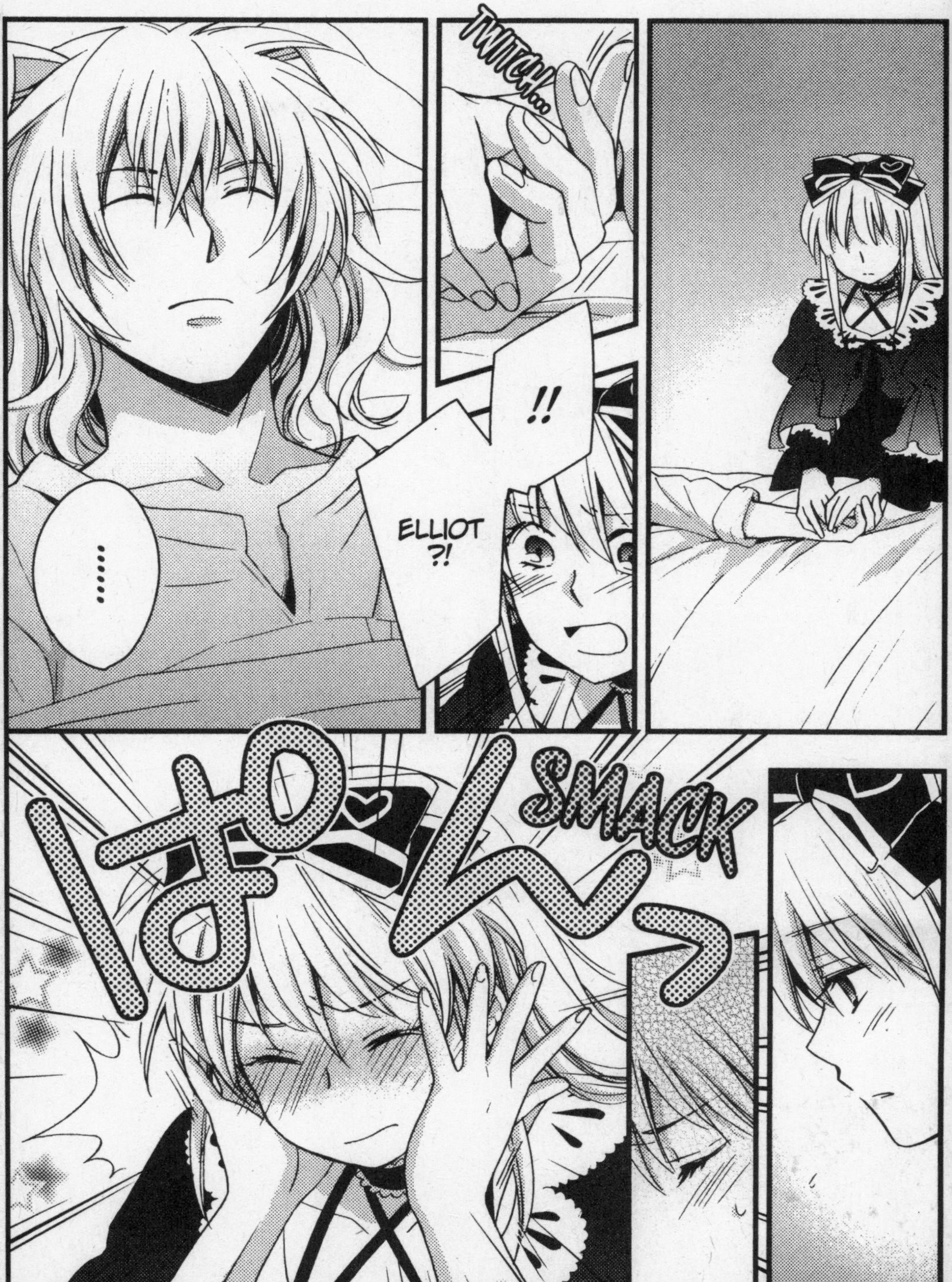
TWITCH...
!!
ELLIOT ?!
......
ぱん〜っ
SMACK

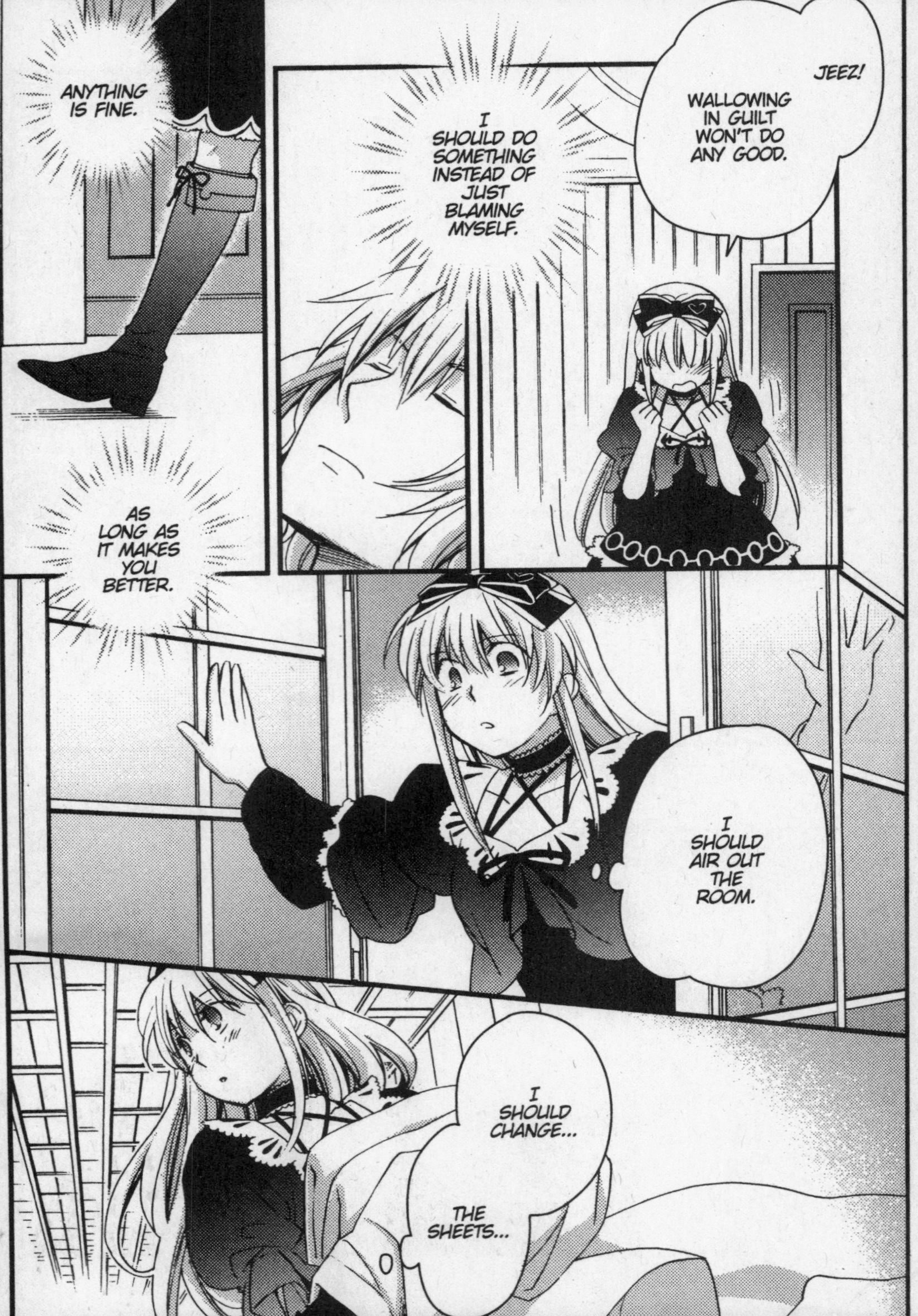
JEEZ!
WALLOWING IN GUILT WON'T DO ANY GOOD.
I SHOULD DO SOMETHING INSTEAD OF JUST BLAMING MYSELF.
ANYTHING IS FINE.
AS LONG AS IT MAKES YOU BETTER.
I SHOULD AIR OUT THE ROOM.
I SHOULD CHANGE...
THE SHEETS...

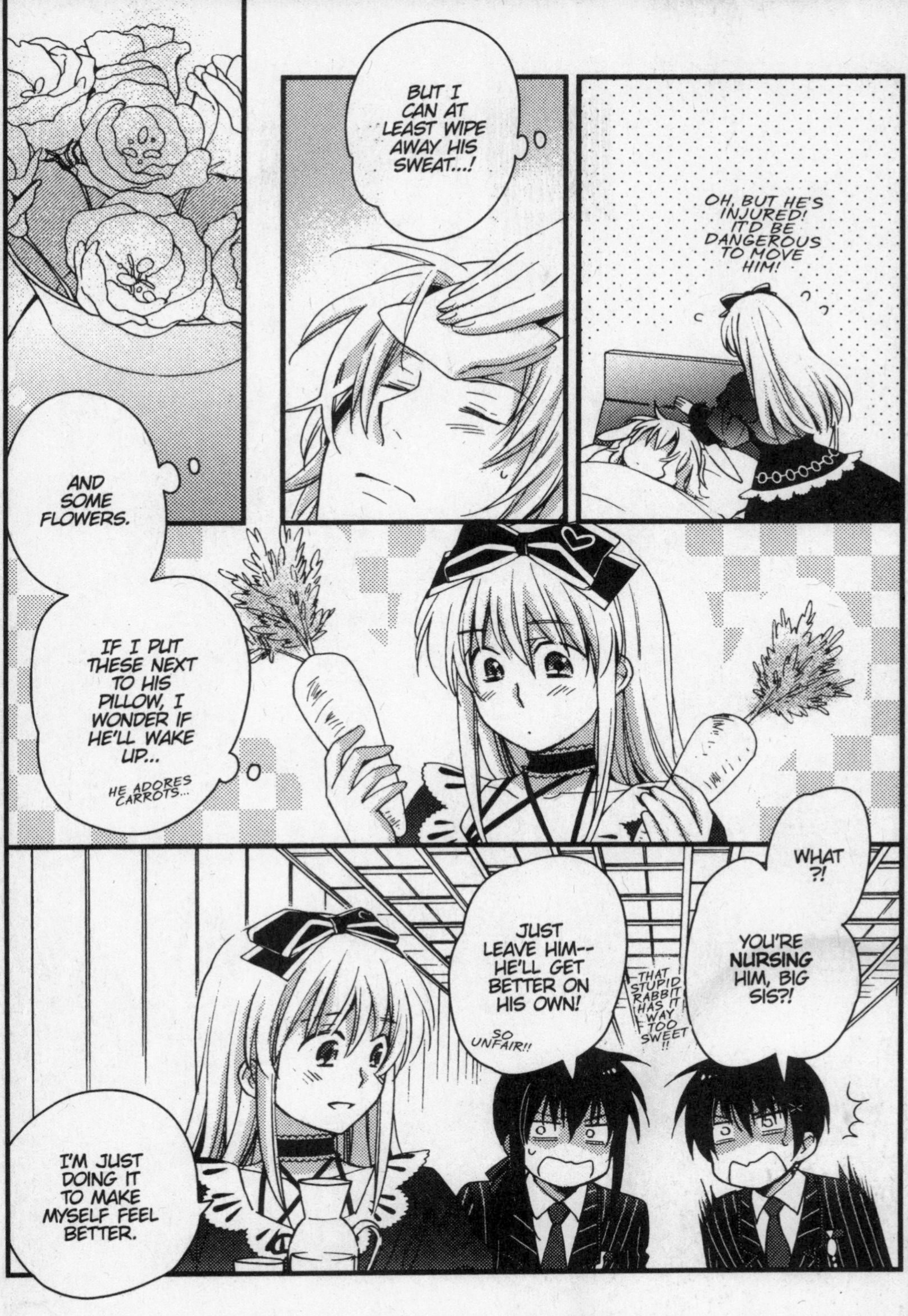
OH, BUT HE'S INJURED! IT'D BE DANGEROUS TO MOVE HIM!
BUT I CAN AT LEAST WIPE AWAY HIS SWEAT...!
AND SOME FLOWERS.
IF I PUT THESE NEXT TO HIS PILLOW, I WONDER IF HE'LL WAKE UP...
HE ADORES CARROTS...
WHAT?!
YOU'RE NURSING HIM, BIG SIS?!
THAT STUPID RABBIT HAS IT WAY TOO SWEET!!
JUST LEAVE HIM--HE'LL GET BETTER ON HIS OWN!
SO UNFAIR!!
I'M JUST DOING IT TO MAKE MYSELF FEEL BETTER.

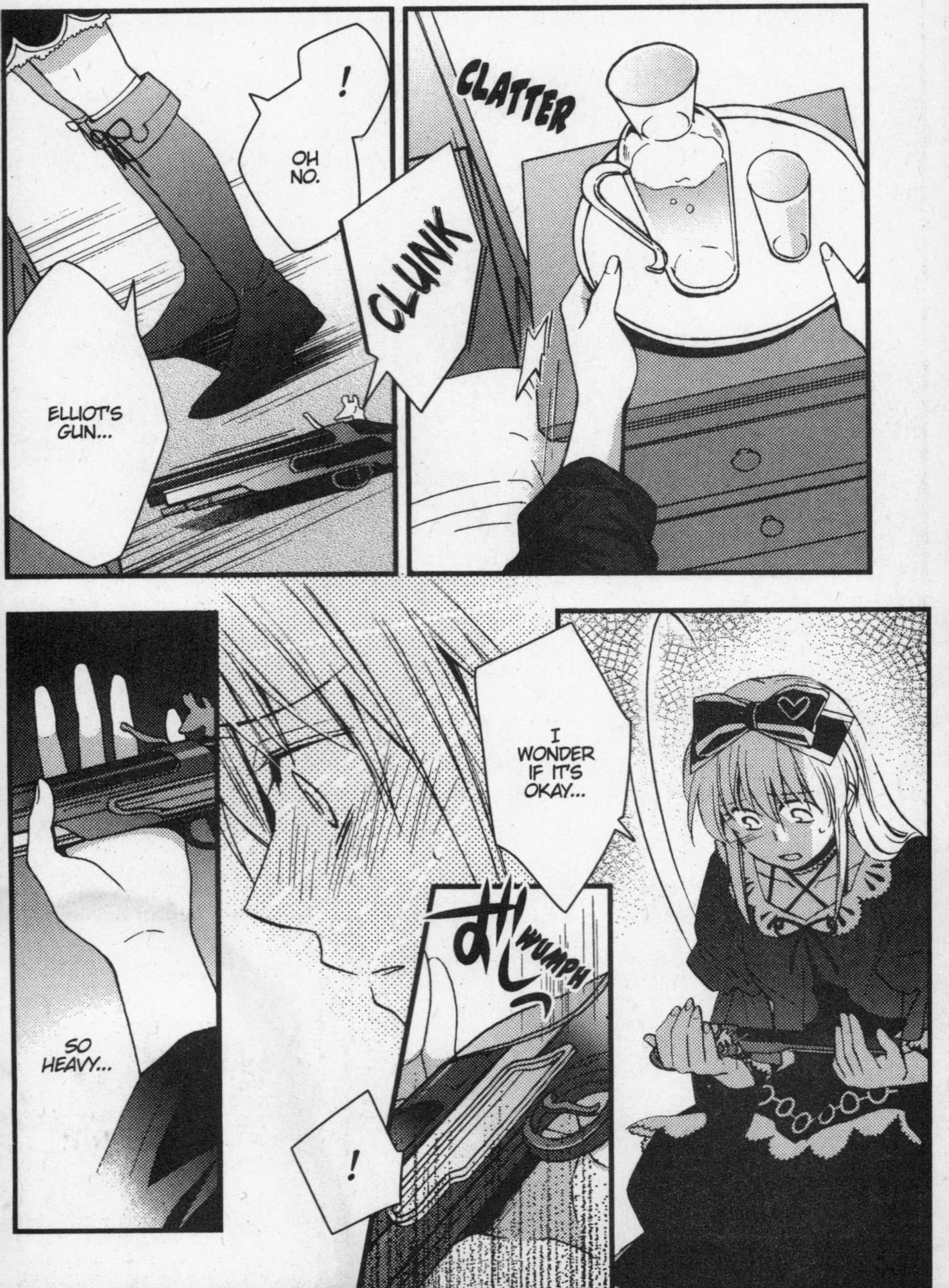
CLATTER
CLUNK
!
OH NO.
ELLIOT'S GUN...
I WONDER IF IT'S OKAY...
WUMPH
!
SO HEAVY...

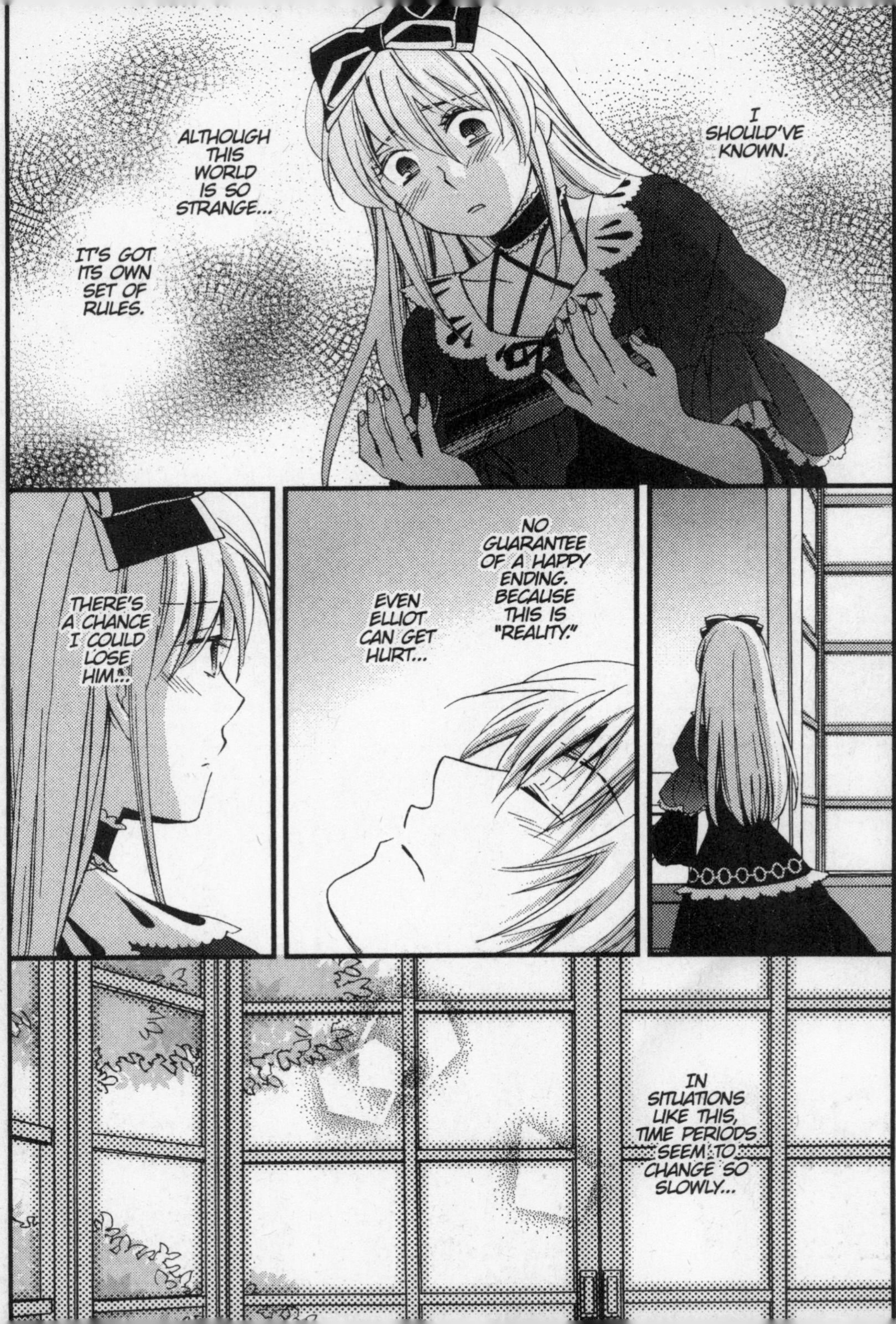
I SHOULD'VE KNOWN.
ALTHOUGH THIS WORLD IS SO STRANGE...
IT'S GOT ITS OWN SET OF RULES.
NO GUARANTEE OF A HAPPY ENDING. BECAUSE THIS IS "REALITY."
EVEN ELLIOT CAN GET HURT...
THERE'S A CHANCE I COULD LOSE HIM...
IN SITUATIONS LIKE THIS, TIME PERIODS SEEM TO CHANGE SO SLOWLY...

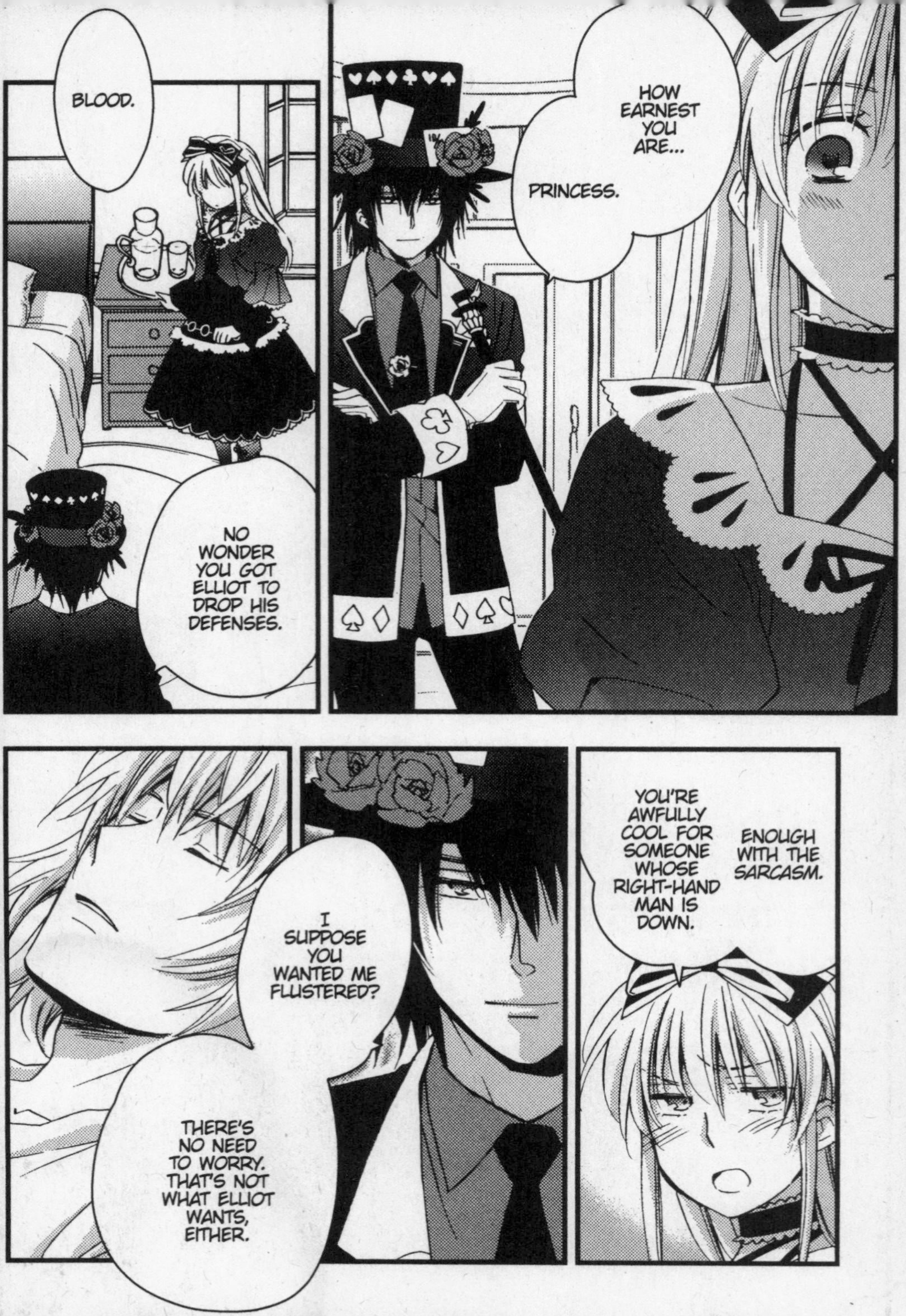
HOW EARNEST YOU ARE...
PRINCESS.
BLOOD.
NO WONDER YOU GOT ELLIOT TO DROP HIS DEFENSES.
ENOUGH WITH THE SARCASM.
YOU'RE AWFULLY COOL FOR SOMEONE WHOSE RIGHT-HAND MAN IS DOWN.
I SUPPOSE YOU WANTED ME FLUSTERED?
THERE'S NO NEED TO WORRY. THAT'S NOT WHAT ELLIOT WANTS, EITHER.

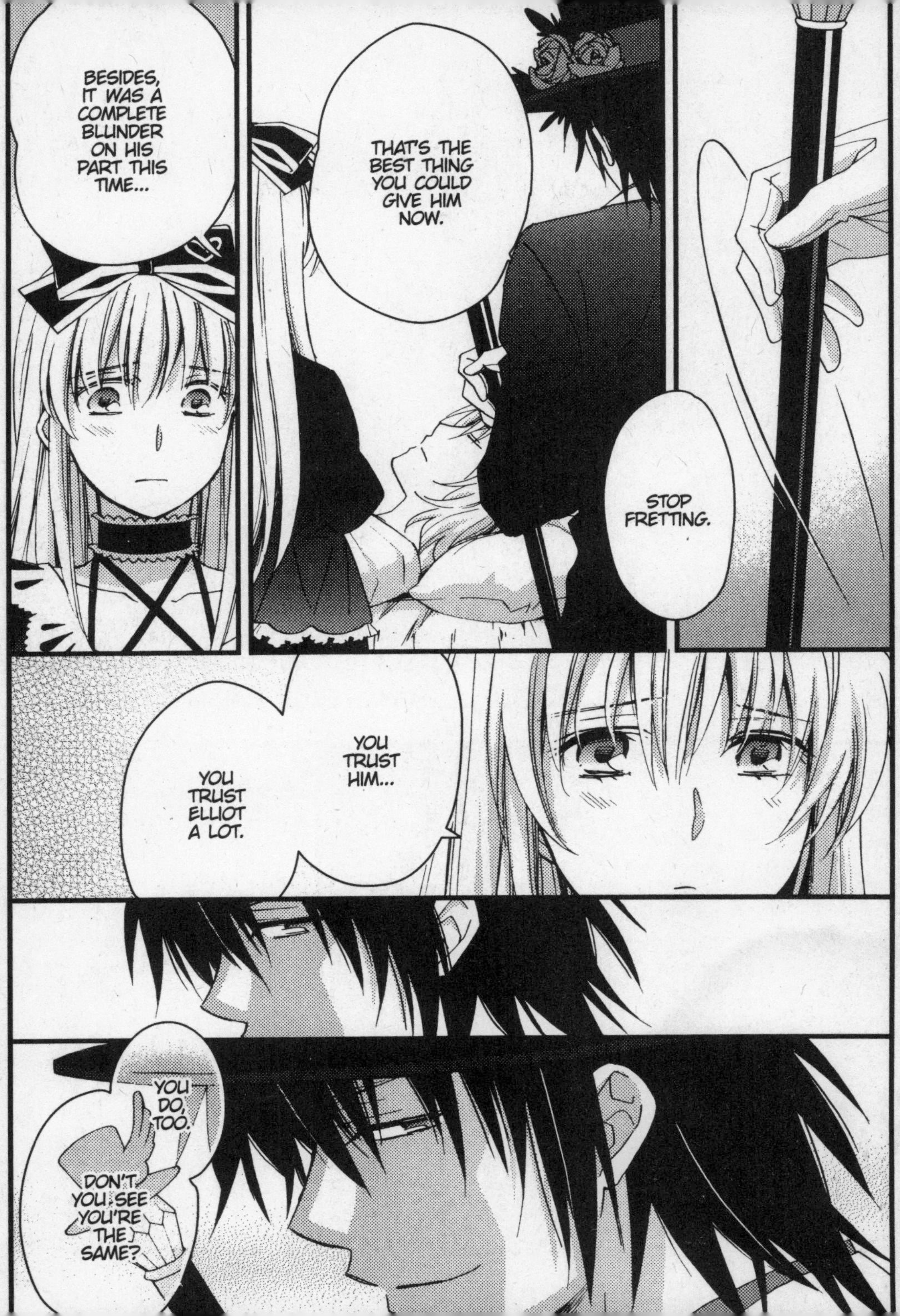
STOP FRETTING.
THAT'S THE BEST THING YOU COULD GIVE HIM NOW.
BESIDES, IT WAS A COMPLETE BLUNDER ON HIS PART THIS TIME...
YOU TRUST HIM...
YOU TRUST ELLIOT A LOT.
YOU DO, TOO.
DON'T YOU SEE YOU'RE THE SAME?

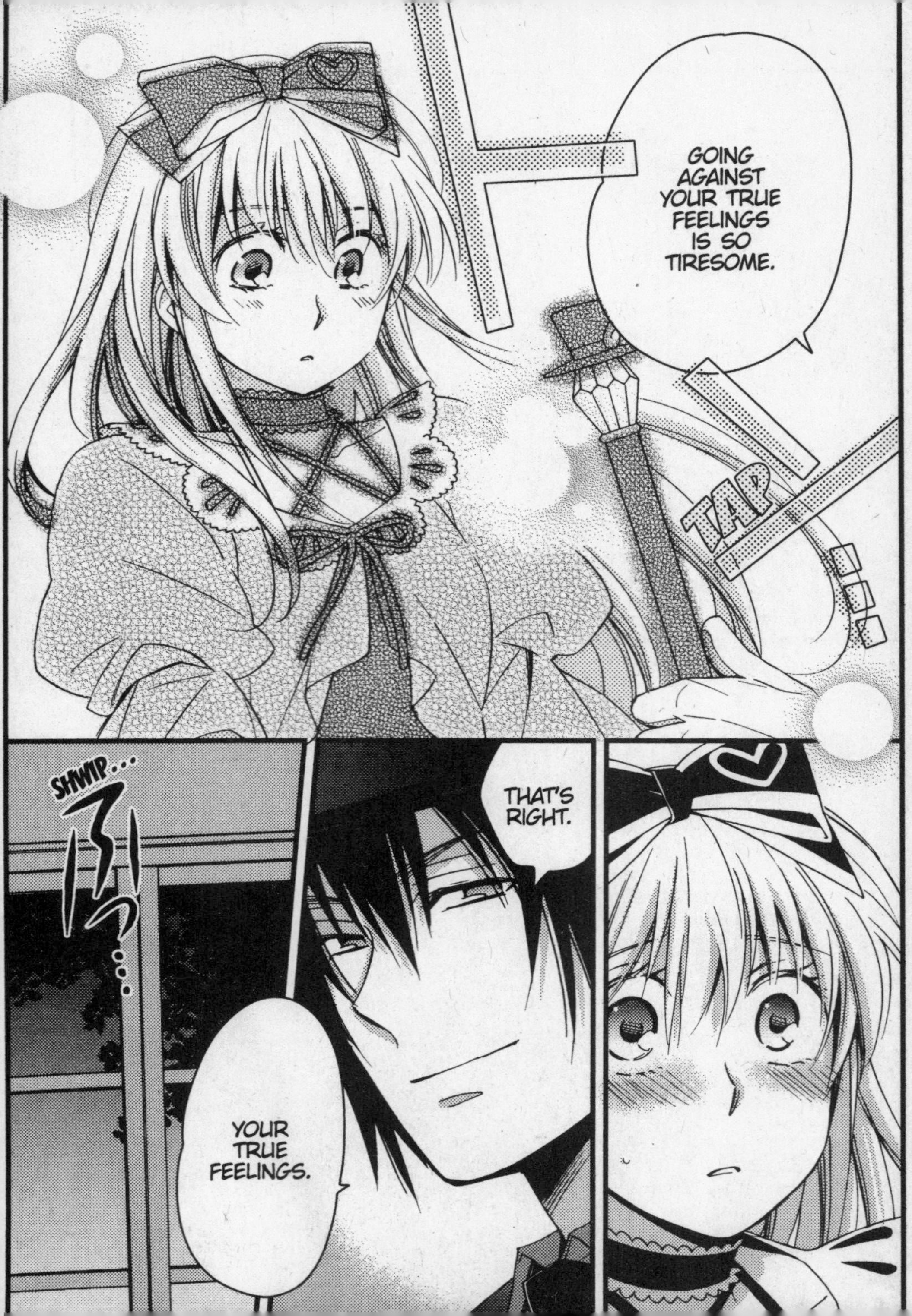
GOING AGAINST YOUR TRUE FEELINGS IS SO TIRESOME.
TAP
...
THAT'S RIGHT.
YOUR TRUE FEELINGS.
SHWIP...

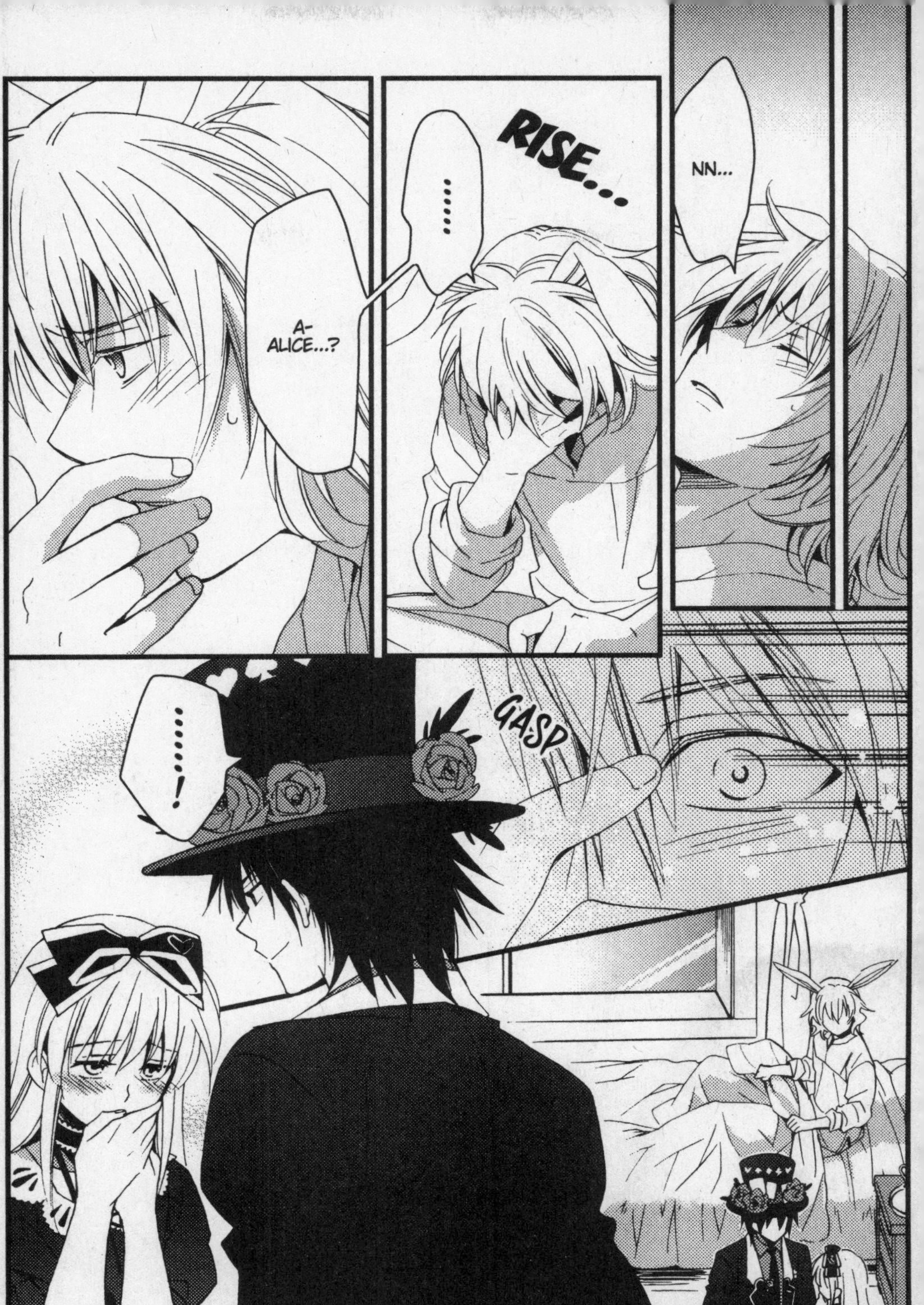
NN...
RISE...
......
A-
ALICE...?
GASP
......!

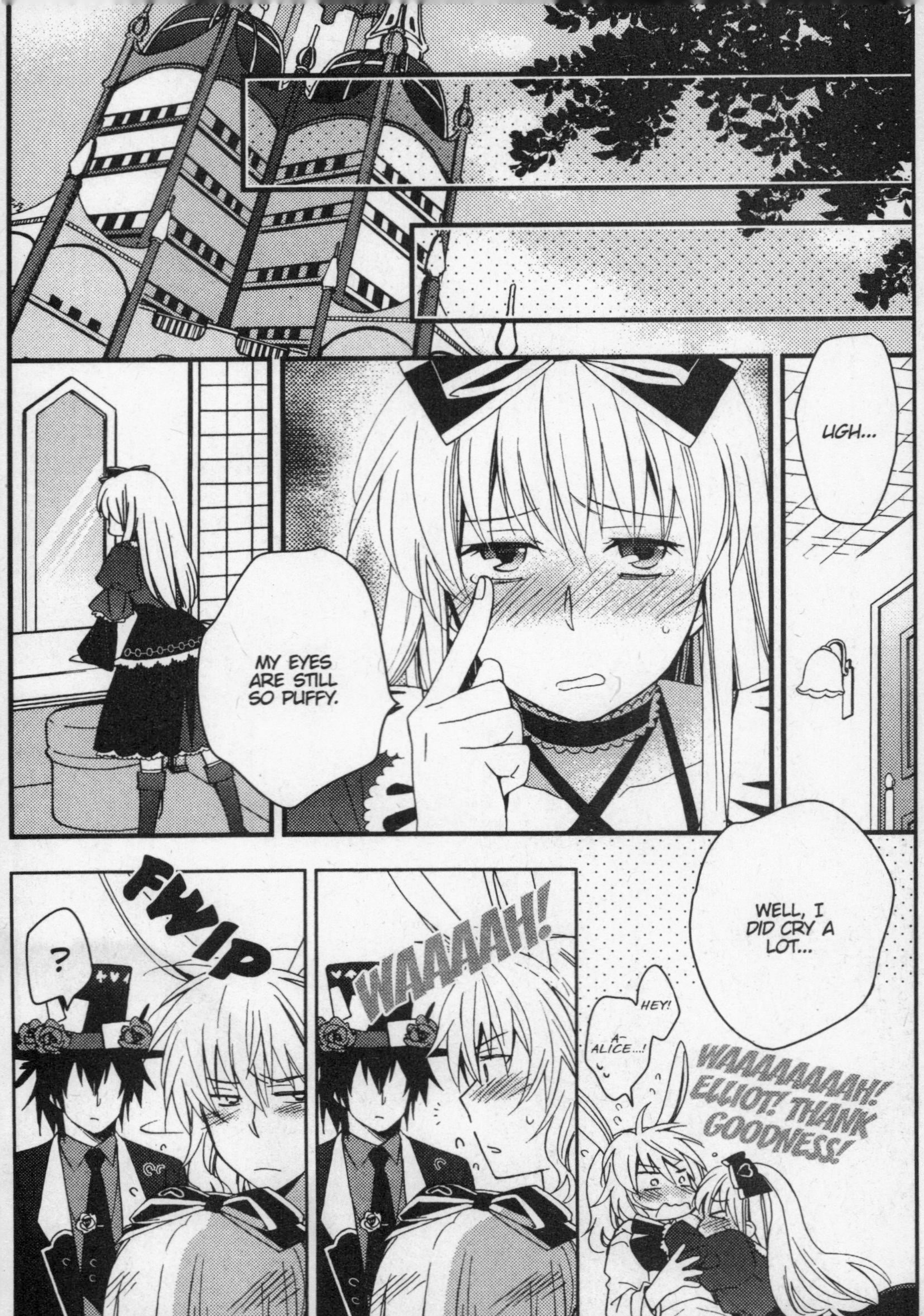
UGH...
MY EYES ARE STILL SO PUFFY.
WELL, I DID CRY A LOT...
WAAAAAAAAH! ELLIOT! THANK GOODNESS!
HEY!
A-ALICE...!
WAAAAAH!
FWIP
?

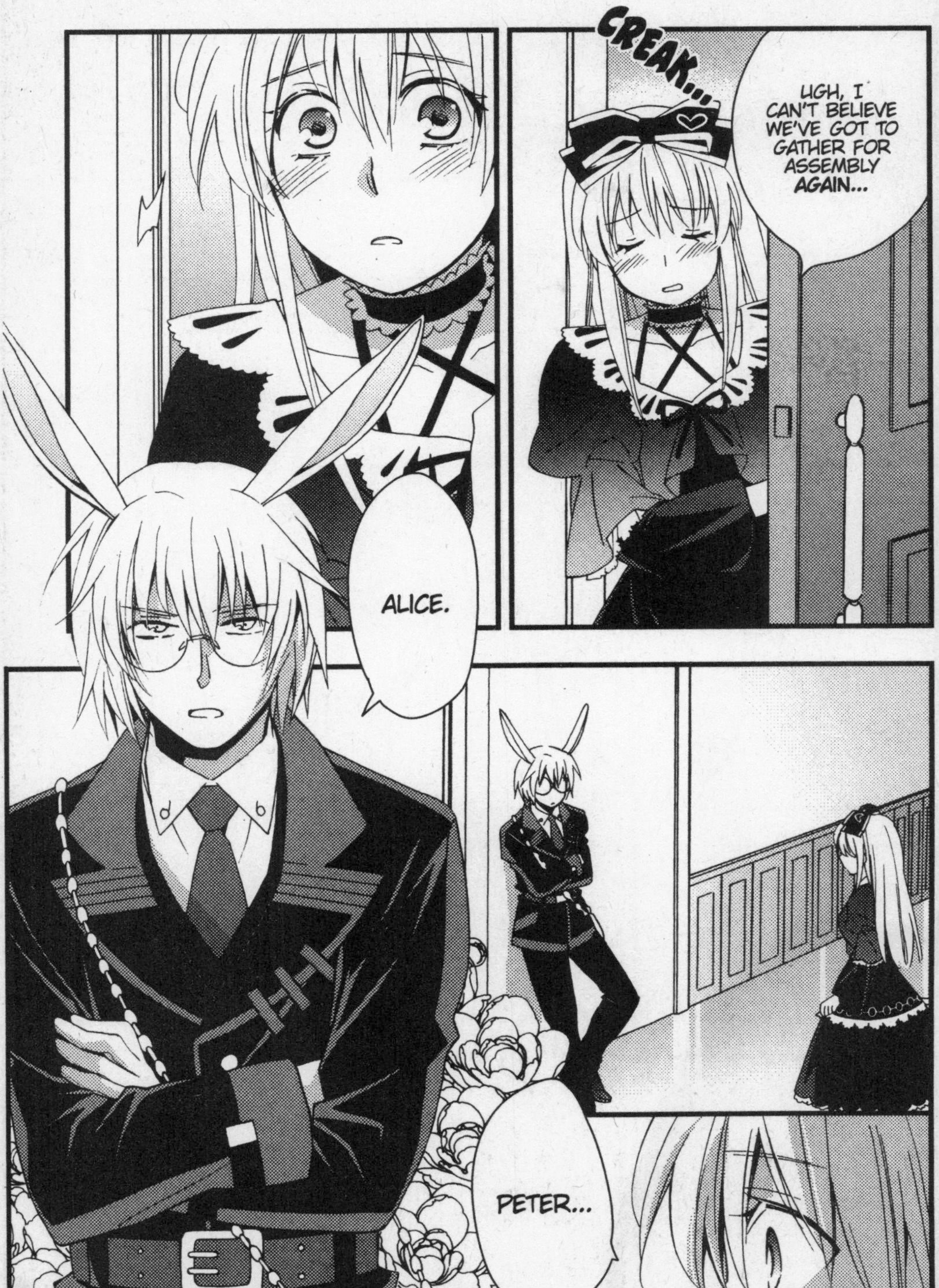
CREAK...
UGH, I CAN'T BELIEVE WE'VE GOT TO GATHER FOR ASSEMBLY AGAIN...
ALICE.
PETER...

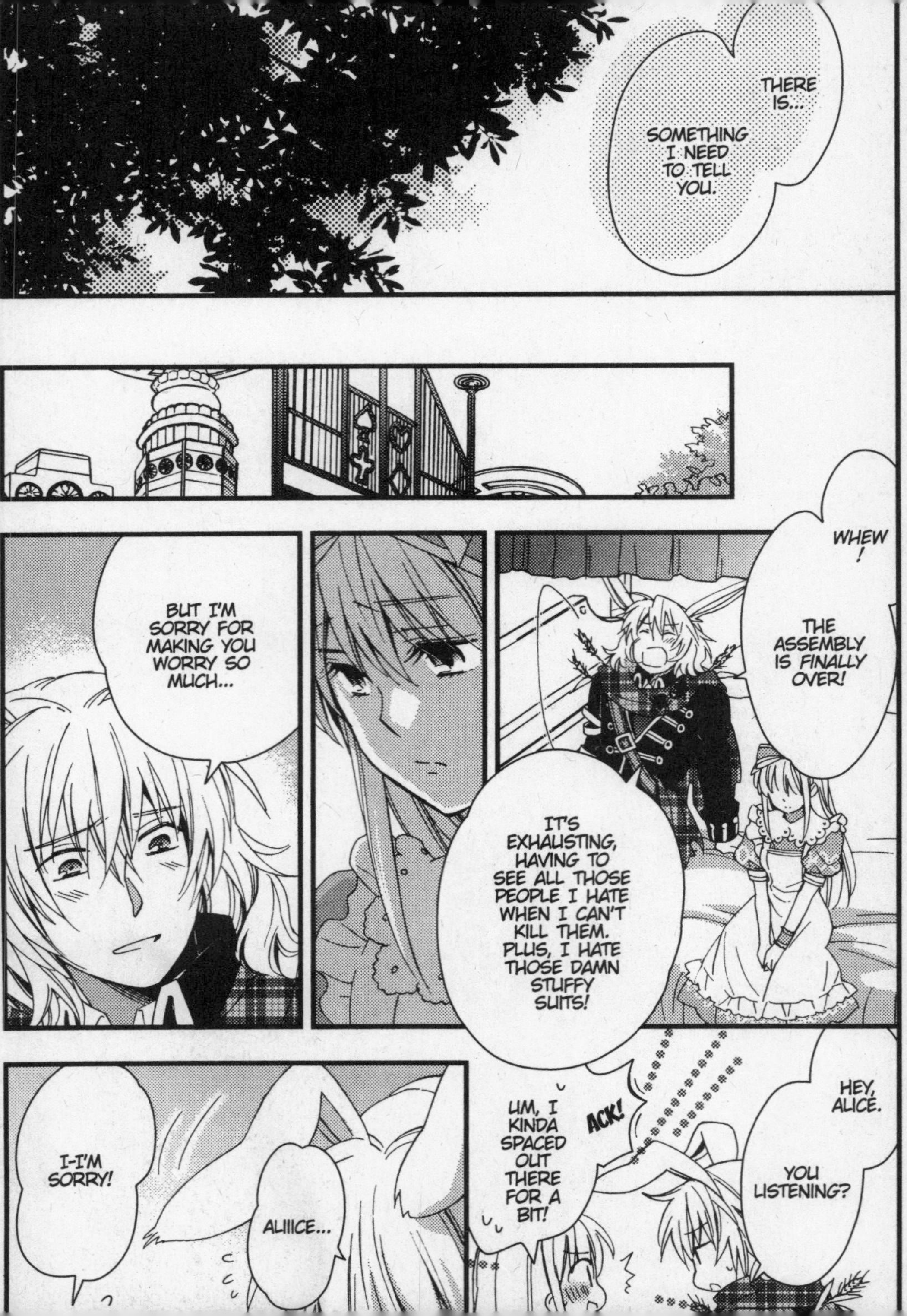
THERE IS... SOMETHING I NEED TO TELL YOU.
WHEW! THE ASSEMBLY IS FINALLY OVER!
IT'S EXHAUSTING, HAVING TO SEE ALL THOSE PEOPLE I HATE WHEN I CAN'T KILL THEM. PLUS, I HATE THOSE DAMN STUFFY SUITS!
BUT I'M SORRY FOR MAKING YOU WORRY SO MUCH...
HEY, ALICE. YOU LISTENING?
ACK!
UM, I KINDA SPACED OUT THERE FOR A BIT!
ALIIICE...
I-I'M SORRY!

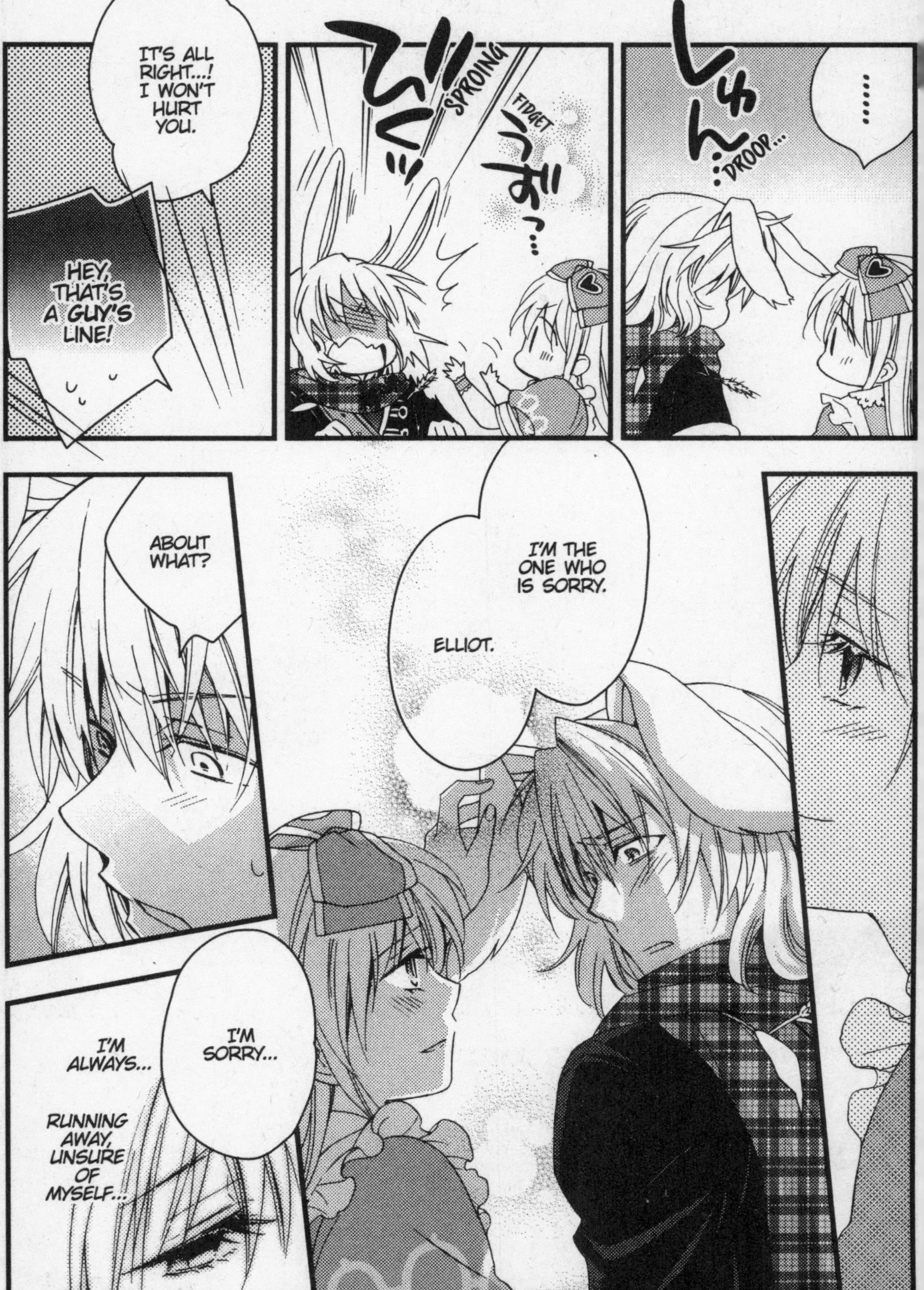

しゅん…
DROOP...
……
びくっ
SPROING
うずっ…
FIDGET
IT'S ALL RIGHT...! I WON'T HURT YOU.
HEY, THAT'S A GUY'S LINE!
I'M THE ONE WHO IS SORRY.
ELLIOT.
ABOUT WHAT?
I'M SORRY...
I'M ALWAYS...
RUNNING AWAY, UNSURE OF MYSELF...

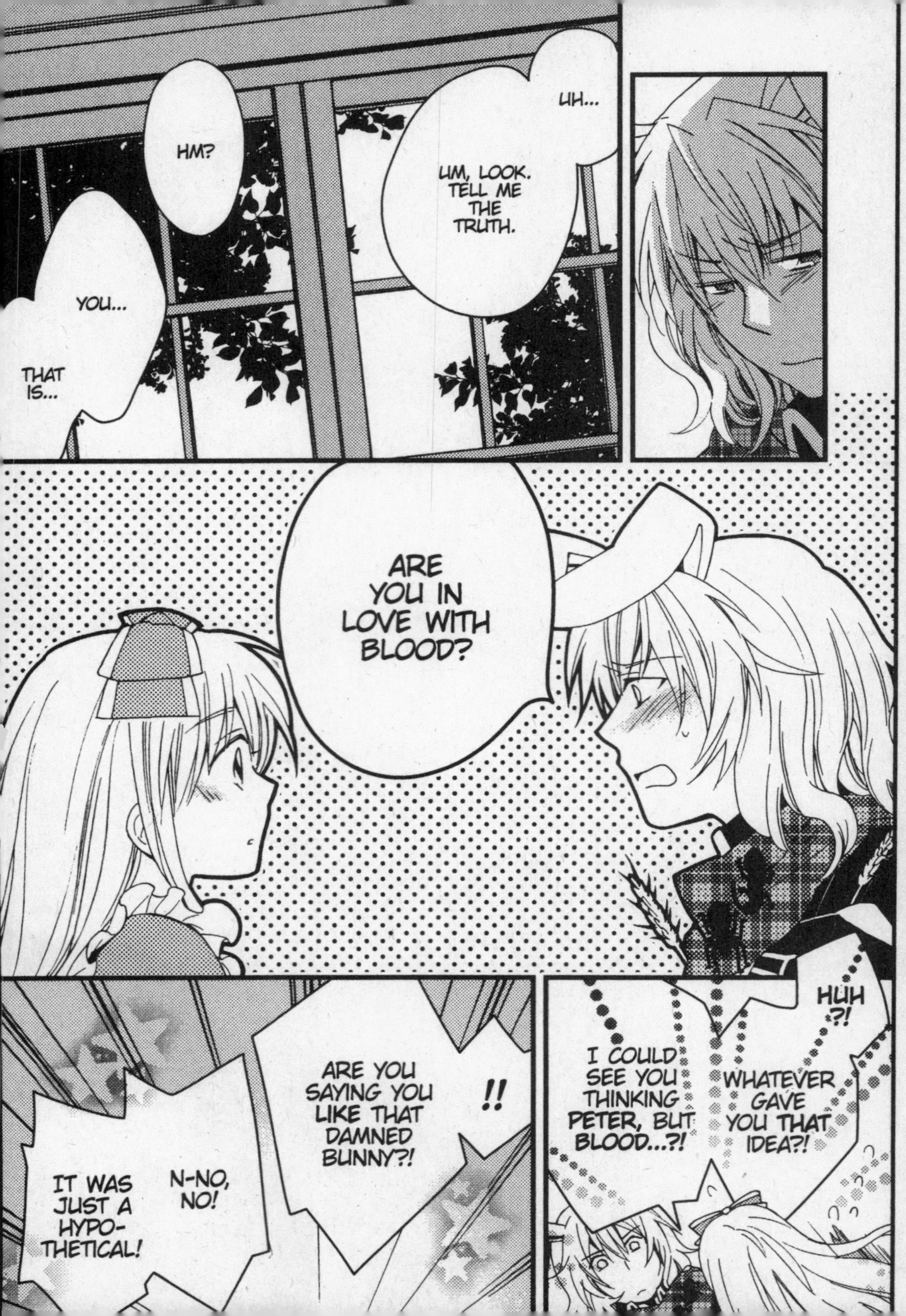
UH...
UM, LOOK. TELL ME THE TRUTH.
HM?
YOU...
THAT IS...
ARE YOU IN LOVE WITH BLOOD?
HUH?!
WHATEVER GAVE YOU THAT IDEA?!
I COULD SEE YOU THINKING PETER, BUT BLOOD...?!
!!
ARE YOU SAYING YOU LIKE THAT DAMNED BUNNY?!
N-NO, NO!
IT WAS JUST A HYPOTHETICAL!

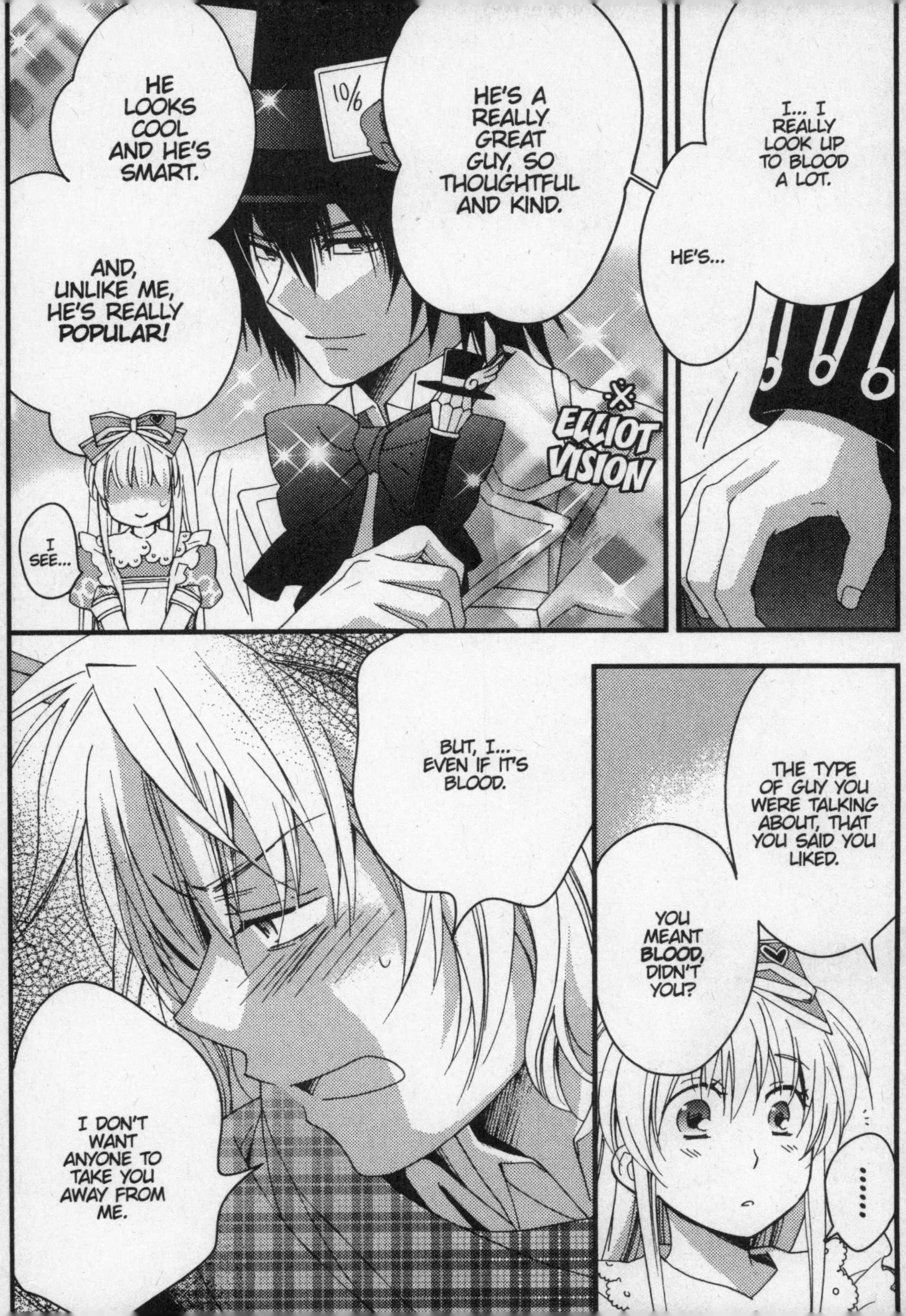
I... I REALLY LOOK UP TO BLOOD A LOT.
HE'S...
HE'S A REALLY GREAT GUY, SO THOUGHTFUL AND KIND.
HE LOOKS COOL AND HE'S SMART.
ELLIOT VISION
AND, UNLIKE ME, HE'S REALLY POPULAR!
I SEE...
THE TYPE OF GUY YOU WERE TALKING ABOUT, THAT YOU SAID YOU LIKED.
YOU MEANT BLOOD, DIDN'T YOU?
......
BUT, I... EVEN IF IT'S BLOOD.
I DON'T WANT ANYONE TO TAKE YOU AWAY FROM ME.

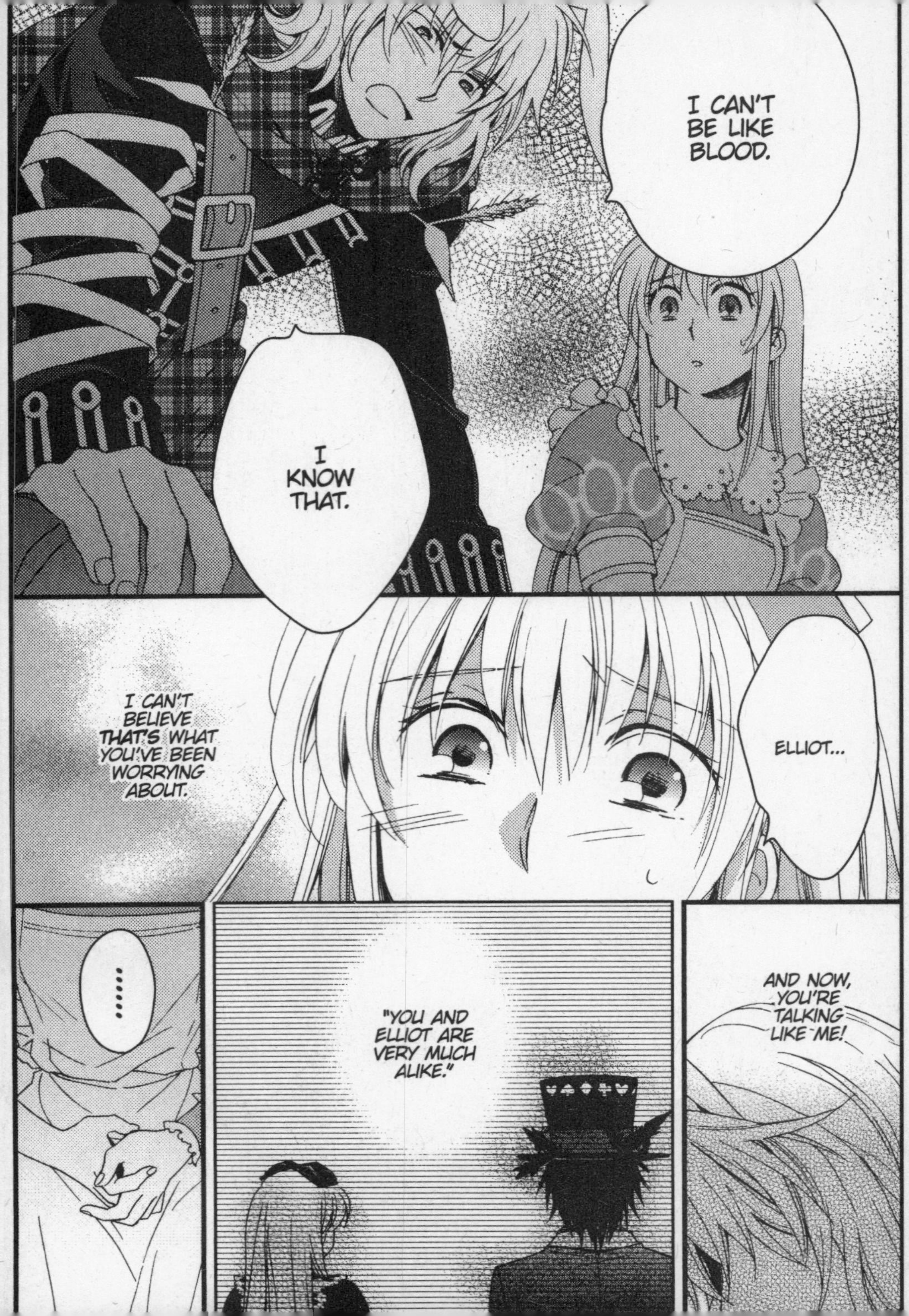
I CAN'T BE LIKE BLOOD.
I KNOW THAT.
ELLIOT...
I CAN'T BELIEVE THAT'S WHAT YOU'VE BEEN WORRYING ABOUT.
AND NOW, YOU'RE TALKING LIKE ME!
"YOU AND ELLIOT ARE VERY MUCH ALIKE."
......

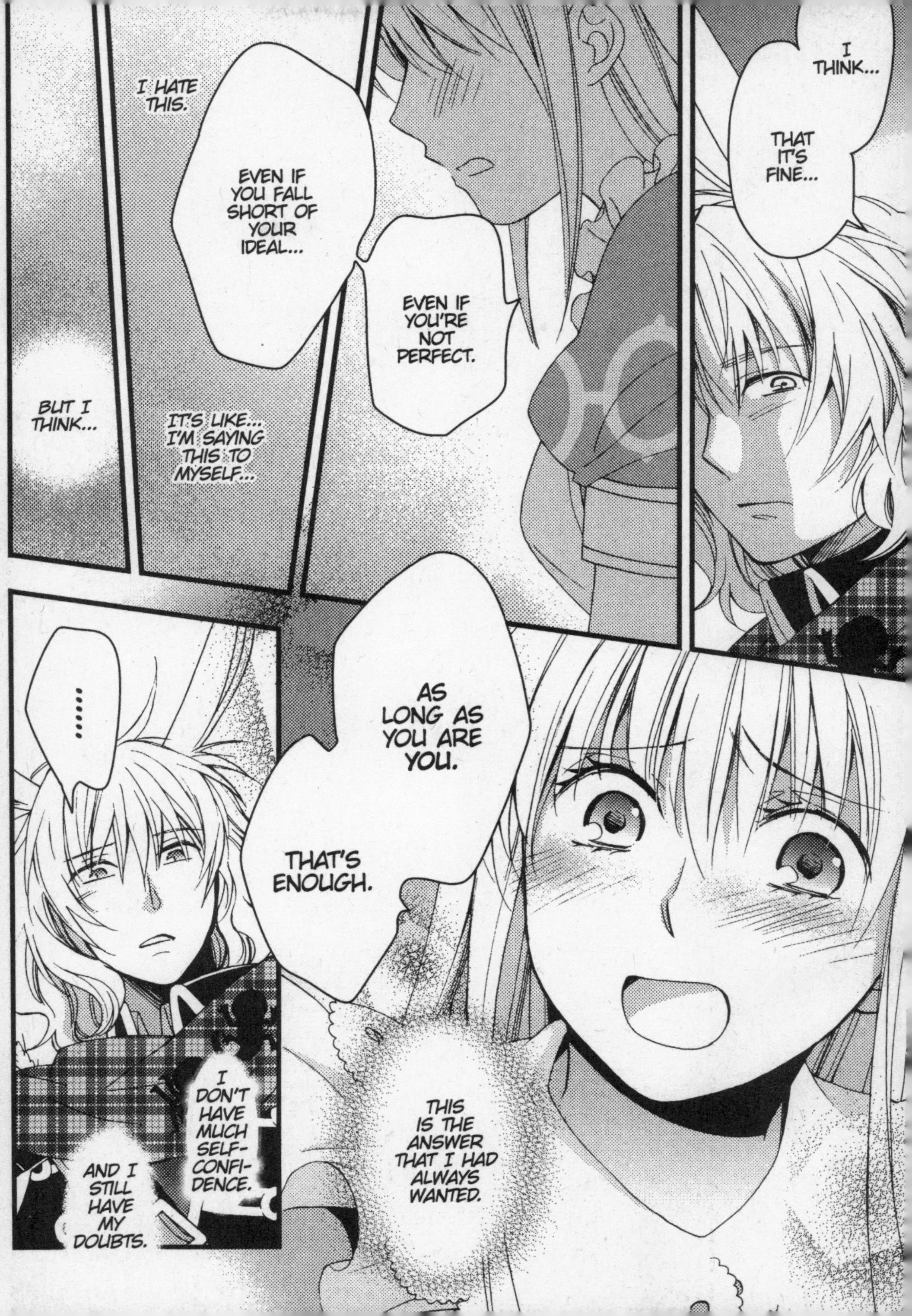
I THINK...
THAT IT'S FINE...
EVEN IF YOU FALL SHORT OF YOUR IDEAL...
EVEN IF YOU'RE NOT PERFECT.
I HATE THIS.
IT'S LIKE... I'M SAYING THIS TO MYSELF...
BUT I THINK...
AS LONG AS YOU ARE YOU.
THAT'S ENOUGH.
THIS IS THE ANSWER THAT I HAD ALWAYS WANTED.
I DON'T HAVE MUCH SELF-CONFIDENCE.
AND I STILL HAVE MY DOUBTS.
......

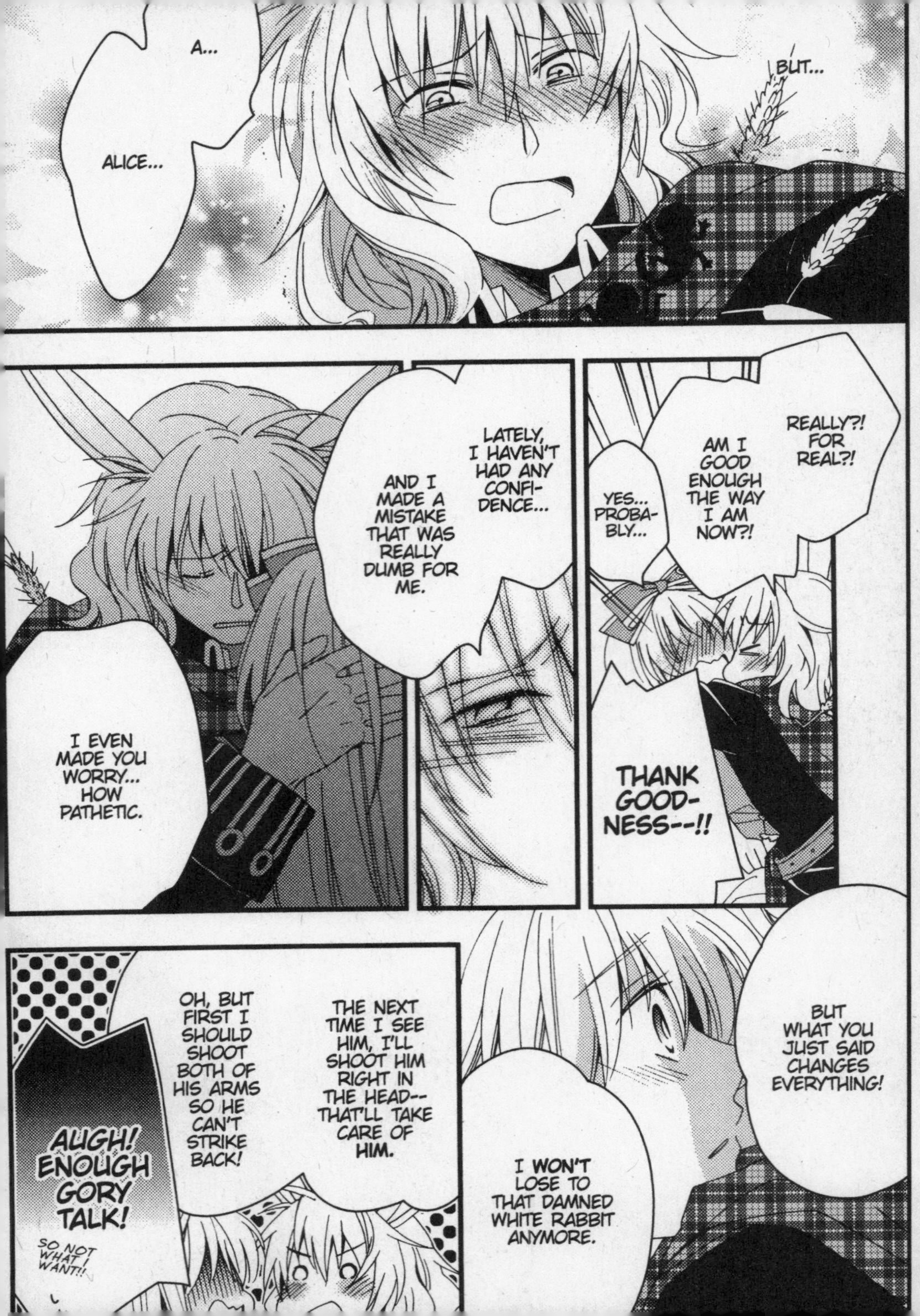
BUT...
A...
ALICE...
REALLY?! FOR REAL?!
AM I GOOD ENOUGH THE WAY I AM NOW?!
YES... PROBABLY...
THANK GOODNESS--!!
LATELY, I HAVEN'T HAD ANY CONFIDENCE...
AND I MADE A MISTAKE THAT WAS REALLY DUMB FOR ME.
I EVEN MADE YOU WORRY... HOW PATHETIC.
BUT WHAT YOU JUST SAID CHANGES EVERYTHING!
I WON'T LOSE TO THAT DAMNED WHITE RABBIT ANYMORE.
THE NEXT TIME I SEE HIM, I'LL SHOOT HIM RIGHT IN THE HEAD--THAT'LL TAKE CARE OF HIM.
OH, BUT FIRST I SHOULD SHOOT BOTH OF HIS ARMS SO HE CAN'T STRIKE BACK!
AUGH! ENOUGH GORY TALK!
SO NOT WHAT I WANT!!

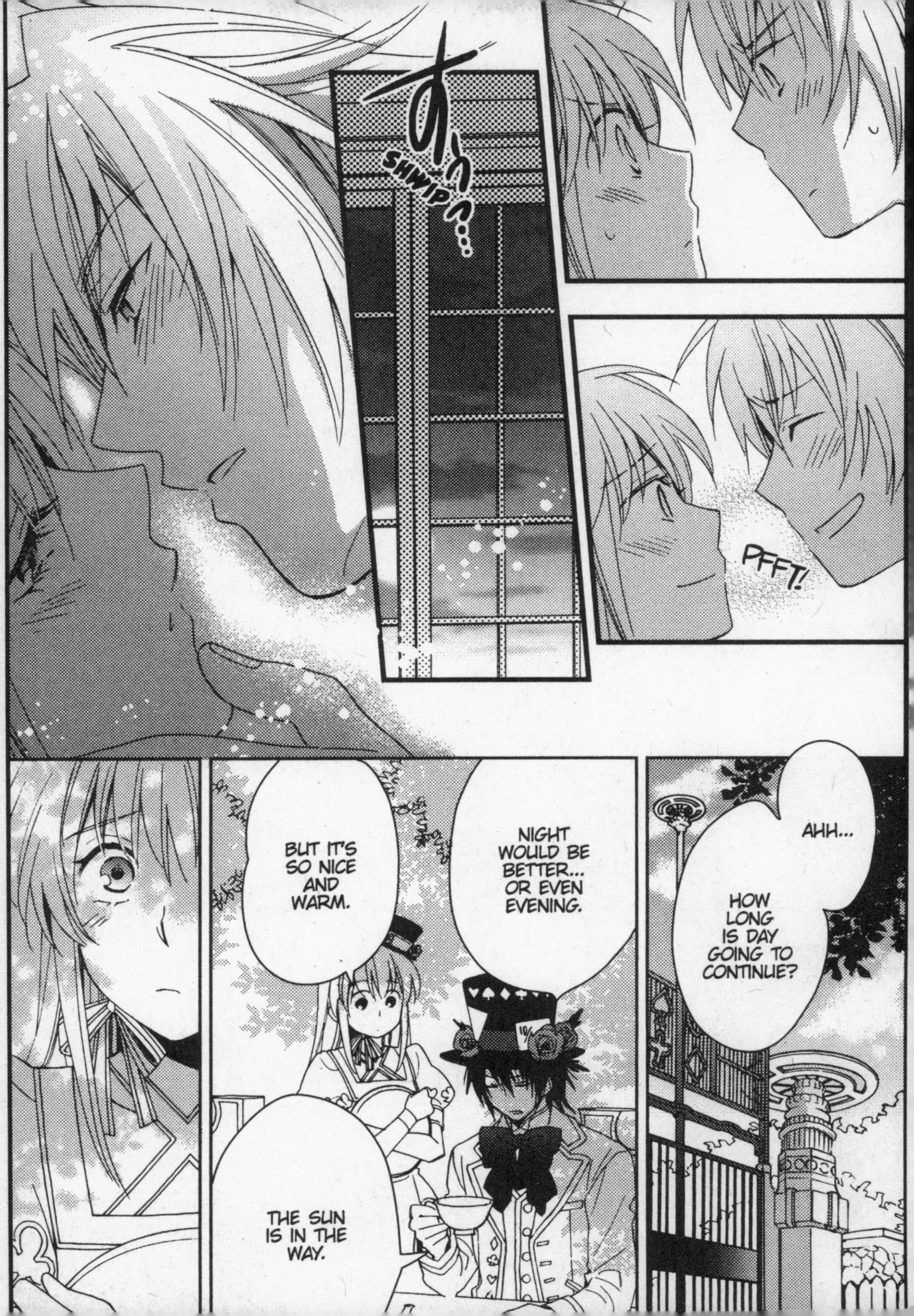
PFFT!
SHWIP...
AHH...
HOW LONG IS DAY GOING TO CONTINUE?
NIGHT WOULD BE BETTER... OR EVEN EVENING.
BUT IT'S SO NICE AND WARM.
THE SUN IS IN THE WAY.

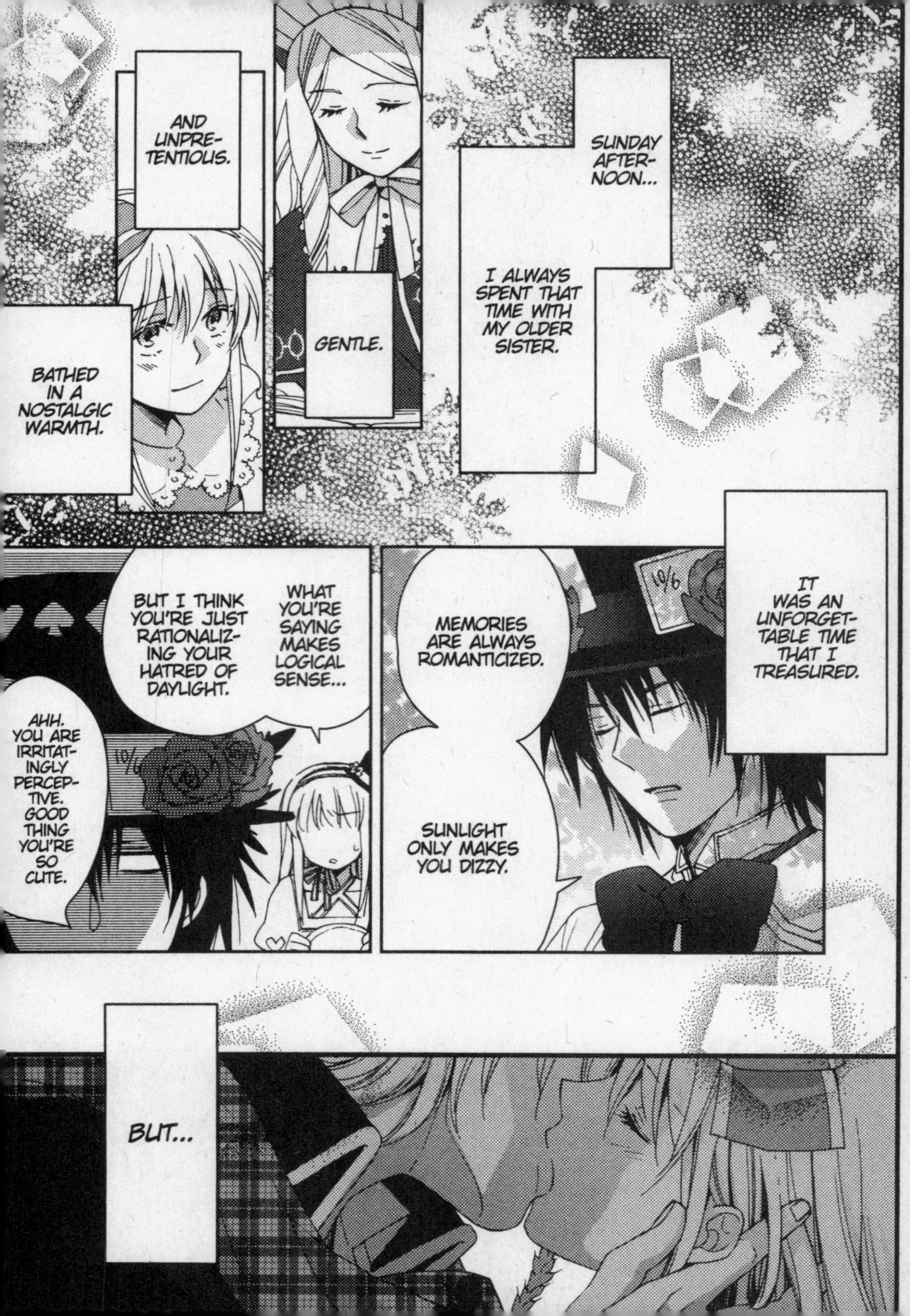
SUNDAY AFTERNOON...
I ALWAYS SPENT THAT TIME WITH MY OLDER SISTER.
GENTLE.
AND UNPRETENTIOUS.
BATHED IN A NOSTALGIC WARMTH.
IT WAS AN UNFORGETTABLE TIME THAT I TREASURED.
MEMORIES ARE ALWAYS ROMANTICIZED.
SUNLIGHT ONLY MAKES YOU DIZZY.
WHAT YOU'RE SAYING MAKES LOGICAL SENSE...
BUT I THINK YOU'RE JUST RATIONALIZING YOUR HATRED OF DAYLIGHT.
AHH. YOU ARE IRRITATINGLY PERCEPTIVE. GOOD THING YOU'RE SO CUTE.
BUT...

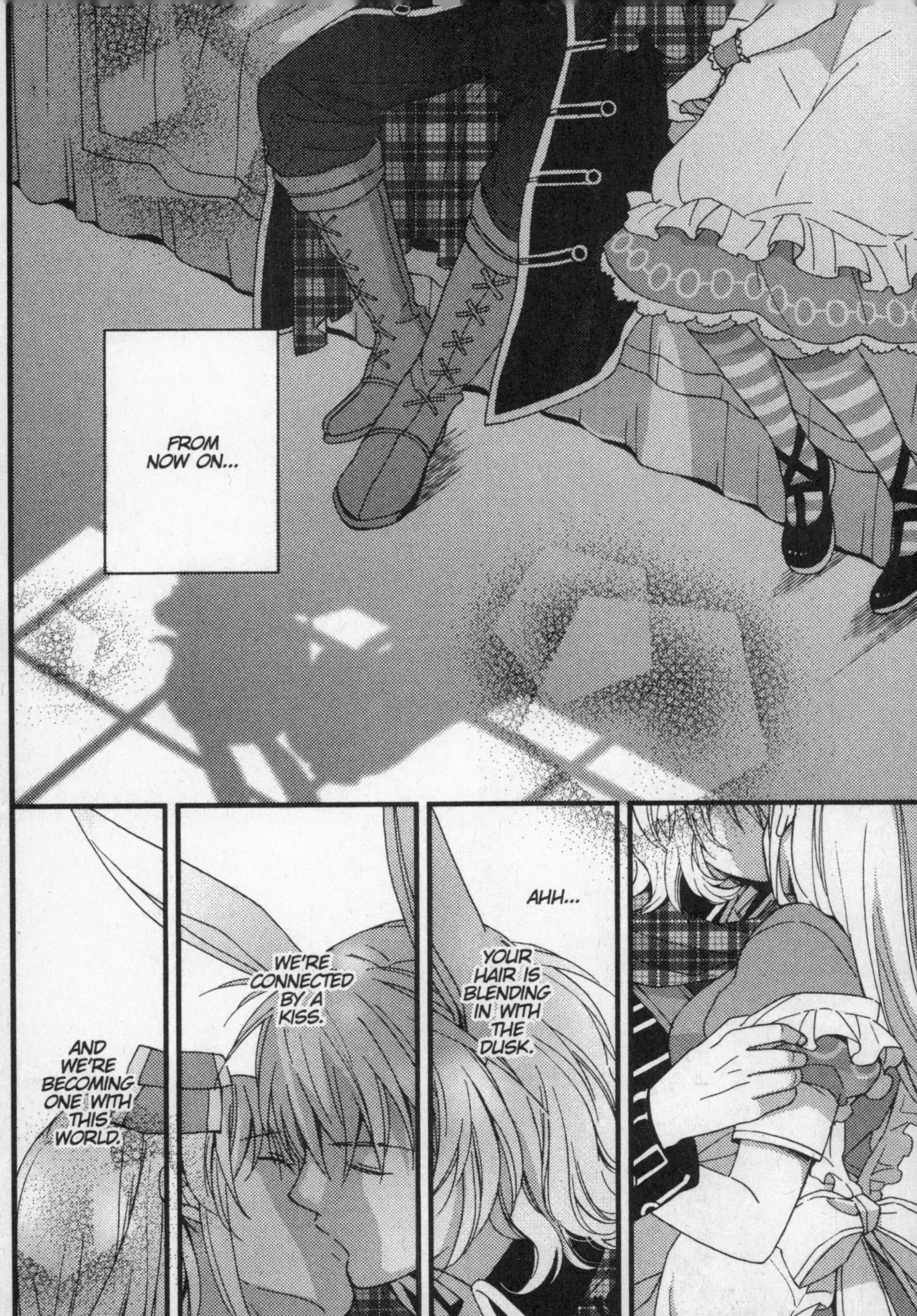
FROM NOW ON...
AHH...
YOUR HAIR IS BLENDING IN WITH THE DUSK.
WE'RE CONNECTED BY A KISS.
AND WE'RE BECOMING ONE WITH THIS WORLD.

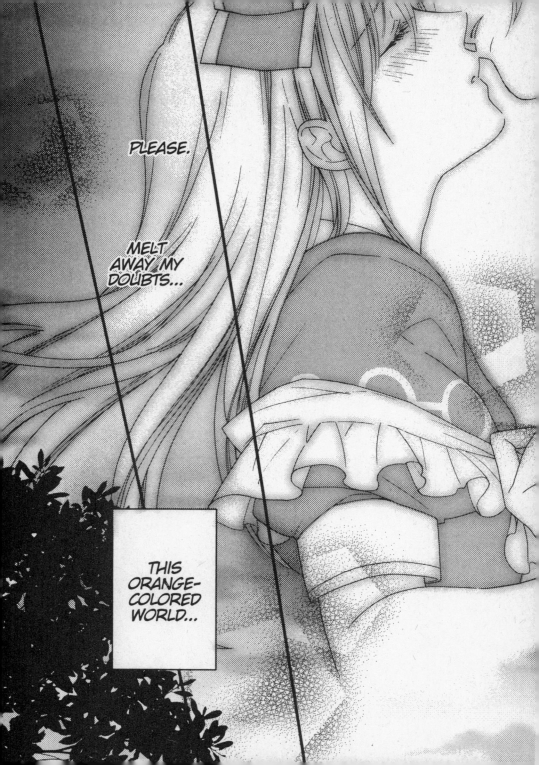

PLEASE.

MELT AWAY MY DOUBTS...

THIS ORANGE-COLORED WORLD...

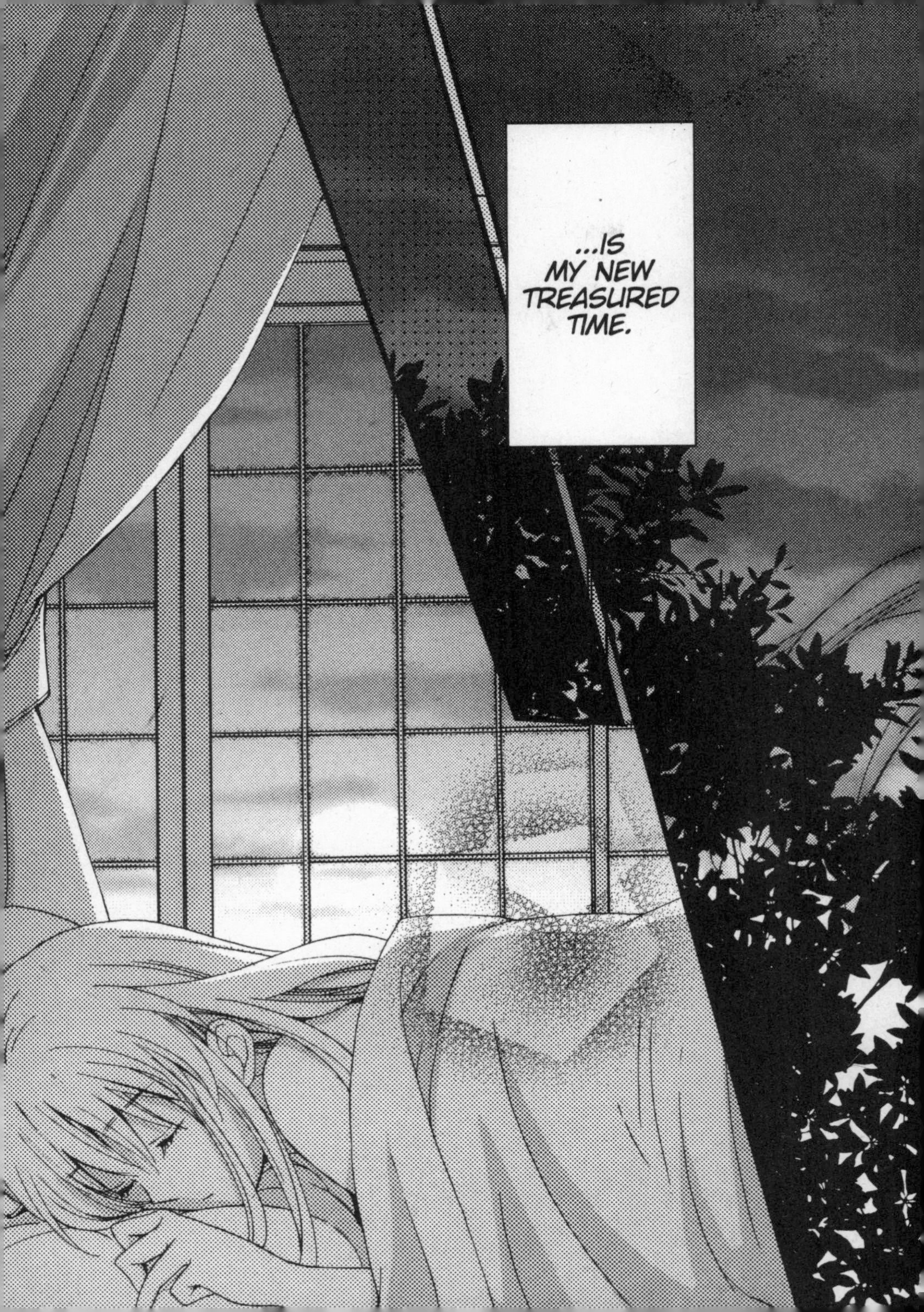
...IS MY NEW TREASURED TIME.

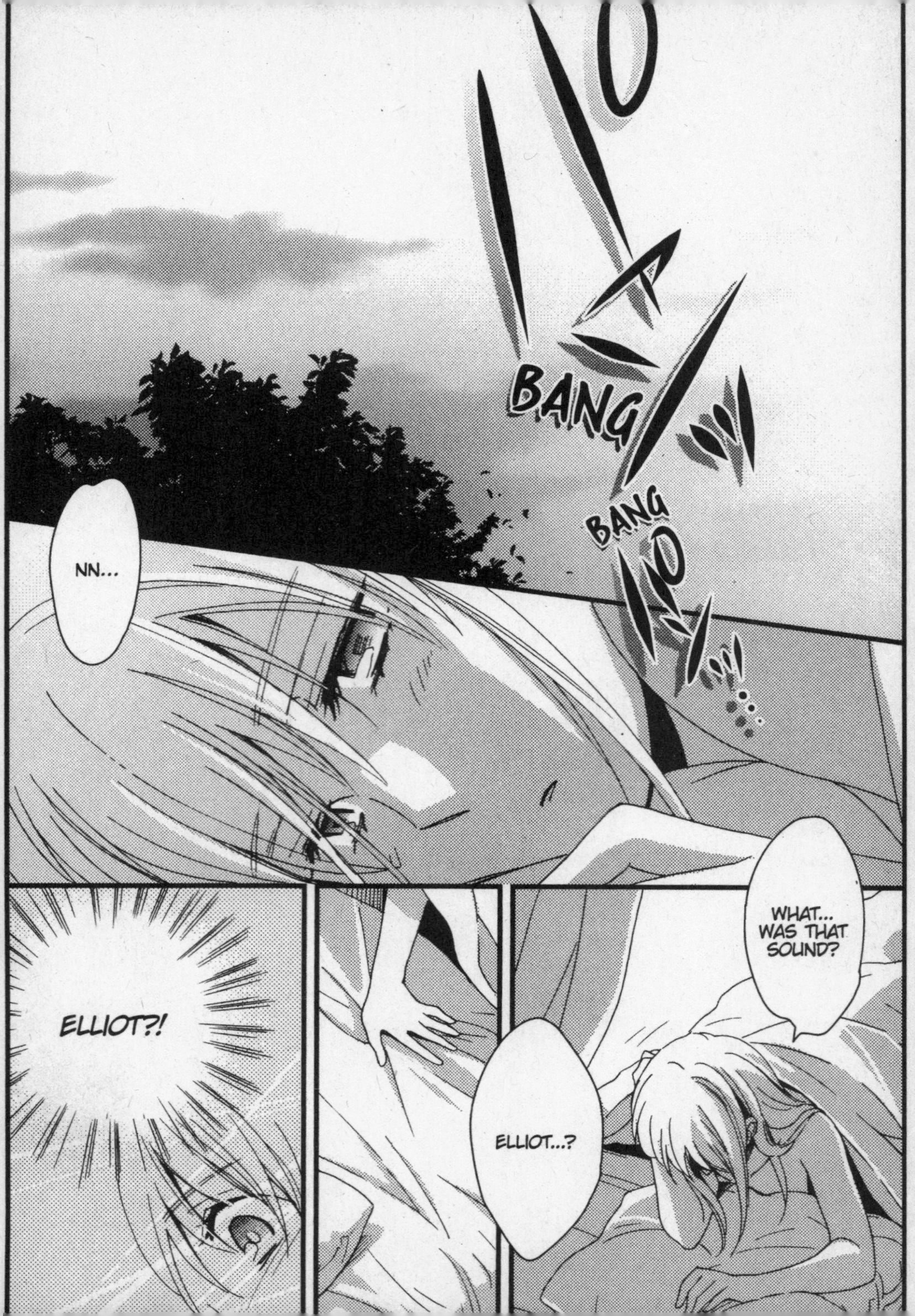
BANG
BANG
NN...
WHAT... WAS THAT SOUND?
ELLIOT...?
ELLIOT?!

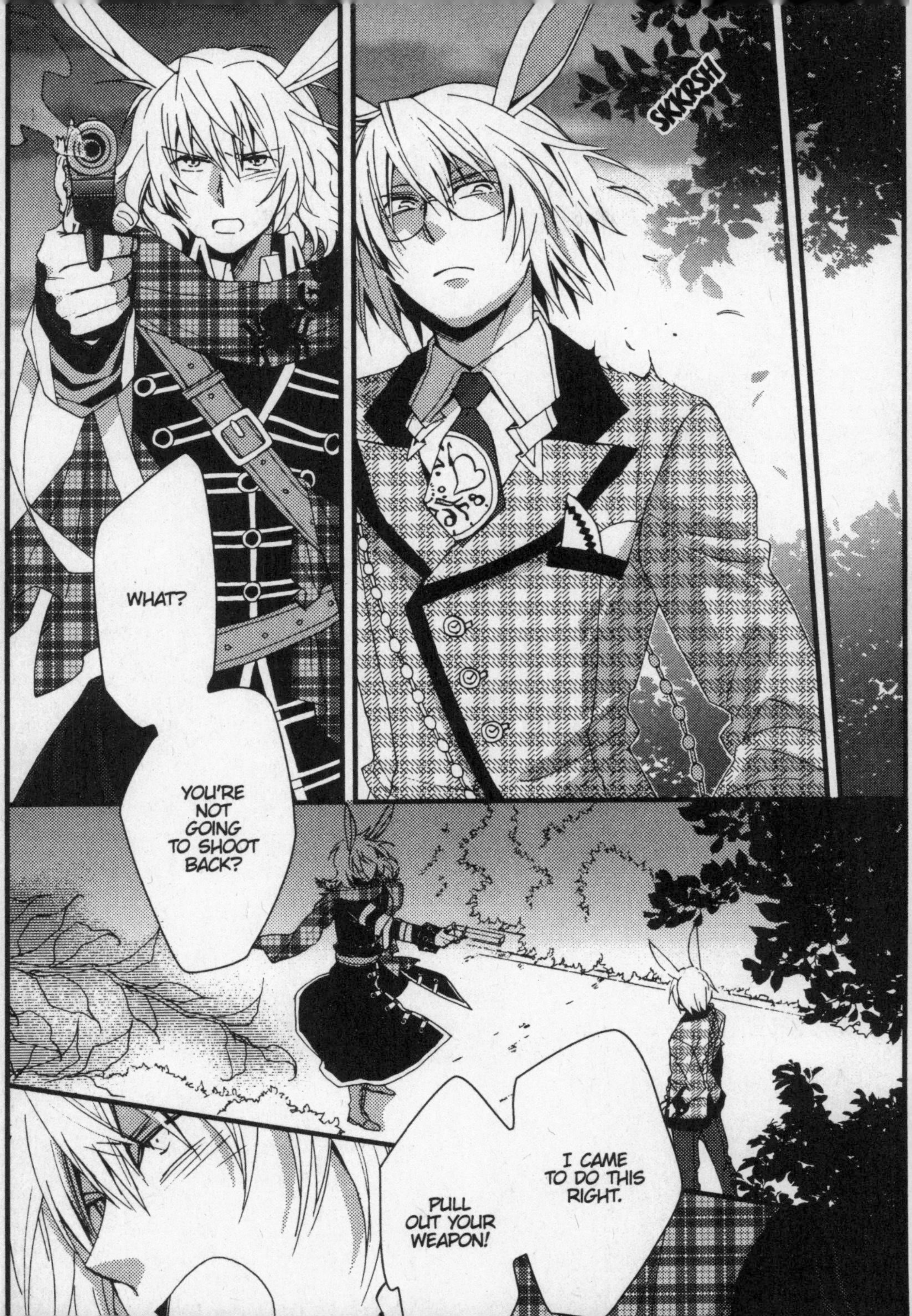
SKKRSH
WHAT?
YOU'RE NOT GOING TO SHOOT BACK?
I CAME TO DO THIS RIGHT.
PULL OUT YOUR WEAPON!

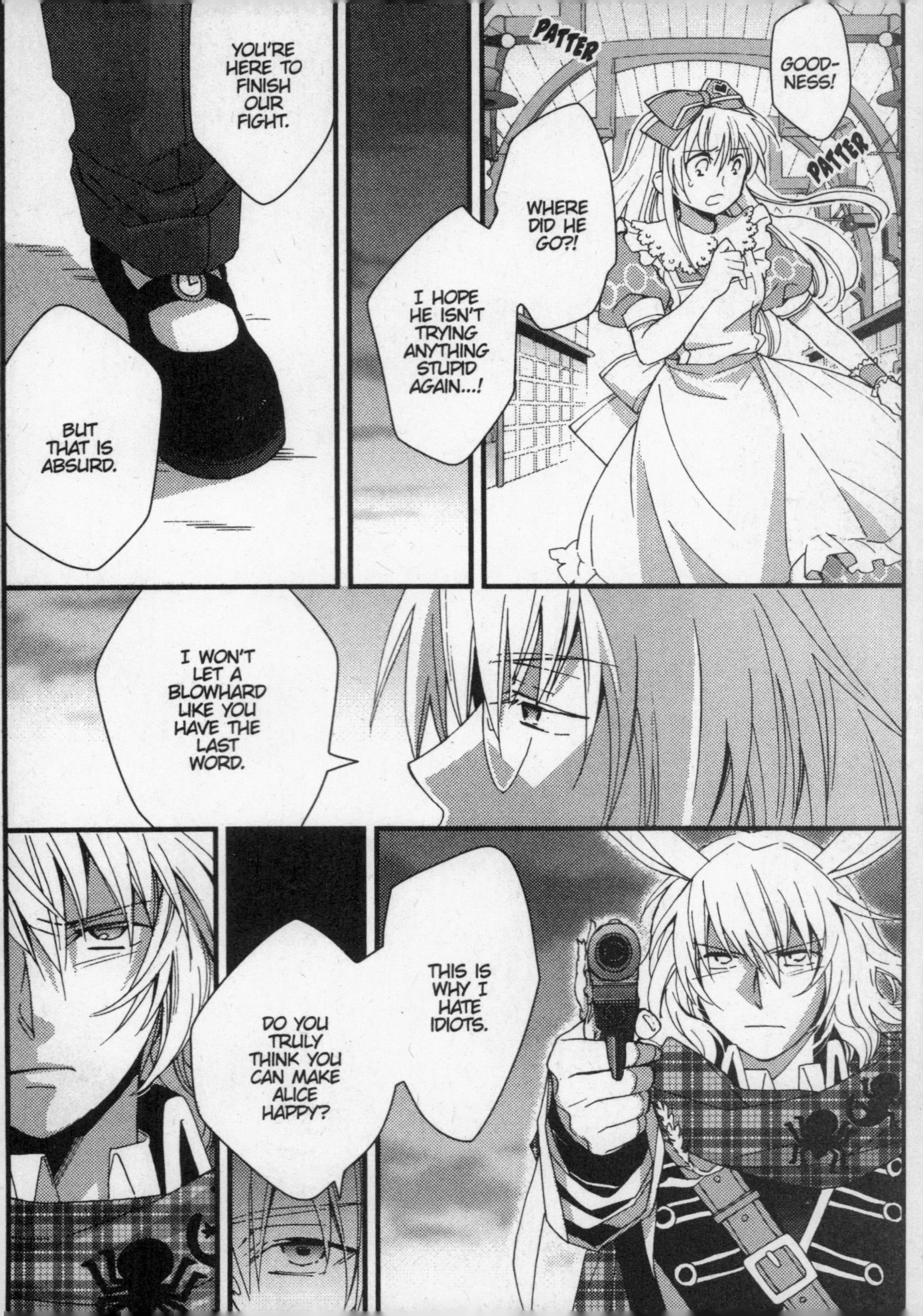
PATTER
GOODNESS!
PATTER
WHERE DID HE GO?!
I HOPE HE ISN'T TRYING ANYTHING STUPID AGAIN...!
YOU'RE HERE TO FINISH OUR FIGHT.
BUT THAT IS ABSURD.
I WON'T LET A BLOWHARD LIKE YOU HAVE THE LAST WORD.
THIS IS WHY I HATE IDIOTS.
DO YOU TRULY THINK YOU CAN MAKE ALICE HAPPY?

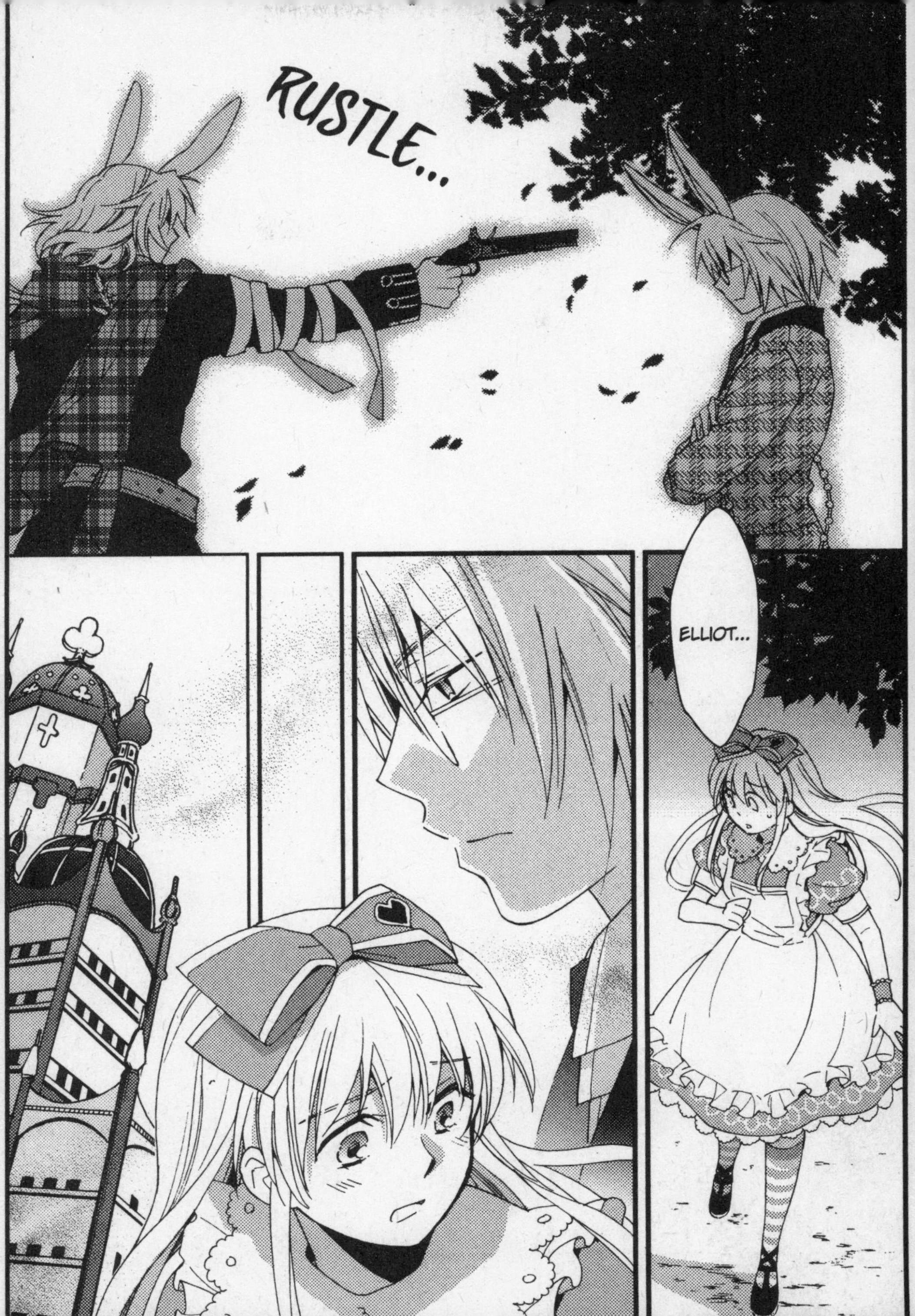
RUSTLE...
ELLIOT...

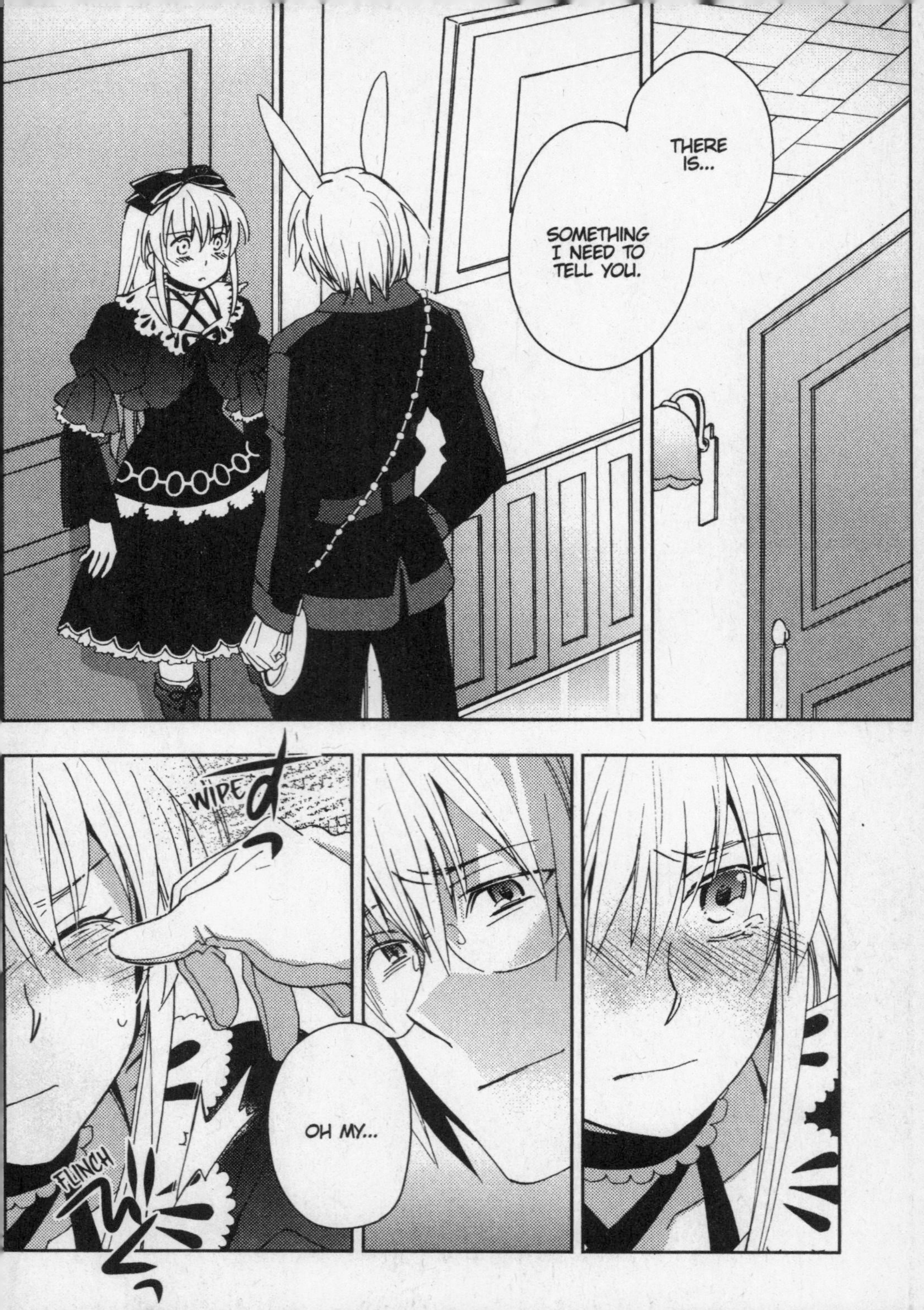
THERE IS...
SOMETHING I NEED TO TELL YOU.
OH MY...
WIPE
FLINCH

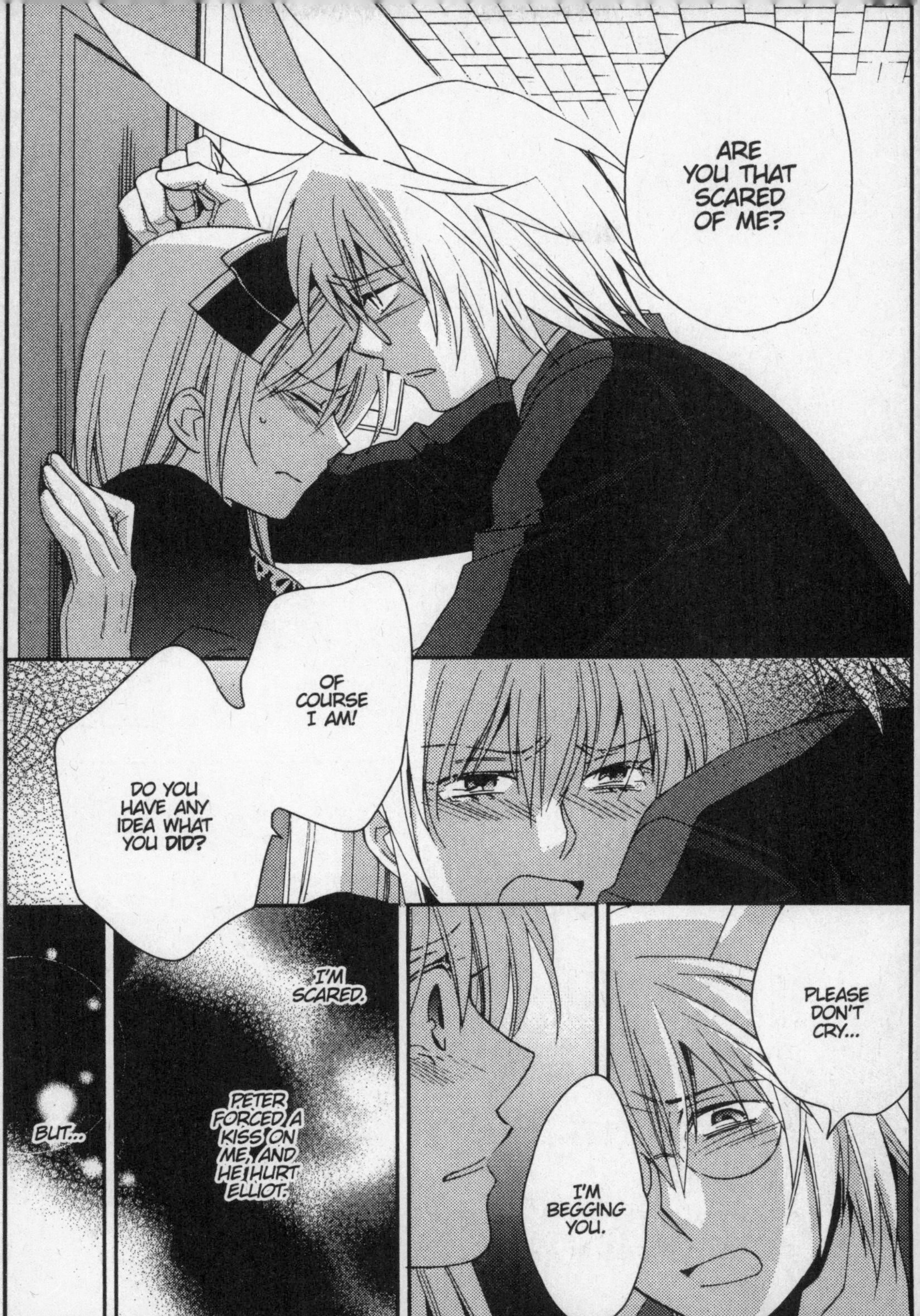
ARE YOU THAT SCARED OF ME?
OF COURSE I AM!
DO YOU HAVE ANY IDEA WHAT YOU DID?
PLEASE DON'T CRY...
I'M BEGGING YOU.
I'M SCARED.
PETER FORCED A KISS ON ME, AND HE HURT ELLIOT.
BUT...

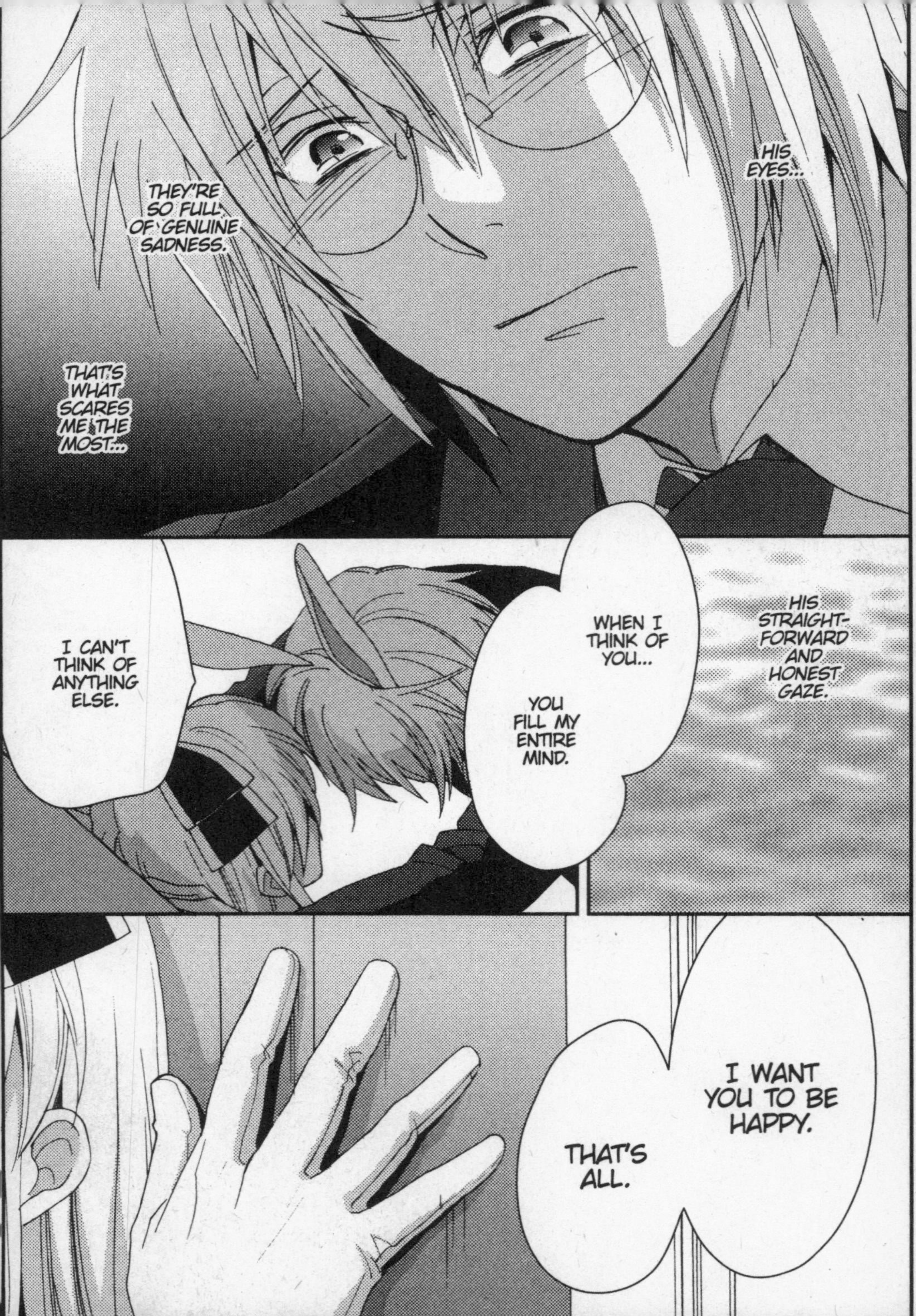
HIS EYES...
THEY'RE SO FULL OF GENUINE SADNESS.
THAT'S WHAT SCARES ME THE MOST...
HIS STRAIGHT-FORWARD AND HONEST GAZE.
WHEN I THINK OF YOU...
YOU FILL MY ENTIRE MIND.
I CAN'T THINK OF ANYTHING ELSE.
I WANT YOU TO BE HAPPY.
THAT'S ALL.

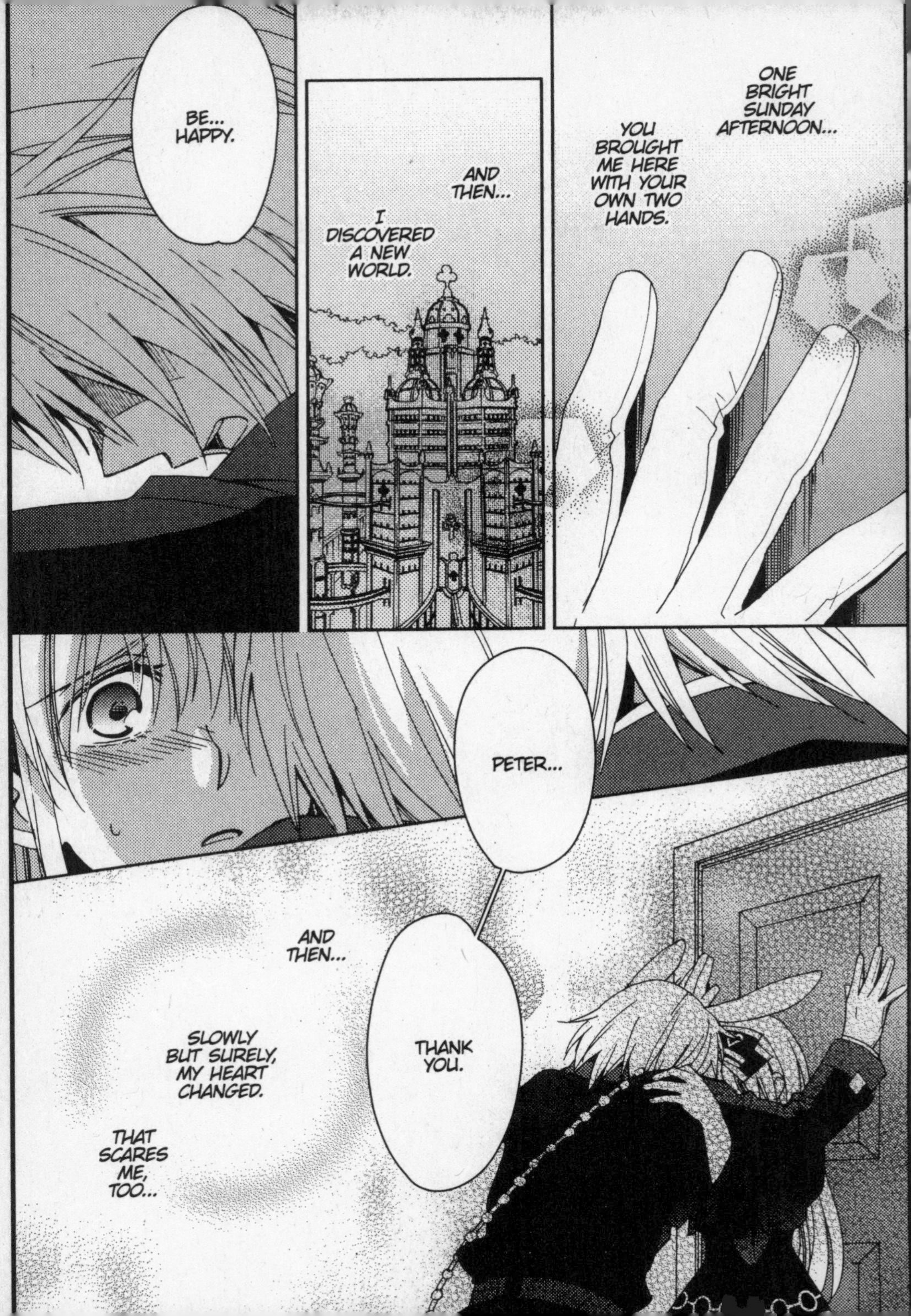
ONE BRIGHT SUNDAY AFTERNOON...
YOU BROUGHT ME HERE WITH YOUR OWN TWO HANDS.
AND THEN...
I DISCOVERED A NEW WORLD.
BE... HAPPY.
PETER...
THANK YOU.
AND THEN...
SLOWLY BUT SURELY, MY HEART CHANGED.
THAT SCARES ME, TOO...

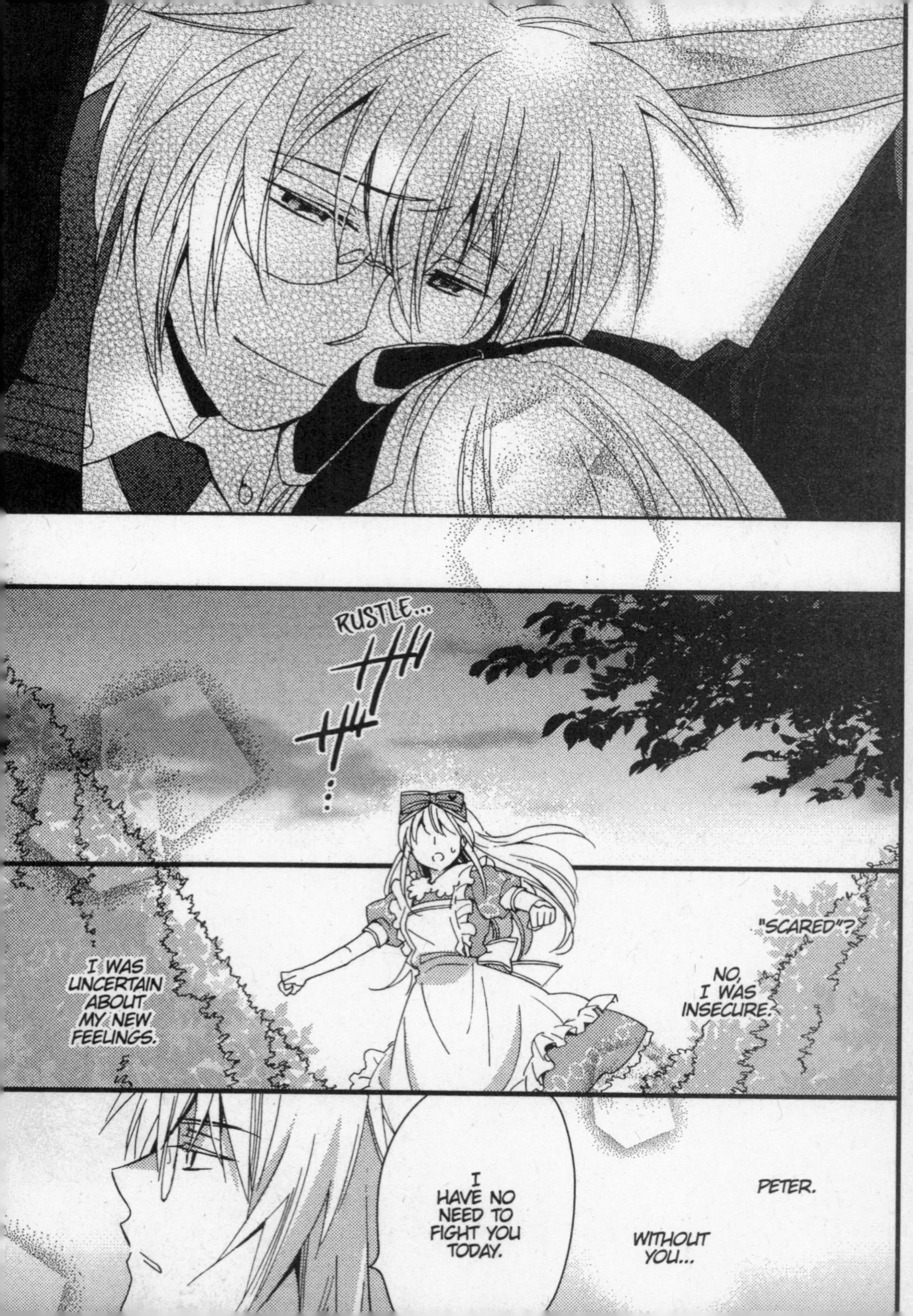
RUSTLE...
"SCARED"?
NO, I WAS INSECURE.
I WAS UNCERTAIN ABOUT MY NEW FEELINGS.
PETER.
WITHOUT YOU...
I HAVE NO NEED TO FIGHT YOU TODAY.

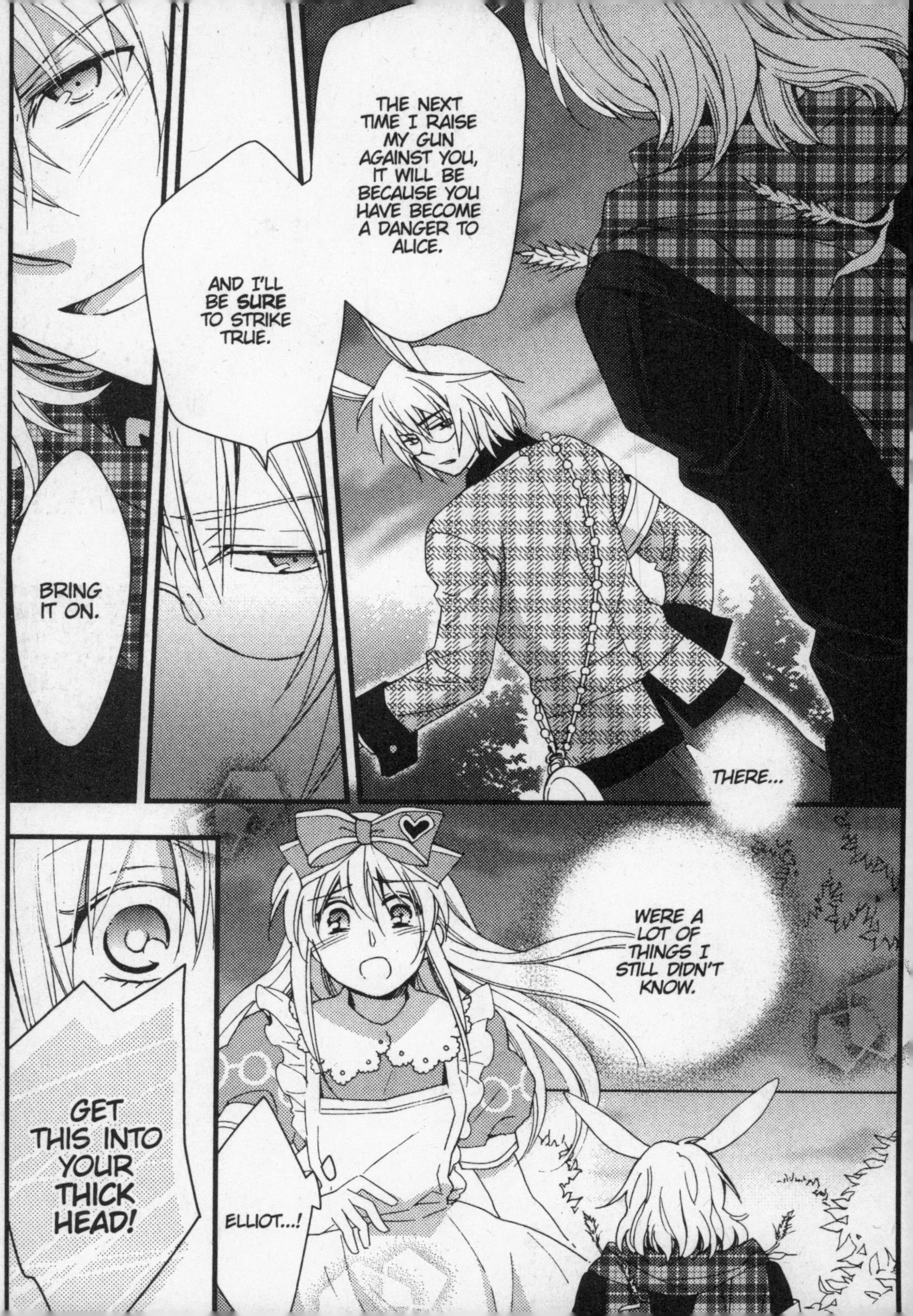
THE NEXT TIME I RAISE MY GUN AGAINST YOU, IT WILL BE BECAUSE YOU HAVE BECOME A DANGER TO ALICE.
AND I'LL BE SURE TO STRIKE TRUE.
BRING IT ON.
THERE...
WERE A LOT OF THINGS I STILL DIDN'T KNOW.
ELLIOT...!
GET THIS INTO YOUR THICK HEAD!

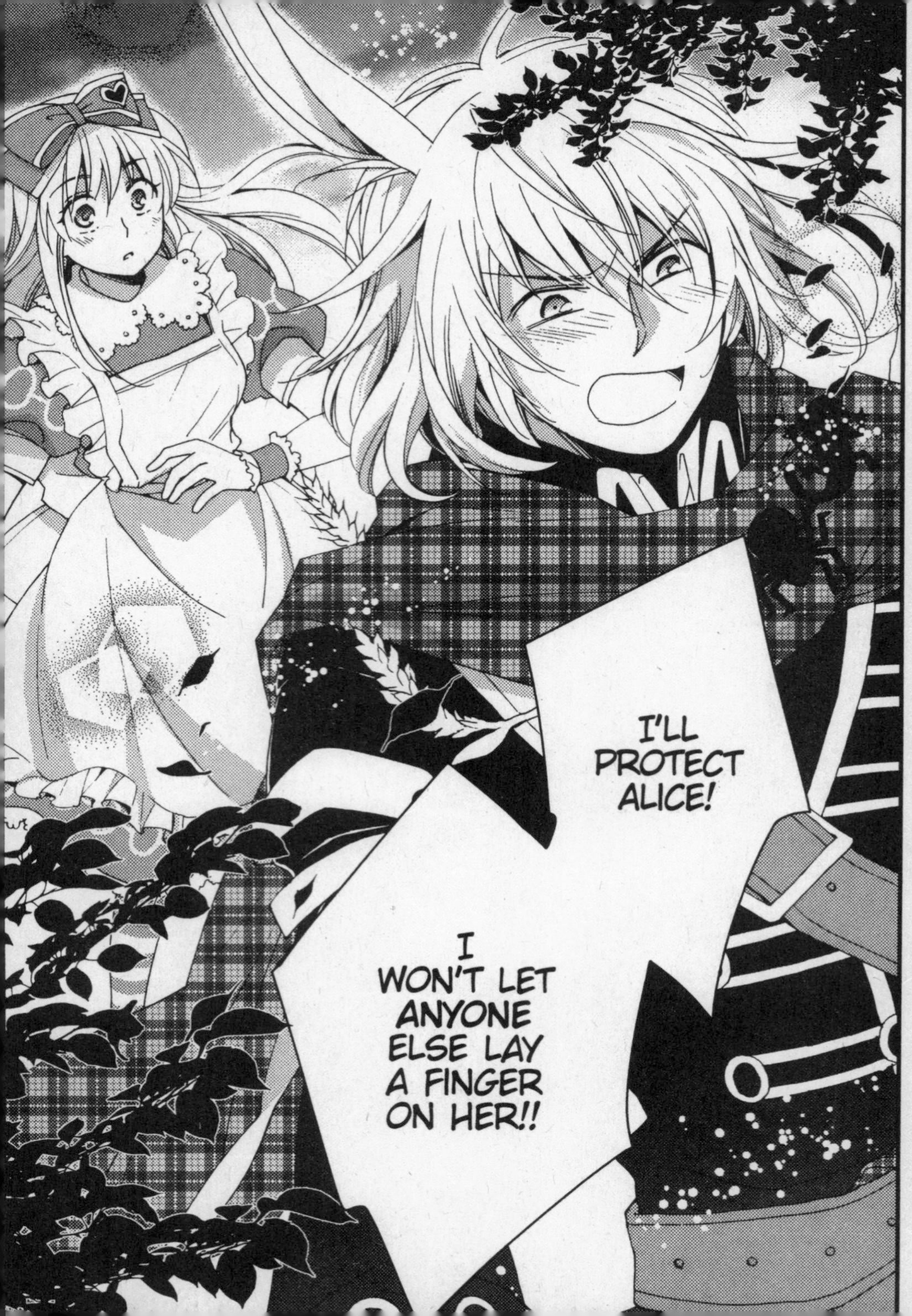
I'LL PROTECT ALICE!
I WON'T LET ANYONE ELSE LAY A FINGER ON HER!!

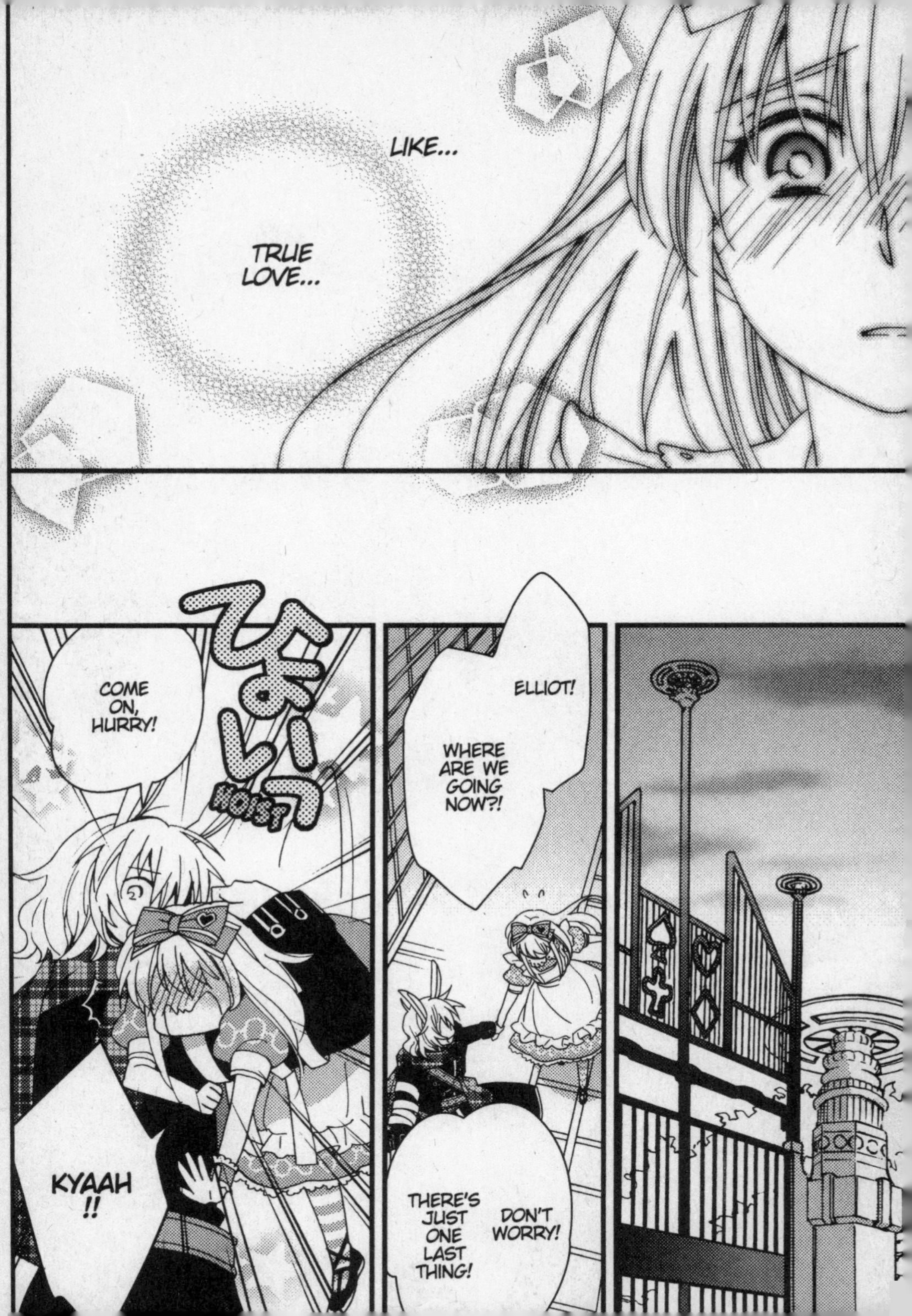
LIKE...
TRUE LOVE...
ELLIOT!
WHERE ARE WE GOING NOW?!
DON'T WORRY!
THERE'S JUST ONE LAST THING!
COME ON, HURRY!
ひょいっ
HOIST
KYAAH!!

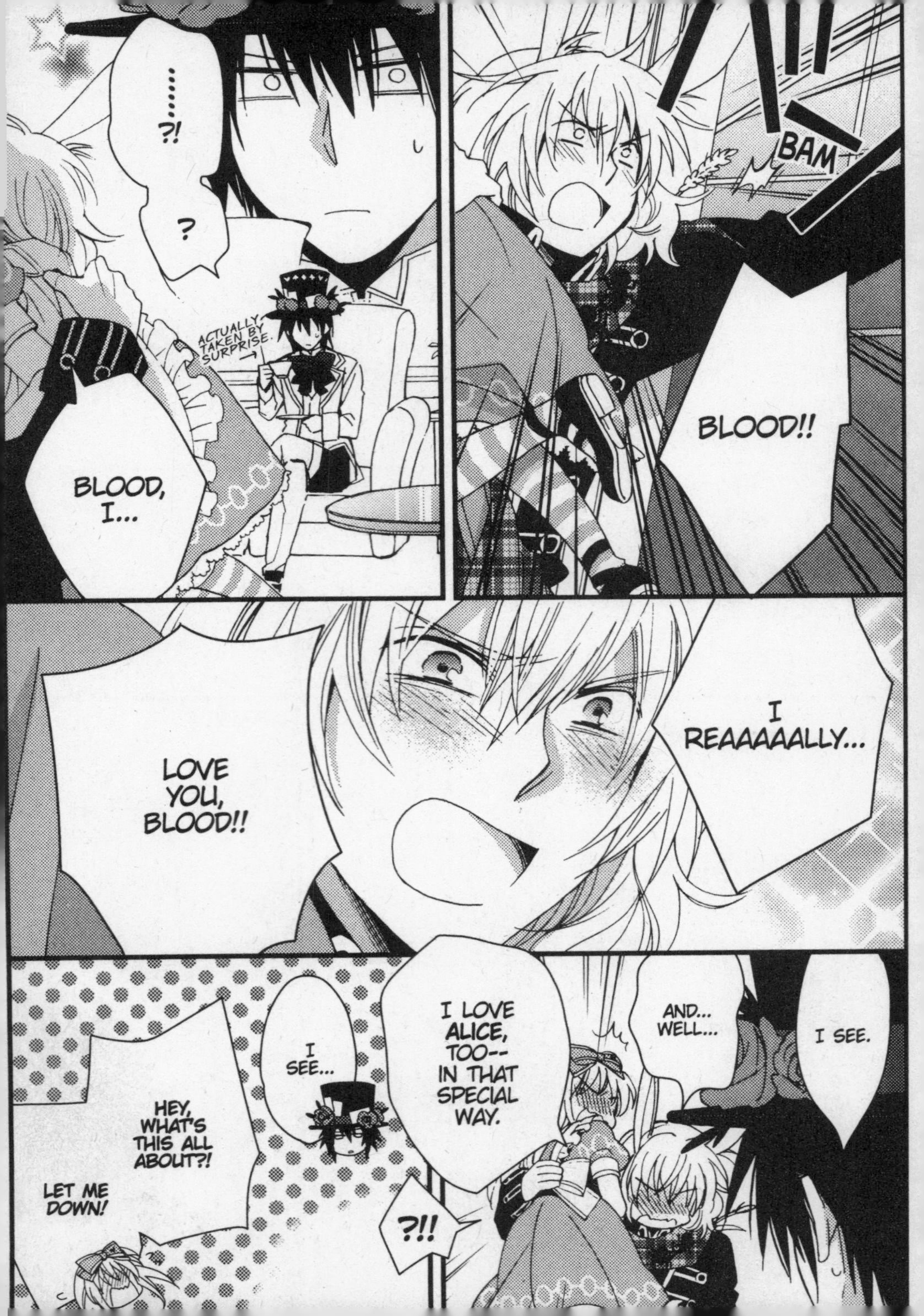
BAM
BLOOD!!
......
?!
?
ACTUALLY TAKEN BY SURPRISE.
BLOOD, I...
I REAAAAALLY...
LOVE YOU, BLOOD!!
I SEE.
AND... WELL...
I LOVE ALICE, TOO-- IN THAT SPECIAL WAY.
?!!
I SEE...
HEY, WHAT'S THIS ALL ABOUT?!
LET ME DOWN!

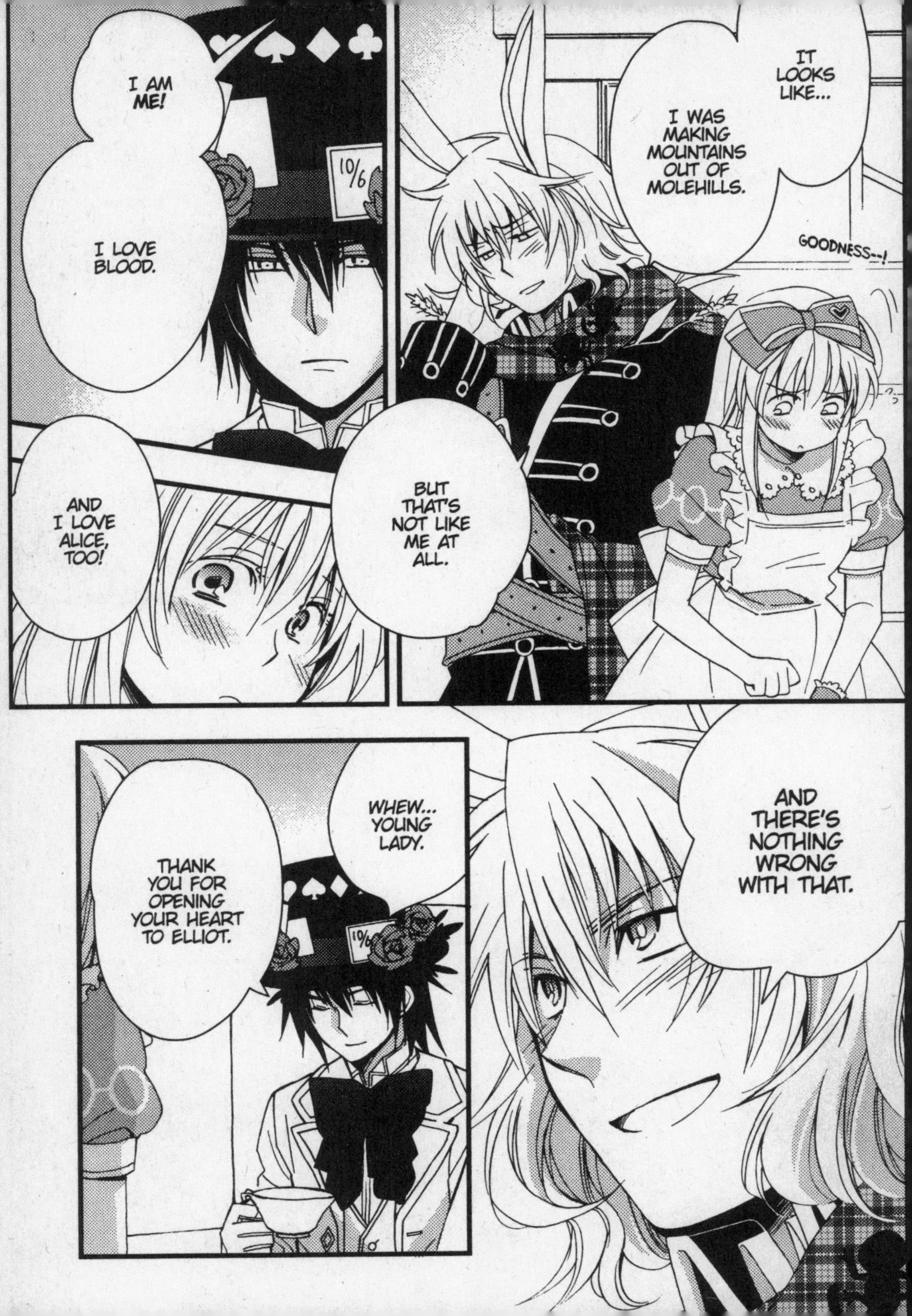
IT LOOKS LIKE...
I WAS MAKING MOUNTAINS OUT OF MOLEHILLS.
GOODNESS--!
BUT THAT'S NOT LIKE ME AT ALL.
I AM ME!
I LOVE BLOOD.
AND I LOVE ALICE, TOO!
AND THERE'S NOTHING WRONG WITH THAT.
WHEW... YOUNG LADY.
THANK YOU FOR OPENING YOUR HEART TO ELLIOT.

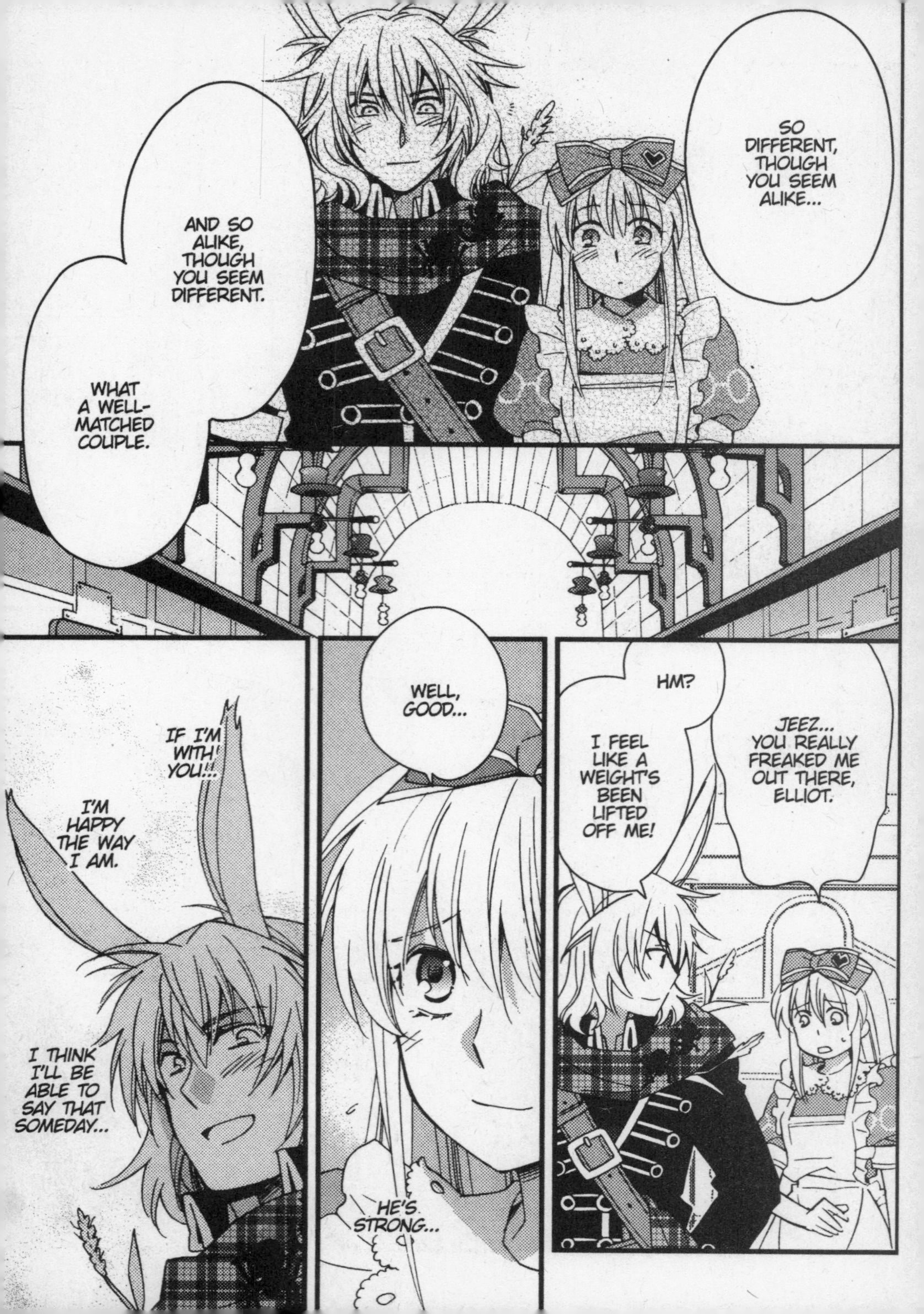
SO DIFFERENT, THOUGH YOU SEEM ALIKE...
AND SO ALIKE, THOUGH YOU SEEM DIFFERENT.
WHAT A WELL-MATCHED COUPLE.
HM?
JEEZ... YOU REALLY FREAKED ME OUT THERE, ELLIOT.
I FEEL LIKE A WEIGHT'S BEEN LIFTED OFF ME!
WELL, GOOD...
HE'S STRONG...
IF I'M WITH YOU...
I'M HAPPY THE WAY I AM.
I THINK I'LL BE ABLE TO SAY THAT SOMEDAY...

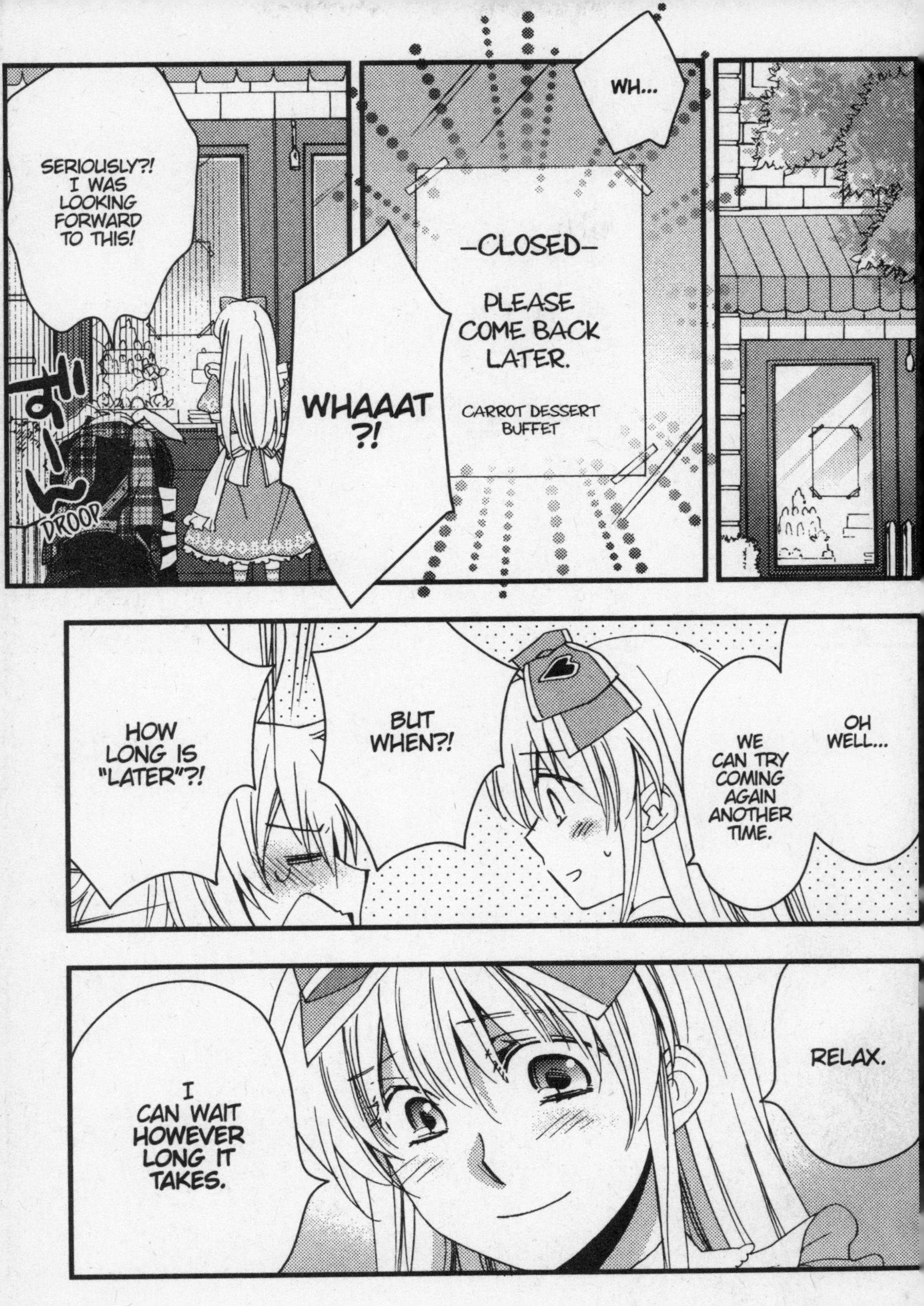
WH...
-CLOSED-
PLEASE COME BACK LATER.
CARROT DESSERT BUFFET
WHAAAT?!
SERIOUSLY?! I WAS LOOKING FORWARD TO THIS!
DROOP
OH WELL...
WE CAN TRY COMING AGAIN ANOTHER TIME.
BUT WHEN?!
HOW LONG IS "LATER"?!
RELAX.
I CAN WAIT HOWEVER LONG IT TAKES.

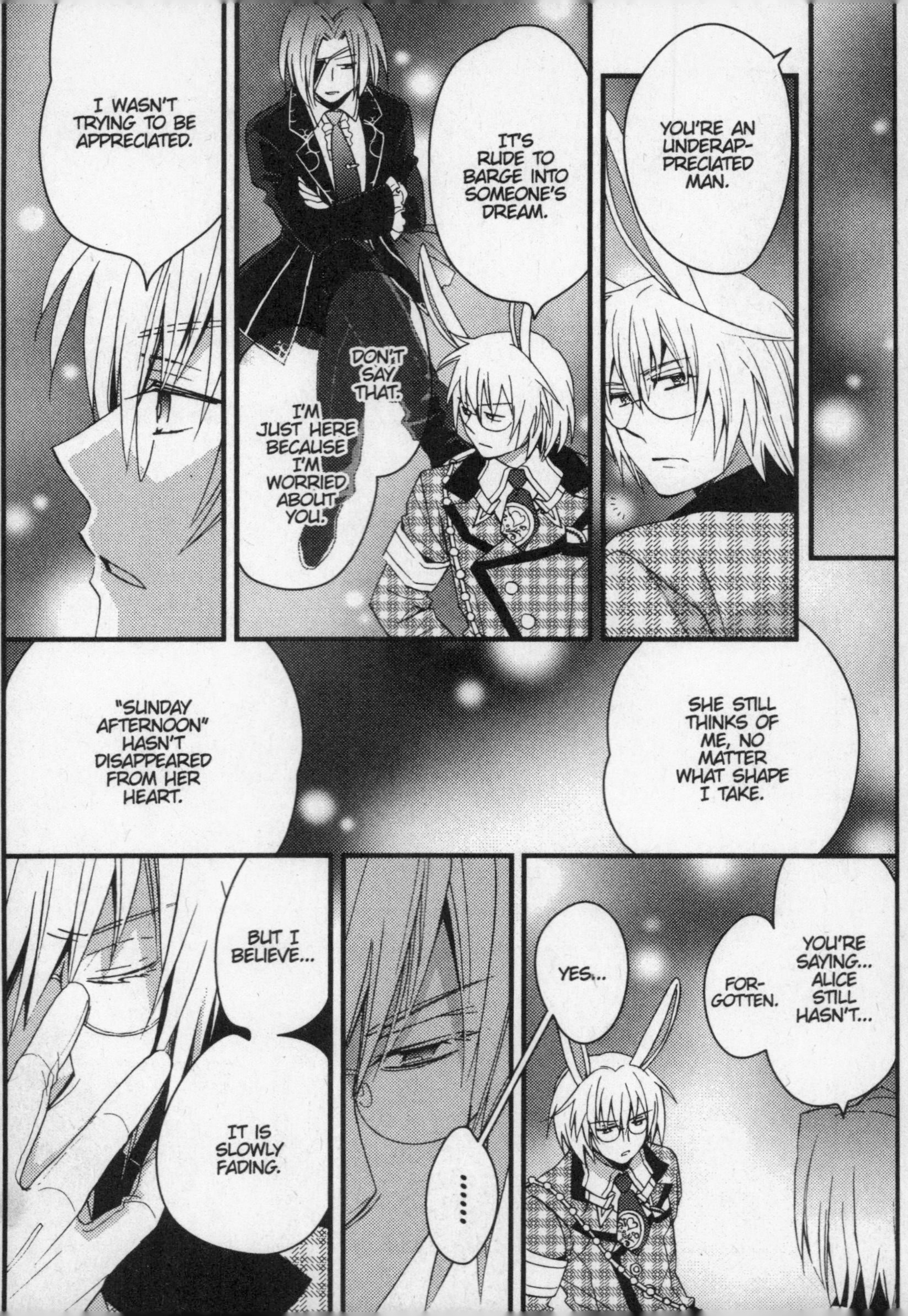
YOU'RE AN UNDERAP-PRECIATED MAN.
IT'S RUDE TO BARGE INTO SOMEONE'S DREAM.
DON'T SAY THAT.
I'M JUST HERE BECAUSE I'M WORRIED ABOUT YOU.
I WASN'T TRYING TO BE APPRECIATED.
SHE STILL THINKS OF ME, NO MATTER WHAT SHAPE I TAKE.
"SUNDAY AFTERNOON" HASN'T DISAPPEARED FROM HER HEART.
YOU'RE SAYING... ALICE STILL HASN'T...
FOR-GOTTEN.
YES...
......
BUT I BELIEVE...
IT IS SLOWLY FADING.

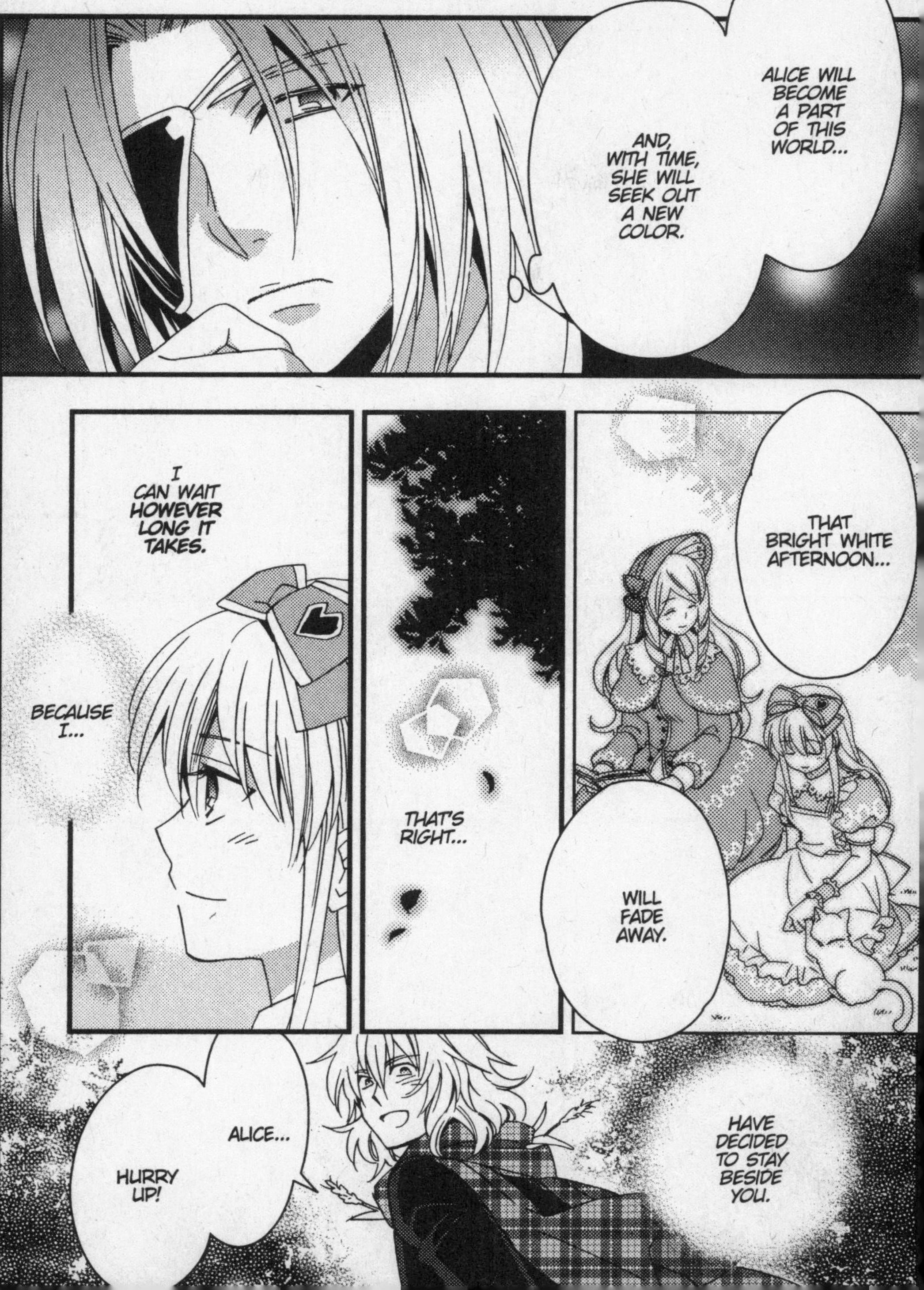
ALICE WILL BECOME A PART OF THIS WORLD...
AND, WITH TIME, SHE WILL SEEK OUT A NEW COLOR.
THAT BRIGHT WHITE AFTERNOON...
WILL FADE AWAY.
THAT'S RIGHT...
I CAN WAIT HOWEVER LONG IT TAKES.
BECAUSE I...
HAVE DECIDED TO STAY BESIDE YOU.
ALICE...
HURRY UP!

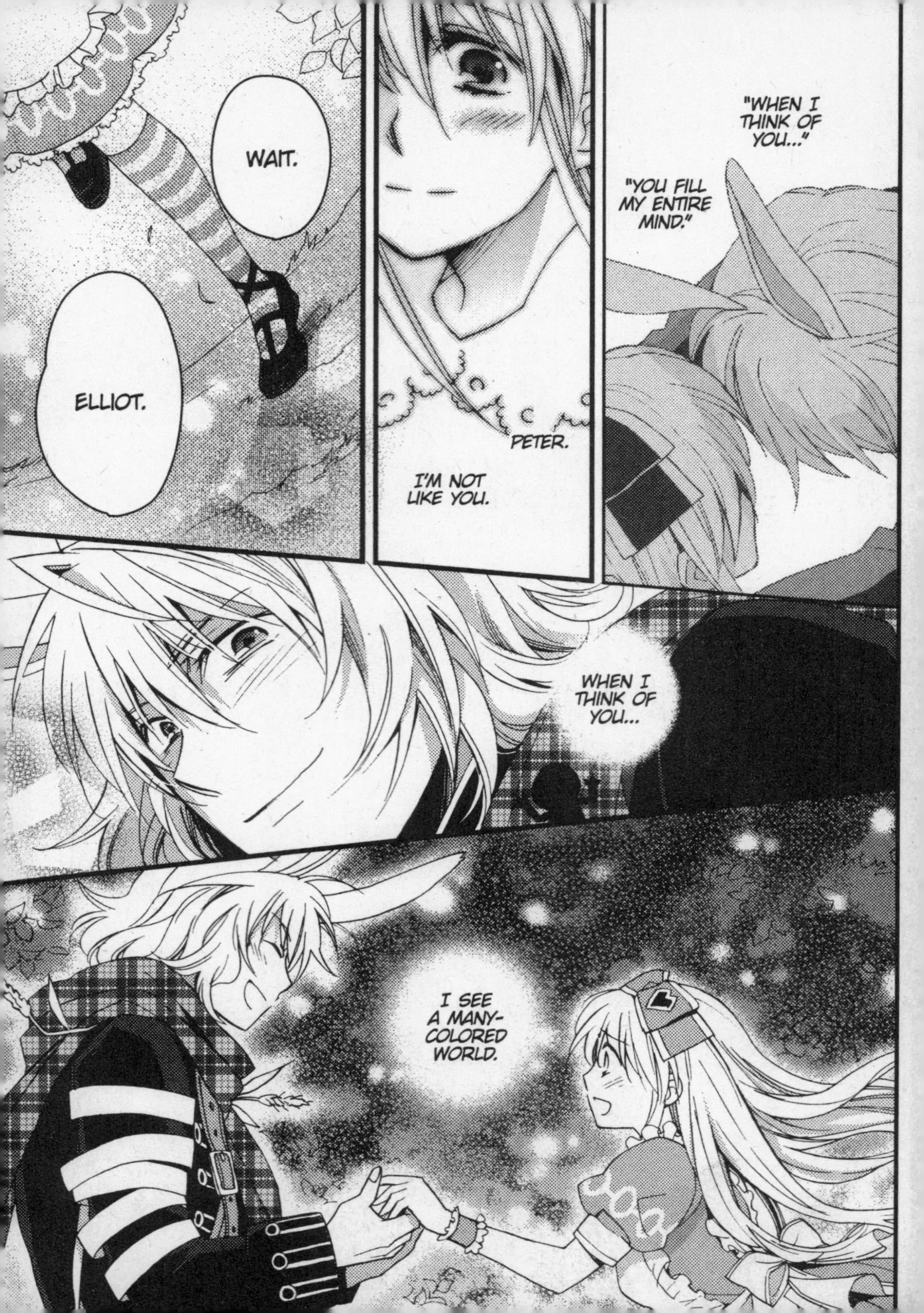
"WHEN I THINK OF YOU..."
"YOU FILL MY ENTIRE MIND."
PETER.
I'M NOT LIKE YOU.
WAIT.
ELLIOT.
WHEN I THINK OF YOU...
I SEE A MANY-COLORED WORLD.

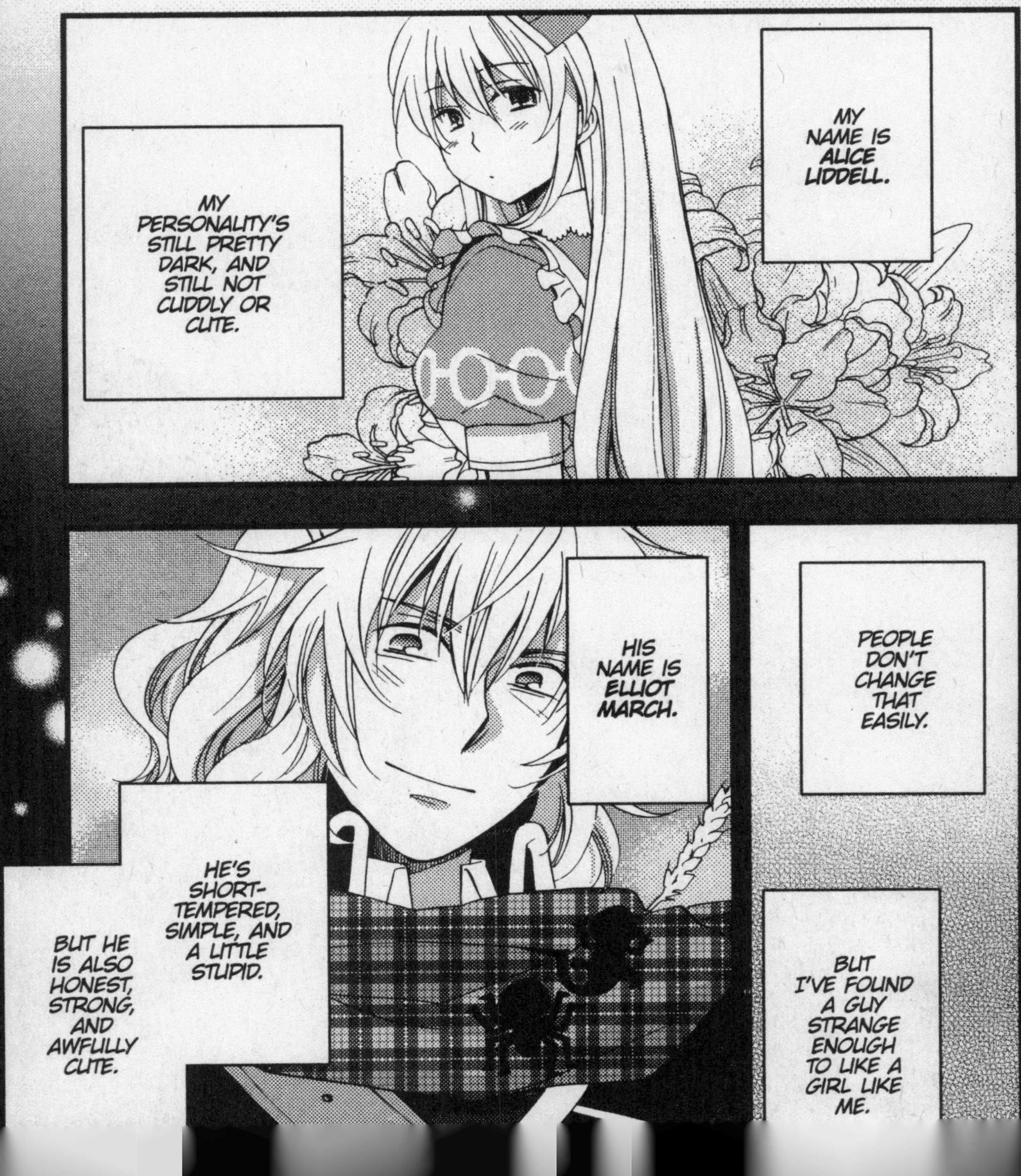
MY NAME IS ALICE LIDDELL.
MY PERSONALITY'S STILL PRETTY DARK, AND STILL NOT CUDDLY OR CUTE.
PEOPLE DON'T CHANGE THAT EASILY.
BUT I'VE FOUND A GUY STRANGE ENOUGH TO LIKE A GIRL LIKE ME.
HIS NAME IS ELLIOT MARCH.
HE'S SHORT-TEMPERED, SIMPLE, AND A LITTLE STUPID.
BUT HE IS ALSO HONEST, STRONG, AND AWFULLY CUTE.

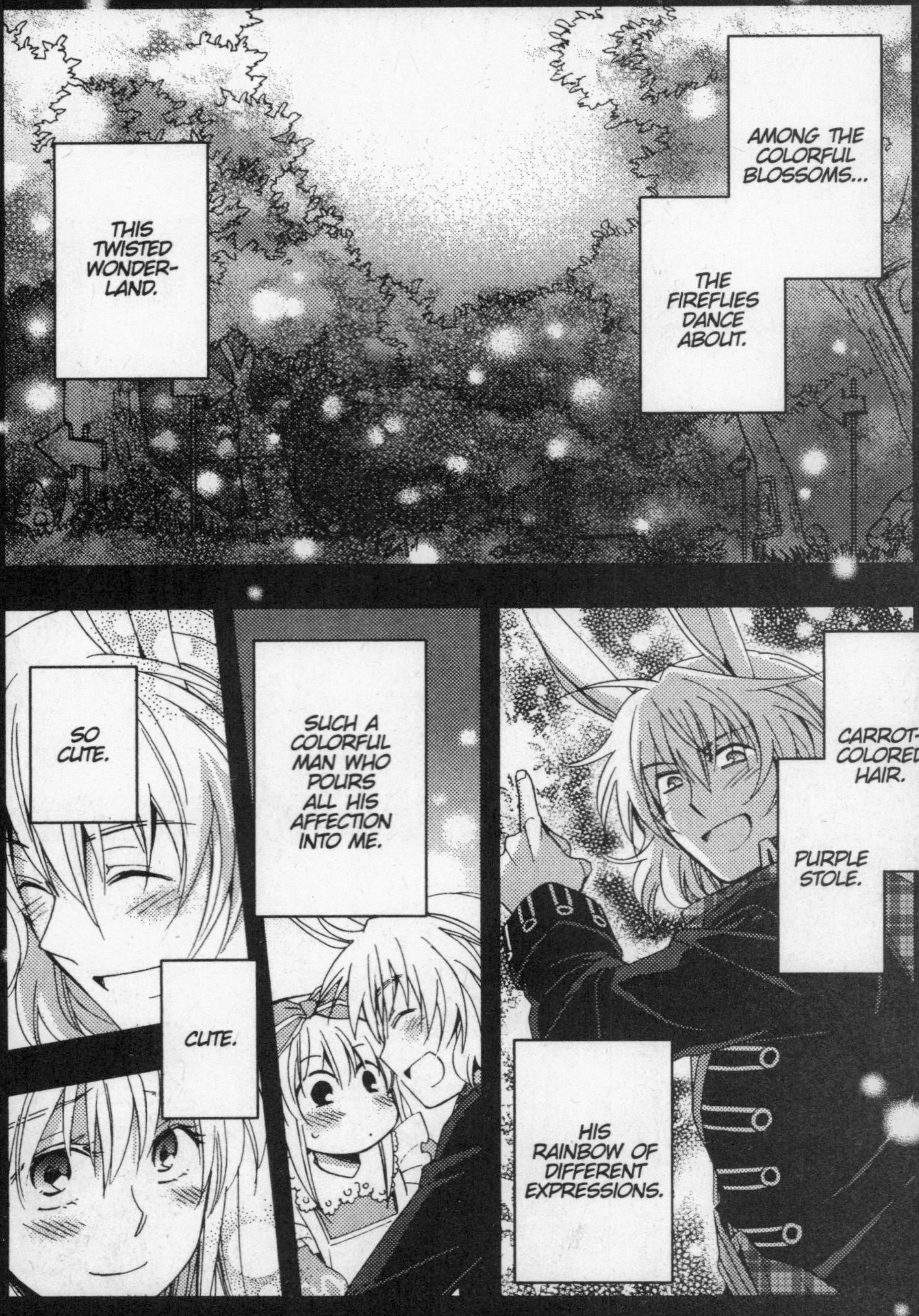
AMONG THE COLORFUL BLOSSOMS...
THE FIREFLIES DANCE ABOUT.
THIS TWISTED WONDER-LAND.
CARROT-COLORED HAIR.
PURPLE STOLE.
HIS RAINBOW OF DIFFERENT EXPRESSIONS.
SUCH A COLORFUL MAN WHO POURS ALL HIS AFFECTION INTO ME.
SO CUTE.
CUTE.

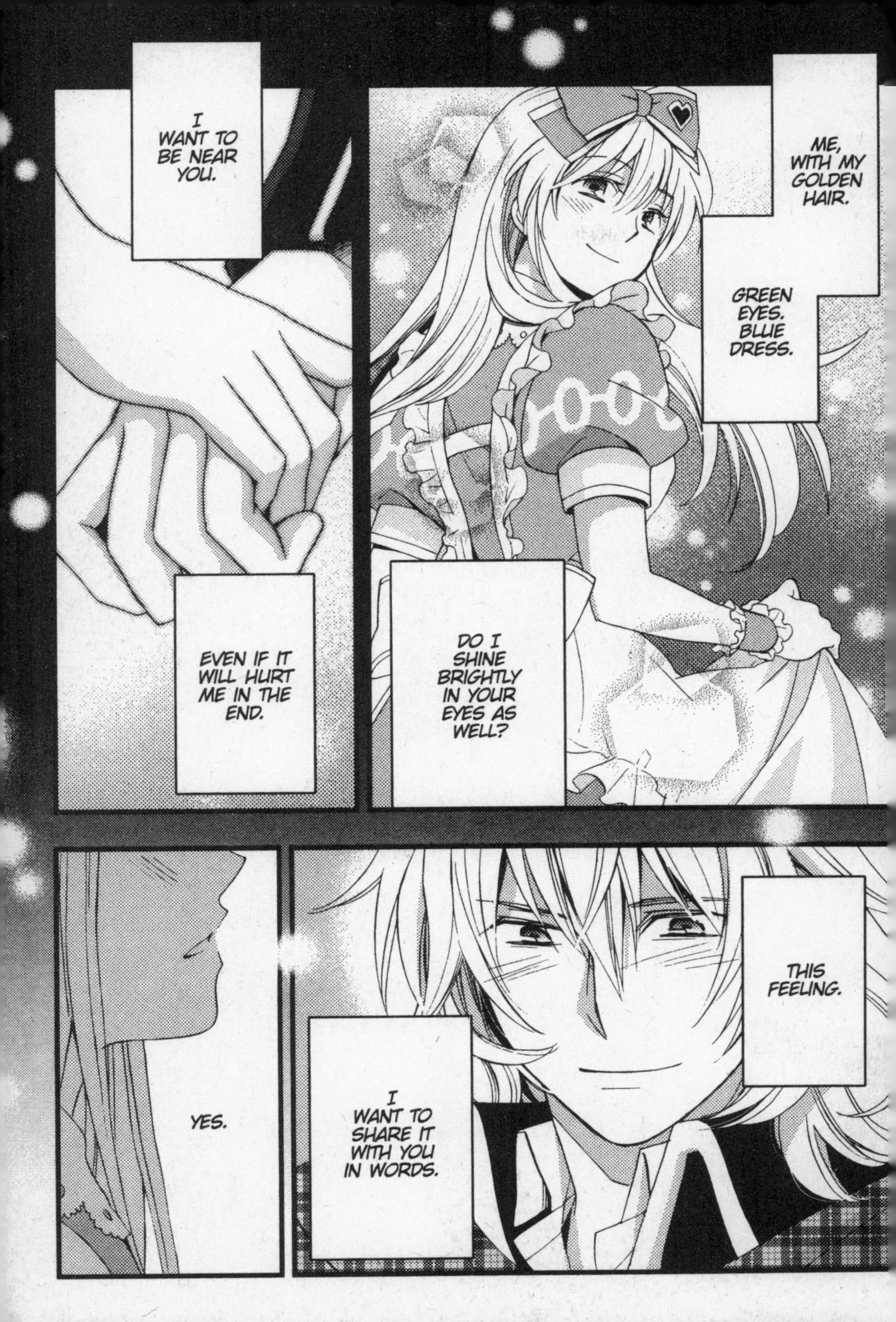
ME, WITH MY GOLDEN HAIR.
GREEN EYES. BLUE DRESS.
DO I SHINE BRIGHTLY IN YOUR EYES AS WELL?
I WANT TO BE NEAR YOU.
EVEN IF IT WILL HURT ME IN THE END.
THIS FEELING.
I WANT TO SHARE IT WITH YOU IN WORDS.
YES.

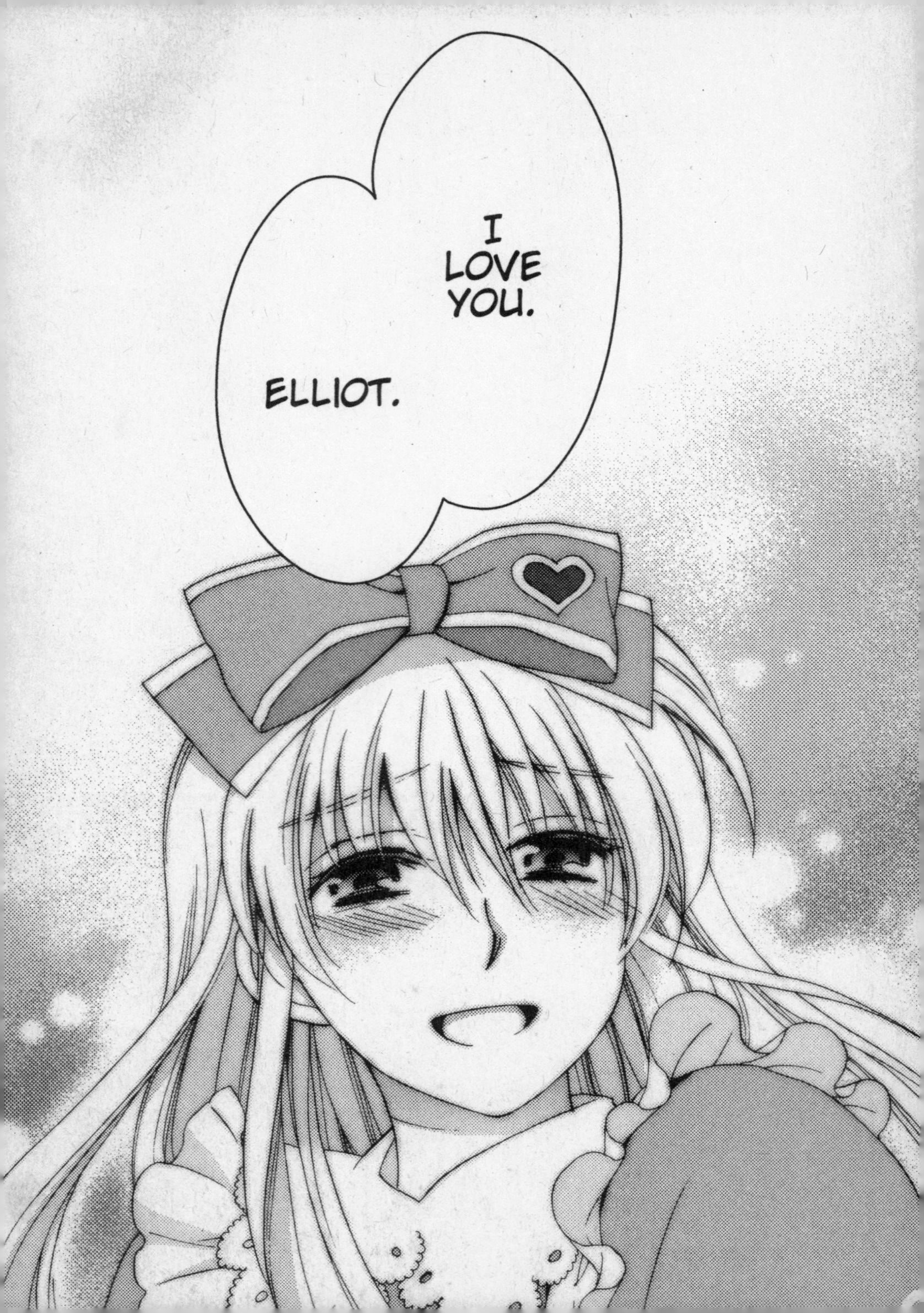
I LOVE YOU.
ELLIOT.

Special Thanks

Shisui
Nagisa
Oumi
Wawa
Mirei
Saaya
Miyako
Harue

QuinRose

And you!

Thank you very much!

Soyogo Iwaki

COMING SOON

APRIL 2014
Alice in the Country of Clover:
Nightmare

MAY 2014
Alice in the Country of Hearts:
Love Labyrinth of Thorns

JUNE 2014
Alice in the Country of Joker:
Circus and Liar's Game Vol. 5

JULY 2014
Alice in the Country of Clover:
Knight's Knowledge Vol. 1